The First British Trade Expedition to China

The First British Trade Expedition to China

Captain Weddell and the Courteen Fleet in Asia and Late Ming Canton

Nicholas D. Jackson

Hong Kong University Press
The University of Hong Kong
Pokfulam Road
Hong Kong
https://hkupress.hku.hk

© 2022 Hong Kong University Press

ISBN 978-988-8754-10-6 (*Hardback*)

All rights reserved. No portion of this publication may be reproduced or transmitted in any form or by any means, electronic or mechanical, including photocopying, recording, or any information storage or retrieval system, without prior permission in writing from the publisher.

British Library Cataloguing-in-Publication Data
A catalogue record for this book is available from the British Library.

Digitally printed

To Lucinda Van Buskirk Jackson,
a steadfast mother and bibliographical mariner,
who kept a battered manuscript from sinking

Hence it is that barbarous empires have never grown to such glory, though of more giant-like stature, and larger land-extension, because learning had not fitted them for sea attempts, nor wisdom furnished them with navigation. Thus, the Persian, the Mogul, the Abyssinian, the Chinois, the Tartarian, the Turk, are called great, but their greatness is like Polyphemus with one eye, they see at home like purblind men near to them, not far off with those eyes of Heaven, and lights of the world, the learned knowledge, whereof is requisite to navigation.

—Samuel Purchas, *Hakluytus Posthumus or Purchas his Pilgrimes* (1625)

Contents

Prologue	1
1. The British in Seventeenth-Century Luso-Dutch Asia	14
2. Enter the Interlopers: Genesis of the Courteen Association, Rival of the English East India Company	34
3. From the Downs to Goa to Melaka, April 1636–June 1637: Mishaps and Breakthroughs along the Way to China	48
4. Welcome to China with Portuguese Characteristics: The Courteen Fleet in Macao Purgatory, July–August 1637	70
5. The *Dragon* Enters the Tiger: The Courteen Fleet in the Bogue and Pearl River Estuary, August 1637	83
6. Captives at Canton: The Crisis of the Courteen Fleet at the Bogue, September–October 1637	93
7. Negotiation and Liberation: Restoration at Canton and Trade at Macao, October–December 1637	107
8. Lessons Learned: The "Anglology" of the Ming?	130
9. Lessons Learned: The Sinology of the Courteens?	157
Epilogue: The First British Trade Expedition to China: A Precursor of the Opium Wars?	176
Appendix: Key Chinese Officials in Ming Documents with English Renderings by the Courteens	185
Bibliography	187
Index	195

Prologue

In late autumn 1637, an English sea-captain at Macao, John Weddell, was compelled to sign a pledge promising both the Chinese and Portuguese that he would never return to China. Captain Weddell kept his word for almost two years. In the spring of 1639, aboard the *Dragon*, he embarked upon the return voyage to England from the Malabar coast of India. Sailing into the ocean towards the Cape of Good Hope: that was the last anyone heard from him. Frances Weddell, with her daughter Elizabeth, would wait again, no doubt patiently, but this time in vain, for the return of husband and father. Some consolation might have been derived from the return of her son Jeremy, who made the voyage to China in the fleet commanded by her husband, but came back to England in another ship, the *Sun*. What happened to the *Dragon* and Captain Weddell "in parts beyond the sea" remains a mystery. After a few more years of waiting, Frances would have to conclude that her husband had been slain by pirates at sea, maybe ambushed by some marauding Dutch, or merely swallowed by the stormy ocean he had crossed multiple times.

While most have never heard of this Englishman and his family from four centuries ago, we may all recognize that we are living in a world still dominated by their language and civilization. We inhabit a planet that was subject to the British Empire, whose foundations were laid by the exertions of such sea-captains as John Weddell. Long before reaching the coast of Ming China in 1637, Captain Weddell had sailed into remote seas and exotic bays and traversed unmapped territories and rivers. Long before launching attacks upon fleets and storming forts and villages in the Pearl River Delta of southeast China, Weddell had successfully commanded ships in naval battles in the Persian Gulf and fought skirmishes along the Malabar coast south of India's Mughal Empire. Absent the audacity and panache of such pioneers; omitting the hardships endured and sacrifices suffered by the likes of Weddell and his family, it is unlikely that the British Empire would ever have arisen. Likewise would it be improbable that we would find that imperial progenitor Weddell's language spread and thriving all over the twenty-first-century world, if not for those globe-spanning and routinely fatal ventures of him and his British contemporaries of the early seventeenth century.

By the time Weddell had received his first commission as a captain for the East India Company (EIC), ventures to India and the Far East were far from extravagant luxuries or quixotic schemes. Governments in Europe, particularly the Habsburg ones, were funding armies and navies with wealth gained from commerce involving Asia. As Alison Games has pointed out: "Nation, region, and the world were all intertwined in this period, as European states and kingdoms struggled for dominance in Europe and turned to overseas holdings to finance or reinforce that power. The power of a state within Europe was necessarily connected to that state's ability to project itself beyond the region."[1] In the 1630s, and for several prior decades, the Portuguese were the only Europeans permitted by the Ming government to reside and trade directly in China. If the post–Zheng He, oceanic-averse Ming Chinese refused to trade with *all* foreigners, that would have been one thing. But to let such Iberians reap massive profits—and fund armies and navies in the European theater—could not be countenanced by Dutch, British, French, or any other Europeans who could be adversely affected by richer, more powerful Spanish and Portuguese. As the seventeenth-century political philosopher Thomas Hobbes formulated the logic in 1640: "It is also a law of nature, *that men allow commerce and traffic indifferently to one another*. For he that alloweth that to one man, which he denieth to another, declareth his hatred to him, to whom he denieth; and to declare hatred is war."[2] Ming Chinese in Guangdong trading exclusively with the Portuguese would be hostility to the excluded British; it was indirectly a policy of bellicosity.

The religious dimension and ramifications of overseas enterprise were also conspicuous, most broadly in the form of a threat to the northwestern European Protestant cause posed by the mighty Roman Catholic, Iberian Habsburg dynasty. The counter-reformational danger served to animate Dutch and British overseas ventures as a way of depriving that dynasty of the wealth—from Mexico and Peru or Asia—that would fund campaigns against them, the Protestant heretics.[3] This consideration obviously applied no less to the East, whether China, the Philippines, or Japan, or from Goa to Melaka to Macao to Manila to Nagasaki. The Elizabethan and Jacobean imperial impresarios Hakluyts and Samuel Purchas were quite deliberate and methodical in articulating a program to promote trade and colonization in order to fortify Protestant rulers and subvert the Roman Catholic monarchs of Spain.[4] To gain profits from Chinese commerce would be, accordingly, a religious, that is, Protestant-contra-Catholic, imperative: to preserve and further the Reformation against Counter-Reforming Habsburgs, with their dynamic and

---

1. Alison Games, *The Web of Empire: English Cosmopolitans in an Age of Expansion, 1560–1660* (Oxford: Oxford University Press, 2009), 14.
2. Hobbes, *Elements of Law*, Part I, Chapter XVI, Section 12.
3. For one spectacular example, take the 1628 Dutch seizure of the Spanish treasure fleet in the Caribbean which would enable the United Provinces to fund a massive campaign to dispossess Habsburg Philip IV of parts of the Spanish Netherlands.
4. "Hakluyt's message of oceanic imperialism [in *Principall Navigations*, 1599] conquered the reading public with such triumphant ease because the public mind was now ready to accept it." Kenneth R. Andrews, *Trade, Plunder and Settlement: Maritime Enterprise and the Genesis of the British Empire, 1480–1630* (Cambridge: Cambridge University Press, 1984), 248. Such a bibliographic conquest required a Protestant public mind.

Prologue

multilingual squads of Jesuit missionaries already stationed in the Americas, Macao, Manila, and Nagasaki—to ensure that the orthodox form of Christianity would be the one that first reached and sustained the natives scattered all over the lands and oceans remote from Rome, Lisbon, Madrid, London, and Amsterdam.[5]

If we agree with Games that "by the middle of the seventeenth century, England had transformed itself from a weak kingdom on the margins of Europe, one struggling to participate in the major overseas opportunities of the period, to a nation able to vie with and sometimes to defeat Dutch, French, Portuguese, and Spanish rivals in their competition for new territory and coveted commodities,"[6] then to John Weddell, Nathaniel Mountney, and Thomas Robinson much credit must be given. Mountney and Robinson were also veteran East India Company (EIC) employees whose vast experience, business acumen, linguistic facility (particularly Portuguese and Malay), and knowledge of Asia led to their assignment in the first British trade expedition to China. The gritty Captain Weddell and these immensely talented, linguistically nimble, and resourceful "factors" (commercial agents): their expedition launched from the Downs in the spring of 1636 was a pioneering effort to bring the Stuart British into a position to compete with those other European peoples in the Far East—most especially, if over-ambitiously, to break into the China-Japan silk-silver trade in which Iberians and Dutch (the latter more as interlopers and pirates) had been participating very profitably. Weddell and all the other captains, mariners, and merchants aboard the Courteen fleet that reached the Pearl River estuary in the summer of 1637 were among the men who transformed England from a marginal European island-kingdom to a key player around the world.[7] The Weddell expedition would contribute to the extension of the oceanic frontier of the inchoate British Empire. But it was a mere beginning, to be sure. Less vaguely, with the long-range in view, this venture launched in 1636 can be recognized as a preliminary China imperial reconnaissance mission of a global endeavor that would lead to the establishment of Hong Kong in the nineteenth century. Moreover, some aspects of this expedition led by Weddell bear strong resemblance to circumstances and features of the Opium Wars that took place two hundred years later in the same area of the Pearl River, the Bogue (虎門 Humen), leading to Canton (Guangzhou).[8]

As that English couple John and Frances Weddell illustrates, the transformation of a marginal, insular European nation into the capital of a global empire exacted

---

5. The Hakluyts and Purchas were less concerned with another, less denominational, religious dimension: the more Iberian-waged Christian-Muslim war from Africa all the way to Melaka.

6. Games, *Web of Empire*, 289.

7. The perplexing phenomenon of a small island-state like England punching so effectively above its weight across the globe is similar to that which prompts Tonio Andrade to raise his question: "The Spanish and the Dutch managed to establish colonies on an island [Taiwan] just a hundred miles from the empire of China, which, with its 150 million inhabitants, was a hundred times larger than the Dutch Republic. How did people from these small European countries establish colonies on an island that had already aroused the interest of merchants from the two most powerful states of East Asia?" *How Taiwan Became Chinese: Dutch, Spanish, and Han Colonization in the Seventeenth Century* (New York: Columbia University, 2008), 2.

8. This notion of the 1637 expedition in China as a sort of precursor of the Opium Wars is elaborated fully in the Epilogue.

much hardship, pain, and sacrifice. Perhaps the only thing that could temper those was the sober anticipation of them: sickness, injury, loss, and death were to be frequent. In the seventeenth century, in whichever hemisphere, high mortality and reasonable probability of failure accompanied ventures of trade, conquest, and colonization. The pioneering Portuguese had a saying: "A India mais vão do que tornam." More seek than return from India. By the Lusitanians, epically eulogized by poet Camoens, made famous by such navigators as Vasco da Gama and maritime *conquistadores* as Afonso de Albuquerque, vessels embarking for the East were likened to coffins: *tumbeiros*.[9] Those British acquainted with the EIC experiences in Asia in the first decades of the seventeenth century were no less capable of noticing the macabre resemblance of containers—and appreciating another Portuguese maxim: "If you want to learn how to pray, go to sea."[10] Scurvy was a staple of voyages to India and beyond. Lack of critical nutrients (particularly vitamin C) was the concomitant of the dearth of fruit, vegetables, and meat.[11] Malaria was also a constant peril. That disease was to decimate Captain Weddell's crew when the fleet was off the Malabar coast of India in the spring of 1637—the *Sun*, commanded by Richard Swanley, would suffer the most: of the 132 who set sail on that ship from England in the spring of 1636, 52 had died of sickness by the end of the China sojourn, in January 1638. A further four drowned. In addition to scurvy and malaria, "the bloody flux" of dysentery (intestinal contamination) and yellow/dengue fever were prolific killers of British and other Europeans desperate or courageous enough to voyage around the Cape of Good Hope to the East.

As one of our most eminent authorities on the British Empire in Asia, P.J. Marshall, has summarized: "To most Europeans, Asian conditions seemed menacingly unpredictable. Ships were at the mercy of typhoons, unknown diseases suddenly carried off men, wars and famines could bring trade to a standstill, and merchants were believed to be harried by capricious and tyrannical governments."[12] Serious and lethal risks had to be routinely undertaken and devastating hazards often run if a global empire was to be achieved. Weddell, Mountney, Robinson, and their colleagues were among those who braved these perils, in a pioneering or "experimental" spirit. Games characterizes the century of 1560–1660 as one of experimentation: "Only with much loss of life and great difficulty did the English learn what kinds of exploitative or extractive activities might succeed in different parts of the world and in different ocean basins, each with their own distinctive existing and

---

9. It has been estimated that not even one-third of Vasco da Gama's crew returned to Portugal in 1499.
10. That fatalities were alarmingly routine aboard the EIC ships, it suffices to browse several volumes of William Foster's *English Factories in India*, where they are casually related nearly every other page.
11. "From the 14th century to the 19th, the range of foodstuffs which could be preserved for use at sea remained the same: salt beef and pork, beer, pease, cheese and butter (all in cask), biscuit, and salt fish. . . . In the best circumstances it appears that in this period victuals could not be relied upon for more than 3 or 4 months." N.A.M. Rodger, "Guns and Sails in the First Phase of English Colonization, 1500–1650," in *The Origins of Empire*, ed. Nicholas Canny (Oxford: Oxford University Press, 1998), 87.
12. P.J. Marshall, "The English in Asia to 1700," in *The Origins of Empire*, ed. Nicholas Canny (Oxford: Oxford University Press, 1998), 266.

Prologue

emerging commercial networks, rivalries, and indigenous populations."[13] The first British trade expedition to China illustrates this truth as opulently as any other venture of that Tudor-Stuart century. Besides this experimental quality of the Courteen enterprise, we are also warranted in emphasizing the improvisational aspects of this British endeavor to establish commercial relations with the Ming Chinese. After categorizing the pioneering, discovery-replete sixteenth century as "an age of first contacts," Timothy Brook classifies the seventeenth as one of *second contacts* and *improvisation*: "It was a time when people had to adjust how they acted and thought in order to negotiate the cultural differences they encountered. It was a time not for executing grand designs, but for improvising. The age of discovery was largely over, the age of imperialism yet to come. The seventeenth century was the age of improvisation."[14] The China expedition of the Courteen Association serves to illustrate and validate that generalization as well. As we watch the quick-thinking, opportunistic, and resourceful Weddell, Mountney, and Robinson recruiting and seizing native pilots and interpreters as their fleet proceeded from Aceh (Sumatra) to Macao and from there to the Bogue, we may certainly recognize many instances of improvisation. Embarking for the East in 1636, Weddell, Mountney, and Robinson were the farthest things from "China hands"—upon arrival at Macao the Portuguese scoffingly referred to them as "novices." None had been in China. None could speak a syllable of Chinese, or decipher the simplest character. Their audacious experiment and improvisation would begin a process that would plant the name of Victoria in the Pearl River Delta.

The trio of ex-EIC employees had been disgruntled enough to switch their allegiance and carry their talents over to an upstart, interloping rival of that older company: the Courteen Association. As L.H. Roper recently noted: "the consistent neglect or dismissal of the Courteen Association in the historiography of the Anglo-British Empire is curious."[15] All the more odd does the oversight appear when just this one, the Weddell expedition of that organization of adventurers, has been described by another scholar, John Appleby, as "an audaciously ambitious attempt to challenge the trading monopoly of the East India Company in Asia."[16] Of course it is far from unreasonable that the EIC has received the lion's share of attention from

---

13. Games, *Web of Empire*, 14.

14. Timothy Brook, *Vermeer's Hat: The Seventeenth Century and the Dawn of the Global World* (Bloomsbury: London, 2007), 21.

15. L.H. Roper, *Advancing Empire: English Interests and Overseas Expansion, 1613–1688* (Cambridge: Cambridge University Press, 2017).

16. John Appleby, "William Courten," *Oxford Dictionary of National Biography (ODNB)*. The neglect also manifests itself in glaring inaccuracies printed even very recently. Publication of typical inaccuracies in treatments of this expedition to China may be seen in the recent book by Adele Lee, *The English Renaissance and the Far East: Cross-Cultural Encounters* (Madison, NJ: Fairleigh Dickinson University Press, 2018). She represents the China expedition as both an EIC *and* a Courteen venture—when the EIC in London was doing everything it could to strangle the Courteen enterprise in the cradle. This lobbying of the EIC against the Courteen Association is covered in Chapter 2. Note that "Courten" and "Curten" are variant spellings found alongside "Courteen" in the seventeenth century; and some scholars since then have used "Courtenians" and "Curtenians" instead of my preferred usage, "Courteens," for its directors, managers, and personnel.

6   *The First British Trade Expedition to China*

scholars interested in the origins or early (and fitful) development of the British Empire, as that company was to become almost synonymous with Asian empire; or that rivals of the EIC, many of whom spent most of their careers as investors and employees of the EIC, have suffered proportionate neglect. Not surprisingly, episodes involving such "interlopers" (as they were called by resentful EIC employers or ex-colleagues) have been relegated to footnotes of the volumes devoted to histories of the EIC. So far, then, it would be apt enough to summarize that the Courteen Association, and its China venture, has constituted merely footnotes in the annals of the EIC—diverting annotations about interlopers; the dubious when not treacherous exploits of commercial traitors and defectors. Nor could one deny that it makes decent sense to regard the rival Courteen Association as some sort of heretical or bastard sect of the EIC.[17]

Yet another avenue available to us in accounting for the historiographical neglect of the Weddell expedition to China is the geographical shift in British imperial focus that was taking place when his fleet left England in 1636. For example, exciting, dramatic, tragic colonizing endeavors in the Atlantic and Caribbean were undertaken in the first decades of the century. These have subsequently outshined and served to obscure some remarkable exploits in the East. Unlike English "factories" (entrepots and trading stations) in the East—whether at Surat, Aceh, or Banten—such colonies attracted fairly considerable migrations of British.[18] Furthermore, in Asia, from about the 1620s to 1680s, concentration on China and Japan would steadily *decrease*: "For all the wide dispersal of its operations across Asia, the [East India] Company's trade in the first decades of the seventeenth century was mainly focused on two areas: the Indonesian archipelago and India."[19] If the Weddell expedition had been more successful at Macao and Canton, things might have been different. Thus, the disappointments and shortcomings of that expedition are very important in any explanation of its neglect in the historical annals. From that perspective,

---

17. That would be an impression warranted upon reading the classic and still not superseded K.N. Chaudhuri, *The English East India Company: The Study of an Early Joint-Stock Company, 1600–1640* (London: Frank Cass, 1965). Recently, in *A Business of State: Commerce, Politics, and the Birth of the East India Company* (Cambridge, MA: Harvard University Press, 2018), Rupali Mishra has provided a well-informed account of the Courteen Association, but not an adequate discussion of its China expedition as commanded by Weddell, nor that expedition's origin in the (Anglo-Portuguese) Goa Convention of 1635. In view of his much wider "macro" and chronological scope, as well as more narrow geographical focus, it is not surprising that David Veevers mentions the Courteen Association and Weddell only in passing in *The Origins of the British Empire in Asia, 1600–1750* (Cambridge: Cambridge University Press, 2020).

18. "Small forays at Sagadahoc (1607), Bermuda (1609), Guyana (1609), Newfoundland (1610), and Plymouth (1620) were soon overshadowed in the 1620s and 1630s by intense colonial activity in the Caribbean and on the North American mainland and by the large-scale migration from England that sustained those ventures." Games, *Web of Empire*, 146. Thus, naturally, L.H. Roper's monograph on seventeenth-century British imperial endeavor, *Advancing Empire*, deals mostly with Atlantic affairs: that is where substantial colonial activity was taking place. As Holden Furber noted long ago: "The interest of the English court and gentry, and a sizeable body of merchants, in colonizing activity in the Caribbean, in Virginia, and Ireland diverted capital and brains from East India trading." *Rival Empires of Trade in the Orient, 1600–1800* (Minneapolis: University of Minnesota Press, 1976), 78.

19. Marshall, "English in Asia," 270.

Prologue 7

neglect may be judged deserved—that is, there was not enough success to be better remembered.

Just as important in explaining the historiographical gap is the fact that the expedition's richest and, by far, most informative record suffered exceptional neglect. An impressively detailed and meticulous account of this venture was written by one of its principal factors, Peter Mundy. The section of his journal that covered his voyage to China as a merchant and linguist of the Courteen Association was only published after World War I. The third volume of *The Travels of Peter Mundy* was published in 1919. Some time after Mundy's death in around 1667 his journal had fallen into the hands of the Worths. From them this global-roaming merchant's manuscript containing his China experience was probably purchased by the legendary bibliophile, Thomas Rawlinson (1681–1725). When the Rawlinson MSS were sold, in 1734, Mundy's journal seems to have landed in the Bodleian Library, Oxford University. There its first editor and publisher Richard Temple found it in the twentieth century.

Several decades before Temple commenced his enormous editorial toil, in 1846, William Desborough Cooley had founded the Hakluyt Society to publish unprinted and rare accounts of medieval and early modern travels and voyages. Temple rendered invaluable service in editing the handsome, map- and illustration-rich multi-volume edition of Mundy's travel journals for that publication series.[20] In the Mundy *Travels* volume pertaining to China, Temple's editorial industry was marvelously wide and deep—covering not only related English but also Portuguese and Spanish and a few Dutch documents. That conscientious work of Temple is debt-inducing in all would-be Courteen historians—myself at the forefront. However, readers seeking a smooth, continuous, and chronological narrative of the China expedition will find themselves often drowning or at least losing their bearings and sense of sequence in copious and discursive footnotes—where the thread can be lost even by the grimly focused, vigilant, and earnest. At the core of this book is a much more consolidated and coherent narrative than that assembled in the Hakluyt Mundy volume.[21]

When Temple introduced the volume of Mundy which recorded the British experience in China in 1637, he noted: "So far as I am aware, beyond the references in Mr. Foster's *English Factories*, Mundy's narrative of his China voyage as a factor in Weddell's ill-fated expedition financed by Sir William Courteen, has received no serious attention from any author except Mr. James Bromley Eames (*The English in China*) who, however, does not seem to have consulted the original MS. or was

---

20. *The Travels of Peter Mundy, in Europe and Asia, 1608–1667, Vol. III: Travels in England, India, China, Etc., 1634–1638* (London: Hakluyt Society, 1919). This volume contains Temple's transcription of the MS Rawlinson A.315 still preserved at the Bodleian Library, Oxford University. I should say Temple-supervised transcription, as in the preface he vouched for the accuracy of E. G. Parker's labor. Nineteenth-century-executed copies of this manuscript are now in the British Library, London.

21. In Chapter 9, I further discuss Mundy, Temple, and related bibliographical matters, as well as offer additional tribute to both. It is there that I also make the case for regarding Mundy as the first English sinologist, *avant la lettre*.

dependent on an inaccurate copyist for his extracts."[22] A century after Temple's remark, not so much has changed. While various historians and writers, Western and Chinese, have consulted the Hakluyt-packaged, Temple-edited Mundy, they have not used and exploited much of his journal, let alone all the other English and European (chiefly Portuguese) documents that yield a rich narrative of the first trade expedition to directly access the Canton market. The older and rival EIC was not in a position to observe the Courteen fleet in China, but correspondence conducted before they reached and after they left informs us, if often only second-hand, of some important details. All students of the early EIC and Courteen Association are enormously indebted to William Foster for the *English Factories* volumes as noted by Temple. From EIC records we also learn much about the genesis of the Courteen Association and some biographical details of its directors, leadership, mariners, and factors.[23]

Most of the Courteen personnel, beyond the trio introduced above, were quondam EIC employees. Besides Peter Mundy, another ex-EIC merchant, members of the Courteen fleet, including its commander, Weddell, and chief factors (and brothers) Nathaniel and John Mountney, as well as Thomas Robinson, left records and accounts of their experience in China in 1637; to wit:

1) Account of the voyage of Weddell's fleet from the 14/24 April 1636 to 6/16 April 1637 (summarized in *Calendar of State Papers*, Dom. Chas. I. CCCLI, No. 30), most likely written by Nathaniel or John Mountney or Thomas Robinson—I attribute to Nathaniel Mountney. This covers the expedition from embarkation at the Downs (April 1636) to its passage through the straits of Melaka (April 1637); I refer to this account as "Voyage of Captain Weddell's Fleet, April 1636–April 1637."

2) Account of the expedition from the Straits of Melaka 6/16 April 1637 to shortly after departure from China in 4/14 February 1638; which was preserved at the India Office in Temple's time and cited by him as *Marine Records*, Vol. LXIII; now preserved in the British Library. While quoted and labeled as "Continuation" by Temple, I will refer to it as the "Voyage of the Weddell Fleet."

3) Weddell's own account of the expedition which in Temple's time was preserved at the India Office as O.C. 1662. I will refer to it as "Weddell's China Narrative, O.C. 1662."

4) A report by Nathaniel Mountney to the Courteen Association, 19/29 December 1637, MS. Rawl. A.299, written just after all trade in China had been concluded. I will refer to this as: Mountney, Rawlinson A.299.

---

22. Mundy, III, Preface, vii.
23. As noted by William Foster: "At the beginning of July 1637 we lose the invaluable aid of the Company's records, for the volume containing the minutes from that point to July 1639 is unfortunately missing." Ethel Bruce Sainsbury and William Foster, eds., *Calendar of the Court Minutes of the East India Company, 1635–1639* (Oxford: Clarendon, 1907), xxiv.

Prologue 9

5) Notes by Thomas Robinson and the Mountneys outlining the prospects of trade in China, Aceh, and Bhatkal in 1637 (PRO, C.O. 77/6, No. 49); which I refer to as "Notes on the Prospects of Trade in China."

6) Set of miscellaneous documents by multiple authors preserved at the Bodleian Library, as MS. Rawlinson, A.399, transcribed and referred to as the "Courteen Papers" by Temple. I will cite them simply as "Rawlinson A.399."

Mundy's and the accounts of his colleagues (as listed above) are far from identical and even contain some important discrepancies—as will be noted throughout my narrative and discussed in Chapters 8 and 9. The journal of Mundy is by far the most detailed and reliable—although there were some important episodes in China that Mundy and Weddell had no opportunity to observe with their own eyes. For example, the experience of the Mountneys and Robinson as captives in Canton (narrated in Chapters 6 and 7) could only be told second-hand by Mundy and Weddell. We are forced to rely on Mountneys and Robinson (and Chinese and Portuguese documents) to relate some significant incidents involving the British in Canton. In case of conflicts between English accounts, Mundy's is the one most worthy of trust and the one to which I have usually accorded benefit of the doubt. Throughout his editing of the multi-volume journal, Temple, an exceptionally conscientious and painstaking editor, repeatedly praised the widely traveled and savvy Courteen merchant for accuracy and disciplined, punctilious, and non-embellishing journalism.[24]

Neglect of the first British trade expedition to China—or at least the absence of a book devoted solely to telling and analyzing its complicated story—is also to be ascribed to the challenge of gathering and mastering all the non-Courteen, non-English sources. As the Portuguese were ensconced in Macao in the coastal province of Guangdong (where Canton—Guangzhou—is capital) decades before this expedition was launched, it is not surprising to find many informative records left by the Lusitanians who greeted the British newcomers. Particularly rich are the *Livros das Monções*, the documents known to English scholars as "Books of the Monsoons." They comprise royal and other official correspondence and dispatches between Lisbon and the Portuguese viceroy stationed at Goa, headquarters of the *Estado da Índia*.[25] As this viceroy supervised (if none too effectively) the Portuguese enclave of Macao, the Weddell expedition is treated in great detail in some documents of this collection. The Hakluyt Mundy editor Temple was able to procure English translations of all the germane Portuguese letters, reports, agreements, and notes extant

---

24. On several occasions C.R. Boxer praised Mundy's sangfroid disposition and noted his consistent reliability and accuracy—whether reporting on matters and events in India or China. Some indicative specimens from just one Boxer book: "the perceptive Peter Mundy"; "Mundy was an exceptionally balanced and judicious observer." *Portuguese India in the Mid-Seventeenth Century* (Delhi: Oxford University Press, 1980), 50.

25. For description and assessment of the *Livros das Monções* see the appendix in George B. Souza, *The Survival of Empire: Portuguese Trade and Society in China and the South China Sea, 1630–1754* (Cambridge: Cambridge University Press, 1986); and C.R. Boxer, "A Glimpse of the Goa Archives," in *Portuguese Conquest and Commerce in Southern Asia, 1500–1700* (London: Variorum Reprints, 1985).

in Lisbon and Goa. Thus, the would-be narrator of Weddell's China expedition may employ what Temple reproduced generously as "Lisbon Transcripts, Books of the Monsoons," in the relevant volume of Mundy's journal.[26] These Portuguese documents are of inestimable value for, as Temple emphasized, neither originals nor copies of the correspondence between the British and the Portuguese and Chinese authorities at Macao and Canton are to be found among the English records.[27]

The most extensive and recent account by a Portuguese scholar, Rogério Miguel Puga, available in English translation and employing all these Portuguese primary sources, is a chapter in his *British in Macau, 1635–1793*.[28] As the title alone would suggest, Puga's purpose, within the scope of a two-century survey, was not to offer a comprehensive account of the 1637 British-Portuguese-Chinese encounter and interactions as initiated by the Courteen interlopers—let alone to explain in much detail how Weddell's fleet was conceived, funded, and organized. The brief narrative and discussion of the Weddell sojourn at Macao which Puga does provide is not informed or supplemented by any of the available Ming primary sources; nor does he grapple with such vexing things as discrepancies between: 1) British vs. Portuguese; and 2) British vs. British (e.g., Mundy vs. Weddell) accounts. Puga's objective did not permit him the luxury of digging deep and turning over every stone to write his rendition of the first British trade expedition to China—no matter how much it revolved around Macao. Similarly, Temple's brief account (much less any other summary of this expedition available in English published since) did not wrestle with all the issues and problems which arise from minute examination and comparison of all the English and Portuguese documents. No less importantly, and, again, like Puga, Temple and all the other English authors of more recent summaries have made no attempt to apply or incorporate the Chinese records—though, as discussed briefly below and at much greater length in Chapter 8, these records are not as abundant as the European ones. None of the English-writing chroniclers, narrators, or commentators on the Courteen China expedition has utilized (or cited and quoted) Ming sources in an attempt to shed further light on British dealings and communications with the Portuguese and Chinese at Macao and Canton. My account is the first English one to utilize and reflect the Ming records as well as all the English and Portuguese primary sources.

As should be clear from considering Chapter 1, when Weddell's fleet arrived in the Pearl River estuary in the summer of 1637, the Dutch were already well and advantageously established across the Taiwan Strait in Zeelandia, southwest

---

26. Temple supervised Leonora de Alberti's Portuguese-English translations of documents from R.A. Bulhão Pato, ed., *Documentos remetidos da Índia*, 5 vols. (Lisbon: Academia Real das Ciências, 1893), Vol. IV.

27. Mundy, Journal, ed. Temple, III, 159, n. 3.

28. Rogério Miguel Puga, *The British in Macau, 1635–1793* (Hong Kong: Hong Kong University / Royal Asiatic Society Great Britain and Ireland, 2013); this is the English translation by Monica Andrade of what was originally published in 2009 by Centro de História de Alem-Mar (CHAM), FCSH-New University of Lisbon, and by Centro Cultural e Científico de Macau (Lisbon, Portugal) as *A Presença Inglesa e as Relações Anglo-Portuguesas em Macau (1635–1793)*.

Prologue

"Formosa" as it had been called by the Portuguese. In that location, however, they only proved a peripheral factor in the story of the British that unfolded in and around the shores of the Pearl River between July 1637 and January 1638. From Goa to Aceh to Melaka to Macao, Courteen relations and interactions with the Dutch were important—and awkward when not tense or hostile—for the two sets of "red barbarians" (紅夷 *hongyi* and 紅毛 *hongmao*), as denominated by the Ming Chinese, vied with one another to outmaneuver and supplant the Iberians in Asia. Chapters 1 and 3 relate key Anglo-Dutch events and issues that arose during the Weddell fleet's voyage around the Cape of Good Hope to India through the Straits of Melaka to China. Similar to how EIC records shed light on the Weddell expedition, the Dutch East India Company (Vereenigde Oost-Indische Compagnie: VOC) records are used at some junctures in the narrative which follows.[29] Once the British were arrived in China, however, the Dutch fade into the background. Accordingly, Dutch primary documents do not contribute in any major way to our account of the British drama in China. The Spanish in Manila were likewise peripheral; Spanish documents, like the Dutch ones, do not offer us significant assistance in telling the story of what happened to Weddell and the Courteens at Macao, Canton, and in between.[30]

In view of such a diversity of documents in multiple languages entailed in telling the story of the British in China in 1637, an observation of the late John Wills recalls itself. In the bibliographical essay appended to his magisterial survey of Sino-Western maritime relations in the sixteenth and seventeenth centuries, he noted: "There is no fully adequate monograph in any language on any major facet of Ming relations with maritime Europeans. The great stumbling block has been the need to make use of European archival and old printed sources and at the same time to have control of the Chinese sources."[31] The "stumbling block"—or, at least, very daunting challenge—of researching the first major episode of Anglo-Chinese relations is rendered smaller by the fact that there are not as many Chinese records as English and Portuguese ones. The scarcity of Ming records on the British presence in Guangdong in 1637, as I will discuss fully in Chapter 8, has more than a little to do with the collapse of the dynasty just six years after Captain Weddell departed Macao with the Courteen fleet in January 1638. As I also explain in that chapter, the Ming government in Beijing had many bigger and more pressing issues and problems to deal with up north, and far from the shores of the Pearl River. Neglect of and commensurately meager reporting on the presence of a small British commercial

---

29. For the Weddell expedition, the most pertinent of such Dutch sources is the *Dagh-Register gehouden int Casteel Batavia*, published at Batavia (Jakarta), Java and The Hague, 1887–1912.

30. That is far from saying that the Dutch and Spanish were unimportant in shaping the conditions and situation in that part of Ming China where the British fleet spent six months in 1637. None of the chapters which follow ought to suggest otherwise. The market and political-diplomatic situation in Macao and Canton were heavily influenced by what the Spanish and the Dutch were doing from their bases in the Philippines and Taiwan.

31. John Wills, Jr., *Cambridge History of China, Ming Dynasty*, Part 2, Vol. 8, ed. Frederick W. Mote and Denis Twitchett (Cambridge: Cambridge University Press, 1998), 995.

fleet in its southeast periphery is to be expected in a Ming China whose regime was confronting the colossal Manchurian nemesis that would become the Qing dynasty.

A handful of Chinese scholars have grappled with the Ming sources that deal with incidents and aspects of the British enterprise in the Pearl River Delta. However, they have not published full or book-length accounts of this expedition, whether in Chinese or English. This is not surprising when we consider that Chinese scholars must wrestle with seventeenth-century English—not that Mundy's or Weddell's is nearly as difficult as Shakespeare's—in addition to the Portuguese records produced by the viceroys of Goa, captain-generals and Senado da Camara of Macao. Our contemporary scholars Wan Ming and Lawrence Wong meet with some formidable linguistic challenges in dealing with these seventeenth-century Western sources. Intermittently in subsequent chapters I comment upon, and at depth in Chapter 8 I discuss the Chinese-language scholarship of Wan, Wong, and some of their peers and predecessors in the Sino-Luso-British field. Here let it suffice to observe that none of them were attempting more than brief accounts or article-length treatments of aspects of the first British venture to China. As they have only endeavored to provide summaries and strictly circumscribed analysis of a few facets, they cannot be faulted very easily for any dereliction of scholarly duty.[32] One could object to minor errors, like Wong's misinforming his Chinese readership that Weddell was still living three years after he was drowned in the Indian Ocean. It would not be too surprising if neither Wan nor Wong read the *Oxford Dictionary of National Biography* articles on William Courteen and John Weddell. As for that reference work's articles on Nathaniel and John Mountney, as well as an entry for Thomas Robinson, there are none to be found. In the same way that the story of the British trade expedition may lead to a recognition of the Mountneys and Robinson sufficient to warrant their inclusion in the next edition of a *Dictionary of National Biography*, on the Chinese side, the roles played in this story by (hitherto obscure) Li Yerong (李葉榮), Chen Qian (陳謙), Zheng Jinguang (鄭覲光), Ge Zhengqi (葛徵奇), and Zhang Jingxin (張鏡心) may lead to their inclusion in the next edition of a dictionary of Ming biography.[33]

---

32. 万明 [Wan Ming], "明代中英的第一次直接碰撞—来自中、英、葡三方的历史记述" [The first direct clash of China and Britain during the Ming dynasty from the historical accounts of the Chinese, English, and Portuguese], 中国社会科学院历史研究所集刊, 第三辑 [*Chinese Academy of Social Sciences Historical Research Journal*] 3 (2004): 56–69; 王宏志 [Lawrence Wang-chi Wong], "通事與奸民：明末中英虎門事件中的譯者" [The Bogue Incident translator, 1637], 編譯論叢, 第五卷, 第一期 (2012年3月) [*Compilation and Translation Review* 5, no. 1 (Mar. 2012)]: 41–66. Professor Wong lists all the Ming primary sources in his Works Cited. Further, Tang Kaijian and Zhang Kun provide a brief but detailed review of these sources and the best of Chinese scholarship in 湯開建、張坤 [Tang Kaijian and Zhang Kun], "兩廣總督張鏡心《雲隱堂文錄》中保存的崇禎末年澳門資料" [Governor of Guangdong and Guangxi, Zhang Jingxin's reports concerning Macao at the end of Chongzhen's reign], 澳門研究 [*Boletim de Estudos de Macau/Journal of Macau Studies*] 35, no. 8 (August 2006): 122–32.

33. Their titles, jurisdictions, and functions within Ming and Guangdong governance are identified and discussed in Chapters 8 and 9. They are also listed in the Appendix, "Key Chinese Officials in Ming Documents with English Renderings by the Courteens."

Prologue   13

Finally, the neglect of the China expedition of the British in 1637 must also be partially imputed to the events of the decade which followed its launch—events in those isles ruled by a dynasty, the Stuart, that fell at about the same time as the Ming under the last, Chongzhen emperor. All over the world, revolts, civil wars, and destruction of kingdoms and dynasties followed swiftly in the wake of the departure of the British from China in 1637. (No, I do not here attempt a post-hoc-ergo-propter-hoc miracle.) These tumults are among the constituents of the famous historiographical constructs: "Seventeenth-Century Crisis" and more recently, and climate-change enhanced, "Global Crisis."[34] While the Weddell fleet was in China, Charles I, beginning late July 1637, was trying to quell disorders in the wake of the introduction of the Scottish Prayer Book.[35] The accounts and memories of that British expedition to China were only among many that got lost in the heads and shuffle of the historical annals, and virtually eclipsed by the chain of events and civil wars which culminated in the decapitation of Charles Stuart in 1649—just five years after the noosed suicide of the Chongzhen emperor in Beijing in 1644. As for the Iberians, in the mid-1630s the Habsburg Philip IV of Spain/Philip III of Portugal had to be most absorbed by issues closer to home arising out of the Thirty Years' War. Like Chongzhen dealing with Li Zicheng and Zhang Xianzhong, domestic rebels, and Manchu invaders; Charles confronting rebellions, civil wars, and strategic and revenue challenges posed by those and the continental war; Philip, jointly ruler of Spanish and Portuguese, could not afford to spend a great deal of time considering minute details of issues pertaining to Asia. In 1637, the same year that Weddell's fleet was arriving at Macao, Philip was facing Portuguese revolts and, three years later, the Catalan revolt. By 1640, the Portuguese had regained independence from the Spanish Habsburgs, under the direction of the House of Braganza. One of that family's princesses, Catherine, would bring Bombay (Mumbai) into the fledgling British Empire as dowry in her marriage to Charles II, son of the royal sponsor of the Courteen expedition—one of whose ships, the *Katherine*, would disappear in the same ocean that swallowed the China-baptized *Dragon* and Captain John Weddell.

---

34. The grand culmination of the conceit is Geoffrey Parker, *Global Crisis: War, Climate Change and Catastrophe in the Seventeenth Century* (New Haven, CT: Yale University Press, 2014).

35. The "St. Giles incident" of 23 July 1637 in Edinburgh sparked the Covenanting movement opposed energetically and polemically by Anglican ecclesiastical scourge of presbyterian nonconformity, Bishop John Bramhall. Nicholas D. Jackson, *Hobbes, Bramhall and the Politics of Liberty and Necessity: A Quarrel of the Civil Wars and Interregnum* (Cambridge: Cambridge University Press, 2007), 32–36.

1

The British in Seventeenth-Century Luso-Dutch Asia

Direct trade between the English and Portuguese can be documented at least as early as the time of King John I of England (1199–1216). The patent roll of the fourth year of his reign refers to commerce between the Atlantic neighbors. King John's fourteenth-century successor, Edward III, expanded opportunities for merchants by signing a commercial accord with the cities of Lisbon and Oporto in 1359. The English king followed up, in 1373, by forging a political alliance with King Fernando of Portugal (1367–1383). This proved crucial for the defense of Portugal against its aggrandizing Iberian neighbor in the east of the peninsula. In 1384, during the Castilian siege of Lisbon, English ships arrived in time to reinforce the Lusitanians. After the siege had been broken, hundreds of English archers played a major role in the Battle of Aljubarrota (1385). The outcome of the battle secured not only the throne of King John (João) I of Portugal (1384–1433) but preserved the small kingdom as an independent nation.[1] That monarch brought the insular English and coastal Portuguese into a long-term alliance by the Treaty of Windsor in 1386.[2] In the following century much larger numbers of English merchants traveled to the bustling entrepot of Lisbon, where they acquired substantial privileges from King Afonso V (1438–1481). By the end of the fifteenth century, some of this English merchant contingent, including their wives and children, had settled in Portugal.[3] It was also during that century that the royalty of the two nations, the houses of Lancaster and Avis, became intertwined by marriage. The illustrious Prince Henry the Navigator of Portugal, the Infante Dom Henrique, was a nephew of the English King Henry IV. That prince's role in paving the way to Portuguese imperial grandeur in the sixteenth century is legendary—if now diminished by some debunking by scholars of the last few decades.

---

1. L.M.E. Shaw, *The Anglo-Portuguese Alliance and the English Merchants in Portugal, 1654–1810* (Aldershot: Ashgate, 1998), 5–6; Malyn Newitt, *Portugal in European and World History* (London: Reaktion, 2009), 43–46; Anthony Disney, *A History of Portugal and the Portuguese Empire: From Beginnings to 1807*, Vol. I (Cambridge: Cambridge University Press, 2009), 120–21.
2. Signed 9 May 1386, the Treaty of Windsor was renewed by monarchs of both countries until 1499.
3. "Although their community in Lisbon was small, by the early seventeenth century, the English were the most prominent of the merchant communities in Portugal." Games, *Web of Empire*, 100.

As Tudor England became more able and committed to emulating the navigational prowess and the commercial and colonial dynamism of the Lusitanians, conflict arose.[4] Piratical raids by the English upon the Iberians plying their trade along the west coast of Africa prompted the Portuguese King Sebastian to incite reprisals against England, and he issued an edict to prohibit all English ships from visiting Portuguese ports, and banning textile and other imports from England. By the middle of the reign of Elizabeth I (1558–1603), England, as a Dutch aider-and-abettor, had become an open (if not firmly committed) enemy of the Habsburg Spanish king, Philip II. This powerful Iberian monarch, ruler of a world empire, exerted himself to thwart any reconciliation between neighboring Portugal and England. But by the end of 1576, Elizabeth and the King of Portugal had signed a treaty to render amicable relations between the two seafaring nations. That treaty was rendered a nullity only four years later, however. In 1578 King Sebastian was slain in the Battle of El Caser-el Kebir. When Sebastian's heir, and uncle, died in 1580, it was Philip II of Spain who inherited the crown to become concurrently Philip I of Portugal. While the coastal European realm of Portugal was nothing vast, its empire was global by this time. Philip II/I inherited an opulent assortment of overseas possessions from Brazil to Africa, from Hormuz in the Persian Gulf to Goa in India, to Melaka on the Malay peninsula, and Macao in China. At Macao on the southeast periphery of Ming China, seventy miles from the provincial capital, Canton (Guangzhou), the Portuguese had established a prosperous commercial enclave in 1557, just a year before Elizabeth acceded to the throne of England.[5]

It was not the Lusitanians so much as an Italian who had sparked the global imagination of the Tudor English. Italians, just as much as any Iberians, had kindled in the English notions of unknown or remote lands of abundant gold and silver, minerals, spices, and commercial opportunity. Christopher Columbus was among the multitude of Europeans who believed the stories about China told by Marco Polo. Fantasies of China derived from the tales of the Venetian Polo stirred in his head as he plotted a voyage to the fabulous land conjured by a mixture of fact and fiction.[6] The Genoese Columbus was to carry aboard the *Santa Maria* a copy of Polo's account of the Far East. Like other Europeans, the English relished

---

4. For English interest in commerce in Guinea and the west coast in the late fifteenth century, see P.E.H. Hair and Robin Law, "The English in Western Africa to 1700," in *The Origins of Empire*, ed. Nicholas Canny (Oxford: Oxford University Press, 1998), 245; for the importance of the Guinea trade in the development of English maritime ventures and clashes between England and Portugal from the mid-sixteenth century, see John W. Blake, *West Africa: Quest for God and Gold, 1454–1578* (London, 1977); and Kenneth R. Andrews, *Trade, Plunder*, 101–15.

5. For the establishment of Macao in the 1550s, C.R. Boxer reviews all the Portuguese and Chinese documents in *South China in the Sixteenth Century: Being the Narratives of Galeote Pereira, Fr. Gaspar da Cruz, O.P., and Fr. Martin de Rada, O.E.S.A. (1550–1575)* (London: Hakluyt Society, 1953), xxxiii–xxxvii. More recently John Wills offered a refined and authoritative summary, *China and Maritime Europe, 1500–1800: Trade, Settlement, Diplomacy, and Missions* (Cambridge: Cambridge University Press, 2011), 35–40.

6. Columbus learned the names of "Cathay" (north China) and "Cipango" (Japan) from the Venetian Marco Polo. For sources accessed by Columbus, see Valerie Flint, *The Imaginative Landscape of Christopher Columbus* (Princeton, NJ: Princeton University Press, 1992).

the account of Polo and closely followed the subsequent exploits of the Italians, Portuguese, and Spanish as the Mediterraneans explored, discovered, and conquered exotic and scarcely imagined parts of the world. Then a pseudo-Englishman Sir John Mandeville contributed something of a sequel to the volume of tales of the Venetian merchant-traveler. A book that was probably read even more than Polo's *Milione*, Mandeville's *Travels*, many of them quite imaginary, and exceedingly far-fetched, was published in England in 1499.[7]

The accounts of Marco Polo and Sir John Mandeville can only have stimulated English curiosity about China and other lands in the Far East. While the English had consumed the Italian's tales, and savored the lore of Mandeville, they tarried well behind the southern Europeans in exploration, enterprise, and conquest in Asia.[8] It was only the voyage of Sir Francis Drake in the years 1577–1580 which furnished the English with some of their own first-hand intelligence about the splendors and prospects of the East and the oceanic geography relevant to reaching and realizing them. Drake's pioneering voyage also engendered more hope that the Portuguese Asian imperial realm, the *Estado da India*, was more vulnerable than previously supposed.[9] Another Englishman, Thomas Cavendish, circled the globe a decade later, in 1586–1588. His report about the voyage offered this intriguing description: "I navigated to the island of the Philippinos hard upon the coast of China, of which country I have brought such intelligence as hath not been heard of in these parts. The stateliness and riches of which country I fear to make a report of, lest I should not be credited."[10] Cavendish's acquisition of such an exotic item as a Chinese map was a sensation in London, and it nurtured amateur and more practical and mercenary collecting.[11] Interest if not confidence in reaching China grew with news of Cavendish's successful trip, coupled with the first major publication in English of a book about China. Provided with a dedication to Cavendish, whom

---

7. There were more than three hundred versions in multiple languages (including Irish and Czech) of Mandeville's tales. Games, *Web of Empire*, 20. Before the close of the seventeenth century, nine English editions had been published. A recent discussion of Mandeville can be found in Ralf Hertel, "Faking It: The Invention of East Asia in Early Modern England," in *Early Encounters between East Asia and Europe: Telling Failures*, ed. Ralf Hertel and Michael Keevak (London: Routledge, 2017), 31, where it is noted that the author claimed he had served the Chinese emperor—and, just as arresting, that "we do not even know whether Mandeville was English at all."

8. Tudor lack of incentive and initiative is discussed by Nicholas Canny, "The Origins of Empire: An Introduction," in *The Origins of Empire*, ed. Nicholas Canny (Oxford: Oxford University Press, 1998), 3–4.

9. Derek Massarella, *A World Elsewhere: Europe's Encounter with Japan in the Sixteenth and Seventeenth Centuries* (New Haven, CT: Yale University Press, 1990), 53.

10. Quoted in Earl H. Pritchard, *Anglo-Chinese Relations during the Seventeenth and Eighteenth Centuries* (Urbana: University of Illinois Press, 1929), 45.

11. "Thomas Cavendish returned to London from his circumnavigation of the globe with a Chinese map of the Ming Empire, a Chinese compass, two Japanese sailors, and three young boys from the Philippines, all captured from a Spanish ship off the coast of Mexico. This was the first of three important maps from China—the second printed by Samuel Purchas in 1625 and the third being John Selden's map—that would shape ideas about East Asia and global trade in London." Robert Batchelor, *London: The Selden Map and the Making of a Global City, 1549–1689* (Chicago: University of Chicago Press, 2014); 65. For this map and fresh discussion of the significance of Cavendish's activities, see 64–76.

he exhorted to further global exploits, in 1588 Robert Parke printed his translation of Mendoza's monumental work of European sinology.[12] First published in Rome in 1585, it was to shape Western views of China throughout the seventeenth century. Richard Hakluyt the younger, recognizing the unique value of Mendoza's encyclopedic scholarship, had urged Robert Parke to undertake a translation. So it was that in London in 1588, the same year as the Armada invasion, the book appeared in English dress as *The Historie of the great and mightie kingdome of China, and the situation thereof: Together with the great riches, huge citties, politicke government, and rare inventions in the same.*[13]

While the English continued to translate Portuguese and Spanish accounts of China and Asia after Parke's rendering of Mendoza's seminal book, they also began to challenge, compete, and clash with them on distant seas and coasts. Along with the Dutch, Britons arose as a formidable threat to Spanish control and Portuguese dominance in both eastern and western hemispheres—in many areas across the untidily arranged Tordesillas globe. Just four years after translating the Spanish Mendoza, Elizabethans captured the Portuguese carrack *Madre de Dios* in the Atlantic. Not only in one stroke did the British enrich themselves prodigiously by a cargo of precious metal as well as merchandise fetched from the East, they also acquired a treasure of knowledge in the form of a book printed at Macao in 1590. This Latin treatise on China ultimately fell into the hands of Richard Hakluyt the younger who published an English version in 1599. It contained the most accurate and freshest information about China for some of its contents were compiled from recent reports by Matteo Ricci and other Jesuits who had penetrated the Middle Kingdom beyond Macao. The British also benefited from similar intelligence-plundering performed by the Dutch. At about the same time as Hakluyt's aforementioned publication, Elizabethans were reading the Dutch Linschoten's divulgence of Asian trade and navigational secrets from the Portuguese-extracted *Itinerario*. Among the most valuable items in that compendium were details about routes that Lusitanians

---

12. The qualification "major" is necessary to register the fact that prior to Parke's translation of Mendoza, a small publication in English appeared. The *Treaty of China*, by the Portuguese Galeote Pereira, was translated from Italian by Richard Eden and Richard Willes and published by the latter as the *History of Travayle in the West and East Indies*, and subsequently by Hakluyt. For the funding and aristocratic patronage of Willes, as well as an inventory and assessment of his motley translations of various Iberians, see Batchelor, *London*, 76–78. For Pereira, who was imprisoned in Fujian from 1549 to 1553, see Boxer, *South China*. Furthermore, the Spaniard Bernardino de Escalante's book on China, *Discours of the Navigation which the Portugales doe Make to the Realmes and Provinces of the East Partes of the World, and of the knowledge that growes by them of the great thinges, which are in the Dominion of China*, published in Seville in 1577, was translated and published in London only two years later by John Frampton, a retired merchant who had done business in Seville. For Frampton's publications, see Batchelor, *London*, 270n54.
13. The paramount influence of Mendoza's sinology, long ago documented by Donald Lach, has been reiterated by Michael Keevak, *Embassies to China: Diplomacy and Cultural Encounters before the Opium Wars* (London: Palgrave Macmillan, 2017), 51; for translations, editions, and European-wide influence, see also Georg Lehner, *China in European Encyclopaedias, 1700–1850* (Leiden: Brill, 2011), 74.

used between China and Japan, as yielded by their rutter books (*roteiros*).[14] As the British had still not come even close to reaching China by the end of the sixteenth century, so they remained totally dependent on their fellow Europeans for information about China.[15] Both the Hakluyts and Samuel Purchas aimed to incite their compatriots to undertake further voyages and enterprise in the Far East, in emulation of the Iberians, Italians, and Dutch.[16] In the last decade of Elizabeth's reign and the two decades of James I's rule (1603–1625), this industrious pair translated and commissioned translations of writings about Asia and China undertaken by other Europeans. They also encouraged the procurement of and subsequently published maps, acquired by fair means and foul.[17]

Not that there were no English whatsoever compiling their own notes about the East. But few wrote from direct access; most merely recorded what was related to them. Ralph Fitch, for example, during his extensive travel in Asia in 1585–1591 had gathered some remarkably accurate information about the Portuguese trade from Macao to Japan—but obviously he had visited neither. Moreover, it was several years after his return that Fitch's not-so-fresh market intelligence was published by Hakluyt: "When the Portuguese go from Macao in China to Japan, they carry much white silk, gold, musk, and porcelain; and they bring forth from thence nothing but silver. They have a great carrack which goes thither every year, and she brings from thence every year above six hundred thousand cruzados; and all this silver of Japan, and two hundred thousand cruzados more in silver which they bring yearly out of India, they employ to their great advantage in China; and they bring from thence gold, musk, silk, copper, porcelains, and many other things very costly, and gilded."[18] Such reporting, whether dependent on or ultimately derived from Iberians or not (or *via* the Dutch or not) bolstered interest and whetted the imperial

---

14. "During five years as secretary to the [Portuguese] Archbishop of Goa, van Linschoten had quietly compiled a dossier on the eastern sea routes which he then smuggled back to Europe, an achievement which may constitute the most momentous piece of commercial and maritime espionage ever." John Keay, *The Honourable Company: A History of the English East India Company* (London: Harper Collins, 1991), 54. The first English captain to voyage to Japan (arriving at Hirado in 1613), John Saris, was to carry a copy of Linschoten.

15. Long ago William Appleton noted this sinological dependence in his generalization: "During the seventeenth and eighteenth centuries a mythical China had been created. Largely a synthetic product, the China that Stuart and Augustan Englishmen visualized was seen refracted through Jesuit eyes." *A Cycle of Cathay: The Chinese Vogue in England during the Seventeenth and Eighteenth Centuries* (New York: Columbia University Press, 1951), v. A more recent literature review that does not contradict Appleton can be found in Lee, *The English Renaissance and the Far East*. Nor is the repose enjoyed by Appleton disturbed at all by Robert Markley's *The Far East and the English Imagination, 1600–1730* (Cambridge: Cambridge University Press, 2006). For more literary views, consult Adrian Hsia, ed., *The Vision of China in the English Literature of the Seventeenth and Eighteenth Centuries* (Hong Kong: Chinese University of Hong Kong Press, 1998).

16. "[English] trading companies [routinely] provided copies of Hakluyt and Purchas to overseas merchants." Games, *Web of Empire*, 21.

17. For published English maps in Jacobean times acquired forcibly and otherwise, see not only Batchelor, *London* but also the same author's "The Selden Map Rediscovered: A Chinese Map of East Asian Shipping Routes, c. 1619," *Imago Mundi: The International Journal for the History of Cartography* 65, no. 1 (2013): 37–63, as well as Timothy Brook, *Mr. Selden's Map of China: Decoding the Secrets of a Vanished Cartographer* (London: Bloomsbury, 2013).

18. These lines were published in the second edition of Hakluyt's *Principall Navigations*, volume II, in 1599.

appetite among the Elizabethans for eastern voyages that might ultimately pave the way to a British version of Goa, Melaka, Macao, or Manila (established by the Spanish in 1571). At all events, by the dawn of the seventeenth century, the British were thoroughly aware of many aspects of the enormously lucrative trade that was being conducted by the Portuguese in the Far East between China and Japan and the Spanish from Manila in the Philippines.

Besides the exploits of roving and marauding pirates and opportunistic privateers, the English executed their first commercial voyage aimed at China in 1596. Then a highly placed courtier of Queen Elizabeth, Sir Robert Dudley funded three ships: the *Bear*, *Bear's Whelp*, and *Benjamin*. The Tudor monarch provided a letter in Latin addressed to the Chinese emperor in which she requested that he accord free trade and related liberties and privileges to her sea-faring subjects. She proffered reciprocation: "We on the other side will not only perform all the offices of a well-willing prince unto your Highness, but also for the greater increase of mutual love and commerce between us and our subjects . . . do most willingly grant unto all and every your subjects (if it shall seem good to your Highness) full and entire liberty unto any of the parts of our dominions to resort there to abide and traffic, and thence to return."[19] Alas, the emperor of China at that time, Wanli (reigned 1573–1620), was never given an opportunity to respond to these Elizabethan overtures of amity. Apparently the fleet of three met terrible mishap and it is thought that a decimated crew, far from reaching China, merely fell into the hands of Spaniards who duly put them out of their misery. While these British had snared some Portuguese ships, disease would later slaughter many of them. In any event, none of this expedition survived to bring back any report about China. The early years of James I's reign saw some British scheming directed toward Asia, including some projecting by aristocrats who were not associated with the recently (1600) founded East India Company; but it seems to have been largely confined to ill-organized and ad-hoc piracy like Sir Edward Michelbourne's in 1604. Having obtained royal license—much to the disgust of the recently chartered EIC—to explore and trade in the East, he ended up raiding ships in the waters of southeast Asia, including Indian and Chinese junks trading among the Spice Islands.[20]

But while entry into Ming China remained just a quixotic aspiration, an Elizabethan, William Adams (1564–1620), had reached Japan in 1600. It is true that he came there as a navigator aboard a Dutch ship—the first non-Iberian and Protestant European ship to anchor in the northeast Asian archipelago.[21] That year the *Liefde* reached the shores of a Kyushu island after a decimating and heroic crossing of the Pacific. A little over a decade later, the recently founded English East India Company, rivalling the Dutch one (VOC), launched a voyage to the East that

---

19. Hakluyt, *Voyages, Travels, and Discoveries of the English Nation* (1810), Vol. IV, 372.
20. Pritchard, *Anglo-Chinese*, 46, 53.
21. Giles Milton, *Samurai William: The Adventurer Who Unlocked Japan* (London: Sceptre, 2003); and for a briefer account, see Massarella, *World Elsewhere*, 71–88.

went as far as Japan. The hope was to participate in (or procure profits indirectly from) the Iberian-dominated Japan-China trade—as the intrusive Dutch had just begun to do at Hirado in 1609, albeit peripherally, but still to the keen chagrin of the Portuguese from Macao and Spanish from Manila.[22] In January 1613, Adams wrote to the EIC personnel at Banten in west Java to encourage his compatriots to voyage to the archipelago up north. The English company's management in Banten, even before receiving communications from Adams, had already commenced preparations to send the *Clove*, a vessel of the EIC's Eighth Voyage, from there to Japan.[23] In this pioneering enterprise, Captain John Saris sailed the *Clove* into a Japanese harbor in June 1613.[24] Armed with a letter from King James addressed to the retired shogun of Ieyasu, Saris journeyed to Edo. By the intercession of Adams, the EIC captain was able to obtain substantial trading privileges for the British, including liberty to settle a trading post at Hirado, a small island off Kyushu, a little north of Nagasaki—where the Dutch had recently arrived, the same Hirado where the Portuguese had maintained a post before being forced to shift to Nagasaki.[25] In the following year Captain Saris returned to London and by pen and tongue rendered the EIC executives an over-optimistic prospectus on commerce in the archipelago.[26]

Following the Adams-facilitated breakthrough of John Saris in Japan, for a decade, 1613–1623, the EIC maintained a handful of staff, the head of whom, Richard Cocks, made notable and persistent efforts to initiate trade in China. President (head merchant) Cocks at Hirado struck up relations with Chinese who traded regularly in Japan—Chinese who traded in Japan without any express authorization from the Ming government in Beijing. There were small Chinese populations doing business at both Hirado and Nagasaki. Cocks became acquainted with Li Dan (李旦), who functioned as the head of the Chinese merchant contingents in Japan.[27] Li Dan could exploit a commercial-piratical network around Xiamen and Quanzhou on the Fujian coast, the area where his younger brother and partner

---

22. For the Dutch presence in Japan in this era, see Adam Clulow, *The Company and the Shogun: The Dutch Encounter with Tokugawa Japan* (New York: Columbia University Press, 2014).

23. *The Journal of John Jourdain, 1608–1617*, ed. William Foster (Cambridge: Hakluyt Society, 1905), 271–72. The two poles of the EIC would emerge as Surat and Banten. At the latter in Java the British found a substantial and wealthy Chinese merchant community with whom EIC personnel regularly interacted.

24. For this English captain's reliance upon Linschoten's *Itinerario*, see C.R. Boxer, *Jan Compagnie in Japan, 1600–1817: An Essay on the Cultural, Artistic, and Scientific Influence Exercised by the Hollanders in Japan from the Seventeenth to the Nineteenth Centuries* (The Hague: Martinus Nijhoff, 1936), 2n2.

25. Massarella, *World Elsewhere*, 131.

26. Besides Saris's letter—and viva voce address upon return from Japan—the EIC received letters about the situation in Japan from Richard Cocks, Tempest Peacock, Richard Wickham, and William Adams. With the assistance of the latter, the shogun Ieyasu composed an epistle in reply to the missive from King James. Massarella, *World Elsewhere*, 131.

27. In the communications of Richard Cocks and the EIC, Li Dan (李旦) appears as "Andrea Dittis" and is also styled "Captain China." For extensive treatment of Li Dan, Iwao Seiichi's article does not appear to have been superseded: "Li Tan, Chief of the Chinese Residents at Hirado, Japan, in the Last Days of the Ming Dynasty," *Memoirs of the Research Department of the Toyo Bunko* 17 (1958): 27–83. The elusive Li Dan has also been examined by Robert Batchelor more recently in the context of the newly discovered Selden Map, whose owner or patron he may have been: "Selden Map Rediscovered," 50.

resided.[28] The landlord of the first house that Captain Saris and the English rented in Hirado was Li Dan.[29] The English chief Cocks lavished considerable sums upon Li Dan to act on his behalf to establish direct commercial relations in China. He erroneously believed that Li Dan wielded influence that reached even into the court of the Wanli emperor. The Chinese merchant explained to Cocks that setting up such a commercial channel would be an extremely delicate and expensive task. Not the smallest part of apprehension, his maneuvering would have to evade the notice and hostility of the monopoly-jealous Iberians: "He [Li Dan] sayeth there can nothing cross us in our pursuit of entrance [into China] but only the Portuguese of Macao and Spaniards of Manila, who have great trade into China, and if they come to the knowledge of our presence will not want to give, largely to cross our proceedings; and therefore hath still desired to pass all in silence."[30] It is most probable that Li Dan merely duped Cocks to enrich himself handsomely, for it is highly unlikely that the former had any influence to exert among high-ranking officials in the Ming China ruled by Wanli. The swindling Li managed to collect plenty of money from an insufficiently skeptical Cocks, who did not procure anything beyond a promise of access to Chinese silk markets (like Canton's) and, even more incredible, a promise of a permanent trading post at Ningbo on the northeast coast of Zhejiang.[31]

Although the EIC Hirado factory proved ephemeral (1613–1623) and not at all lucrative, it did bear some significance for Stuart commercial interest and prospects in China. From an advantageous if transient position in Japan the British were able to cull more critical details about commerce involving China—context and dynamics of the trade, traffic, and piracy between Macao/Canton-Japan, Macao/Canton-Manila, Fujian-Manila and Fujian-Japan. It was from Hirado that EIC staff endeavored to make contacts in order to commence direct trade somewhere in China. Letters by King James were even prepared in the event of an opportunity to communicate with the Wanli emperor.[32] The EIC Japan factory, then, ought to be regarded as a very concerted if remote effort to penetrate China; all the exertions and ordeals of Richard Cocks and his colleagues constitute an initial stage of a long trial-and-error process that would establish direct trade with China. The brief career of the Hirado factory is also important as a chapter and dimension of Luso-British relations. Tempers were rising and direct conflicts were emerging between these western Europeans as both sought profits from the same Chinese, Japanese, and other Asian markets.

---

28. Tonio Andrade, *How Taiwan*, 43–47, provides a rich account of the Quanzhou (Fujian) native Li Dan's early enterprises as a merchant trading in China, Japan, Taiwan, Philippines, and Southeast Asia—and anatomizes his pirate-trader duality. Andrade focuses on Li Dan's associations with the VOC in Taiwan, after the EIC had shut down its Hirado station in 1623.
29. The house was located in Kibikida, where Chinese were settled. Li Dan charged them ninety-five real of eight per month. Massarella, *World Elsewhere*, 109.
30. Quoted in Puga, *British in Macau*, 19.
31. Puga, *British in Macau*, 19.
32. Massarella, *World Elsewhere*, 253.

By the time the EIC had planted its trade station in Hirado in 1613, the Portuguese had to worry about British competition not only in Japan but also in various maritime regions between the Red Sea, Persian Gulf, west coast of India, and Malay-Indonesia. The Lusitanians were already well-established along that coast of India, where, at Goa, they maintained their imperial (*Estado da India*) capital. As the first two decades of the seventeenth century unfolded both the British and Dutch were sending ever more ships and ever savvier mariners and factors to that coast—to participate in the textiles and spices (especially pepper) markets. To the port of Surat, in the Gujarat region—north of the Portuguese at Goa—the EIC was dispatching small numbers of ships within the first decade of its founding in 1600. For centuries Gujarat had functioned within a larger maritime network of trade that encompassed the Red Sea and Persian Gulf and crossed the Indian Ocean to southeast Asia. This was a network that had, more recently, come to be dominated when not diverted by the Portuguese. The British and Dutch could expect only a cool interloper's welcome into this maritime commercial realm. The EIC's choice of Surat as their Indian focus followed from the fact that the Portuguese dominance did not extend into Gujarat. Surat was administered only loosely by the Mughal emperor—that is, by governors appointed but not closely supervised by him. By obtaining favor of the Mughals, this English company could establish itself as a counter, European alternative to the Lusitanians at Goa and along the Malabar coast farther south down the coast.[33] The British made several diplomatic attempts to the consternation of the Portuguese. These Iberians were to offer sturdy opposition when the British under James I attempted to gain a secure position in northwest India through the embassy of Sir Thomas Roe to the court of the Mughal emperor, in the years 1615–1619. Into the 1620s the EIC would continue to jostle and vie with the Portuguese in the northwest of India, and probe possibilities along the coast to the south.

To the west of the Mughals, for a century the Lusitanians had dominated the sea-borne commerce of the Persian Gulf—in the wake of Albuquerque's exploits there in the early 1500s. In 1622, the EIC contributed a small squadron to combine with an army of land-based Safavid Persians, under the Shah Abbas, to undertake a successful siege of the Portuguese-controlled island of Hormuz. John Weddell, a veteran sea-captain of the company, served as commander of the squadron in the Anglo-Persian military-naval operation to expel the Portuguese from the Persian Gulf.[34] This ouster of the Portuguese signified "the turning point in the struggle

---

33. Marshall, "English in Asia," 270–71; Bruce Watson, "The Establishment of English Commerce in North-Western India in the Early Seventeenth Century," *Indian Economic and Social History Review* 13, no. 3 (1976): 375–91; for the planting of the EIC factory at Surat, see William Foster, ed., *The Voyage of Thomas Best to the East Indies, 1612–1614* (London: Hakluyt Society, 1934).
34. For a vivid account of Weddell's outstanding leadership at Hormuz in 1622, see Keay, *Honourable Company*, 104–8.

for power between English and Portuguese in the Gulf."[35] The joint siege ended decades of Portuguese commercial hegemony in the area.[36] Just a few years after the Portuguese had been thrust out, Captain Weddell commanded English ships in an Anglo-Dutch squadron that patrolled the gulf to prevent the Portuguese from recovering their dominant position. The EIC had assigned him command of the *Royal James* in the fleet that sailed for India in March 1624. Arriving at Surat, in September of this year he was ordered to sail the company's fleet to Gombroon (Bandar Abbas) to join with the Dutch squadron to engage with the Portuguese. Weddell played the key role for the British in an intense naval combat that lasted three days and left the Portuguese fleet vanquished and its remnants forced to retreat to Goa.[37] Among EIC captains of the 1620s, Weddell was probably the greatest scourge of the Lusitanians in the Arabian Sea and Indian Ocean.

By the second decade of the seventeenth century, while the British had clearly become more than a small pest of the Portuguese in parts of Asia, it was the Dutch who constituted their great nemesis. The Dutch were intriguing against, assaulting, and dislodging the Portuguese in many areas which the latter had settled and fortified in the previous century. Yet while the Portuguese (and Spanish) might have lumped the Dutch and British together indifferently as heretic, Protestant thorns in their sides, the two northern European peoples proved to be consistently uneasy and erratic allies against those Iberians. In the first two decades of the seventeenth century the Dutch and British were jostling and jockeying for positions in some of the same areas—places where Iberian presence was slender or its influence waning. This pair of imperialist upstarts often founded factories—trading stations—very near each other. While the VOC had founded its headquarters at Jakarta on Java—to be in convenient position to control the production and trade of nutmeg, mace, and clove of the Spice Islands to the east—the EIC established a smaller base a little west, at nearby Banten by 1619. After the VOC governor general Coen had seized the port of Jakarta he christened it "Batavia," the Latin rendering of Holland. Batavia would serve not only as a major naval base for the VOC but also its shipbuilding complex and all-purpose entrepot. From this location the Dutch governor-general and his Council of the Indies would be able to supervise and coordinate activities of VOC factories and settlements from India to Japan. The location of the Dutch headquarters in Java had also been chosen as a place where the company would be

---

35. C.R. Boxer, "Anglo-Portuguese Rivalry in the Persian Gulf, 1615–1635," in *Chapters in Anglo-Portuguese Relations*, ed. Edgar Prestage (Westport, CT: Greenwood, 1971), 53.
36. For the strategic importance of Hormuz to the Portuguese, see M.A.P. Meilink-Roelofsz, *Asian Trade and European Influence in the Indonesian Archipelago between 1500 and about 1630* (The Hague: Martinus Nijhoff, 1962), 190.
37. Key operations of the Anglo-Dutch Defence Fleet between the Persian Gulf and northwestern India (Gujarat) in the 1620s are described by Boxer, "Anglo-Portuguese Rivalry." Weddell frequently commanded in such joint squadrons. In 1625–1626, for example, he led the flagship *James* with *Jonas, Anne, Falcon*, which were coupled with six Dutch ships commanded by Cistiens. See Foster, *English Factories, 1624–1629*, 105–17; and Furber, *Rival Empires*, 47–48.

able to receive highly profitable commodities and merchandise coming from the north, whether from Chinese or Japanese sources.[38]

Even before the VOC had situated its headquarters at Jakarta, the British were causing trouble and disquiet. Conflicts of commercial interest between these two Protestant peoples sometimes escalated into rather nasty and bloody clashes. By 1610 the British and Dutch merchants, agents, and mariners collided in the Spice Islands as the latter tried to impose contracts upon native rulers that required them to submit their nutmeg and mace crops exclusively to the VOC. To preserve their monopolistic regime, the Dutch blocked and attacked EIC ships when they attempted to do business with native rulers and merchants. The Indonesia-Spice Islands area was to be the theater where the worst of the violence was enacted. By the late 1610s, the Dutch were proving especially ferocious as they attempted to achieve supremacy in the Banda Islands, where natives had allied with the British newcomers to maintain or retrieve their freedom and independence. From about 1617 to 1620, the Dutch harassed, detained, and assaulted the British and their ships, while they lobbied, intimidated, or coerced the natives.[39] The most notorious of the Dutch savagery practiced upon the subjects of James I came a few years later at Amboina, where in 1623 about a dozen English were summarily executed after arousing suspicions of a plot to overthrow the Dutch.[40]

Despite such episodes of violence or exercises in cruelty, the Dutch and British could still keep squarely in view their mutual interest in maintaining trust and cordiality and cooperating against the Iberians in various regions of Asia. Moreover, even when they might be inclined to engage in more hostility with one another, they would still be constrained by their sovereigns back in Europe to maintain concord. By the Treaty of Defence, agreed at London in 1619, the rival East India companies were henceforth to conduct trade in the Spice Islands as partners. The VOC and EIC were engaged in skirmishes into April 1620 when communication arrived in Java that accords had been signed at Westminster on 7 July 1619. By this entente the Dutch, who had acquired the stronger position in the region, would be entitled to two-thirds of the spices while the British would be allotted the other third. Of even more relevance to the Portuguese in China and Japan and Spanish in the Philippines, the VOC and EIC were to form a joint "Fleet of Defence" to operate

---

38. Andrade, *How Taiwan*, 258. At Jakarta in 1619 a sizeable Chinese community was already settled, mostly migrants from Fujian, many of whom were employed on sugar plantations or in the timber industry. Chinese commerce at Batavia and an account of the significant Fujianese diaspora in Java can be found in Leonard Blussé, *Strange Company: Chinese Settlers, Mestizo Women, and the Dutch in VOC Batavia* (Dordrecht and Riverton: Foris, 1986).

39. Vincent Loth, "Armed Incidents and Unpaid Bills: Anglo-Dutch Rivalry in the Banda Islands in the Seventeenth Century," *Modern Asian Studies* 29, no. 4 (1995): 705–40.

40. While Rupali Mishra recently offered a fresh contextualization of the Amboina Massacre and early Stuart Anglo-Dutch relations in *Business of State*, 209–24, there are now two rich volumes to supplement: Adam Clulow, *Amboina, 1623: Fear and Conspiracy on the Edge of Empire* (New York: Columbia University Press, 2019); and Alison Games, *Inventing the English Massacre: Amboyna in History and Memory* (New York: Oxford University Press, 2020).

in Asian waters, consisting of twelve ships, whose commanders would receive this instruction: "If you meet Portuguese, Spaniards or their adherents anywhere, assault and surprise them."[41] While an Anglo-Dutch fleet was dispatched against the Portuguese on India's Malabar coast in 1621, most operations of this joint squadron were executed farther east, in the vicinity of Macao, Taiwan, Japan, and Manila.[42] In this period of Anglo-Dutch naval alliance (or at least cooperation) in Asia, in the early 1620s, the British seized Iberian ships, occasionally confiscating the latter's silver, whether obtained from Japan or the Americas, as well as such goods as Chinese silk and porcelain.

Throughout the 1620s the Dutch were more wide-ranging and aggressive than the English.[43] In 1622, the same year the Portuguese lost Hormuz by the joint-operation of EIC captain John Weddell and Shah Abbas of Safavid Persia, the Dutch invaded Macao. In June, under the direction of Cornelis Reijersen, eight fully armed VOC ships, with a thousand men ready to land, aimed an amphibious assault at the enclave in the Pearl River estuary. Only after a battle lasting several days were the Dutch, having lost hundreds of men, forced to withdraw into the Taiwan Strait, where they anchored at the Pescadores Islands.[44] While naval partners by the Treaty of Defence, the British did not join in this June 1622 Dutch ambush of Macao: the assault was not an operation of the dual Fleet of Defence.[45] After their unsuccessful venture to take Macao, the Dutch would station themselves for a few years in the Pescadores near Taiwan—eighty miles from the mainland, thirty miles from the island.[46] Their fortified position in those islands and then even stronger presence and projection at Port Zeelandia in southwest Taiwan put them in striking distance of key ports of the Fujian and Zhejiang coasts, and it was conveniently located in relation to both Japan and the Philippines.[47] Thus, they could cruise and prey in several directions and intercept Asian and Iberian vessels navigating the main routes. As more than a thick thorn in the Iberian side, from the 1620s to 1660s they menaced, sabotaged, and diverted commerce involving China, Japan, and southeast

---

41. C.R. Boxer, *The Great Ship from Amacon: Annals of Macao and the Old Japan Trade, 1555–1640* (Lisbon: Centro de Estudos Historicos Ultramarinos, 1959), 98.

42. Massarella, *World Elsewhere*, 271–72. For further details about operations carried out by Dutch and English ships between Japan and Macao and Manila in the early 1620s, see 271–74. As C.R. Boxer noted, "One of the main objectives of the Fleet of Defence was to disrupt the Chinese junk trade with Manila, and forcibly divert it to Batavia, Bantam, and other places frequented by the Dutch and English." *Great Ship from Amacon*, 104.

43. One telling statistic is that in the year 1621 the VOC had sixty-seven ships in Asian waters to the EIC's twenty-five. This numerical advantage only increased in the next few decades. Furber, *Rival Empires*, 270.

44. Wills, *Cambridge Ming*, Vol. 7, 602–3.

45. "Reijersen's orders [from Governor-General Coen] were explicit. The English company was not to be permitted to assist in the attack on Macao in order to deprive it of any claim to a share of the spoils or right of dual occupation in the event of victory." Massarella, *World Elsewhere*, 300.

46. By contrast with Taiwan, the Pescadores were under the (loose) jurisdiction of the Ming. "Since the Song dynasty (960–1279), Penghu was administered off and on under Quanzhou [Fujian] prefecture, and thus remained, however tenuously, integral to the empire." Hang Xing, *Conflict and Commerce in Maritime East Asia: The Zheng Family and the Shaping of the Modern World, c. 1620–1720* (Cambridge: Cambridge University Press, 2016), 36.

47. Andrade, *How Taiwan*, 11.

Asia. During these decades the Dutch conducted operations from Batavia and Taiwan that particularly disrupted and impaired Lusitanian trade between Macao, Manila, and Japan. The VOC was determined—and possessed of more organization and wherewithal than the EIC—to re-channel much of the most highly profitable, silk-and-silver traffic, to enrich the Dutch at the expense of the previously dominant, monopolistic Iberians.[48] In the same spirit the VOC, as directed from Batavia, would also attempt to choke and seize Portuguese Melaka: the key Malay port between India and the Far East.

By the mid-1620s the Dutch plagued the Iberians in Macao, Manila, and Japan as well as Chinese merchants and pirates from Zhejiang and Fujian—and caused headaches and policy-debates among the Ming authorities appointed to govern the coastal zones of those provinces.[49] But in these decades it was clearly the Portuguese who were most adversely affected by the Dutch. The VOC regularly undertook to intercept, blockade, and waylay the Lusitanians to prevent them from operating on the routes from Goa to Cochin (Malabar coast) to Melaka to Macao to Japan. In 1627, just five years after the failure of the Macao invasion, the annual and immensely lucrative China-Japan voyage of Portuguese galliots could not be launched from that Chinese location because of a blockade maintained all summer by a Dutch squadron.[50] It was because the Dutch remained by far the most formidable antagonist and imperial rival in Asia that the Portuguese decided in the 1630s to seek some sort of alliance or accommodation with the British. Increasingly beleaguered by the venturesome and aggressive VOC, the Iberians were compelled to contemplate the forging of an entente with the EIC and British, as the lesser threat to their already eroding *Estado da India*. Presumably the British would be amenable as rivals and sometimes fellow victims of the Dutch; certainly, the Jacobean and then Caroline British bore grudges against the Dutch arising out of many incidents before and after the Amboina atrocity of 1623. Back in Europe, where Stuart Great Britain and Portugal-Spain had been at war intermittently through the 1620s, as one peripheral dimension of the Thirty Years' War (1618–1648), a treaty of November 1630 formally ended the Anglo-Iberian conflict. Charles I's policy harked back to and rekindled his father, James I's *hispanófilo*-tending continental alliance preference.

This 1630 accord resuscitated the "firm peace and concord" that James and the Habsburg Philip III of Spain (Philip II of Portugal) had signed. This agreement

---

48. "There can be no shadow of a doubt that the primary goal of the Dutch in Taiwan was to usurp the places occupied by both Macau and Manila in the silk-for-silver trade run by the merchants of Fukien and Kwangtung." Cheng Wei-chung, *War, Trade and Piracy in the China Seas, 1622–1683* (Leiden: Brill, 2013), 116.
49. Wills, *Cambridge Ming*, Vol. 7, 602–3. The headaches of the Ming imperial and provincial authorities (in Fujian especially) were induced not simply by the Dutch but by all the Chinese pirates, smugglers, and corrupt local officials who were willing to collaborate with those "red barbarians." Such collusion and variety of clandestine operations are thoroughly examined in the first few chapters of Cheng, *War, Trade and Piracy*; many of the same phenomena and episodes are covered in the extensive scholarship of Tonio Andrade—see, for example, his "The Company's Chinese Privateers: How the Dutch East India Company Tried to Lead a Coalition of Privateers to War against China," *Journal of World History* 15, no. 4 (2004): 415–44.
50. Boxer, *Great Ship*, 114.

covered the overseas possessions of both parties, to expand free trade and furnish mutual protection of their Asian establishments and markets against the Dutch.[51] By 1632, the Portuguese viceroy at Goa, Conde de Linhares, was writing to commend to Philip IV of Spain (Philip III of Portugal) an overture made by the president of the EIC Surat factory to formalize friendship and free trade between Portuguese and British in India.[52] First and foremost the viceroy reasoned that such cooperation leading to expanded commerce would significantly augment his sovereign's customs revenues.[53] The EIC chief at Surat, William Methwold, determined that some type of commercial accord with the Portuguese based at Goa would be of considerable benefit to the company.[54] It was regarded as a way of reviving the fortunes of the EIC in India which had been declining in the previous several years, especially in the wake of the famine that struck in the early 1630s.[55] Of the two sides, perhaps the Portuguese at Goa were the more eager to forge an accord.[56] For by the early 1630s the Lusitanians were suffering much more at the hands of the Dutch than the British were. In the 1630s the VOC was regularly maintaining blockades that obstructed when they did not strangle ports, key trade routes, and operations of the Portuguese.[57] Particularly smothering and obnoxious were such blockades set up around the imperial capital, Goa. By the mid-1630s the Dutch would be forming effective obstruction if not blockades in the straits of Melaka, the narrow passage

---

51. The thirty-four articles of the 1630 entente are neatly summarized by Puga, *British in Macau*, 142n67.

52. The origin and logic of the Anglo-Portuguese convention of 1635 is explicated by Anthony Disney, *Twilight of the Pepper Empire: Portuguese Trade in Southwest India in the Early Seventeenth Century* (Cambridge, MA: Harvard University Press, 1978), 148–54, who relates that even as early as the 1620s members of the Council of Portugal had proposed rapprochement with British to counter Dutch.

53. Puga, *British in Macau*, 23–24.

54. William Foster, ed., *English Factories in India, 1634–1636: A Calendar of Documents in the India Office, British Museum and Public Record Office* (Oxford: Clarendon, 1911), vii–x. "Linhares himself explained the reasons for the English factory's desire for a truce: the English had 'neither fortress nor sure haven' in India, being dependent solely on the goodwill of the Moghul authorities at Surat. They were hard-pressed by the Dutch competition, were forced to concentrate on the silk trade with Persia where they bought dear and had to sell cheap, and they could not fill their ships through this trade alone. The use of Portuguese ports and the right to trade there would therefore be most useful to them." Disney, *Twilight*, 198n52.

55. "The great scarcity of merchandise occasioned by the late famine and pestilence in India has caused the Company's fourteen ships at present in those parts to lie idle." A Court of Committees, 7 March 1636, in Sainsbury and Foster, *Court Minutes of EIC, 1635–1639*, 163.

56. That the Portuguese took the initiative is claimed in Captain Weddell's review a few years later: "At last peace *was sought for by you* for two or three years, the procurers being padres and persons of your own nation [notably Father Paulo Reimão], and was concluded in the city of Goa in December 1634, by the Conde de Linhares your viceroy and the president of the English nation [Methwold]." Weddell to City of Macao, 27 September/7 October 1637, *Lisbon Transcripts*, I.O. Records, vol. IV; emphasis added. But as Disney relates: "The initial peace feeler seems to have been made in May 1631 by Thomas Rastell, president of the EIC factory at Surat, through the local Jesuit provincial, Padre Antonio de Andrade. [The viceroy of Goa] Linhares' first reaction was understandably cautious." *Twilight*, 150. Rastell was Methwold's predecessor at Surat. Puga notes in similar vein: "The proposal was initially conveyed to Goa by two Jesuit informers loyal to the viceroy who were in Surat, António Pereira and Paulo Reimão. In August 1633, Joseph Hopkinson and the Council of Surat informed Father Paulo Reimão that once Portugal and England joined forces 'we would be lords of all India and neither Moor nor Dutch would be able to withstand.'" *British in Macau*, 142n68.

57. Fellow subjects of Philip IV, the Spaniards in the Caribbean, in the other "Indies," were suffering from other (non-VOC) invasive Dutch: "By 1635 the maritime and commercial supremacy of the Hollanders in the West Indies could not be denied." Andrews, *Trade, Plunder*, 302.

connecting the Indian sub-continent and the Far East.[58] With the tenacious Dutch hounding and intercepting Portuguese vessels all around Asia, how was the viceroy to continue communicating and conducting exchange with Macao and other locations in the east? How could the Portuguese transport their silver money, materials, military/naval supplies, and general merchandise without suffering seizure or destruction by the Dutch? Among the most critical issues was the Conde de Linhares's inability to receive shipments of firearms and ordnance from Macao. The chief at Goa depended upon artillery products, particularly bronze cannons, manufactured at the foundry in that south China enclave.[59]

Preoccupied with acute security and logistical problems like these, the viceroy at Goa, the Conde de Linhares, entered into negotiations with William Methwold, primarily hoping to have the EIC transport essential items between Goa and Macao. For the British the obvious attraction was expansion of trade to parts of India and the Far East where previously they could expect only hindrance and hostility from the Portuguese and the latter's native allies. To negotiate the accord with the viceroy, Methwold traveled from Surat to Goa in the *Jonas*, commanded by Captain Weddell, scourge of the Portuguese and hero of Hormuz, accompanied by three other EIC ships. Nathaniel Mountney, veteran factor, accompanied Methwold and Weddell.[60] The viceroy, after conferring with his council, considered himself warranted to devise an accord—"a cessation of arms and union"—as a logical Asian extension of the November 1630 Treaty of Madrid: "till such times as the said most illustrious Kings of England and Spain shall reciprocally declare themselves each to other that they are not pleased therewith; and it shall so continue six months after such notice shall be given unto the Viceroy of India and the President of the English nation then being in India, that so the merchants may have time to retire and withdraw their merchandises."[61] Although Weddell did not sign the accord, he had accompanied President Methwold to a private conference with the viceroy shortly before it was finalized and subscribed.[62]

---

58. Sanjay Subrahmanyam, *The Portuguese Empire in Asia, 1500–1700: A Political and Economic History* (London: Longman, 1993), 169.
59. "Macao had become one of the most important cannon production centers of all Asia, and some of its products were shipped back to Europe itself." Tonio Andrade, *The Gunpowder Age: China, Military Innovation, and the Rise of the West in World History* (Princeton, NJ: Princeton University, 2016), 198.
60. Mountney's first visit of Surat occurred at least twenty years earlier. From there he returned to England in the EIC *Hope* in the year 1616.
61. This convention, as transcribed by the EIC's Benjamin Robinson, was signed by the Conde de Linhares, with members of his council serving as witnesses, and Methwold, Mountney, Turner, Martin, and Cooper. "The Accord between the Viceroy of Goa and the English President and Council [of the EIC], 10/20 Jan. 1635, PRO, C.O. 77, Vol. VI, Nos. I, I I–V.
62. "We were received and dined at Sr. Jeronimo de Sozah's house, who is Auditor General [*Vedor da Fazenda* of Goa], a man of quality and great estate, unto whom we were much obliged. And about three of the clock in the afternoon were admitted into the Viceroy's presence, where he vouchsafed unto the President and Captain Weddell a long conference, renovating for the most part his former discourse, and assuring us that, although the King of Spain might seem to dislike this act of his, yet he would confirm it because the Viceroy had done it." President Methwold and Messrs. Mountney, Turner, Martin, and Cooper, aboard the *Jonas* in Goa Road, to the Company, 19/29 January 1635, Foster, *English Factories, 1634–1636*, 98.

The British in Seventeenth-Century Luso-Dutch Asia 29

With the cape merchant Mountney, Weddell sailed for home in the *Jonas* after all the negotiations and meetings with the Portuguese at Goa had been concluded. They were back in England by the summer of 1635. But would their king, Charles I, and his counterpart, the Iberian monarch Philip IV, ratify the provisions made by their imperial representatives in western India? Reconfigurations and vicissitudes of the Thirty Years' War in Europe would encourage the monarchs to enhance their alliance—to commend ratification of the Goa entente. In May 1635 France declared war on Habsburg Spain and, increasingly subsidizing and partnering with the Dutch, the Bourbon monarchy would contest Philip's control of territories in the Netherlands.[63] Confronted by a two-headed, Franco-Dutch monster, it was prudent for the Habsburg ruler to keep the British at least neutral. Charles I, for his part, was disaffected by recent actions taken by the Dutch. The Stuart king had reason to be increasingly irritated by aggressive and intrusive operations of Dutch ships in the English Channel.[64]

Letters took several months to travel from India to western Europe, and royal deliberations on their proposals could not presume to be expedited as a top priority. The viceroy at Goa and President Methwold at Surat would not wait for official approval to initiate what was conceived as a mutually beneficial Anglo-Portuguese operation. The Conde de Linhares was desperate to obtain materials and weapons from Macao and Methwold and the EIC were eager to probe or open new avenues of commercial opportunity in Lusitanian spheres of influence in India, Malay-Indonesia, and China. As Great Britain and the United Provinces of the Netherlands were still officially at peace, the VOC would not prey upon and seize EIC ships as it would any Portuguese vessel. So a British ship could be chartered to run a Portuguese errand from Goa through the straits of Melaka to southern China. In the process of performing this service, the British might achieve the goal of entering or at least becoming more intimately acquainted with the commerce emanating from Canton. Perhaps the EIC agents could make some direct contact with the local Ming merchants and mandarins, in hopes of paving the way to future, more extensive and lasting commercial relations. Thus, one of the company's largest ships (nine hundred tons), the *London*, was designated and a veteran captain, Matthew Wills, appointed to sail from India to Macao in order to transport to Goa metals (copper and iron) and military equipment (mainly artillery pieces from Bocarro's foundry)

---

63. Parker, *Global Crisis*, 235. On 26 May 1635 France declared war in response to the Habsburgs' 26 March invasion and occupation of the territory of its ally, the Elector of Trier (and bishop of Speyer) Philipp Christoph von Sötern, who had placed himself under French protection in 1632. In 1634 Louis XIII and Cardinal Richelieu were to increase subsidies in support of Dutch operations against Spain in the Low Countries. However, the joint Dutch-French campaign of 1635 in the Netherlands was to fail.

64. For the menacing of the Dutch in the Channel and North Sea in the mid-1630s, see Kenneth R. Andrews, *Ships, Money and Politics: Seafaring and Naval Enterprise in the Reign of Charles I* (Cambridge: Cambridge University Press, 1991), 134–36.

urgently needed by the viceroy for activities in and around the capital of the *Estado da India*.[65]

While the British ship would be doing primarily Portuguese business, Captain Wills and the chief factor Henry Bornford, expected to ascertain details about the current China market if not the contacts necessary to participate in it. In April 1635 the *London* set out from Surat on this novel Luso-British venture to circumvent the increasingly suffocating blockades of the Dutch. Captain Wills would receive navigational guidance from an experienced Portuguese pilot and the EIC factor Bornford would be accompanied by a veteran *Estado da India* merchant, Gaspar Gomes, both selected by the Conde de Linhares. The EIC was promised 10 percent of all profits made by the various exchanges and transactions of the voyage. According to the viceroy, the British pledged to refrain from any intercourse with the Chinese once arrived at Macao. They also consented, he claimed, not to disembark once in China.[66] But quite to the contrary, the EIC president at Surat seems to have informed Wills and Bornford that at least a small number of the EIC personnel would be permitted to go ashore and set up at least a temporary residence.[67] However differently the Conde de Linhares and President Methwold at Surat construed the terms of the arrangement, it was an entirely separate question as to how the Lusitanians at Macao would treat the hybrid creature, a Portuguese-guided *London*. Equally distinct and just as crucial was the question how the Ming officials at Macao and Canton would greet this novel Anglo-Portuguese enterprise. The official policy of the Ming government in the reign of the Chongzhen emperor remained: trade with Europeans was to be restricted to the Portuguese (佛朗機 *folangji*) settled in small numbers at Macao.[68] When the English vessel arrived at Macao at the end of July 1635, the Portuguese in the city were not delighted to see the Protestant heretics so easy to mistake for the "red-barbarian" Dutch. Nor were the Chinese enclave's government and senior merchants innocent of the cynicism that the viceroy of Goa might well be pursuing the Crown's and his own interests too much at the expense of their own. Most worrisome was the prospect of the British using this escort errand as a way of personally intruding into the Chinese market. Thus, only after initial opposition were members of the opportunistic EIC allowed to come ashore. While the Portuguese officials permitted the *London* to anchor, they ventured to deceive

---

65. Matthew Wills had commanded the EIC *Dolphin* in 1623 and 1624. In 1625, 1627, and 1631, he made voyages for the company to Surat and Banten. In 1634 he was chosen admiral of the fleet bound for Surat and was subsequently presented with a piece of plate "with the Company's arms graven thereon" on account of his "good services in the fight against the Portugals" on Swally Sands—just beyond Surat. Description of the *London* is in Foster, *English Factories, 1634–1634*, 95.

66. For instructions sent in May 1635 by the viceroy of Goa to the captain-general of Macao, Manuel Ramos, as to how the Portuguese at Macao were to treat the EIC of the *London*, see Puga, *British in Macau*, 30–31. Among the directions most emphasized was not to let the British communicate directly with any Chinese. Of course, this would be in keeping with the viceroy's scheme to avoid detection and concomitant taxation and assessment of fines by the Ming authorities of Canton.

67. "Instructions" in Foster, *English Factories, 1634–1634*, 105–6.

68. Nor, under the Chongzhen emperor (1627–1644), had Ming decrees (海禁 *haijin*) which entailed prohibition of maritime trade with Japan been rescinded.

the Ming mandarins, their overlords: the captain-general of the enclave, Manuel Ramos, reported that the vessel was a galleon of Philip IV's Armada, dispatched to Macao to bolster its defense against attacks by the Dutch and British barbarians.[69]

According to Ramos, in his later review of the episode, both Captain Wills and chief factor Henry Bornford tried immediately to gain access to and communicate directly with the Chinese and, while the Ming officials were measuring the ship to assess customs fees, even took the opportunity to present a petition to a mandarin— a petition requesting a spot somewhere in the Pearl River estuary to set up a base for future trade. The sojourn of the EIC *London* at Macao lasted about three months. As Ramos's report indicates, Bornford did not squander the opportunity to gather information about China while trying to make contacts and exploring new commercial possibilities. When, upon return to Surat, the pioneering factor rendered a report to the company, he emphasized that: "the averseness of the Chinese to intercourse with foreigners is exaggerated by the Portuguese, who also abuse other nations to the Chinese in order to keep trade to themselves." With regard to the possibility establishing trade relations with the Chinese, even more promisingly, he related: "When the mandarin came down for the [measuring] of the ship, we closed more nearly with those that were chief about him, as to question whether the King's [emperor's] license were not procurable to our further and free trade with them; who to this answered that it was in the power of the mandarin to effect, provided there must be a sum of money given him, which he nominated 2,000 tael."[70] The EIC factor professed himself confident that profitable exchange with the Chinese might by-pass Macao: "He [Bornford] himself does not doubt, if he be allowed to make a second trial, to do some acceptable service herein, and to experience so far as that you might know another way better to that trade than Macao, there being many convenient islands and ports in the mouth of the river of Canton." This mouth of the Pearl River was Ming's "Tiger Gate" (虎門 Humen), Boca do Tigre to the Portuguese—and would, much later, be called "the Bogue" by the British.

As for intelligence gathering, Bornford must have learned many more details about aspects of the Canton-Macao-Japan trade, including current prices and goods in high demand. This configuration of commerce was still extremely lucrative for the Portuguese of Macao and Chinese officials and merchants at Canton.[71] Since the administration of the Chongzhen emperor in Beijing had not lifted its ban on Chinese merchants trading with Japan, the Portuguese at Macao were still serving as the middlemen and reaping nearly monopolistic profit.[72] The same year, 1635, that Captain Wills and Bornford spent three months surveying the scene at Macao

---

69. Puga, *British in Macau*, 31.

70. Henry Bornford at Surat to the Company, 19/29 April 1636, Foster, *English Factories, 1634–1636*, 226–30.

71. Many Cantonese merchants regularly shipped their goods to Japan through the Lusitanians of Macao. Chinese-Portuguese partnership in Japan-related commerce was common. Boxer, *Great Ship*, 13.

72. Subrahmanyam, *Portuguese Empire*, 104–5.

and the Pearl River estuary, their Portuguese contemporary Antonio Bocarro was present to observe:

> Of all the voyages which are made from this city of the Name of God [Macao], it is clear that the chief and most important is that of Japan, whither go yearly four pinnaces laden with silks of various kinds, taking 10 or 12 days on the outward voyage, and eight to ten on the return; by staying in Japan for about a month, a good market is secured for all these commodities, which include, in addition to the silk, much gold, and much China root, all of which are exchanged for some of the mass of natural silver there is in Japan; in addition we export the aforesaid copper which is specified in the regulations, much camphor, and furthermore many gold lacquered cabinets.[73]

Bornford would have learned, or confirmed first-hand, that at Canton (and elsewhere in southeast China), many Chinese were ever eager to purchase or trade for spices (pepper, nutmeg, clove), and luxury items like sandalwood (from Timor). The Portuguese were still bringing large quantities of silver (in bullion and specie) from Japan. In exchange for that silver and other commodities, the Portuguese were regularly obtaining at Canton silk (wrought and raw), porcelain, gold, cotton goods, zinc, alum, and radix.[74]

After lading the metals, munitions, and other cargo items requested by the viceroy of Goa, the *London* sailed away from Macao on 20 October 1635. The following month, the EIC ship barely passed unmolested the irritated Dutch: "The Hollanders reluctantly let her pass . . . although 'laden to sinking point with the goods of our mortal enemies the Portuguese,' as their commander bitterly reported to Batavia."[75] Reaching Surat at the end of March 1636, Bornford prepared the very positive report and prospectus some of whose lines we have reviewed above. He and his colleagues in India proposed that the EIC launch another venture to China—but not one that would anchor at Macao. Instead, it was suggested that the British should try to by-pass the Portuguese enclave and aim to set up their own, independent venue to conduct trade. Optimally, they would acquire a much more convenient place, perhaps nearer to Canton, closer to the mouth of the Pearl River, which flowed around that provincial capital.[76]

Not long after the departure of the *London,* and as the factor Bornford might have been drafting his report to the directors of the EIC, the captain-general, Manuel Ramos, wrote from China to his imperial superior, the new viceroy of Goa, Pero da Silva—who had just replaced the Conde de Linhares. The tenor of this report by the Macao governor was sharply admonitory: the British were obviously intent on taking yards wherever permitted inches. According to Ramos, EIC personnel had

---

73. Antonio Bocarro, "Descricao de Macau, em 1635," quoted in C.R. Boxer, *Macau na Epoca da Restauracao* [Macao three hundred years ago] (Lisbon: Fundacao Oriente, 1993), 40–41.

74. Souza, *Survival of Empire,* 46.

75. Boxer, *Fidalgos in the Far East,* 113.

76. William Foster, *England's Quest of Eastern Trade* (London: Adam and Charles Black, 1933), 326–27.

tried strenuously to obtain permission directly from the Chinese to send a few ships as early as the following year (1636). Even more alarmingly, they had impetuously proposed to Ming officials the building of a handful of houses, from which they would undertake to sell goods to the Chinese at half the price the Portuguese of Macao had been charging. The brazen British interlopers offered large sums to a Guangdong official as annual payment to trade on terms similar to those enjoyed by the Lusitanians. In the same account dispatched to the viceroy of Goa, Ramos related that when the Portuguese at Macao discovered this bold and monopoly-busting proposition conveyed by the EIC, they prevailed upon the Chinese official at Macao with a bribe. Apparently, the silver-swayed Ming official consented to deceive Bornford into thinking that he, this mandarin, would go to the provincial capital to lobby for the British.[77]

77. Puga, *British in Macau*, 34.

2

Enter the Interlopers

Genesis of the Courteen Association, Rival of the English East India Company

While it had been the East India Company's president at Surat, William Methwold, who had worked to reach an accord with the Portuguese in Goa to facilitate British trade in India and the Far East, it was not that commercial entity but a rival back in London, the Courteen Association, which would organize the first British trade expedition to reach China. At the end of 1635, after the EIC *London*'s sojourn at Macao under the aegis of the Lusitanians, proposals for further voyages from Surat and Goa in combination with these Iberians were discussed in London by the directors. Anticipated difficulties, particularly those which could come from Dutch interference, rendered the executives of the EIC reluctant to plan or authorize anything from England. After heated debate, the directors resolved to let Methwold exercise his own discretion in negotiating any further ventures to China in concert with or with the approval of the Portuguese.[1] Evidently the EIC deemed the January 1635 entente, the Goa Convention, an unsure foundation for a China enterprise that would constitute a sequel to the *London*'s voyage. Near the end of this year the company directors wrote a letter to Lord Aston, English ambassador at Madrid. Along with their posting him, as directed by Lord Cottington, Chancellor of the Exchequer, a copy of the agreement for a truce and cessation of arms signed at Goa, still pending ratification by Charles I and Philip IV, they pointedly raised the question whether this could substantially improve the company's commercial prospects in and beyond India. For now, it was their understanding that they could *not* assume assistance or cooperation on the part of the Portuguese subjects of Philip at Goa, Cochin (Malabar), Melaka, or Macao: "As the said agreement contains no plain declaration for the settling of commerce in those parts more than is provided for in the 7th Article of the Peace made between the said Kings the 15th November, 1630, they do not find it safe to trade upon such a basis; and therefore they beseech His Lordship to negotiate with the King of Spain for such a declaration as may warrant their safe commerce in those parts."[2]

Meanwhile, in the summer of 1635, EIC captain John Weddell, hero of the 1622 Anglo-Persian siege of Portuguese Hormuz, and just recently Methwold's

---

1. A Court of Committees, 27 November / 7 December 1635, *Court Minutes of EIC, 1635–1639*, 120–21.
2. EIC to Lord Aston at Madrid [ca. December 1635], *Court Minutes of EIC, 1635–1639*, 139.

Enter the Interlopers

companion at the signing of the Goa accord, was on very acrimonious terms with the company in London. The EIC ship he was commanding in 1633 had accidentally burned down while anchored off Surat. For this catastrophic loss he had been blamed by the company directors, who demanded that he answer for himself in London. He thought this most unjust: no dereliction of his could be detected by anyone acquainted with the circumstances of the ship's fiery destruction.[3] Thus, in 1635, the veteran commander returned to London bitterly resentful: for all the valuable services rendered to the company over two decades, he had been rashly reproached, denied all grace and benefit of the doubt. Weddell's revenge upon the company was ripe for prosecuting upon arrival in England. On the voyage home he had been working out a plan for a venture that would threaten or seriously injure the interests of the company that had treated him so shabbily. He had a veteran merchant of the EIC to serve as his partner. Nathaniel Mountney, another distinguished and aggrieved employee of the company, had also attended with Weddell and Methwold, the negotiations of the pact made at Goa. Indeed, Mountney himself was one of the English representatives to sign the document there. Mountney and Weddell, returning to England on the same ship in 1635, had connections with men on intimate terms with Charles I.

Upon his return to the English Channel in the EIC *Jonas* at the end of July 1635, Weddell was treated to a cordial welcome by Sir William Monson. That year Monson had been selected to serve as vice-admiral of the first fleet funded by the highly controversial revenue-raising program, Ship Money.[4] The vice-admiral wrote on behalf of Weddell to Charles I's Secretary of State, Sir Francis Windebank. In his letter to Windebank, Monson indicated that Weddell had a lucrative scheme to propose to the king: a voyage to the East that would yield profits greater than any the EIC had achieved so far. Monson instructed Weddell to meet with the secretary at the earliest opportunity.[5] Besides conferring with Windebank, Weddell might well have gotten into touch with Sir Endymion Porter, a very influential insider in the court of Charles at Whitehall.[6] This courtier, a member of the royal household as Groom of the Bedchamber, seems to have taken a strong interest in launching an enterprise which would exploit the freshly devised convention with the Portuguese. Given that the commercial venture of Captain Weddell and Nathaniel Mountney would rely upon the accord with the Iberian authorities, it was probably not irrelevant that Porter had *hispanófilo* pedigree. Indeed, in 1623, he had accompanied young Charles to Madrid, when the then Prince of Wales made the trip to arrange

---

3. *Court Minutes of EIC, 1635–1639*, xv–xvi. Weddell was subsequently fully vindicated, as it was officially established that he could not have been held in any way negligent for the loss of the ship.
4. Andrew Thrush, "William Monson," *ODNB*. For the origins and a savvy appraisal of the Ship Money program, see Andrews, *Ships, Money and Politics*, 128–59.
5. Sir William Monson to Secretary Windebank, 1 August 1635, *Calendar of State Papers, Domestic*, CCXCV, 311.
6. "[Porter] had more access to confidential information than most courtiers. He regularly received a great number of letters from suitors who wanted him to present their petitions to the king, or influence Charles in their favour." Ronald Asch, "Endymion Porter," *ODNB*.

marriage to a Habsburg princess—an episode known as the "Spanish Match."[7] Long prior, early in the reign of James I, Porter had resided in Spain as a member of the second Count of Olivares's household, serving the latter's heir, Don Gaspar de Guzmán. Guzmán, as the grand Count-Duke of Olivares, was to be Philip IV's most powerful minister. In dictating and managing relations with Great Britain in the 1630s, Olivares depended upon Porter as a well-informed confidant within the Caroline court.[8]

It should not have been too difficult to interest Charles I in such a promising, customs-enhancing venture at a time when royal finances were strained to the breaking point—his regime was approaching the parliamentary confrontation and constitutional crisis which would yield to armed defiance and civil war, and lead to his own trial and execution for treason in 1649. By the summer of 1635, the Stuart monarch was settled into what historians style his "Personal Rule," governing without parliaments, undertaking ad hoc measures like "forced loans," and embarking upon the Ship Money program mentioned above. As another potential source of revenue, the king must have been intrigued by an enterprise that would differ from the previous ones carried out by the older overseas trading company, the EIC. Most notably, it had been conceived and projected to exploit the recently established entente with the Portuguese. Assistance and facilitation by the Iberians would, among other things, allow the subjects of Charles in Asia to better compete with the aggressively aggrandizing Dutch of the VOC. The presence, power, and profits of the Hollanders in the East remained decidedly superior to that of the British.

This novel enterprise would not be the first of Endymion Porter's projecting of privateering or commercial ventures to the East.[9] Earlier in the year, in the spring of 1635, he had obtained a royal commission for the London merchants, Thomas Kynaston and Samuel Bonnell. Their expedition would not be focused on commerce. Two small vessels, the *Samaritan* (250 tons) and the *Roebuck* (100 tons), would prey upon Arab or Muslim ships, as reprisal for recent attacks upon the British. The widely roving Barbary corsairs had been marauding, capturing, and enslaving hundreds if not thousands of European Christians—at least decent pretext for retaliating upon the members of *any* Muslim nation with which Great Britain had no formal or previously established commercial relationship.[10] Both

---

7. "Although the prince's journey to Spain was a complete failure, Porter's standing with the future king was improved, having acted as an important intermediary between the prince and the Spanish court in Madrid, and having demonstrated his knowledge of works of art, so important to Charles I." Asch, "Endymion Porter," *ODNB*.
8. Bearing comparison to Porter, Francis Cottington, Chancellor of the Exchequer, was something of a "Spain hand." He had served two of James I's ambassadors at Madrid, Sir Charles Cornwallis and Sir John Digby. In determining British foreign policy, particularly with respect to the Habsburg powers, Cottington played a major role. Fiona Pogson, "Francis Cottington," *ODNB*.
9. Porter has received more attention, at least recently, for his involvement in a Madagascar colonization scheme, as described at length by Games, *Web of Empire*, 181–208.
10. Foster, *English Factories, 1634–1636*, xix. By this time, hundreds of Charles I's subjects were living in slavery in north Africa.

Enter the Interlopers

ships, well-furnished for attack, were authorized by Charles to fly flags of the Royal Navy; and all compatriots of the commander of the ships were instructed to obey and assist this captain in cases of any exigency or difficulties arising on the seas or coasts.[11] But in the late months of 1635 the EIC was still unaware of the activities of those ships, so it could concentrate instead on thwarting the new rival venture of a fleet to the East to be led by Captain Weddell and Nathaniel Mountney.

Fresh from his collaboration with Kynaston and Bonnell, Porter turned for further funding and management to the superior of those overseas-commerce agents, the Anglo-Dutch magnate Sir William Courteen.[12] A Dutch immigrant, collaborating with his brother and partner Peter still based in Zeeland, he was among the elite merchant-adventurers of London: "Of all the ship-owning traders of London the wealthiest and the most ambitious in maritime enterprise were the Courteens."[13] Courteen's scope was global. For decades he had been orchestrating diverse and ambitious overseas ventures, whether colonizing or trade; fishing, whaling, or salt commerce; in such far-flung places as Caribbean islands (like Barbados) or American and African coasts. He stepped up to serve as Porter's partner and to assume the major responsibility for financing and managing the ambitious enterprise that would parallel and rival the EIC. Courteen's role was crucial: besides sheer wealth and invaluable experience handling many large-scale mercantile and financial operations, he was connected to those within whispering distance of the king.[14] In addition to his acquaintance with Porter, Courteen benefited from a long relationship with another Caroline figure of considerable clout, Thomas Howard, Earl of Arundel.[15]

---

11. Foster, *English Factories, 1634–1636*, xx; Deed of Covenant between Endymion Porter and Thomas Kynaston and Samuel Bonnell, 31 May 1635 [O.S.], is reproduced in *Court Minutes of EIC, 1635–1639*, 58–59.

12. *Court Minutes of EIC, 1635–1639*, xv–xvi. Kynaston was an assistant of the government financier, Sir Abraham Dawes; Bonnell had previously served as an agent for Courteen. Robert Brenner, *Merchants and Revolution: Commercial Change, Political Conflict and London's Overseas Traders, 1550–1653* (Princeton, NJ: Princeton University Press, 1993), 170. Brenner identified several powerful merchants in London who, though more focused on Atlantic colonial ventures, may have collaborated with Courteen. Their personal and business relationships with him cannot, however, be clearly established (173–76). One of those merchants was probably Maurice Thompson, who seems to have invested or supported Courteen in some way. Andrews, *Ships, Money and Politics*, 57–58.

13. Andrews, *Ships, Money and Politics*, 51; Andrews emphasizes the extent of Sir William's ship-owning and the affluence which allowed him to maintain thousands of employees. Along with Sir Paul Pindar, Courteen had loaned astronomical sums to both James and Charles. This was recognized by the Lord Treasurer in July 1625, when Courteen was commended as a subject who "freely lends his money for supply of the King's instant occasions, and that without interest of the old debt." *Calendar of State Papers Domestic, 1625–1626*, 74. Surely any gratitude to Courteen that burdened Charles would have helped him overcome EIC objections to chartering the rival group.

14. Roper, *Advancing Empire*, 16, 29. Roper, who has emphasized the global scope of his commercial ambitions, notes that as a sponsor of overseas ventures, Courteen was second to only the Earl of Warwick and his circle. Most recently Rupali Mishra has offered an extensive discussion of the origins as well as relations of the Courteen Association with Charles and the EIC in *Business of State*, 272–301. What her account conspicuously lacks is treatment of the 1635 Goa accord background—surely a factor, if not the major one, in the rise of this EIC rival.

15. Games, *Web of Empire*, 186.

Courteen with his partners and associates aimed to obtain a charter to trade in India, southeast Asia, China, and Japan, in all places where the older company had not already established a factory (trading station) or long-term relationship with a native ruler. To compete alongside and surpass the EIC, this new outfit would need veteran mariners and Asia-acquainted merchants. Every captain who would be appointed to a ship of this upstart company's fleet had previously commanded for the EIC. A mere glance at the roster of the navigational and mercantile personnel and staff of the Courteen Association is enough for us to label it a sort of who's-who of dissatisfied and disgruntled ex-EIC. Like John Weddell, Captain John Carter, who would be commander of the Courteen's *Katherine*, had been blamed by the EIC for losses and punished for alleged misbehavior while he had served as master's mate in the company's *Swallow* a few years back. He was accused of being drunk and ordering the firing of cannon that caused the conflagration which destroyed his and then Weddell's ship, the *Charles*, which were then, in 1633, anchored off the coast of Surat.[16] By the time he joined the new company as commander of the *Katherine*, Carter already had nearly twenty years of experience as a mariner for the EIC. Most pertinent for the China-aiming Courteen venture, he had navigated in the seas of the Far East. Carter was master of the EIC *Unicorn* sailing from Banten to the company's Hirado station in Japan, in 1620, when the ship was swept up in a storm that wrecked the vessel on or near the Guangdong coast, in the vicinity of Macao.[17] Another veteran captain of the EIC, Richard Swanley had only recently (1632–1635) commanded the *Jonas* and was with Weddell (*Charles*) and Carter (*Swallow*) off the coast of India just prior to the commencement of the Courteen enterprise. Swanley had served several years under Weddell, and most notably fought alongside him in the battles against the Portuguese in the Persian Gulf in the early 1620s; Swanley played a major role in the naval engagement against the Lusitanians off Gombroon.[18] Edward Hall, who would captain the Courteen *Planter*, was an EIC mariner with substantial navigational experience in eastern seas and had just served under Weddell on the return voyage from India in 1635.[19]

Not only accomplished and battle-hardened captains but top factors (merchants and commercial agents) and high-level administrative and clerical personnel of the EIC proved logical and easy Courteen recruits for their feeling undervalued

---

16. "[Carter] petitions for the remainder of his wages, detained because of the burning of the said ship [*Swallow*]; refused, he being one of the four sent home prisoners, being drunk when the accident occurred. He denies having been drunk or giving order for shooting the ordnance that fired the ship, but is told that it is usual for mariners to lose their pay if their ship perishes, and that he has fared well to be left unquestioned on the return of the Commission from India." A Court of Committees, 19/29 August 1635, *Court Minutes of EIC, 1635–1639*, 82.

17. May 1637, Mundy, *Travels*, vol. 3, 141; Massarella, *World Elsewhere*, 271–72. Carter and the rest of the crew and passengers of the shipwrecked *Unicorn* were subsequently snared by the Portuguese and taken to Macao.

18. Michael Baumber, "Richard Swanley," *ODNB*.

19. Edward Hall had served as mate in the EIC *Star* bound for Madras in 1631 before returning to England as master's mate in the *Royal James* in 1633. In 1634 he was master's mate of the *Jonas* and served under Weddell in the voyage home from India in 1635.

Enter the Interlopers

or mistreated by the older company.[20] Early in 1636 Henry Glascock, an India hand with several years' experience, was hired as a Courteen factor after being punished and fined by the EIC for some alleged misbehavior. At the end of 1635 he had re-applied for a position with the older company but had been rejected.[21] Many of these EIC employees who went over to the Courteen Association were merely seeking better opportunities, higher salaries, or just trying to avoid shrunken paychecks. As the early 1630s had not been as productive as the late 1620s, the EIC was drastically economizing and cutting salaries in 1635.[22] This year eighteen members of its London staff were forced to take a pay cut.[23] Nathaniel Mountney's older brother John, also a long-time EIC employee, mainly as an accountant, had suffered a significant diminution in wage.[24] When meeting with the directors of the company to inform them of his decision to resign and work for the Courteen Association, he complained that his EIC salary could not cover even his ordinary expenses.[25] In reply the executives expressed their sense of his ingratitude for their having employed him since a mere youth.[26]

Thomas Robinson, who would emerge as the ace linguist-factor of the Weddell expedition to China, was also an EIC veteran. As the lingua franca on many coasts of Asia was a modified Portuguese, the Courteen Association would need Robinson's EIC-acquired prowess in that tongue to deal with many complicated situations.[27] Like the other EIC-turned-Courteen captains and factors, in his two decades of service in India, Sumatra, Java, and at Makassar (Spice Islands) he had suffered

---

20. The case of the Courteen Association richly illustrates Philip Stern's generalization: "Some of the most problematic 'interlopers' in Asia were disgruntled, dismissed Company factors, captains, and governors, who had either returned to England or kept up their private 'country' trade and permanent residence elsewhere in Asia." Philip J. Stern, "Company, State, and Empire: Governance and Regulatory Frameworks in Asia," in *Britain's Oceanic Empire: Atlantic and Indian Ocean Worlds, c. 1550–1850*, ed. H.V. Bowen, Elizabeth Mancke, and John G. Read (Cambridge: Cambridge University Press, 2012), 138.

21. A Court of Committees, 13 November 1635, *Court Minutes of EIC, 1635–1639*, 116.

22. David Veevers has stressed the weakness and fragility of the EIC throughout the 1620s and 1630s in *Origins of the British Empire in Asia*, Chapter 1.

23. Keay, *Honourable Company*, 127. Presumably most of those eighteen switched to the Courteen Association; instances of this EIC-Courteen transfer are recorded in documents edited by William Foster in the *English Factories* and *Court Minutes of EIC, 1635–1639*.

24. In December 1635 John Mountney's salary was cut from fifty to forty pounds. *Court Minutes of EIC, 1635–1639*, 135.

25. The customary stinginess and policy of meanness practiced by the EIC directors towards its current and former servants is emphasized by Massarella, *World Elsewhere*, 328.

26. A Court of Committees, 4 March 1636 [O.S.], *Court Minutes of EIC, 1635–1639*, 162–63. The father of John and Nathaniel, Richard Mountney, was an even more important and veteran administrative officer ("husband") of the EIC in London, whose salary was drastically reduced in preceding years—from 200 to 150 pounds. He had been an employee of the company since 1607. "Mr. Mountney, the Husband, being discontented at the lessening of his salary, and having lately very much neglected his work, the Court resolves to dismiss him. He is summoned, and required to deliver up his keys; and after some excuses he willingly surrenders them." A Court of Committees, 13/23 July 1636, *Court Minutes of EIC, 1635–1639*, 185. For a follow-up meeting on Richard Mountney's dismissal, see A Court of Committees, 20/30 July 1636, *Court Minutes of EIC, 1635–1639*, 186. In August he offered to resume his post at his original, lowered salary, but the company snubbed him. By this time both his sons were Courteens.

27. "The Portuguese had made their language in its 'creole' form the *lingua franca* of commerce and diplomacy throughout the East." Furber, *Rival Empires*, 26.

many reproaches, accusations, punishments, and even imprisonment at the hands of his EIC supervisors. One of these supervisors, Richard Wylde, who had been EIC president at Surat, referred to Robinson as "one of the most shameless and impudent rascals." Another boss, Henry Hawley, EIC president at Jakarta, whom Robinson served as secretary, described him as a "gamester," exceedingly susceptible to "vice and idleness" and "prodigal and contentious above measure."[28] But neither Wylde nor Hawley denied his commercial acumen or his exceptional abilities in both European and Asian languages. Peter Mundy and Anthony Vernworthy were other EIC factors who had acquired facility in multiple languages and extensive commercial practice before turning to employment with the Courteen Association. Mundy had recently completed more than five years working for the EIC in Surat, where he had picked up Gujarati and improved his Persian—to add to his proficiency in Spanish, French, Italian, and Portuguese.[29] The widely traveled, culturally nimble, and diplomacy-adept Mundy seems to have been less estranged from than bored by the EIC.[30] In December 1635 he opted to join the Courteen venture as a more imaginative enterprise than any the EIC was currently undertaking: "[At London] I found two good businesses on foot, one for India by the Company, the other a fleet setting forth by Sir William Courteen, upon an unknown design, so resolved on the latter."[31] Evidently, Mundy was much intrigued by the prospect of a pioneering voyage that would go well beyond the EIC's present purview. Another highly accomplished commercial agent for the Courteen Association, Anthony Vernworthy, had worked more than a decade for the EIC as a factor in Banten, Jakarta, and Makassar—a resumé similar to that of Thomas Robinson. Like Mundy, he had the option of signing another contract with the old company but found the Courteen enterprise more appealing.[32]

Captains, mariners, and factors were not the only EIC employees attracted to the fresh and more ambitious Courteen enterprise. Some of the company's veteran clergy proved no less eager to enlist. William Courteen's ships would maintain the

---

28. Mundy, *Travels*, vol. 3, 463.
29. Mundy, *Travels*, vol. 3, xlviii. Prior to his employment with the EIC in the late 1620s, Mundy had spent four years as a factor in Istanbul of the Ottoman Empire. He had begun his career by serving several years in Spain as a commercial agent. During his five years in India (1628-1633), if not earlier, Mundy became acquainted with Captain Weddell and Nathaniel Mountney—and several other future Courteen leaders. His references to earlier encounters of Weddell may be found at *The Travels of Peter Mundy, in Europe and Asia, 1608-1667*, vol. 2: *Travels in Asia, 1628-1634*, edited by R.C. Temple (London: Hakluyt Society, 1914), 21, 303. Mundy referred to fellow Courteen factor and India hand Henry Glascock as "an old friend and acquaintance of mine." They had been at Surat together for a few years.
30. Opportunities to develop his diplomatic finesse during his tenure at Surat were plenty. On one occasion Mundy was dispatched to the court of the Mughal emperor at Agra, where the building of the Taj Mahal had just begun.
31. Mundy, *Travels*, vol. 3, 13–14. The EIC ventures that failed to interest Mundy were the late 1635 voyage of the *Swan* to the Coromandel coast of India, and the dispatch of the *Mary* to Surat and *Hart* to Banten early in 1636.
32. In February 1636 Vernworthy had been nominated as a factor for the EIC establishment at Banten, but declined the offer. Mundy, *Travels*, vol. 3, 21n1. Prior to commencing employment with the EIC in 1624, Vernworthy had spent several years assisting a Spanish merchant in New Spain (Mexico).

Enter the Interlopers

same Anglican standards of piety during the voyages: services, including sermons, would be rendered twice a day to merchants and crew.[33] Arthur Hatch, an EIC chaplain with decades of experience, was the perfect choice for Captain Weddell—a commander never careless in his exercise of clerical patronage. In 1623 Weddell had rejected a candidate for chaplain, Patrick Copland, who had once been reproved for delivering a sermon that had "disanimated" an EIC crew when confronting hostile Hollanders.[34] Arthur Hatch was a well-traveled and versatile churchman who had served the EIC even as remotely as Hirado in Japan with John Saris.[35] As the fleet led by Weddell would entertain the hope of visiting Japan after trading in China, Hatch could be particularly useful as an advisor. In his Japan tour Hatch would also have gained familiarity with Chinese merchants, like Li Dan (see Chapter 1), who were stationed or regularly visited southern ports of the archipelago.[36] A decade after his service there, he preached and prayed aboard ships commanded by Captain Weddell in the late 1620s and early 1630s. Upon signing his third contract with the EIC, he had embarked with Weddell on the *Charles* in 1632. When, in 1633, that ship was burned off Surat, all of Hatch's property went up in flames. Along with Weddell and Nathaniel Mountney in the *Jonas*, he had returned to England in 1635. On the voyage home, more than likely Hatch would have participated in any discussion of a venture encompassing not only China but Japan.

Unable to invoke or enforce any sort of "non-compete" clause, the directors of the EIC were livid at what they considered the disloyalty and betrayal of their former employees, whether mariners, merchants, or clergy: "By their dealings, [they shall] ruin our whole trade, although there is not one of them but have had his bringing up, maintenance, and preferment by us and in our service; yet thus ungratefully

---

33. "You are in the first place to provide that God be duly served in all your ships twice a day according to the liturgy of the Church of England." Instructions for John Weddell and Nathaniel Mountney, by commission of Charles I, under our royal sign and signet, 12/22 December 1635, PRO, C.O. 77/6, No. 12.

34. Haig Smith, "'God Shall Enlarge Japheth, and He Shall Dwell in the Tents of Shem': The Changing Face of Religious Governance and Religious Sufferance in the East India Company, 1610–1670," in *The East India Company, 1600–1857: Essays on Anglo-Indian Connection*, ed. William Pettigrew and Mahesh Gopalan (London: Routledge, 2017), 100. As Copland was a Presbyterian who became Congregationalist ("Independent") in the 1630s, Weddell seems to have been demonstrating his own Anglican orthodoxy. For Copland's distinguished career, including service in Japan, see Massarella, *World Elsewhere*, 240.

35. To well-traveled and versatile we may add *durable* to our characterization of Hatch, as "9 out of 45 (20%) chaplains who held EIC posts before 1666 died on the voyage out and back or in India. Of these 45, a few had multiple visits, including Arthur Hatch, who signed up for three voyages between 1618 and 1633." Games, *Web of Empire*, 232–33. For more on the career of Hatch and profiles of other clergy of the early EIC, see Daniel O'Connor, *The Chaplains of the East India Company, 1601–1858* (London: Bloomsbury, 2011). The only other clergyman in Courteen's Weddell fleet that I have been able to identify is a Mr. Hudson, a preacher who would be assigned to the pinnace *Anne*.

36. Enlisting with the EIC in 1618, Hatch was chaplain of the *Palsgrave* that reached Japan in 1619. He returned to England in 1623. On his return he rendered Samuel Purchas an account of Japan, printed in *Purchas His Pilgrimes*, ed. 1625, Vol. II: "A Letter touching Japon with the Government, Affaires and later Occurents there, written to me by Master Arthur Hatch, Minister, lately returned thence," dated "From Wingham in Kent the 25 of November 1623." According to Derek Massarella, Hatch's little Japan survey was commissioned by Purchas and proves comparable in insight to the much better-known set of observations made by Richard Cocks. *World Elsewhere*, 331.

they deal with us."[37] If treason could be committed against a company, the EIC executives would have charged the Courteens with that; the latter were usurping the monopolist's throne of Asian trade. The EIC considered that it had undertaken all the toil, trouble and risks, expended the money, and extensive investment to make commerce possible in India and elsewhere in Asia. The Courteen Association would be reaping where it had not sown. The competition from the new organization would surely lead to considerable reduction of profits. Supposing what was plausible enough, that the new enterprise would bring back to London and Europe many of the same commodities that the EIC was already fetching, how could prices not drop significantly, and profit margins not narrow? On Indian and other Asian coasts, would not natives exploit multiple, competing merchants to raise prices of their commodities, and lower their offers to purchase? As the governor of the EIC would remonstrate with members of the Privy Council, the trading of the Courteens "will raise the price of all goods there [in the East], and when they return to England so lower the price here that the Company will lose heavily, and be greatly prejudiced and unable to continue the trade."[38]

Certainly the Courteen Association was not the first rival with which the EIC had had to contend. During the reign of James I, various upstarts and competition were suffered and overcome. As noted in Chapter 1, the company had been much vexed when the Stuart king authorized Sir Edward Michelbourne to launch an expedition to the East in 1604. This was construed as a violation of the company's exclusive charter. Just a few years later the directors started a lawsuit in the Admiralty Court against Michelbourne for a series of piratical exploits that compromised their trading relations around Asia. Even more substantially were EIC interests assailed by James when, in 1617, the same monarch consented to grant some of his courtiers a patent to adventure under the name Scottish East India Company. The EIC was able to swallow and digest this Scottish version of itself only by bribing the courtiers and undertaking to loan James a large sum.[39]

As we saw in the previous chapter, it was an EIC ship, the *London*, which had reached and traded on a small-scale in Macao in 1635, after its president of Surat, William Methwold, had arranged the entente with the Portuguese viceroy at Goa. The EIC lobbied its sovereign strenuously but in vain to deprive Courteen of license to dispatch ships to the East to exploit this modest breakthrough into the Luso-Chinese domain. The EIC executives submitted more than one petition, pleaded directly with the king's highest ministers and members of his Privy Council, and

---

37. Foster, *English Factories, 1634–1636*, 261.
38. A Court of Committees, 9/19 December 1636, *Court Minutes of EIC, 1635–1639*, 207.
39. Andrews, *Trade, Plunder*, 278. For the failure of a Scottish East India Company to materialize, also see Games, *Web of Empire*, 8, where it is noted that Scots were notably numerous as participants—mariners, merchants, and soldiers—in ventures of the EIC (and VOC), as well as enterprises of the Portuguese, Spanish, and French. There would be Scots aboard the Courteen ships. Rupali Mishra has more recently offered an account of the ephemeral Scottish EIC in *Business of State*, 162–77.

even separately appealed to the Archbishop of Canterbury, William Laud.[40] On one occasion, the director of the company spent most of a day squatting in desperation at the king's residence. Over several hours he and his deputy languished in exasperation at Whitehall only to be crowned with mortification by a curt reception and dismissal by Charles himself in the evening: "Mr. Governor [Maurice Abbot], with Mr. Deputy, Alderman Abdy, and Mr. Mun, went yesterday to Whitehall and waited all the morning, being sermon day, hoping through favour of Lord Cottington and Mr. Secretary Coke to gain private access to the King and deliver to him the Company's petition concerning Sir William Courteen's voyage, and to be able to speak more fully on that matter; but it was not until after dinner that he presented the petition to His Majesty, who took it from his hands but gave no answer to it, though they waited all the afternoon."[41] The king may well have appreciated the hostility of the EIC and was probably not surprised by the vigor of the endeavor of its directors to dissuade him from countenancing the allegedly interloping enterprise. Yet he had plenty of answers to the objections of the Elizabethan-chartered overseas trading company.

Since the latter had not succeeded in establishing many large trading stations (factories) in Asia, there was plenty of opportunity for an alternative company to try different tactics, probe unexplored areas, and initiate and cultivate more relationships. Indeed, it was recognized that in the first decade of Charles's reign (1625–1635), there had been considerable "decay of trade." The number of ships sent to the East by that company had steadily declined in the last few decades: from fifty-five in 1611–1620, to forty-six in the 1620s, to only thirty-five for the entire 1630s.[42] As P.J. Marshall has pointed out: "The twelve separate voyages sent out between 1601 and 1612 had made handsome returns, but those who contributed to the second joint stock of £1,629,040 between 1617 and 1632 consistently lost money. When a third

---

40. "Mr. Governor [Maurice Abbot], hearing that the Lords Grace of Canterbury [William Laud] was in private council with the King, determined to wait on him at Lambeth [Palace] and desire his favourable intervention with His Majesty, and at seven o'clock this morning went and was admitted, and informed him of the matter, but his Grace had to be with the King at half-past seven o'clock, and so took a copy of the petition, promising to read it and speak to the King and Lords about it and desired that Mr. Sherburne should attend tomorrow to hear their answer." A Court of Committees, 9 March 1636, *Court Minutes of EIC, 1635–1639*, 164.

41. A Court of Committees, 9 March 1636, *Court Minutes of EIC, 1635–1639*, 164. Lords Cottington, Windebank, Coke, and Archbishop Laud were the chief targets of the EIC lobbying campaign. From 1635 Laud acted as Lord Treasurer while he was archbishop of Canterbury; Sir Francis Windebank was not only Secretary of State but commissioner of the treasury. Sir Francis Cottington, Chancellor of the Exchequer, and Sir John Coke, himself previously Secretary of State and Lord Privy Seal, were also commissioners of the treasury. The following documents pertain to actions taken by the company to prevent Courteen from receiving royal authorization, all reproduced in *Court Minutes of EIC, 1635–1639*: A Court of Committees, 15 January 1636, 141–42; "The Remonstrance of the EIC to the King, Jan. 1636," 143–44; A Court of Committees, 17 February 1636, 157; A Court of Committees, 7 March 1636, 163; A Court of Committees, 9 March 1636, 164; A Court of Committees, 11 March 1636, 165; A Court of Committees, 7 October 1636, 197–98; A Court of Committees, 9 December 1636, 207.

42. Chaudhuri, *English East India Company*, 215–23.

joint stock was launched in 1631, it too returned poor results."[43] Furnished with a different foundation from which to launch initiatives—the 1635 Goa entente— another venture of his subjects would have some fresh chances to make some inroads where the older organization of investors and projectors had failed.[44] As Charles and his counselors surveyed the map of Asia, they could descry sizeable vacuums that the EIC had been unable to fill. Would it be unfair to let others try to set up factories and forts in different and more advantageous locations along the coasts of Asia, where the older overseas trading company was remiss or had squandered its opportunities?

The Stuart monarch was even entitled to some indignation, as he compared his government's condition with those of his peers on the continent. The EIC's shortcomings and inefficacy had deprived him of much potential revenue— while the Dutch East India Company, by contrast, was yielding the rulers of the United Provinces more and more wealth from commerce and conquests in the East. Likewise, from India, China, Japan, and the Philippines, the Portuguese and Spanish subjects of his European sovereign peer, Philip IV, were enriching a monarchy—which, in 1635, needed prodigious sums to finance campaigns and battles at a critical juncture of the Thirty Years' War. Nor had the EIC discovered the northeast or northwest passage—neither of which had yet been convincingly diagnosed as delusional. So, among other things, it would have appeared equitable and just to permit another set of British adventurers to launch a probe for that ever-elusive corridor, while their mariners and merchants opened or deepened trade in places not tried or effectively exploited by the older mercantile organization.[45] Charles was careful to clarify that he was not chartering the Courteen Association to supplant the EIC. As he emphasized, there was plenty of space and opportunity for both of them to co-exist (if not cooperate) in Asia. In the Royal Commission authorizing the Courteen entity, Charles scrupulously instructed this new configuration of adventurers "not to prejudice the trade of our East India Company." Moreover, if nature did abhor a vacuum, then the Courteen Association's *not* exploiting room left by the EIC would only facilitate further expansion and aggrandizement of the Dutch, from India to Japan.[46]

---

43. Marshall, "English in Asia," 274. Such a trend of contraction served as warrant for the Courteens to argue that they would be filling voids, not jostling with or displacing the EIC.

44. In characterizing the provisions of the Goa Convention of 1635, Charles laid emphasis on the novel China prospect: "truce and free trade not only at Goa . . . *but also at Chine*."

45. In the Royal Commission dated 12/22 December 1635, Charles expressly authorized the Courteen Association "to search for the Northeast passage to the North part of the Californias on the backside of America."

46. It probably contributed to the defeat of the EIC lobby that the company could not present a united front against the Courteen Association: "Its [the EIC's] position was damaged by rumours that some of its own members were adventurers with Courten." Appleby, "William Courten," *ODNB*. From this not implausible rumor our impression of EIC-Courteen fluidity is only fortified. Many EIC members had (and would have) investments in other overseas companies. This was established long ago by Theodore K. Rabb, *Enterprise and Empire: Merchant and Gentry Investment in the Expansion of England, 1575–1630* (Cambridge, MA: Harvard University Press, 1967); and more recently discussed by Brenner, *Merchants and Revolution*.

Enter the Interlopers

However tenacious and robust the animosity of the EIC, the Courteen Association's Asian fleet would sail with the full measure of blessing and support of Charles I. In April 1636 the Courteen ships commanded by John Weddell would sail from the Downs with hopes of reaching and trading in China. The commercial expedition was enabled by pledges of royal patronage. The monarch had not merely assented but committed to help fund it. Promising disbursement of £10,000 from his own coffers, he was projecting himself as a major investor.[47] Nor were his highest ministers personally or financially detached, as the Secretary of State, Sir Francis Windebank contrived an arrangement to profit himself individually by this new venture.[48] The captains, crew, staff, and factors of Weddell's fleet would sail with the assurance and arrogance that they were the envoys of the king of Great Britain, fully backed by his administration. As more than merely private, rather as royal trade delegates: that is how the Courteens expected to be treated by fellow Europeans and Asians. In December 1635 Charles provided Captain Weddell and Courteen's chief factor, Nathaniel Mountney, with full panoply of permissions and licenses, empowered by His Majesty's signatures.[49] Even a royal seal was commissioned to be cast for use by Weddell for documents that would need to be produced when unforeseeable situations and emergencies on the high seas arose. The Courteen ships commanded by Weddell would sail fully under the Stuart aegis.[50] In case of battle Weddell was expressly authorized to unfurl the royal flag of Charles. While

47. To give some idea of the value of £10,000 in 1635: that sum would be enough to pay the salaries of about four hundred merchants or one hundred sea captains for one year. In 1627 Peter Mundy had received employment in Surat from directors of the EIC, having engaged for £25 annually for a five-year term. There were EIC factors in India in the 1620s being paid as little as £10 per annum. In October 1627 the accomplished commander Richard Swanley had proposed to "serve the Company in the Indies at 10 pounds per month," but was requested "to bethink himself of a less demand." He was ultimately hired at £100 per year. Geoffrey Parker in *Global Crisis* estimated that in the 1630s £5,000 was the equivalent of 2014's £1 million. So, Charles I's projected investment could be counted in today's terms as well above £2 million. Furnishing and equipping Weddell's fleet of four ships and two pinnaces cost more than £120,000 pounds. Courteen covered the majority of that amount. It was reported that Sir Paul Pindar, at the prompting of Charles I, loaned Courteen about £36,000 to amass that total. *Court Minutes of EIC, 1635–1639*, xix, 275. More investors can be found listed in W.R. Scott, *The Constitution and Finance of English, Scottish, and Irish Joint-Stock Companies to 1720*, 3 vols. (Cambridge: Cambridge University Press, 1910–1912), II, 113.

48. "Undertaking to allow a share of profits to Sir Francis Windebank," 7/17 December 1635, *Court Minutes of EIC, 1635–1639*, 124.

49. "We the King by these presents under our Royal Signature and Signet give you not only license and express command, but also full power and authority . . . to undertake a voyage to Goa, the parts of Malabar, the coast of China and Japan, there to trade." Royal Commission, 12 December 1635. Transcripts of all documents concerning the investment and authorization of Charles are easily accessible as edited by Temple in Mundy, *Travels*, vol. 3, Appendix A, 429–45.

50. Rupali Mishra has rightly emphasized the unprecedentedly regal, more potent, authorization of the Weddell fleet in comparison with any enjoyed by the EIC: "The letters provided Courten, Weddell, and their associates [conveyed] additional powers that the Company did not have." *Business of State*, 283. Among the privileges conferred by Charles upon the Courteen Association was license to transport the sum of £40,000 in gold and silver bullion without having to pay more than negligible customs fees. Similarly, the Courteens had obtained special permission to carry ordnance and exceptionally large quantities of munitions—the latter particularly requested by the Portuguese viceroy of Goa, Conde de Linhares, at the signing of the accord in January 1635.

commercial ambassadors of sorts, they could act as his navy in the event of any clash or altercation upon oceans, in bays, and at ports and coasts.

Yet as they set out for India, China, Japan, and beyond, the Courteen fleet could not be confident that even their own compatriots, their former colleagues, would be friendly. Suppose their fellow Stuart subjects, EIC captains and factors in the East, attempted to hinder or spoil their business? Further, although an agreement between British (as represented by Nathaniel Mountney) and Portuguese had been signed the previous year at Goa, it was far from clear that the Lusitanians should be depended upon to honor it. And if they chose to flout it, or practice obstruction by some pretense, perhaps violence could not be avoided. The hostility of the EIC to the Weddell expedition might also deprive the Courteen commander of leverage vis-à-vis the Iberians. As the Portuguese would be fully cognizant of the resentment and enmity between the EIC and Courteen Association, so those subjects of Philip IV stationed and operating in Asia could more comfortably decline either to facilitate or assist in the achievement of Weddell and Mountney's objectives there. Such uncooperative or obstructive conduct would be tantamount to doing the rival EIC a favor—and thereby obtaining for the Portuguese some good-will from that older company in the future. In any event, as Weddell's fleet of the Courteen Association was to approach China in the summer of 1637, the British in the East could certainly not present a united front, either to the Portuguese or the Ming officials of the province of Canton (Guangdong)—or to the Dutch sea-captains prowling and marauding in the straits of Melaka and Taiwan and in the East China Sea.

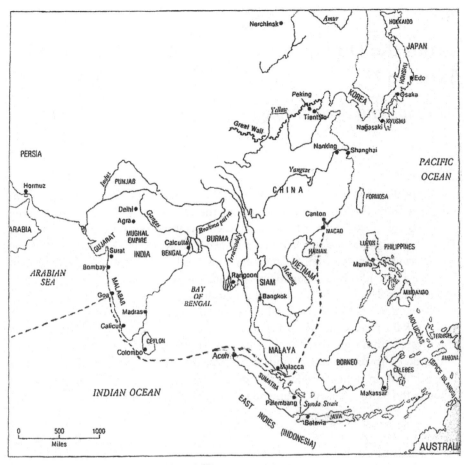

Map 2.1: The Courteen Fleet's route to China, 1636–1637
Goa, October 1636; Aceh, May 1637; Macao, July 1637

3

From the Downs to Goa to Melaka, April 1636– June 1637

Mishaps and Breakthroughs along the Way to China

Flying the flag of King Charles I, the Weddell expedition of the Courteen Association departed from the Downs at 3 o'clock on the afternoon of 24 April 1636.[1] The fleet was comprised of four large ships, each weighing several hundred tons, the *Dragon*, *Sun*, *Katherine*, and *Planter*, and two pinnaces (100–250 tons), the *Anne* and *Discovery*.[2] In the English Channel on 28 April, patriotism prompted Captain Weddell in the admiral *Dragon* to fire cannon at a French ship: "Neglecting his duty to the King's flag, [it] was taught better manners."[3] Weddell's second-in-command was Richard Swanley in the vice-admiral, the *Sun*; Captain John Carter led the rear-admiral *Katherine*, while Edward Hall commanded the *Planter*. By 10 May 1636 the ships were within sight of the Canary Islands. The pinnace *Discovery* was discarded and ordered to return to England on 14 June after it had proven too much of a laggard.[4] Within sight of England that pinnace was captured by Turkish pirates and taken to the Barbary coast.[5] Meanwhile, the *Katherine* was separated from the other

---

1. "Voyage of Captain Weddell's Fleet, April 1636–April 1637." The EIC's *Royal Mary*, bound for India, had departed four hours ahead of Courteen's fleet. All dates New Style (Gregorian) unless otherwise indicated. Those aboard the *Mary* inferred from the provisions and merchandise taken by the Courteen ships that Weddell would go to Goa.
2. The *Dragon* was an old vessel that had probably spent much of its career in the Atlantic; it seems to have come from a Levant Company adventurer: "John Fowke, a Levant Company trader who carried on a thirty-year legal battle with the EIC over disputed debt obligations, became involved with Sir William Courteen when Fowke and his partner William Clobbery, the great colonial trader and Kent Island leader, fitted out their ship *Dragon* for Courteen's use in his interloping fleet of 1635–1636." Brenner, *Merchants and Revolution*, 173. As of 1635 the *Katherine* was being used by Courteen in the Atlantic. It was at the Azores in September of that year. Andrews, *Ships, Money and Politics*, 89. Mundy described both the *Dragon* and *Katherine* as "old and long out." In other words, they were at least fifteen years old when they sailed for Weddell in 1636. As for the *Sun*, Mundy noted it was "Dutch-built."
3. "Voyage of Captain Weddell's Fleet, April 1636–April 1637."
4. Martin Milward was captain of the *Anne* and Mr. Richardson captain of the other pinnace, *Discovery*.
5. It is only from Peter Mundy's 1650-penned appendix to his travel journal that we learn: "June the 4th[/14th] 1636: in a gale of wind we left the *Discovery* (a victualler) behind, of whom we understood afterward she steered home again, and being near the landsend of England, she was taken by Turkish pirates and carried for Barbary." Mundy, *Travels*, vol. 3, 424. Mundy embarked from the Downs as principal factor of the *Planter*. For the capture and enslavement of English sailors by Sallee (Morocco) / Barbary corsairs in 1635–1636, see Andrews, *Ships, Money and Politics*, 170.

From the Downs to Goa to Melaka

vessels by storms but did not turn back—or fall into the claws of corsairs.[6] The storms cost the *Sun* at least one of its staff: the ship's trumpeter's mate was drowned in May 1636 in what Peter Mundy described as a "tornado."[7]

Having crossed the equator on 22 June, three months after embarking from the Downs, on 4 August the fleet sailed round the Cape of Good Hope. East of the Cape, on 30 August, the British fleet, minus the *Katherine*, encountered a huge, 1,600-ton Portuguese carrack, carrying 800 men, including the new archbishop of Goa, Dom Fr. Francisco dos Martyres.[8] Thomas Robinson, factor and Portuguese-fluent linguist, traveling aboard the Swanley-commanded *Sun* with 131 other men, went aboard a barge to communicate with the carrack's captain. From the latter the Courteens received some disquieting news: Conde de Linhares, viceroy of Goa, the man with whom Captain Weddell and Nathaniel Mountney had negotiated the 1635 Anglo-Portuguese accord, had left that office to return to Portugal.[9] On the spot, the British commander composed a letter to the new viceroy, Pero da Silva, to be conveyed to Goa by this carrack.[10]

A week after encountering the Portuguese ship, the Courteen fleet anchored a little northwest of Madagascar, at Anjouan among the Comoro Islands, 4 September 1636.[11] Shortly before this stop Weddell and Mountney endeavored to prepare a friendly reception for their fleet in India from the EIC president at Surat, William Methwold. To their collaborator in the forging of the Anglo-Portuguese entente they wrote from aboard the *Dragon* on 29 August to inform him of their present location and expectation of reaching Goa within a month or two. Weddell and Mountney hoped the missive would establish a communication channel that could be used through the duration of their expedition. The ex-EIC veterans conceded that he might be disturbed to hear of their new, non-EIC venture; so they hastened to emphasize their justification, through their king's will and favor: "Let His Majesty's [Charles I's] pleasure and the good terms and satisfaction which we received in England suffice to resolve you (as it hath done us) that all our intendments are both

---

6. "Yesterday received a packet dated from the island of Mayo, May 13[/23], from Captain Carter, commander in the *Katherine*, who has been separated by a storm from the fleet. Captain Weddell has appointed their rendezvous to be beyond Cape Bona Speranza." Thomas Kynaston and Samuel Bonnell to Edward Nicholas, 10/20 August 1636, PRO, East Indies, Vol. IV, B, No. 20, *Court Minutes of EIC, 1635–1639*, 190–91.

7. Mundy, *Travels*, vol. 3, 28–29.

8. "Voyage of Captain Weddell's Fleet, April 1636–April 1637." Later, on arrival at Goa, Mundy was able to go aboard this carrack and provide this description: "She is said to be of 1600 tons, of a strange form, her beakhead in such a manner and so capacious that would [measure] near 20 tons, and the biggest longboat in our fleet would easily lie in her forechains; 12 main shrowdes of a side; steered below with tackles fastened to her tiller: all monstrous methought." Mundy, *Travels*, vol. 3, 60.

9. "Voyage of Captain Weddell's Fleet, April 1636–April 1637."

10. Mundy, *Travels*, vol. 3, 32.

11. "Voyage of Captain Weddell's Fleet, April 1636–April 1637." Arrival of the Courteen fleet at Anjouan was also recorded by William Bayley in his journal kept aboard the EIC's *Mary*, during its voyage to Surat: "Aug. 26[/ Sept. 5], 1636: reached Johanna [Anjouan]. Aug. 27[/Sept. 6], 1636: Captain Weddell arrived with the *Dragon*, *Sun*, and *Planter*, having touched nowhere on his way from England." Foster, *English Factories, 1634–1636*, 306. It was evidently this ship, the *Mary*, which would transport the letter of Weddell and Mountney at Anjouan to Methwold at Surat; see below for that correspondence.

fair, just, and honest."[12] To satisfy Methwold that this was no distortion or fabrication, they accompanied this note with a copy of the letter penned by their sovereign, Charles I, addressed to all EIC personnel stationed in Asia. In this communication dated 30 March 1636 (O.S.), referring to his own "particular interest" in the success of the Weddell expedition of the Courteen Association, the monarch commanded "the President and Council of Our East India Company residing in the Indies" to facilitate the operations of the Courteens by providing food, refreshment, and supplies as occasion might necessitate. In this same royal directive, Methwold and all his other EIC subjects residing in Asia were commanded not to impede any of the interests or pursuits of the Courteens.

By 16 October 1636 the Courteen fleet could glimpse the western coast of India, and the following day it anchored some small distance from Goa. On 18 October the fleet, bereft of the *Katherine* and the pinnace *Anne*, both of which had fallen behind, reached Fort Agoada in the Goa bay.[13] The Portuguese carrack carrying the new archbishop of Goa had arrived just four days before the Courteens.[14] When the British fleet reached the coast of India, William Methwold at Surat was ready to issue a most uncordial welcome. Upon learning that his old colleagues had arrived at Goa, Methwold, writing in private capacity, addressed the Courteen commander: "From the particular respect which I profess to owe you, I address these lines to congratulate your safe arrival in India. I cannot say welcome because you bring ruin to the honourable company whom I serve."[15] Methwold and the rest of the EIC employees in the East had previously been ordered by the London directors not to facilitate or advance the commerce of their old colleagues. Methwold also dispatched a long reply to the letter Weddell and Mountney had sent him from Anjouan via the EIC *Mary*. Writing on behalf of himself and the EIC council at Surat, Methwold expressed his shock and disgust at the behavior of Weddell and Mountney. He did acknowledge that the Courteen fleet sailed to the East with full approval of the king; and the company staff at Surat would cooperate with Weddell and Mountney and the Courteen Association insofar as obeying their monarch required it.

---

12. Captain John Weddell and Nathaniel Mountney, aboard the *Dragon* at Johanna [Anjouan], to the President at Surat, 29 August [8 September] 1636, Foster, *English Factories, 1634–1636*, 284.

13. "Voyage of Captain Weddell's Fleet, April 1636–April 1637" gives 6/16 October against Mundy's 8/18. Mundy relates that the *Katherine* and *Anne* arrived at Goa on 23 October / 2 November. Mundy, *Travels*, vol. 3, 49. According to the "Voyage of Weddell's Fleet, April 1636–April 1637," the *Katherine* arrived at Goa on 24 October / 3 November and the *Anne*, commanded by Martin Milward, on 25 October / 4 November. The *Katherine* had reached Anjouan just a day after the *Dragon*, *Sun*, and *Planter* had left it. This ship commanded by John Carter arrived at Goa neither having lost any men nor carrying any sick ones.

14. From later correspondence we learn that the Dutch had targeted this carrack. Evidently Jakob Cooper's VOC fleet at Goa was to have raided this large ship: "We now know for certain that the carrack which was expected from Portugal arrived in Goa on the [10/]20th Oct. [1636]. We arrived 20 days later, and that fat prize escaped us." Cooper to Heren XVII, 7 December (N.S.) 1637, *Hague Transcripts*, 1st ser., Vol. X, No. CCCXLII.

15. President Methwold at Surat to Captain Weddell at Goa, 24 October / 3 November 1636, Foster, *English Factories, 1634–1636*, 317.

Methwold tried to appeal to his old colleagues by defying them, from their own extensive experience, to deny the simple proposition that the commercial sphere of India "will not endure competition of the same nation." Venting his spite, he also taunted Weddell and Mountney with the promise that the new viceroy at Goa, Pero da Silva, would not be receptive to their overtures, no matter how warranted by the recently inked Anglo-Portuguese accord: "You will not find Goa such as you formed to yourselves in your private counsels." Nor, he gloated, should they expect to be successful at obtaining sufficient quantities of pepper down south, on the Malabar coast, to lade any of their large ships. As for more ambitious and novel schemes in the Far East, they might as well promptly abandon any hope of finding the Portuguese hospitable or cooperative. He prophesied that no matter how eloquent or imperious their letter of introduction and authorization from Charles I, they would discover the Portuguese at Macao and elsewhere to be indifferent when not hostile. In this epistolary diatribe, Methwold did not omit to advertise the ingratitude and betrayal of the EIC by Weddell and Mountney. They understood perfectly well how this new Courteen venture would hazard what their old (his present) employer had labored decades to establish.[16] They were trying to exploit what he personally had been most instrumental in achieving: an unprecedented and transformative entente with the Portuguese executive of the *Estado da India*.

EIC president Methwold's lecture in ethics irked Captain Weddell. His retort to the letter was a tirade drenched in sarcasm and spiked with rebuke. Penned aboard the *Dragon* anchored off Goa the following month, in November 1636, Weddell chided his old colleague for contemptible indulgence in self-pity ("your pretended misery") for the plight of the EIC in Surat and the Malabar coast. Besides scolding Methwold for disingenuous courtesy and hollow welcome, he assured his old associate that neither he nor Nathaniel Mountney was in the least bit perturbed by the president's "peremptory jeering menaces." More placidly and gravely, Weddell promised to requite Methwold should he or any EIC personnel in Surat practice any ploys to obstruct or sabotage the Courteen ventures: "Be assured that if ever you attempt the least underhand injury by your supposititious tricks, though it never come to perfection (which indeed we fear not) either you or yours shall answer it."[17] In a separate letter, from Weddell and Mountney to the president and council at Surat, the tone was more conciliatory. The Courteen leadership conceded that they would add to market competition, but only marginally, to no very detrimental degree. Moreover, they assured their old colleagues stationed at Surat that they "intend not to trade in any place where the Honourable Company have factories,

---

16. President Methwold and Council at Surat to Messrs. Weddell and Mountney, 24 October / 3 November 1636, Foster, *English Factories, 1634–1636*, 314–16. Methwold noted in this communication that Henry Bornford would be conveying the message to the Courteens and that the latter could take the opportunity to discuss any unfinished business with Bornford. It was the same Bornford who had been the chief factor aboard the EIC *London*, which had sojourned at Macao the previous year, August–October 1635. See Chapter 2.

17. Captain Weddell, aboard the *Dragon* in Goa Road, to President Methwold, at Surat, 29 November / 8 December 1636, Foster, *English Factories, 1634–1636*, 321–22.

unless we be either thither invited by the prince of the country or impulse by urgent necessity. . . . [A]ll parts and ports of India, China, Japan, etc., are as free to the one of us as to the other, and if there be any priority it inclineth to your side; and so far will we be from giving you disturbance in your trade as that, unless some extraordinary accident compel us, we will not touch in any of your ports." Conversely, Weddell and Mountney were incensed by the insinuation that they had committed some sort of treason. The Courteen leaders mordantly answered the charge that they were EIC ingrates or traitors: "If fines and public undeserved reproaches, instead of remuneration for honest service, be the East India Company's favours and honours (as nowadays they are) we pray God keep both you and us from such indulgences. . . . But blame us not, nor brand us with the title of mercenaries, if, being commanded upon an honest and lawful design, we have embraced a better master's better pay; which we believe yourselves would have done, especially after such unkind (that we give it no worse epithet) and unconscionable usage." In retort to the gloomy prognostications of Methwold, Weddell and Mountney emphasized that they were undaunted and unfazed by Iberian imperial vicissitudes or personnel changes in India: the fact that there was a new viceroy at Goa was known to them long before they neared the coast of India: "We should indeed be miserable if we depended either on one port or one person." Weddell and Mountney professed themselves quite confident that they could cope with the challenge of adjusting to such alterations in India and beyond. Nor did they suppose that their success in India, China, or anywhere else hinged entirely upon the favor of the Portuguese.[18]

Whatever effect such letters of Weddell and Mountney might have had upon Methwold and the other EIC factors at Surat, the latter had not been the only ones in Asia who had been instructed by the company's directors in London not to be very hospitable to the Courteens. Months before the fleet arrived at Goa, those directors had also written to the president and staff at their other main factory in the East, at Banten in Java, in order to inform them of the voyage of the Weddell fleet. The president and his staff were not to grant any aid or supplies to the Courteens should the latter summon sufficient impudence to request it.[19] In May 1636, the company in London had also dispatched a letter in the same vein to its merchants based in Persia, at Gombroon in the Persian Gulf. Should the interlopers visit that port, "we hope they will find small trade to bid them welcome or encourage them to come again, but if any of them should come thither, you . . . will be so careful of our good as to prevent them both in selling and buying or in transporting of Moors and Persian goods from that port unto any other place."[20] Weddell and Mountney ought

---

18. Captain Weddell and Nathaniel Mountney at Goa to the President and Council at Surat [undated; probably end of November 1636], Foster, *English Factories, 1634–1636*, 322–24.
19. EIC to the President and Council at Bantam, 29 February / 10 March 1636, Foster, *English Factories, 1634–1636*, 173.
20. EIC to the agent and factors in Persia, 25 May / 4 June 1636, Foster, *English Factories, 1634–1636*, 260–61. Recall that while the company had dispatched the *Mary* to Surat, its *Hart* was sailing for Banten in the spring of 1636.

to have anticipated, and probably did expect, that such orders might be transmitted to their old colleagues.

At least Weddell and Mountney had reason to expect a decent welcome from the viceroy of Goa, for they were bringing supplies badly needed by the head of the Portuguese empire of the East: metal (copper and lead), munitions, and naval supplies (especially cordage). As the Courteen commander noted, upon signing of the accord in January 1635: "Your worships [Portuguese at Goa] asked for a quantity of stores, munition, etc., from our land, required by the galleons or fleet, which were granted, but not before special license had been obtained from our king, these being forbidden stores."[21] In exchange, the Courteens expected to receive a sizeable lading of pepper as well as some quantity of cinnamon. Robert Moulton, master of the admiral *Dragon*, Weddell's right-hand man on that ship, with the head merchants of the *Sun*, Anthony Vernworthy and Thomas Robinson, were dispatched in the barge to go ashore and present a letter of introduction to the new viceroy, Pero da Silva.[22] This little delegation discovered that the latter was in mourning at the death of his brother in Portugal, news of which had only just reached him. The Courteen envoys were forced to wait a few hours in an antechamber of his palace before a page of the viceroy came to inform them that his master would speak to none below the rank of captain. Moulton proceeded to the chamber of the viceroy and delivered the letters. The viceroy only condescended to utter a brief welcome before dismissing Moulton with the promise of a reply in the next few days.[23]

The day after Moulton's meeting with Pero da Silva, Captain Weddell and the head merchants and captains of the fleet came ashore. Weddell presented the letter of King Charles addressed to the viceroy, along with the Stuart monarch's gift to him: a gold chain with a pendant, a portrait of that sovereign and his French queen, Henrietta Maria.[24] Philip IV of Spain had conferred upon Pero da Silva authority to exercise his own discretion in dealing with any British visitors invoking the Anglo-Portuguese accord of 1635.[25] After the viceroy convened the council and read the English letter to the senators, they held a lengthy discussion. Their decision was to grant the British ships commerce and let them rent a house in Goa from which to conduct their business. The house would also serve the Courteens as a warehouse for

---

21. Copy of the second letter sent by the English [written in Spanish], 27 September / 7 October 1637, *Lisbon Transcripts*, I.O. Records, Vol. IV. A special dispensation had been procured from Charles I to authorize Weddell and Mountney to export both silver bullion and military/naval supplies.

22. "7[/17] Oct. 1636. Anchored in Goa Road, and sent three men ashore with a letter to the Viceroy. On their way they paid a visit to the General of the Portuguese fleet, Don Francisco Telles de Meneses." "Voyage of Captain Weddell's Fleet, April 1636–April 1637."

23. "Voyage of Captain Weddell's Fleet, April 1636–April 1637."

24. 8/18 October 1636, Mundy, *Travels*, vol. 3, 47. Obviously the letter of Charles addressed to the viceroy of Goa was prepared in such a way as to apply regardless of the identity of the man occupying that office.

25. "And as your Majesty [Philip IV] was pleased, by a letter which came in the *Sao Joao de Deus*, to leave this matter to me, until such time as a decision shall be arrived at, I thought fit to communicate the matter to the Senate [Senado da Camara] that assists me, causing the letter to be read to them and instructing them to advise me what should be done." Letter from the viceroy of India to the king [of Spain], 22 February / 4 March 1637, *Lisbon Transcripts, Books of the Monsoons*, book 37, fol. 481.

54   *The First British Trade Expedition to China*

their goods while they endeavored to make contracts. So, with the house appointed, the British could start unloading cargo from the ships at anchor. The viceroy would arrange to purchase the goods that the Courteen merchants brought expressly to sell to the Portuguese at Goa, including sails, lead, anchors, cannon balls, and other naval supplies.[26]

A few weeks later, on 9 November 1636, while the Courteens, supervised by Nathaniel Mountney, were occupied in arranging transactions in the Portuguese-Indian city, a fleet of ten Dutch ships approached to blockade the harbor of Goa.[27] After the Dutch had anchored close enough to fire cannon at the Portuguese forts in the bay, the viceroy in town prepared to counter with Portuguese vessels, including the large carrack recently arrived. At the same time he pleaded with the British, by mediation of the old acquaintance of Weddell and Mountney, Padre Paul Reimão, to sally forth with the Lusitanian ships to disperse the VOC fleet.[28] The Courteen refusal to participate in an operation to repulse the Dutch greatly upset the viceroy, who now wrote to convey his consternation to Weddell. As the British had been received into the harbor as friends, so he might reasonably expect them to help him secure it. If they were this species of friend, he suggested, then they would most appropriately depart. As the Courteens were now made keenly to feel like unwanted guests, they hastened to conclude their business in Goa.[29] But they were still stuck waiting for the large quantity of pepper and cinnamon promised to come from the Portuguese, out of Malabar and Ceylon (Sri Lanka), as exchange for the metal, munitions, and nautical supplies they had brought from England. By December 1636, Weddell's patience must have been all but exhausted and his suspicion growing that he was waiting in vain for the shipment of pepper and cinnamon sufficient to lade the pinnace *Anne*. By the middle of the month, at latest, the commander was most likely conferring with Nathaniel Mountney about the coordinates of their next move.

As subsequent events suggest, they were probably discussing what were the best options for obtaining pepper elsewhere on the western coast of India, south of Goa.[30] For if the Portuguese would not deliver the quantity of pepper the former had promised in exchange for bringing the metal, munitions, and other supplies from England, then the Courteens would need to procure that spice

---

26. Letter from the viceroy of India, Pero da Silva, to the king [of Spain], Philip IV, 4 March 1637 [22 February, O.S.], *Lisbon Transcripts, Books of the Monsoons*, book 37, fol. 481.
27. "We entered the bay of Goa in the afternoon of November the 9th. We saw 14 vessels lying under the fort Aguada [in Bay of Goa], viz. six galleons, one carrack of 900 tons, two pinnaces and five English vessels [*Dragon, Sun, Katherine, Planter, Anne*], also a large number of frigates impossible to count." Jakob Cooper to the VOC governor-general at Batavia, dated the *Utrecht*, at anchor in the Bay of Goa, 4 February 1637 (N.S.).
28. For the Dutch Jesuit Paulo Reimão's role in facilitating the Goa Convention of 1635, see Chapter 1.
29. 30 October / 9 November 1636, "Voyage of Captain Weddell's Fleet, April 1636–April 1637."
30. In Weddell's later letter to the EIC president at Surat, William Fremlen (successor of William Methwold), he wrote that the Courteens had been promised at least a pinnace-full of pepper from Malabar but that subsequently the Portuguese lied to the effect that it had been a bad year for that spice, such that they could not supply him with such a quantity. Captain Weddell, aboard the *Dragon* off Cannanore, to President Fremlen at Surat, 29 January / 8 February 1639, "Weddell's China Narrative, O.C. 1662."

From the Downs to Goa to Melaka 55

themselves—presumably somewhere in Malabar. Yet all the while they were frustrated at the obfuscating and stingy behavior of the Lusitanians, the British were careful not to display any signs of favoring or abetting the Dutch in the latter's attempt to suffocate Goa. For example, in early January 1637, a Portuguese vessel had gone out to the blockading fleet under a white flag to ransom two captives. When the boat returned with a letter from a Dutchman addressed to the British, Captain Weddell submitted it to his host, Pero da Silva, for review.[31] Likewise, when Weddell's fleet took its departure weeks later, the British were to deliver a note to Mascarenhas, Portuguese captain of the fort at Agoada in the bay of Goa, conveying to him some strategic intelligence they had recently acquired from the Dutch.[32] During November and December 1636 the Courteens also maintained some contact with their former colleagues north of Goa, Methwold and the EIC staff at Surat. On the first of December a company ship from there had arrived at Goa. Among the men aboard was Henry Bornford, the man who had served as chief factor of the *London* on its trip to Macao in 1635.[33] When the Courteens conversed with him, and if they informed him of their China ambitions, might he have offered some fresh tips on how to approach the Portuguese and Chinese at Macao?

After much haggling at the eleventh hour with the royal financier/treasurer (vedor da fazenda) at Goa, Jose Pinto Pereira, about the pricing of such items as the large quantity of cordage brought by the Courteens, the latter finally left the town to embark from the bay. Riding as factor aboard the *Planter*, Peter Mundy summarized the unpleasant sojourn of the Courteens at the capital of the *Estado da India*:

> We failing of our expectation, wanting our good friend el Conde de Linhares, and finding nothing but delays, fair words and breach of promises, perceiving their intent, unwilling to have us intermeddle with their trade for hindering their particular [interests], having brought and delivered them sundry stores and munition according to their requiry and contract, as cordage, lead, shot, anchors, ironwork, pitch, tar, etc., we demanded satisfaction for the same and leave to depart, which accordingly was granted us.[34]

---

31. "Voyage of Captain Weddell's Fleet, April 1636–April 1637."
32. Mundy, *Travels*, vol. 3, 71. This letter of Weddell to Mascarenhas, 23 January / 2 February 1637, is treated in full below. Mascarenhas was himself to become viceroy of Goa in 1644.
33. Most probably on this occasion Methwold, through Bornford, was seeking the EIC share of profit from the *London*'s errand to Macao: "Henry Bornford, who has been sent chiefly to clear accounts with the *Vedor da Fazenda*." President Methwold and Council at Surat to Messrs. Weddell and Mountney [at Goa], 24 October / 3 November 1636, Foster, *English Factories, 1634–1636*, 316. In a letter to the viceroy of Goa the following year, 1637, Methwold was still pleading: "Although a great service was done to the late Viceroy [Conde de Linhares] by the dispatch of the *London* to Macao, the English have hitherto had a very poor return. . . . [S]ince her return the money due on that account has been detained at Goa, besides another sum due to the English." President Methwold at Ahmadabad to the viceroy of Goa, 25 July 1637, *Lisbon Transcripts, Books of the Monsoons*, book 40, fol. 321.
34. Mundy, *Travels*, vol. 3, 66. Weddell specified "40,000 shot and cordage of all sorts which we brought you." John Weddell off Honawar to Dom Filippe Mascarenhas [at Goa], 23 January / 2 February 1637 (O.C. 1587), Foster, *English Factories, 1637–1641*, 7.

Therefore, it was with a decidedly sour Goa aftertaste that the Courteens would now face squarely the blockading Dutch. As already hinted at above, Weddell carefully endeavored to avoid getting entangled in, or injured collaterally by, the Luso-Dutch stand-off in the bay of Goa. The British had closely observed various defensive sallies of the Portuguese and sea skirmishes that ensued. Albeit as only commercial allies of the Lusitanians, the subjects of Charles I probably did not count upon the VOC commanders to be friendly. But more clearly, they did not anticipate an assault.

Setting sail on the 27th of January 1637, Captain Weddell dispatched the factor-linguist Thomas Robinson and Robert Moulton in a barge to the Dutch fleet stationed around the bay. They carried the letter of their monarch addressed to the VOC governor-general of Batavia and all the Dutch captains and factors. The Dutch admiral, Jakob Cooper, convened his fleet council and opened the letter. Composed in English, Robinson translated the lines into Latin, from which the Dutch chaplain translated them into Dutch. The commander of the Dutch signed an acknowledgment of receipt, and a copy of the Dutch translation was produced to be forwarded to the governor-general at Batavia. Shortly afterwards, Cooper came to visit Weddell aboard the *Dragon*: "Their Admiral came on board to see me, and there was not any word of discontentment used amongst us, the Admiral striking his flag when we came within shot, in honor of the King's [Charles I's] colours . . . and the next day we had divers of their captains aboard us."[35]

From the Dutch, Weddell learned not only details about damage and casualties sustained by them in recent skirmishes with Portuguese galleons but also some of their plans for strangling the capital of the *Estado da India*. After sailing away from Goa, the British commander secretly conveyed some of this intelligence to the Portuguese commander Mascarenhas. Weddell related to this captain that the Dutch claimed to have lost but several men from their battles in and near the bay of Goa. He mentioned to Mascarenhas his low estimate of the VOC fleet: "Their ships are not of the force I took them to be, nor their ordnance very great; some few brass pieces they have very good." More importantly, Weddell informed the Portuguese captain that the Dutch were planning within a year or two to lay siege to Goa not only by blockade but by land, in partnership with "the Mogul or neighbor people . . . [or the] Moors which are about Goa." At all events, Weddell reported, the Dutch told him that "they had order from their employers in Europe to lie before Goa these three years; and the next year do purpose to have 16 ships to lie before it." In the same communication to Mascarenhas, Weddell claimed that the Dutch were "much discontented" upon learning (via the same Portuguese factor, Gaspar

---

35. John Weddell off Honawar to Dom Filippe Mascarenhas [at Goa], 23 January / 2 February 1637 (O.C. 1587), Foster, *English Factories, 1637–1641*, 7; Jakob Cooper to Heren XVII, dated Batavia, 7 December 1637 (N.S.), from *Hague Transcripts*, 1st ser., Vol. X, No. CCCXLII. Cooper's distinguished career as a blockader for the VOC, at both Goa and Melaka, is noted by Peter Borschberg in *The Singapore and Melaka Straits: Violence, Security and Diplomacy in the Seventeenth Century* (Leiden: KITLV Press, 2010), 166; Borschberg has recently studied Cooper's published and unpublished correspondence now in the archives at The Hague. For in-depth analysis of Dutch blockading in the 1630s, see 157–88.

Gomes, who had sailed aboard the *London* to Macao in 1635) that the Courteens had brought a large quantity of metal, munitions, and naval supplies to the viceroy of Goa. To Cooper's dismay and exasperation, the Dutch were not authorized to thwart or punish the British for significantly bolstering the military and naval capabilities of the Iberian arch-enemy: "They told me [Weddell] that had we been laden with Portugals' goods that they had no commission to meddle with us."[36]

That the VOC captains were not authorized by the Heren XVII in Amsterdam to take violent action against the British, whether of the EIC or Courteen species, was crucial as the latter sailed away from Goa with intent to pass through Melaka and enter the China seas. Captain Weddell learned from the commander managing the Dutch blockade at Goa that: "they have lying before Malacca eight sail of ships; on the coast of China four sail; before the islands of the Moluccas [in Spice Islands] four sail."[37] Conversely, what intelligence did Cooper acquire from Weddell? Did the Dutch admiral on this occasion learn that the Courteen fleet would within months be approaching the Melaka maritime passage west of the VOC headquarters at Batavia? As for Portuguese intelligence, did Pero da Silva, viceroy of Goa, already know or strongly suspect Weddell and Mountney's design to sail to China and then Japan? Judging by the imperial governor's letter to Philip IV in March 1637 (just after the British ships had left Goa), it would seem that he did *not* know of Weddell and Mountney's notions of taking the fleet all the way to Macao. Yet the Courteens do not seem to have been trying to keep secret their ambition to trade in China. For example, in February or March of that year, not long after leaving Goa, they would tell the nayak of Ikkeri (the ruler served by the governor of Bhatkal in Malabar) that they were headed for China in the upcoming months. And in negotiating with the king for the establishment of a factory on or near the coast, from where they could regularly and directly access the pepper market, they offered to bring back goods from China per his request. Moreover, it seems likely that Weddell made no attempt to conceal his oriental scheme from the Dutch. VOC captain Jakob Cooper reported that as the Courteen fleet departed Goa: "they said they intended to sail to Achin [Aceh, Sumatra], from thence to Malacca, and then to Macao."[38]

At Goa Weddell and Mountney had expected to procure a cargo of pepper and cinnamon to load at least a pinnace of the fleet. Disappointed on this front, the Courteens remained committed to the plan of sending back to London at least one ship with such bulk commodities from the western coast of India.[39] With the EIC already ensconced at Surat, north of Goa, it was logical to seek a commercial

---

36. All quotations in this paragraph are taken from John Weddell off Honawar to Dom Filippe Mascarenhas [at Goa], January / 2 February 1637 (O.C. 1587), Foster, *English Factories, 1637–1641*, 7–8.

37. John Weddell off Honawar to Dom Filippe Mascarenhas [at Goa], January / 2 February 1637 (O.C. 1587), Foster, *English Factories, 1637–1641*, 8.

38. Cooper to Heren XVII of the VOC, dated Batavia, 7 December 1637 (N.S.), from *Hague Transcripts*, 1st ser., Vol. X, No. CCCXLII.

39. Pepper was by far the EIC's biggest import from the East in the first four decades of the seventeenth century. Chaudhuri, *English East India Company*, 140.

sphere or presence south of the Portuguese capital, along the Malabar coast. Over that region, its peoples and their commerce, neither the Mogul emperor nor the Portuguese viceroy exercised control; only the latter had some pretensions in that direction.[40] So it made perfect sense that, embarking from Goa on 27 January 1637, the British fleet proceeded to sail down the coast to anchor at Bhatkal about a week later. It was a port three miles up a river from the coast and for the previous few centuries had been within the jurisdiction of Hindu Vijayanagar rulers. In this era, when the Courteen fleet arrived, it was prospering as a supplier of pepper, rice, and sugar to both Goa and Hormuz; Bhatkal could also be a reliable source for a diverse array of calicoes, another very vendible item—for a few decades the EIC in Surat had been focused on obtaining calicoes and indigo from there.[41] In fact, before establishing themselves at Goa in 1511, the Portuguese had themselves set up a factory at Bhatkal—not far from Calicut, famous as the terminus of the epic voyage of Vasco da Gama.[42] And since Bhatkal was not far down the coast from Goa, anyway, the Portuguese plausibly viewed it as falling within their sphere of influence.[43] In that case, engaging in commerce at such a location, the Courteens would be encroaching upon at least a de facto Lusitanian domain of trade.[44] It was precisely his awareness of Portuguese jealous sensitivity to Malabar pepper commerce in the vicinity of Bhatkal that prompted William Methwold to boast to the viceroy of Goa that the EIC had courteously and virtuously refrained from entering or probing that market.[45]

Since the Courteen fleet abounded in captains, mariners, and merchants who had already served in and around India in recent decades, this British contingent sailing down the Malabar coast would have carried a very good sense of what they could expect next. For instance, they would have been thoroughly aware of the pirate infestation, as some of the Courteen captains had dealt and clashed with such marauders in the 1620s and 1630s. On 3 February 1637 the fleet anchored at Bhatkal. Officers of its governor and representatives of Vira Bhadra, the nayak of Ikkeri, that

---

40. "The Malabar region was, and long had been, divided into a series of petty kingdoms and lordships, none of which exercised authority over more than a few hundred square miles of territory. It possessed no power comparable to the major Moslem states of the Deccan or even the Hindu princedom of Ikkeri." Disney, *Twilight*, 8.

41. In the later report rendered by Nathaniel Mountney, "Notes on the Prospects of Trade in China," the cape merchant indicated that Bhatkal would also be a good source of incense. Incense was always vendible in China, among other places.

42. "Calicut's commercial predominance in Malabar had been broken in the 16th century by the Portuguese promotion of Cochin." Disney, *Twilight*, 9–10.

43. "Onor [just a little north of Bhatkal on the Kanara coast] became Portugal's principal port of export for Kanara pepper, and for much of the first half of the seventeenth century the single most important Portuguese supply port for pepper anywhere in Asia." Disney, *Twilight*, 5.

44. By contrast, the EIC could not raise a syllable of protest at any supposed trespass by the Courteens: "The EIC never had any trade or factory there [Bhatkal] (nor at Cannanore or Cochin, or anywhere nearer to those parts than Surat); neither can Mr. Courteen's factory any ways prejudice that Company." Mr. Courteen's factory at Bhatkal [March 1638?], PRO East Indies, Vol. IV, B, Nos. 53, 53 I–II.

45. "[Methwold] declined invitations to trade on the Malabar coast for pepper, lest the Portuguese should object." President Methwold at Ahmadabad to the viceroy of Goa, 25 July 1637, *Lisbon Transcripts, Books of the Monsoons*, book 40, fol. 321.

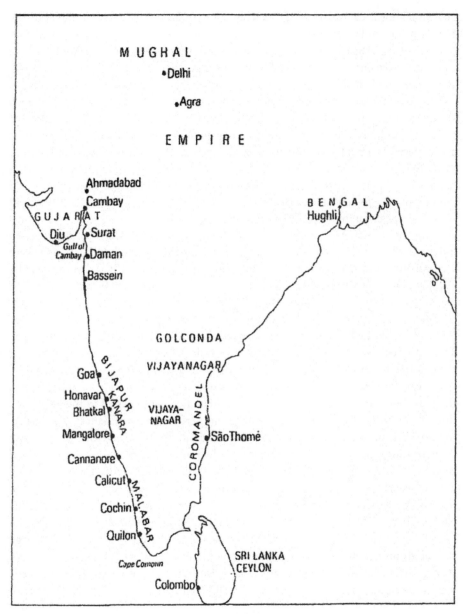

Map 3.1: Bhatkal, location of the first Courteen factory Established April 1637

governor's lord, came aboard to welcome them. These officers and agents of the Hindu prince indicated they would be able to purvey pepper in quantity sufficient to lade at least a pinnace. The Indians in Bhatkal were chiefly interested in the metal that the Courteens could supply. They were most eager to acquire lead by exchange of pepper. The British indicated their commitment to planting a small trade station as a long-term base for transacting similar business in the future. A few days later, 6 February, a tentative or oral commercial accord was achieved. Later that month or in early March, the Courteens would send a small delegation, furnished with some gifts, as well as a pledge to deliver a cannon, to Vira Bhadra, the nayak of Ikkeri, in order to receive official license to trade and, more ambitiously, permission to erect a factory building.[46] For the moment they began to unload the lead that would fetch enough pepper to lade at least one of the ships. As it turned out, the quantity would even be large enough to provide for the *Planter*.[47]

For the diplomatic-commercial mission to the nayak of Ikkeri (in the modern Shimoga district of Mysore), two of the most distinguished India hands were chosen: the factor-linguist Thomas Robinson of the *Sun* and Peter Mundy of the *Planter*. Both had very recently spent a few years in India as employees of the EIC. Accompanied by two servants, they would, on first contact with this sovereign, merely present a drawing of the cannon, which would arrive later. On 3 March they set out from coastal Bhatkal to inland Ikkeri. By 6 March, they had arrived to enjoy an enthusiastic welcome, though the prince himself was observing rites of grief at the death of his nurse, buried the same day. While the ritual of mourning prevented the nayak from receiving the envoys, they had lodging and provision appointed to them as they awaited an audience. The next day they were invited to the palace for dinner as well as theatrical entertainment and performances of dance. After greeting and kissing the hand of the sovereign they presented fine cloth as well as a sketch of the cannon. Instantly he promised to meet their demands and invested them with ceremonial robes. On 9 March they were summoned for more intimate entertainment and negotiation. Hosting Robinson and Mundy in private chambers, the nayak "with a long wand in his hand reaching from dish to dish . . . invit[ed] us to taste thereof. After supper he firmed his grant to our demands and sent it to the Governor of Bhatkal by ourselves." The provisions of that grant included "a large plot of ground, lying very commodiously by the river side, to build us a house, the ruined parts whereof will afford us squared stone enough for that purpose; moreover, in the same patent he hath given us timber (of which there is no want) and all

---

46. 27 January / 6 February 1637, "Voyage of Captain Weddell's Fleet, April 1636–April 1637." "This nayak Vira Bhadra was nominal vassal of the kings of Vijayanagar, but by 1637 the latter were effectively ruling only the princedom of Chandragiri." Disney, *Twilight*, 2.

47. "10/20 Feb. 1637: Having decided to dispatch the *Planter* to England, they began to land their lead. Found that pepper came down very slowly, partly because recent disputes with the Portuguese had diverted the trade into other channels. No stock is ever kept at the port, as the latter has no defences to secure goods from the Malabars [pirates] and others. It was determined to send an embassy to court to treat for a settled residence; also to give the King a piece of ordnance." "Voyage of Captain Weddell's Fleet, April 1636–April 1637."

materials, we paying only for laborers hire, which in these parts is very cheap." The Hindu prince promised that they could procure from 1,500 to 2,000 "candills" of pepper yearly.[48] They would enjoy the exclusive right to export that spice. For his part, he expressly requested them to bring horses (from Persia and Arabia) and to convey exotic rarities from both England and the Far East.[49]

Concluding such a convivial and fruitful commercial embassy, by 12 March Robinson and Mundy had returned to Bhatkal. In receipt of authorization from the nayak of Ikkeri to establish a factory, Captain Weddell, Nathaniel Mountney, and the rest of the council conferred to determine which factors should be stationed at Bhatkal while the fleet sailed farther east.[50] It was determined that the director of the new factory would be Anthony Vernworthy, merchant of the *Sun*. He would be assisted by another veteran factor (and friend of Peter Mundy), John Fortune of the *Planter*. Since the *Planter* would be sailing back to England with the cargo of pepper, another experienced factor from that ship was selected, the *Planter*'s purser (accountant), George Wye.[51] For further staffing needs of the new factory, a Dutchman from the same ship, a young steward named Peter Van Dam was chosen. On 16 March 1637, Vernworthy, Fortune, and Wye journeyed to the nayak of Ikkeri to iron out the details of the arrangements for their establishment at Bhatkal and the commercial transactions to be practiced on the Malabar coast.[52]

When on 12 March Robinson and Mundy returned from their visit to Vira Bhadra, the nayak of Ikkeri, they were deeply distressed to learn that dozens of the crew aboard their ships had been afflicted with malaria. Mundy described the decimation: "At our arrival [at Bhatkal] we understood that since our departure thence very strong pestilential fevers [malaria] had been in the fleet, especially aboard the *Sun* and our ship *Planter*, so that many died thereof. That morning word was brought that our boatswain was dead, and within an hour after came tidings that Mr. John Hill [*Planter*'s master] was departed this life."[53] Mundy, maintaining his journal aboard the *Planter*, then elaborated upon the toll taken by disease and accident since the Courteen fleet embarked from the Downs a year earlier, in April 1636. It seemed to him that, like barnacles, some sort of curses had latched onto Captain Richard Swanley's *Sun* and Captain Edward Hall's *Planter*: "About 80

---

48. The Portuguese form of *kandi*, commonly rendered as "candy." This "candill," equal to about four Portuguese quintal (130 lbs.), was thus approximately 500 lbs.

49. "Voyage of Captain Weddell's Fleet, April 1636–April 1637." For import of Arabian and Persian horses by rulers in Vijayanagar, see M.N. Pearson, *The Portuguese in India* (Cambridge: Cambridge University Press, 1988), 50.

50. In the Royal Commission of 12/22 December 1635, the fleet's council to assist them in leadership ("advice and consent") had been prescribed as six mariners and six merchants to be selected by Weddell and Nathaniel Mountney. In case of delicate matters requiring strict confidentiality, the council was to consist of five: Weddell, Mountney, and three others of their choosing. Mundy, *Travels*, vol. 3, Appendix, III, 434–35.

51. A purser's many and heavy responsibilities aboard the ship are summarized by Massarella, *World Elsewhere*, 144–45.

52. An apothecary, joiner, and smith were chosen as well; the total number of Courteens assigned to the Bhatkal station was fifteen. "Voyage of Captain Weddell's Fleet, April 1636–April 1637."

53. Mundy, *Travels*, vol. 3, 94.

62 *The First British Trade Expedition to China*

persons dead in the fleet since our coming from England. I say that we have already lost out of our little ship *Planter* most of our principal officers, viz., the master and boatswain aforementioned, the surgeon, cooper, boatswain's mate, our armourer, all our quarter masters (I think). I say all these and others have been buried in 10 months out of the said ship. The *Sun* hath lost about 30, and in all the whole fleet to this day near upon fourscore, the sickness yet continuing."[54] Thus, many of the key mariners as well as invaluable craftsmen perished in the maelstrom of malaria that assailed the Courteen fleet off the coast of Malabar in the spring of 1637. Meanwhile, the *Dragon, Katherine,* and *Planter* were still anchored near Bhatkal, while Captain Weddell had dispatched the *Sun* and pinnace *Anne* south along the coast towards Cochin, not only to refresh the sick and obtain potable water and fresh victuals, but also to look for further pepper supplies to lade the *Planter*.[55] On 29 March the *Dragon, Katherine,* and *Planter* departed Bhatkal to follow, and hopefully rejoin, the *Sun* and *Anne*. Several days later, anchoring at Chirakall ("Mondelly") on 3 April, letters left by the *Sun* and *Anne* notified Weddell that these ships had sailed for Cannanore, farther south down the coast towards Calicut.

Captain Weddell and Nathaniel Mountney were obviously concentrated on the task of getting the *Planter* laden as soon as possible for a return voyage to England. They were also occupied by the task of procuring more provisions and water for the ailing men among the fleet. At Cannanore, where the Portuguese maintained a dominant presence, and farther down the coast, at Cochin, the British endeavored to supplement the large quantity of pepper already obtained at Malabar. Along with food, chiefly beef and pork from bullocks and hogs, a considerable amount of cinnamon was procured at Cannanore through the efforts of Thomas Robinson.[56] The cinnamon would help complement the pepper to furnish an ample cargo for the return of a ship to Europe. The fully laden *Planter* was finally dispatched for England 6 April 1637. Commanded by Robert Moulton, who had embarked from the Downs the previous year as master of the *Dragon* under Weddell, it transported 150,000 pounds of pepper, 17,000 pounds of benzoin, 7,000 pounds of cinnamon, and 3,000 pounds of myrrh, besides smaller amounts frankincense and gumlack, as well as some samples of calicoes.[57] Moulton would also carry a report back to the directors of the Courteen Association to inform them of what had been suffered and accomplished in the past year, since the fleet's departure from the Downs in

---

54. Mundy, *Travels*, vol. 3, 94.
55. "Voyage of Captain Weddell's Fleet, April 1636–April 1637."
56. From Mundy we learn more details: "Here was bought a parcel of cinnamon to help make up the *Planter's* lading at 35 Royal of eight per quintal [c. 130 lbs.], to pay part in Royal and part in lead at 9 Royal per quintal; and by virtue of a letter from Don Phillippe Mascarenhas before mentioned, there were sent aboard some bullocks and hogs gratis." Mundy, *Travels*, vol. 3, 112. From this detail about Mascarenhas, we might venture that it was critical that the Courteens carried a letter of introduction from him—no doubt earned, in part, by providing the latter with some intelligence concerning the Dutch as the Courteen fleet departed blockaded-Goa. We might speculate that this Courteen-Mascarenhas contact was an instance of the policy of the viceroy of Goa being undermined by subordinate naval and civil officers.
57. Mundy, *Travels*, vol. 3, 113.

April 1636. Among the breakthroughs and exploits of the Courteens on the Malabar coast in the spring of 1637, the EIC would, by early 1638, learn of the new factory at Bhatkal.[58]

Since Bhatkal was quite far from Surat in Gujarat, the directors of the EIC may not have been very indignant or agitated when they found out about the new Courteen trade station. Not surprisingly, the viceroy of Goa, Pero da Silva, on the other hand, was disconcerted upon learning details of the enterprises carried out by the Courteens on the Malabar coast in the months since leaving his Dutch-blockaded Portuguese city. When, in April 1637, the viceroy penned his reply to the letter of Charles I which had been delivered by Captain Weddell, he complained of the British activity on the southwest coast as seriously detrimental to the interests of the Portuguese. The latter had already made a quasi-monopolistic arrangement to buy all the pepper in the region; the Courteens jeopardized it by purchasing the commodity for themselves at a lower price.[59] Likewise, in an October 1637 letter to his own monarch, the viceroy decried Courteen commerce in Bhatkal and shady dealings with the Malabar pirate Babarat at Cannanore.[60] He deplored and emphasized the extreme degree to which this harmed Lusitanian traffic in pepper, as the Courteens were significantly driving up its price.

---

58. Sir John Pennington, aboard the *Swiftsure* in the Downs, to the Lords of the Admiralty, 19/29 January 1638, PRO, East Indies, Vol. IV, No. 50: "Announcing the arrival of the *Planter*, belonging to Sir William Courteen, laden with pepper and other commodities. They have settled a brave factory [at Bhatkal] eight degrees from any other, and Captain Weddell has gone for China with the rest of the fleet." *Court Minutes of EIC, 1635–1639*, 291. The EIC took notice of the *Planter's* lading upon its return to England: "Malabar pepper is in demand here [London]; and it would be well to send some vessels along the coast to collect a quantity, following the example of Weddell, who has laden the *Planter* with 150,000 lb. of pepper, 17,453 lb. of benzoin, 7,349 lb. of cinnamon, and 3,166 lb. of myrrh, besides gum-lac, cassia fistula, and some samples of calicoes." EIC to the president and council at Surat, 16/26 March 1638, Foster, *English Factories, 1637–1641*, 57–58. "Cassia fistula" might be *cassia lignea*, a coarse type of cinnamon; *gummalacca* is a red-colored substance often used as a varnish—a red lacquer; benzoin: odoriferous resin, much used in medicine and production of incense in the seventeenth century.
59. 13/23 April 1637, O.C. 1597, *Lisbon Transcripts, Books of the Monsoons*, book 38, fol. 285. In a letter several months afterward, Pero da Silva, viceroy of Goa, implied that the Courteen success in obtaining the comprehensive favor and contracts from the nayak of Ikkeri (not least the patent to set up the Bhatkal factory) was achieved by misrepresenting themselves as associates of the Portuguese: "Weddell has defamed the Portuguese both to the Dutch and to Vira Bhadra Nayak, from whom he has obtained permission to build a factory at Bhatkal. That Nayak declares that he only admitted the English under the impression that they were the friends of the Portuguese, and that he will expel them if the Viceroy desires it." Pero da Silva, viceroy of Goa, to President Methwold at Surat, 11/21 November 1637 (O.C. 1605), transcribed at Foster, *English Factories, 1637–1641*, 31–32.
60. That the Courteen fleet cut an intimidating figure is suggested by the fact that this infamous Malabar buccaneer Babarat (Baba Rawat) omitted to ply his trade there in the spring of 1637; see Mundy, *Travels*, vol. 3, 108–9. That Babarat was formidable is indicated by Mundy: "a notable archpirate of which nature there are others on this coast, so that few vessels can escape them except they go under convoy of the Portugals" (109). Judging by Mundy's notes Malabar was a coast infested by pirates in these years. For a specimen of their exploits, Mundy relates: "Particular men met with sundry China commodities, as green ginger in excellent curious porcelain jars, also porcelain cups and dishes, for some of the Malabar pirates had taken a Portugal vessel which came from Malacca, wherein were certain Dutchmen taken by the Portugals in the straits of Malacca. These were all taken again by the Malabars as aforesaid, who sold the goods ashore hereabouts [near Cannanore]; we saw some of it also at Mondillee [Chirakall]" (110).

If in China, in subsequent months, the Courteens were to complain that the Portuguese slandered them, in India, Pero da Silva complained in his letter to Philip IV that these British had corrupted the natives with vilification of the Portuguese: "Not only did they go to Canara to buy the pepper which by ancient contracts is ours, allying themselves with a pirate by name of Babia . . . but they also endeavored to make enmity between us and Vira Bhadra Nayak [king of Ikkeri] and the neighboring kings by spreading evil report of us among them."[61] For the Iberian monarch's better understanding of the situation, the viceroy elaborated that the British had exchanged copper and lead with the king of Ikkeri for pepper; and that after the British had made such deals, this local ruler set a higher price on the spice in negotiating with the Portuguese. He also noted that the British had corrupted Vira Bhadra with various gifts and the cannon. On account of such mischief, "contrary to the friendship they owed us," and so damaging to Portuguese interests—and ultimately adversely affecting the monarch's revenue—his viceroy wrote, "to prevent matters from taking a wrong course and being settled to our prejudice (for experience had shown me that friendship with these people [British] could not include commercial relations with them, but merely a cessation of hostilities and a preservation of peace until such time your Majesty shall issue other directions more to your service), I sent orders to all the captains of fortresses not to permit any commerce with the said English, nor any alterations or innovations beyond the said peace and cessation of hostilities."[62]

When would the viceroy of Goa have sent such an anti-British directive to the Portuguese at Macao? Presumably it was dispatched months before this epistle addressed to Philip IV in October 1637. Likely enough Pero da Silva transmitted a message to this effect to Macao by March 1637—the moment he learned details of what the interloping Courteens were doing on the Malabar coast. Perhaps such a directive would have been received by the captain-general of Macao Domingos da Camara de Noronha by the end of June, when the Courteen fleet would be arriving at that Portuguese enclave in south China. Meanwhile, one may surmise that the EIC was adversely affected by the Courteen activity on the Malabar coast insofar as it may have persuaded the Portuguese to be more hostile to *all* British, that is, all subjects of Charles I. At least one EIC communication indicates that the Portuguese had become less willing to cooperate north of Malabar: "The boat returned with provisions, the Portugals using our people very courteously, but are very cautious and would not admit of the buying of one piece of stuff or [a] pair

---

61. Viceroy of Goa, Pero da Silva to Philip IV, 5 October 1637, *Lisbon Transcripts, Books of the Monsoons*, book 40, fol. 116.

62. Viceroy of Goa, Pero da Silva to Philip IV, 5 October 1637, *Lisbon Transcripts, Books of the Monsoons*, book 40, fol. 116. But the executive of the *Estado da India* hastened to qualify that he would still enforce civility so as not to violate the 1635 Goa accord: "However, should any of the English vessels put into port, compelled by stress of weather or other necessities, I ordered that they should be supplied with what was available, in accordance with the treaty, but that they should not be allowed to remain longer than was necessary to execute repairs, nor to buy or sell anything whatever, and on no account was any vessel, either great or small, to be sold to them until such time as we receive definite orders from Your Majesty."

of sheets, by reason Capt. Weddell hath broken the articles of peace in landing of men at Bhatkal to the Portugals great hindrance."[63] This stands securely as evidence that the viceroy of Goa's anti-Courteen initiative was heeded by at least some of the Portuguese in India—if not by Captain Mascarenhas, who may have assisted Weddell and Mountney in trading in the southwest beyond what Pero da Silva would have wished.

At all events, after the icy and evasive treatment accorded by the Portuguese viceroy and general disappointment at Goa, the Courteens along the Malabar coast had achieved the solid consolation of a new factory at Bhatkal before Weddell sailed the fleet farther east. The Courteens had resolved to set up a station somewhere between southwest India and China. In the Indonesian-Malaysian archipelago, the Dutch were already at Batavia (Jakarta) on Java, and the EIC was still nearby at Banten. Sumatra, much closer to Bhatkal, was an obvious possibility. At Aceh ("Achin"), on the northern end of the island, pepper could be procured in considerable quantities. Besides the luxury item of elephant's teeth, several other very profitable spices and commodities were available at the same location: clove, nutmeg, tin, camphor, brimstone, and lignam aloes among them. The Muslim "king" (sultan) of Aceh Iskandar Muda was the dominant ruler of the island of Sumatra in the early seventeenth century. The very first EIC voyage, the fleet commanded by James Lancaster, went to Aceh as a major source of pepper. In recent decades the sultan had proven receptive to the subjects of the Stuart monarchs, having greeted them as a foil to the odiously imperious Portuguese and increasingly intrusive Dutch. Just recently, in 1629, Iskandar Muda had launched a prodigious but disastrous naval invasion of Melaka to dislodge the Portuguese.[64] As Nathaniel Mountney himself later noted: "The King of Achin being possessed of the most part of the island [Sumatra], and also of several kingdoms on the main about Molucca, [is] very ill-affected both to the Portugal and Dutch."[65] Iskandar Muda's hospitality to the EIC in the recent past was such that Captain Weddell and Nathaniel Mountney could reasonably have entertained hopes of obtaining permission to establish a small establishment of their own in or near Aceh. Nor would the Courteens be encroaching upon any interest of their domestic rival, for the older company had not recently maintained any presence there—the older overseas firm was still concentrated at Banten in Java.

---

63. William Bayley's Account of the Voyage of the EIC *Mars* from Surat to Armagon, 4/14 November 1637, Foster, *English Factories, 1637–1641*, 21–22.
64. Souza, *Survival of Empire*, 15, 93. For an outline of Aceh's relations with the Lusitanians from mid-sixteenth to mid-seventeenth century, see 93–96. For Aceh's relations with Europeans in the first decades of the seventeenth century, see Borschberg, *Singapore and Melaka Straits*, 166–69. For British relations with Aceh's ruler under James I, see the introduction to *The Voyage of Thomas Best to the East Indies, 1612–1614*, ed. Foster (London: Hakluyt, 1934). For Iskandar Muda's intriguing proposal of alliance with James I via marriage see Massarella, *World Elsewhere*, 238–39.
65. "Notes on the Prospects of Trade in China." Mountney did enter an important qualification: "At Achin they [the Dutch] have now a factory, but that King [Iskandar Thani] neglecteth their league and friendship offered against the Portugals, his quondam enemies, and no doubt that when we [Courteens] follow a close trade in his country, he will give them leave to go home."

The last stop along the Malabar coast for the Courteen fleet was Cochin. By 1503 Afonso de Albuquerque had set up a small Portuguese fort at this location, not far from Vasco da Gama's dramatic Calicut landing. Until 1511, when Goa was acquired, Cochin had served as the capital of the fledgling *Estado da India*. Here at Cochin, at least one Jesuit would take the opportunity to ride with the British as they sailed farther east. The Jesuit wanted to travel to the key Malaysian port of the Lusitanians, Melaka. But before embarking from the Malabar coast for the northern tip of Sumatra, on 7 April 1637, Captain Weddell received some shocking news. He learned that just a few months ago, in December 1636, the sultan of Aceh, Iskandar Muda, and his son had been murdered. The plan to visit Aceh was not abandoned. It must have been assumed that no matter the identity of the new ruler, he would be receptive to the British as a counterweight to the Portuguese and Dutch in Melaka and Java—even if the British were at least ostensibly (or at least commercially) allies of those Iberians.

Arriving 1 May 1637, the new sultan of Aceh, Iskandar Thani, proved quite accommodating to the Courteens.[66] He immediately adopted commercial-friendly policies to attract foreign merchants to the port city. He had rescinded the anchorage fees that the previous sultan had levied.[67] The day after their arrival, the Courteens were granted an audience with the new sultan. The latter was amenable to their proposal to found a new factory in his northern port of Sumatra. In the ensuing days, the Muslim ruler treated the British generously and entertained them with such exotic spectacles as elephant gladiatorial combat.[68] The Achinese staged buffalo fights, and one of those beasts was presented to Captain Weddell as a gift to take aboard the *Dragon*.[69] The commander and his council now had to determine whom to assign to the new factory. This would be a smaller operation than the one they had just set up at Bhatkal. Edward Knipe, one of the head merchants of Captain John Carter's *Katherine*, was chosen to manage the Aceh post. To assist him, the purser of the *Anne*, Richard Bourne, and another factor, Andrew Cornworth, would remain in this Sumatra location.[70] Knipe, Bourne, and Cornworth, with two attendants, were charged with receiving and handling the pepper that the Courteens were owed for giving the sultan Iskandar Thani metals (especially iron), pieces of artillery, and cloth.[71] The Aceh factory of the Courteens could be critical in the future China commerce they were projecting. As Nathaniel Mountney later expounded

---

66. Iskandar Muda had appointed his son-in-law heir, in response to his own son's plotting to poison him. The son-in-law who ruled as Iskandar Thani was son of a sultan (Ahmad Shah II of Pahang) from the Malaysian peninsula whom Iskandar Muda had captured in 1617.
67. Mountney, Rawlinson A.299.
68. "Voyage of Captain Weddell's Fleet, April 1636–April 1637."
69. As noted above, more than three decades earlier James Lancaster's EIC fleet had enjoyed an enthusiastic reception at a visit of Aceh. They too were treated to the diversions of elephant and buffalo fighting by the ruler who dominated Sumatra before Iskandar Muda, Ala-uddin Shah. Keay, *Honourable Company*, 16–20.
70. Cornworth may have been the same merchant who appears in the EIC records as "Carnwath": see *Court Minutes of EIC, 1635–1639*, 288.
71. "Voyage of Captain Weddell's Fleet, April 1636–April 1637"; Mountney, Rawlinson A.299.

the logic of maintaining a trading post on Sumatra: "This factory will not only serve for a rendezvous to our shipping until we have a fortified island or fort on the coast of China, but also for a refreshing place for all our ships going and coming from China."[72]

After an eleven-day stay on Sumatra, and probably with the destination of Macao now dominating their thoughts, the British of the *Dragon, Sun, Katherine,* and *Anne* departed Aceh on 12 May 1637.[73] They would now be contemplating the challenge of passing through the strait of Melaka (the narrow channel between modern Indonesia and Malaysia), where they would expect to encounter the Portuguese and the marauding and blockading Dutch. The passage through the strait turned out to be less eventful or stressful than Weddell and his fellow captains may have anticipated.[74] They passed unmolested by the Dutch. The reception of the British granted by the Portuguese at Melaka was remarkably cordial, even if the latter had received the directive of the viceroy of Goa concerning what treatment to give these new Protestant allies—to wit, not to be very accommodating or commercially helpful. Arriving 9 June 1637, Nathaniel Mountney later recalled that they experienced a "very kind welcome from the Captain-General and a large present of beefs, etc., provisions for the refreshing of our people."[75] At Melaka Weddell took the opportunity to careen the ships and procure more potable water and victuals. The other important business was to recruit an experienced pilot who could guide the fleet from Melaka through the treacherous passages exiting what is now Singapore. Presumably such a knowledgeable mariner would also be able to assist them in approaching and maneuvering around Macao in China, in the waters just south of the Pearl River estuary.[76] The fleet weighed anchor on 4 June 1637. Along with their new Portuguese "mestizo" pilot, the Courteens transported

---

72. "Notes on the Prospects of Trade in China." Sensitive to the possible impropriety of encroaching upon an EIC sphere on Sumatra, Nathaniel Mountney, in the same document pointed out: "They [the EIC] had [a presence] at Achin, but many years since neglected and given over." Less than a year after the Courteens had set up their factories at Bhatkal and Aceh, Charles I ordered the EIC not to infringe: "As we formerly wished you to be careful not to prejudice the trade of our EIC in the Indies, so we have now commanded that Company not to trade at Bhatkal or elsewhere on the coast of Malabar, or in the East Indies where they had none and you have settled factories." Charles I to Captain John Weddell, Commander of the Fleet whereof the *Dragon* is admiral, employed by His Majesty to the Indies, 14/24 March 1638, PRO Dom. Chas. I, Vol. CCCLXXXV, No. 72.

73. Mundy, *Travels*, vol. 3, 137; Mountney, Rawlinson A.299.

74. The summer of the previous year was much tenser and dangerous for the Dutch and Portuguese in the straits of Melaka. For 1636, see Boxer, *Great Ship*, 149. Less than four years later, in 1641, the Dutch would snatch Melaka from the Portuguese, who had occupied this strategic location since 1511. The situation in the straits of Melaka during the first four decades of the seventeenth century is described vividly by Peter Borschberg, *Singapore and Melaka Straits*; for the circumstances the Courteens would face, consult especially his Chapter 5, "VOC Blockades in the Singapore and Melaka Straits: Diplomacy, Trade and Survival, 1633–41."

75. Mountney, Rawlinson A.299.

76. In addition to this "slender" pilot, the Courteens benefitted from a Spaniard taken aboard Captain Richard Swanley's *Sun* on the voyage from Melaka to Macao: "Bartholomeo de Roboredo a Jesuit that came with us from Malacca, and a Spaniard, a sergeant major that came on the *Sun*"; "[The Spaniard] was also our pilot coming hither from Malacca." 29 September / 9 October 1637; 30 November / 10 December 1637, Mundy, *Travels*, vol. 3.

a few Jesuits.[77] Evidently, the pilot was "slender" to the point of inept, for the British only narrowly avoided shipwreck: "This day coming forth of the old strait, through negligence of our pilot (being a Portugal mestizo taken in at Malacca as a passenger) we were in some danger when we thought ourselves most secure. For he directed us on the starboard shore when we should [have] kept the larboard side."[78]

A few weeks after leaving Melaka, the British encountered a Japanese junk which had just embarked from Cambodia and was on the way to Cochinchina (present-day south Vietnam), where a small Japanese community was settled. From the men in this junk they learned that these Japanese in Cochinchina were Christians who had fled their homeland about six years ago, when the Tokugawa ruler Ieyasu further intensified persecution of adherents of that foreign faith.[79] Only a day after meeting with the Japanese junk, as the Courteen fleet continued its northward voyage to Macao, a Dutch ship embarked from Jakarta made contact with the British ships.[80] A few VOC vessels were sailing towards the southwestern coast of Taiwan (Formosa), where the Dutch now had a port, Zeelandia, from which they were roaming, raiding, and trafficking from Macao to Fujian to Manila to Nagasaki. The Dutch ships sailed parallel to the Courteen fleet for several hours through the South China Sea, before halting to anchor on a shore somewhere south of the island Hainan, while the *Dragon*, *Sun*, *Katherine*, and *Anne* maintained their northern progress. The VOC contingent would lie in wait to ambush any Portuguese vessels sailing to or from China.[81] Several days later, on 2 July 1637, the Courteen fleet descried the east coast of Hainan, the periphery of the Ming Empire.

---

77. According to Mundy, two Jesuits were picked up at Melaka and brought to Macao. Mundy, *Travels*, vol. 3, 162. One of these was Bartholomeo de Roboredo.
78. Mundy, *Travels*, vol. 3, 147. It seems almost identical peril was posed to the EIC *London* on its voyage to Macao in 1635: "[Th]e ship [was] nearly lost in the Straits [of Singapore] by the fault of the Portuguese pilot." President Methwold at Ahmadabad to the viceroy of Goa, 25 July 1637, *Lisbon Transcripts, Books of the Monsoons*, book 40, fol. 321.
79. 16/26 June 1637, Mundy, *Travels*, vol. 3, 154.
80. That Captain Weddell would not have worried about any assault from the Dutch is suggested by a letter of his old colleague Methwold. Writing just a few weeks after this Courteen encounter with the VOC, Methwold informed Pero da Silva, viceroy of Goa: "Molestation by the Dutch is not to be feared, as they have orders not to interfere with English ships." President Methwold at Ahmadabad to the viceroy of Goa, 25 July 1637, *Lisbon Transcripts, Books of the Monsoons*, book 40, fol. 321.
81. "There came up with us a Dutch vessel come from Batavia and bound for Taiwan, a place of theirs on Isla Formosa on the coast of Chincheo [Fujian] in China. She kept company with us half a day and then stood in to the shore to await for Portugals that come this way bound for China. She had a consort not far off." 17/27 June 1637, Mundy, *Travels*, vol. 3, 155.

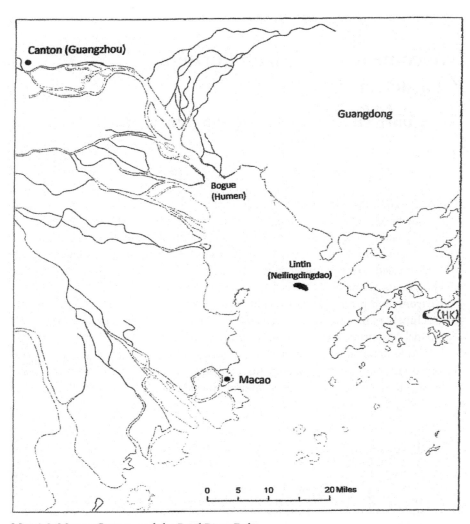

Map 3.2: Macao, Canton, and the Pearl River Delta

4

Welcome to China with Portuguese Characteristics

The Courteen Fleet in Macao Purgatory, July–August 1637

On 7 July 1637 the Courteen fleet of four ships, the *Dragon*, *Sun*, *Katherine*, and *Anne*, anchored at a small island three leagues south of the Portuguese settlement of Macao.[1] The British issued a friendly salute of cannon, which prompted the Lusitanians to send a detachment in small vessels to inform them that they should proceed no farther until directed otherwise by the captain-general of Macao, Domingos da Camara de Noronha.[2] He expressly ordered the Courteens not to move from their present spot just below Macao. The next day, 8 July, the British sent a detachment of three men to meet with Camara de Noronha.[3] Captain Weddell and Nathaniel Mountney selected John Mountney, the fleet's principal accountant and older brother of Nathaniel; Thomas Robinson, an ace Portuguese-fluent factor; and Peter Mundy, one of its chief merchants, conversant in both Iberian languages. They carried with them both the letter written on their behalf by Charles I, addressed to

---

1. Mundy, *Travels*, vol. 3, 158. While the Courteens refer to this island as "Castro," the Chinese scholar of late Ming foreign policy, Wan Ming, identifies this place as Hengqin Island (橫琴島 Hengqindao). 万明 [Wan, Ming], "明代中英的第一次直接碰撞—来自中、英、葡三方的历史记述" [The first direct clash of China and Britain during the Ming dynasty from the historical accounts of the Chinese, English, and Portuguese], 中国社会科学院历史研究所集刊, 第三辑 [Chinese Academy of Social Sciences Historical Research Journal] 3 (2004): 58. For Chinese (dynastic and lunar) dating of the fleet's arrival, see 59n2. As both Wan and 王宏志 [Wong, Lawrence Wang-chi], "通事與奸民：明末中英虎門事件中的譯者" [The Bogue Incident translator, 1637], 編譯論叢, 第五卷, 第一期 (2012年3月) [*Compilation and Translation Review* 5, no. 1 (Mar. 2012)]: 41–66, judge the dating provided in Mundy and the Courteen accounts more reliable than those in the Ming records, the narrative in this and the following chapters will omit lunar calendar dates.
2. Mundy, *Travels*, vol. 3, 158. The Courteen author, most probably Nathaniel Mountney, of "Voyage of the Weddell Fleet," described this captain-general as "a *mulatta* of a most perverse and peevish condition, reported to have been a tinker." Appointed by the viceroy of Goa the previous year, he had replaced Manuel da Camara de Noronha. Sailing from Goa early in 1636, he stopped in Manila and met with the Spanish governor before arriving at Macao in a galliot. *Lisbon Transcripts, Books of the Monsoons*, Vols. IX and XI, Letters of the Viceroy to the King of 8 March 1636 and 31 August 1638 [N.S]. The mulatta-tinker epithet of Mountney might have been more insulting than false: "Local gossip in this instance was not altogether wide of the mark, for the Captain-General had indubitably been born on the wrong side of the blanket. His father, Dom Manoel da Camara, albeit of noble blood, was also a dignitary of the Church, being Canon of the Cathedral of Braga, whilst his mother, Catherine Pires, was a humble peasant woman—possibly even a tinker's daughter." C.R. Boxer, *Fidalgos in the Far East, 1550–1557: Fact and Fancy in the History of Macao* (The Hague: Nijhoff, 1948), 131.
3. Mundy, *Travels*, vol. 3, 159.

the captain-general, and a shorter address from Weddell.[4] These letters were submitted in the hopes that the Portuguese would facilitate trading from Macao or elsewhere in the Pearl River estuary. Weddell's note explicitly recalled the signing and import of the of the Goa Convention of 1635. It further outlined the fleet's recent activities in Goa, Malabar, Cochin, and Melaka, while emphasizing that the viceroy in India had welcomed them into his port.[5] The three envoys in Macao were graciously received and obtained promise of an answer by the following day. They were then conducted to the Jesuit college Madre de Deus at the Church of Saint Paul, where they were treated to a banquet of sweet meats and fresh fruit. The Jesuits had incurred some debt to the Courteens for transporting a few members of their order from Cochin and Melaka. Among other things at the Church of Saint Paul, they sampled lychee, an exotic delicacy hitherto unknown to the British palate.[6]

Upon this visit, Peter Mundy was able to verify that the Portuguese had on hand six ships anchored at Macao waiting to lade goods from Canton (Guangzhou); the cargo, mostly silk and porcelain, would then be taken to sell and trade in Japan, mostly for silver bullion. Mundy heard that there was some delay in delivery of these goods because Ming officials in Canton—up the Pearl River, about a hundred kilometers northwest of Macao—would not release the merchandise and commodities until the Lusitanians had paid a large fine for having recently violated a regulation pertaining to ship-building. Apparently, the Portuguese had constructed a vessel that exceeded the size limit imposed by the Chinese authorities. Mundy learned that the latter had placed such restrictions on both ships and buildings constructed in Macao and regularly assessed fines for infractions.[7]

The captain-general at Macao penned a response to the British monarch's letter the same day as its personal delivery by Mundy, John Mountney, and Robinson. He and the other Portuguese officials of the Senado and senior merchants at Macao recognized Weddell's fleet as a trade mission from Charles I—not simply a private, company venture.[8] He also composed a reply to Weddell's note in which he stated that though he personally would be glad to assist the British, he had been authorized to do so neither by his king, Philip IV, nor his imperial superior, the viceroy of Goa, Pero da Silva. He expressed annoyed puzzlement that the British had not discussed their trip to Macao with the latter, for, as they themselves related, they

---

4. Copy of the King of England's Letter, dated 20 February 1635 [2 March 1636], *Lisbon Transcripts, Books of the Monsoons*, book 41, fol. 200.
5. Copy of the first letter written by Captain Weddell to the Captain General, Domingos da Camara de Noronha, 7 July 1637, *Lisbon Transcripts, Books of the Monsoons*, book 41, fol. 199.
6. Mundy, *Travels*, vol. 3, 159, 162.
7. Mundy, *Travels*, vol. 3, 165.
8. *Lisbon Transcripts, Books of the Monsoons*, book 41, fol. 201. As the Portuguese expressly acknowledged in another document: "The ships were your Majesty's [Charles I's] and were not owned by the English India Company, and their capital was part of the Royal Exchequer"; "to serve your Majesty, the ships and their cargoes being yours." Letter from the City of Macao to the King of England, 24 December 1637, *Lisbon Transcripts, Books of the Monsoons*, book 41, fol. 220.

had been at Goa three months.[9] Why had they not obtained the approval of the captain-general's superior before coming to China? Was it not true that the last time a British ship, the *London*, came to Macao, two years ago, it had carried letters and instructions from Goa—that is, explicit authorization from the Conde de Linhares, the viceroy who signed the Anglo-Portuguese accord with William Methwold and Nathaniel Mountney? There was even further warrant for him not be receptive, the captain-general pointed out to the British. As a consequence of the Lusitanians letting the vessel *London* come to Macao two years prior, the Portuguese at Macao had been subjected not only to reproof but a heavy fine at the hands of the Ming authorities at Canton. The Lusitanians, after all, were neither at liberty nor enjoyed the discretion to host other Europeans in China as they deemed fit; they themselves were merely renting a plot on the periphery of the Ming realm of the Chongzhen emperor. All this was emphasized by the captain-general. Notwithstanding such weighty considerations and reservations, Camara de Noronha professed himself willing to send Weddell any provisions or supplies that were urgently needed. Beyond that, he insisted, his hands were tied, as being unauthorized by the viceroy or his king to do more.[10]

On 8 July, the captain-general also sent his deputy, the procurador of Macao, the highest legal authority and second most powerful official in the city, to deliver these points viva voce to Weddell aboard the admiral *Dragon*.[11] While presenting the Courteens with a gift of pigs and oxen, the procurador emphasized that the Portuguese of Macao were not at liberty to facilitate the enterprise because the British did not possess the requisite authorization or permission from the viceroy at Goa. Nor, he stressed, would the Chinese consent to other foreigners trading at Macao.[12] Thus, he was merely reiterating the points already conveyed in the captain-general's written response. He further remarked that there would be no adequate supply of goods for the British from the nearby provincial capital, Canton: this year there was hardly enough for the Portuguese to lade their own six ships currently waiting for the raw and wrought silk and porcelain which they would transport on their voyage to Deshima.[13] The procurador did assure Weddell that arrangements would be made for additional provisions to be sold to the British to meet their present needs.

---

9. Domingos da Camara de Noronha to the Commander of the English Fleet, 28 June / 8 July 1637, *Lisbon Transcripts, Books of the Monsoons*, book 41, fol. 201.
10. Domingos da Camara de Noronha to the Commander of the English Fleet, 28 June / 8 July 1637, *Lisbon Transcripts, Books of the Monsoons*, book 41, fol. 201.
11. "[The procurador] began to unfold a tedious lamentable discourse, as false as prolix." "Voyage of the Weddell Fleet."
12. Mundy related for 29 June / 9 July: "The city sent our Admiral etts. a present of refreshing, viz., 8 beeves, 8 hogs, 8 jars sweet meats, 8 bags bread, with a proportion of fruit." Mundy, *Travels*, vol. 3, 169.
13. Mundy, *Travels*, vol. 3, 168. These were six Portuguese *galiotas*; a *galiota* was usually between three and four hundred tons. Deshima, not Nagasaki, because by an imperial edict of 1636 the Portuguese were thrust out of the latter.

The British ships drew closer to Macao to take the Portuguese up on the offer to sell them more provisions. It is likely that some of the Courteen captains and crew knew the basic geography of Macao and the small islands in its vicinity, if not also some of the waters and terrain of the Pearl River Delta. The Conde de Linhares, viceroy of Goa at the time of the *London*'s trip to Macao in 1635, had remarked that the British were already familiar with the location.[14] They also had their Portuguese mestizo pilot picked up from Melaka in June. The fleet comprised of four vessels halted at a spot within a league of the city, anchoring at Taipa Island, on the doorstep of Macao. The procurador supervised a patrol to prevent any venturesome Chinese from selling to the British—encircling and shielding each of the British ships—in order, as the Courteens claimed, to subject them to monopoly prices: "[In] matter of refreshing [provisioning], if we came nearer (which we did), he would provide for us. And this he very worshipfully and like a true Hebrew indeed performed, at 2 and 3 times the value on shore, and to the end that none might cheat us but himself, there was a strict watch of boats placed about each ship, not permitting so much as a poor fisherman to supply us with the value of 6*d*."[15]

When the captain-general learned that the British had moved their ships from their original position (橫琴島 Hengqindao), without permission, he issued an order to be circulated that no one from the city, whether Portuguese or Chinese, was to make contact with the visitors without his express authorization. He had commissioned a small fleet of patrol boats to prevent anyone from approaching the anchored Courteen fleet, whether in pursuit of mere communication or some transaction of commerce.[16] The boats keeping guard upon the British provoked complaints from not only these recently arrived Europeans. There were thousands of Chinese in Macao (and plenty elsewhere in the Pearl River estuary) eager to make contact and trade with the British. After these Chinese protested at the guard boats' blocking their access to the Courteens, the captain-general relented: "Certain Chinese wished to communicate with the newcomers. . . . We decided that we could not prevent the Chinese, this port being theirs, but we sent word to the British that the Chinese only came to deceive, and therefore warned them to be careful in their dealings."[17] So it was that on 11 July the British received their first Chinese visitor: a mandarin of some sort came accompanied by some of his minions.[18] Apparently, they came on behalf of this mandarin's superior, an official in Canton (Guangzhou),

---

14. "According to the viceroy, the English already knew the environs of Macau, given the countless voyages they had undertaken, including from Japan, together with their former allies, the Dutch." Puga, *British in Macau*, 28. It will also be recalled that the captain of the *Katherine*, John Carter, had shipwrecked in the EIC *Unicorn* near Macao in 1620, when on a voyage from Banten to the Hirado factory. For the British in Hirado in the 1610s and 1620s, from which experience much was learned about the China situation, see Chapter 1.

15. "Voyage of the Weddell Fleet."

16. Domingos da Camara de Noronha to Viceroy of Goa, 27 December 1637, *Lisbon Transcripts, Books of the Monsoons*, book 41, fol. 191.

17. Domingos da Camara de Noronha to Viceroy of Goa, 27 December 1637, *Lisbon Transcripts, Books of the Monsoons*, book 41, fol. 191.

18. Mundy, *Travels*, vol. 3, 171.

74   *The First British Trade Expedition to China*

curious to know the purpose of their visit. As related by Mundy, the factor who had just visited Macao with John Mountney and Thomas Robinson: "There came a China mandarin aboard with other Chinese and, as they said, to know our intents and demands that accordingly they might certify their master who is a great mandarin at Canton. He was appareled in a gown or coat of black sarsanette or tiffany, and under that other garments with strange attire on his head he had carried before him a broad board written with China characters, it seems the badge of his authority and commission. The rest were as strangely accoutered."[19] Presumably on this occasion communication was conducted between Chinese and British by use of mediating Portuguese, for English was known to no Chinese either at Macao or Canton.

On 22 July cargo ships (*lanteas*) from Canton came down to Macao carrying the goods for the Portuguese to load their six galliots for the Japan voyage.[20] Mundy and his Courteen colleagues assumed that rapport would improve and trade at Macao might open after these ships for Deshima had been dispatched. They could not, however, be optimistic that the Lusitanians would become any less hostile to the achievement of their most ambitious endeavor: to make acquaintance with Ming officials and Canton merchants and establish a more than temporary commercial relationship. With the Courteens expecting these six ships to depart within a few days, Captain Weddell took the opportunity to do a little "spring cleaning," that is, to careen and repair parts of the ships damaged by the rough sea-faring. The commander of the fleet was not content to rely on some sort of post-Japan-departure easing and mellowing of the Portuguese. For on the evening of the same day as the arrival of the cargo ships from Canton, the pinnace *Anne*, freshly careened, was sent north into the Pearl River estuary beyond Macao in the direction of the provincial capital. The purpose was to probe and survey the coasts, and explore the possibility of trading with the Chinese without the mediation of the Portuguese. The *Anne* was to be commanded by John Carter, captain of the larger vessel, the *Katherine*, which would remain at anchor below Macao. Thomas Robinson and John Mountney would lead this detachment with a crew of about fifty sailors, and the pinnace would be accompanied by two small boats, the barge and skiff of the *Dragon*.[21] They sailed towards the northeast of the estuary and after two days reached the Bogue—that is, the entrance of the Pearl River called the Tiger's Mouth (or Tiger's Gate; 虎門

---

19. 1/11 July 1637, Mundy, *Travels*, vol. 3, 171. From his subsequent, 12/22 July, entry we learn that this mandarin came at least one more time: "the aforesaid Mandareene . . . who came twice." "Sarsanette" refers to a fine soft silk; tiffany (epiphany silk), a thin transparent silk. After Mundy described the appearance of the mandarin from Canton on 1/11 July, his next journal entry was not made till 11/21 July. That length of interval is abnormal in his journal.

20. *Lanteas* were broad-beamed river transport vessels used to bring merchandise purchased by Portuguese at Canton down to Macao. For this and other Portuguese nautical terminology, see the glossary in Souza, *Survival of Empire*, Appendix.

21. Mundy, *Travels*, vol. 3, 173. It may be more than a coincidence that Carter, the man who had shipwrecked in the EIC *Unicorn* (in which he served as master) near Macao in 1620, was the captain chosen to command this excursion of the *Anne*. He was the only Courteen captain who had some (very meager) navigation experience around or near the Pearl River estuary.

Humen) by the Chinese and Boca do Tigre by the Portuguese—probably anchoring at or near Chuanbi (穿鼻).[22]

Waiting there for favorable wind and tide, on the morning of 24 July a Chinese fishing junk was spotted. Robinson went after it in the barge in hopes of recruiting a pilot and interpreter to assist them in an excursion up the river to Canton. He went aboard this junk but failed to obtain such guides; later, in the evening, he boarded a similar boat, only to be disappointed again in this errand of recruitment. But the next morning, 25 July, a small boat approached them near Chuanbi, and its occupants consented to be towed by the barge to the *Anne*. These Chinese fishermen came aboard and sold the Courteens some provisions. More importantly, one of these men offered, for five silver dollars (*real* of eight), to guide them up the river to the provincial capital: "One of them [Chinese fishermen] made signs to carry them to Canton and to bring them to speech of the mandarins."[23] That night, by assistance of their native pilot, Captain Carter and the Courteen crew moved farther up the river, anchoring the *Anne* perhaps in the vicinity of another small island, present-day Aniangxie, a little north of Chuanbi.[24] Early the next morning, a Sunday, John Mountney and Thomas Robinson went for shore in the barge, flying a white flag for peaceful intercourse. In the bay, agents or messengers of the man they took to be the "captain of the emperor's junks" motioned for them to land. After disembarking on a sandy beach, they were escorted over some hills and led to a harbor. They were then conducted onto one of the junks anchored in the harbor. But on this occasion, without interpreters—and the Chinese unable to use Portuguese—the two parties could only exchange gestures, "dumb shows," of courtesy and cordiality. Robinson and Mountney were transported back to the *Anne* in one of the Chinese boats, accompanied by several men they classified as "petty mandarins."[25] That afternoon, Captain Carter pushed the pinnace even farther up the river, three leagues, before anchoring somewhere beyond Tiger Island (大虎 Dahu). During this short trip the Courteen reconnaissance contingent passed what appeared to be an abandoned fort ("a certain desolate castle").[26]

On 28 July the progress of the *Anne* up the river towards Canton was halted by a fleet of about twenty junks. This fleet was commanded by the officer whom

---

22. "Voyage of the Weddell Fleet." Chuanbi is Mundy editor Temple's conjecture. Neither Portuguese nor Chinese sources indicate the precise location of the *Anne* in July 1637. English "Bogue"—which only became current well after this British expedition—is an approximation/corruption of Portuguese "boca." Chuanbi is now known as Weiyuan Island (威遠島 Weiyuandao).

23. All of this paragraph draws from Mountney's "Voyage of the Weddell Fleet"; only Weddell's account ("Weddell's China Narrative, O.C. 1662") presents the detail that the "fisherman agreed to show them the way in to the river of Canton for 5 reals of 8." But Weddell was not on the spot: he was with the rest of the fleet still anchored below Macao.

24. "Voyage of the Weddell Fleet" states that the *Anne* "anchored in the river near unto a harbour called Lampton, which is a station for their prime men of war of the king's [emperor's] armada, as Chatham is in England for his Majesty's ships." Aniangxie (阿娘鞋) is Anung-hoi/Anunghoy in non-pinyin approximations.

25. "Voyage of the Weddell Fleet." As Mundy was not a participant in the *Anne's* excursion, his journal does not provide us with any details of this first British passage in the Pearl River.

26. "Voyage of the Weddell Fleet."

they understood to be vice-admiral of the provincial navy, that is, the deputy of the "Champin," the latter taken by the Courteens to be the highest ranking naval officer in the region, whose jurisdiction covered the Pearl River and its estuary.[27] The British were asked to anchor; after doing so, Mountney and Robinson went aboard one of the Ming junks to meet with the admiral.[28] On this occasion, the two sides were able to communicate, if imperfectly, by assistance of fugitive African slaves from Macao, previously owned by the Portuguese, who had fled to Canton and learned Chinese. These interpreters would convert Chinese to Portuguese for English ears and Robinson's Portuguese into Chinese for comprehension by the Ming naval officers.[29]

The Chinese naval commander ("Champin") commenced his discourse by reproving the British for their brazen intrusion into the Bogue and demanding to know who had guided them up the river. Robinson answered that they came as representatives of the king of Great Britain, a Western monarch who wished to establish amity and enter into commercial relations with the emperor of China and his subjects. In interest of achieving this, Robinson explained, he had been granted license to conclude agreements with the Chinese. The fond and honorable hope of the British sovereign and themselves, his subjects, was to establish the same sort of commercial arrangement as that currently enjoyed by the Portuguese at Macao. Robinson flatly denied that they had been guided by a native Chinese pilot; rather, they had relied upon their own navigational instinct and geographical wit. The Ming "Admiral of the Seas" (how they glossed "Champin") appeared mollified and offered to arrange for a small junk of his fleet to transport a three-man contingent of British up to Canton on condition that these bold intruders of the Bogue would agree to proceed no farther with the *Anne*.[30]

So that night, 28 July, Captain Carter, John Mountney, and Thomas Robinson went aboard a Chinese junk of about thirty tons with the hope of reaching the provincial capital.[31] There they would try to meet the viceroy of Canton and present him with a petition requesting a license to trade. The following day the Chinese-escorted Courteens stopped about five leagues from Canton—the "First Bar," as later British referred to it. Here they received a message from the "Hai-tao" ("Hitow"), a customs

---

27. "Being under sail with a fair wind and tide, a fleet of about 20 sails of tall junks, commanded by Champin's (the Admiral of the Seas) deputy, passing down from Canton, encountered our people, and in courteous terms desired them to anchor, which accordingly they did." "Voyage of the Weddell Fleet."
28. "Presently John Mountney and Thomas Robinson went aboard the Admiral, the Chief Mandarin." "Voyage of the Weddell Fleet."
29. "Certain negroes, fugitives of the Portugals . . . interpreted between them." "Voyage of the Weddell Fleet." In their account the Portuguese at Macao also described these African interpreters: "Among the Chinese there are certain negroes who have fled from us, who speak our language and wear our dress." Letter from the City of Macao to the King of England, 24 December 1637, *Lisbon Transcripts, Books of the Monsoons*, book 41, fol. 220.
30. "Voyage of the Weddell Fleet."
31. "The same night Captain Carter, Thomas Robinson, and John Mountney left the pinnace with order to expect their return, and being embarked in a small junk of 30 tons, proceeded towards Canton, with intent to deliver a petition to the viceroy for obtaining of license to settle a trade in those parts." "Voyage of the Weddell Fleet."

official and naval officer ranking above the "Champin," who ordered the junk carrying Carter, Mountney, and Robinson to halt. If they would return to the *Anne* and evacuate the river with the pinnace (at present anchored somewhere in the Bogue), then they would receive assistance from Chinese officials down at Macao in obtaining from the "subordinate viceroy for trade" ("Quan Moan") a warrant to trade. The Courteen delegation readily consented to do as directed and Carter, Mountney, and Robinson were carried back down the river to the pinnace.[32]

On 1 August Captain John Carter sailed the *Anne* out of the Pearl River and southwest, across the estuary to rejoin the fleet anchored at Taipa, a few leagues south of Macao. In the morning of the same day as the return of the pinnace, the captain-general of Macao had sent a message to inform Captain Weddell, still with the anchored *Dragon*, *Sun*, and *Katherine*, that the Ming naval fleet had taken the *Anne* and thrown the whole British crew into jail and confiscated all their goods and money.[33] When, later the same day, the Courteen pinnace came into sight of Macao, the Portuguese governor promptly dispatched a message to the commander in the *Dragon*, explaining that he had been misinformed by some Chinese. When the *Anne* returned from its reconnaissance on 1 August, Captain Carter, John Mountney, and Robinson briefed Captains Weddell and Richard Swanley of the *Sun*, and Nathaniel Mountney, cape merchant. They reported that, according to the natives they met in the Bogue and Pearl River, the Portuguese had been misinforming the Chinese about the intents of the Courteens. The Lusitanians had told the Chinese that the British, carrying neither money nor cargo, were merely marauders, coming not with any design to engage in any substantial trade but only to prowl and raid and plunder—just like those other violent barbarians, the Dutch, whom the Ming referred to as "red barbarians" (紅夷 *hongyi*). By the end of July, then, the Courteens were convinced that while their fleet had been anchored for weeks just below Macao, the Portuguese had been diligently slandering them throughout the Pearl River Delta.[34]

Back at Macao, on 25 July, just a few days after the *Anne* had begun her excursion towards Canton, as described above, a delegation of three Ming officials from Macao led by a superior of theirs from the provincial capital came aboard the *Dragon* anchored at Taipa: "They came in a big vessel with a kettledrum and a broad

---

32. "19/29 July 1637: The next day they arrived within 5 leagues of Canton, whether it seems the rumour of their coming and fear of them was already arrived, so that from a message from Hai-tao ["Hitow"] . . . they were required in friendly manner to proceed no further, but to repair aboard, with promise of all assistance in the procuring of licence from Quan Moan, the subordinate viceroy for trade, if they would seek it at Macao by the solicitation of some they should find there and would instantly abandon the river." "Voyage of the Weddell Fleet." Identifications and variant spellings of the Ming official titles by the British are given in Chapters 8 and 9; a list of the Chinese officials involved is presented in the Appendix, "Key Chinese Officials in Ming Documents with English Renderings by the Courteens."
33. Mundy, *Travels*, vol. 3, 174–75.
34. According to Mundy, reporting on the intelligence gained by the *Anne*'s excursion: "22 July [1 August] 1637: There came to them [Carter, Robinson, John Mountney] sundry officers, and many of the king's men of war [junks] came about them, and they were told by the Chinois how the Portugals should report us to be pirates and that we came only to rob and spoil, bringing neither money nor goods." Mundy, *Travels*, vol. 3, 175.

brass pan [gong], on both which they beat, keeping time together. They had also on their vessel certain flags and streamers."[35] These mandarins had received reports and heard various rumors about these foreigners which they sought to check and verify. They also came to survey the ships, weaponry, cargo, and silver money of the Courteen fleet.[36] It may have been just after this meeting with the Chinese aboard the *Dragon*, while the *Anne* was still up at the Bogue, that the captain-general of Macao dispatched the Jesuit Bartolomeo de Roboredo and a Spanish sergeant-major, as well as some senators of the city (members of the municipal council, the Senado), to urge the British "to put no trust whatever in the Chinese, who would seek by some trick to get them all within their power."[37] The Jesuit Roboredo and the Spaniard had been among those transported by the Courteens from Melaka in June. Through their previous acquaintance with the British during the voyage up to China, they must have developed a rapport that could have been expected to facilitate credence.[38]

After 2 August, the Courteens seem to have entertained some expectation of receiving more hospitable treatment from the Portuguese at Macao. For at that date the Japan fleet had finally embarked upon its voyage north. The Iberians would now be relieved of the anxiety that the Courteens would meddle with or block these ships. The British understood that upon their arrival back in July, the Portuguese had been constantly worried that the Protestant interlopers would impede or delay the business of lading and launching those six ships set to sail for Deshima. The Lusitanians may well have feared worse: that, frustrated and desperate enough, the Courteens would detain and take their Japanese fleet hostage.[39] That was unlikely, however, on account of the Anglo-Portuguese accord. Such offensive action would blatantly violate the spirit if not letter of the entente signed at Goa. The plight of the still-unladen Portuguese Japan fleet at Macao had been among the reasons which had been given to Captain Weddell in order to excuse the Portuguese for not offering

---

35. 15/25 July 1637, Mundy, *Travels*, vol. 3, 174. The same day Mundy noted: "Today came a vessel from Macassar belonging to the Portugals and entered the town." He would report that as of 17/27 July 1637 three men in the fleet had died since arriving at Macao.

36. This is most likely the meeting with Chinese officials described by the Portuguese as follows: "To effect their purpose, they [British] entered into negotiations with two petty mandarins of this port [Macao], who have no power, asking them to come to the ships and speak with them, which they did various times, and by their advice they left here and proceeded to the mouth of the River of Canton, the mandarins having promised that there they would be admitted to the same conditions of trade as ourselves." Letter from the City of Macao to the King of England, 24 December 1637, *Lisbon Transcripts, Books of the Monsoons*, book 41, fol. 220.

37. Domingos da Camara de Noronha to Viceroy of Goa, 27 December 1637, *Lisbon Transcripts, Books of the Monsoons*, book 41, fol. 191.

38. "Bartolomeo de Roboredo a Jesuit that came with us from Malacca, and a Spaniard, a sergeant major that came on the *Sun*." 29 September / 9 October 1637, Mundy, *Travels*, vol. 3; the *Dagh-Register gehouden int Casteel Batavia* records Roboredo's presence at Banten as late as March 1637. The Spaniard had served as the Courteen fleet's pilot in navigating the passage from Melaka to Macao: "[He] was also our pilot coming hither from Malacca." 30 November / 10 December 1637, Mundy, *Travels*, vol. 3.

39. Several subsequent communications of the Portuguese at Macao explicitly indicated their concern that the British could interfere with or seize the Japan ships—whether upon their being laden by the *lanteas* from Canton or, as we shall see, upon their return a few months later.

him and Nathaniel Mountney more access to commerce at the British arrival in the beginning of July. So the British were not operating irrationally to entertain some notion that opportunity to trade at or from Macao might come as soon as the Japan fleet departed. In previous weeks the Courteen fleet anchored at Taipa had heard rumors, and may even have received communication from some residents of the city, that they (British) would be granted liberty to trade at Macao once the Japan ships departed.[40] Instead of welcome news of an alteration and relaxation in the posture of the Portuguese, on 5 August Weddell received an alarming message. The letter from the procurador of Macao conveyed a warning that the Chinese intended to launch a fire-ship attack to annihilate the Courteen fleet.[41]

The following day, 6 August, a delegation of Macao merchants was dispatched by the captain-general to confer with the British. The Portuguese remonstrated: the Courteens had no reason to be irritated by any behavior of the captain-general and his council. Domingos da Camara de Noronha had already fully and clearly explained the situation: he had no authorization from his superiors to facilitate trade, and the Chinese would permit no other European nation to trade—not even their fellow Iberians and fellow subjects of Philip IV, the Spanish. To illustrate their own strict observance of the Ming rules and regulations, the Portuguese cited the fact that just a few years ago a Spanish ship from Manila was repulsed by Lusitanian cannons when it approached Macao to trade.[42] When the Spaniards subsequently lodged a protest with their joint Habsburg monarch, Philip declined to censure or punish the Portuguese for violently repelling the Spaniards. Instead, the Iberian king recapitulated that the Portuguese at Macao were to preserve their monopoly privileges and the Spaniards were not permitted to send any more ships from Manila to trade at Macao or anywhere else in the Pearl River estuary. The Lusitanians of Macao emphasized this point that however much they shared the same monarch, their fellow Iberians in the Philippines were not authorized to come to Macao to trade: "Even the Spaniards who inhabit the country nearby cannot carry on trade in this land, because of the harm it will do to us; and therefore it is not permitted to

---

40. "At night departed the Japan fleet to sea on their voyage. And now expected we open admittance of trade, as we were encouraged by common report and private letters from some particulars only, but from the General of the City [captain-general] not a word since the last letter which was a mannerly denial of trade under excuse that for want of order from the superiors, viz., the King of Spain and Viceroy of India, he could not do us that good office which otherwise he willingly would." 23 July / 2 Aug. 1637, Mundy, *Travels*, vol. 3, 180. "Private letters from some particulars only" refer to residents (merchants presumably) of Macao communicating to the British with neither the authorization of the captain-general nor the Senado.

41. "There came a letter from the procurador of Macao advising us to look to ourselves; that he was told the Chinois had an intent to fire us if they could." 26 July / 5 Aug. 1637, Mundy, *Travels*, vol. 3, 181.

42. "Some 5 or 6 years since, as they relate, a Spanish ship coming from Manila was not suffered to enter but kept out with their ordnance, nor suffered to trade." 26 July / 5 August 1637, Mundy, *Travels*, vol. 3, 181. This was most probably a reference to the incident of April 1634, involving the governor of the Spanish settlement in north Taiwan (Keelung/Jilong 基隆), Sergeant Major Alonso Garcia Romero, whose galleon sailed into the harbor of Macao on the pretext of escaping typhoon. Boxer, *Fidalgos in the Far East*, 136.

them."[43] Furthermore, as the Portuguese propounded and pleaded, currently there were neither commodities nor manufactures sufficient in quantity at Macao to lade any of the British ships.[44] Thus, the Portuguese could conclude by professing themselves sorely baffled and vexed at the arrival, let alone lingering, of the Courteens. They renewed their request that Captain Weddell sail the fleet away from China as soon as possible.

Evidently, some of the crews on the British ships had grown desperate after about a month anchored and stagnating off Macao at Taipa. For on 8 August, two days after this meeting with the representatives of the captain-general and city, the Portuguese returned to Weddell five runaways (including a Frenchman) from Macao. This turned out to be only one round of a larger series of exchanges. The British had seized a few Portuguese who had been on the boats which patrolled and monitored the anchored fleet; they were released when the Portuguese brought the Courteen fugitives.[45] It is likely, however, that more members of the Courteen fleet had fled to Macao than were returned to the fleet. Nathaniel Mountney's later account records that the Portuguese returned only the scoundrels and rascals among the Courteen defectors.[46] Some fugitives who fled the Portuguese to join the British were to be of enormous value. Among them would be at least one who would serve as interpreter when dealing with the Chinese in subsequent encounters. A native Chinese man from coastal Fujian, the Ming province bordering Guangdong in the north, was taken aboard one of the Courteen ships at this juncture.[47]

By 8 August Captain Weddell, Nathaniel Mountney, and the fleet's council had held a discussion that concluded with a resolution to disregard and bypass the obstructionist Portuguese of Macao and to try independently and directly to engage the Chinese in Canton. Visits from Ming officials within the first weeks of their arrival at Macao indicated a willingness of at least some Chinese to entertain their offers—not excluding bribes—and to open commercial channels for the newcomers.

---

43. Letter from the City of Macao to the King of England, 24 December 1637, *Lisbon Transcripts, Books of the Monsoons*, book 41, fol. 220. For further examples and discussion of Portuguese thwarting Manila-launched Spanish ventures to trade directly with the Chinese near Macao and Canton, see Souza, *Survival of Empire*, 80. The late sixteenth-century (1598) violent and successful Portuguese opposition to a Spanish attempt to establish themselves on an island in the Pearl River estuary is analyzed by Paulo Jorge de Sousa Pinto, "Enemy at the Gates: Macao, Manila and the 'Pinhal Episode,'" *Bulletin of Portuguese/Japanese Studies* 16 (2008), 11–43.
44. The Portuguese stressed "the slender quantity of goods which they might expect this year from Canton for Japan." "Voyage of the Weddell Fleet."
45. 29 July/ 8 August 1637, Mundy, *Travels*, vol. 3, 181–82.
46. The "runaways were found . . . to be good for nothing (as commonly such people are) and therefore we obtained this courtesy to have them delivered, although since they [Portuguese] have inveigled and concealed better able men whom we could never recover." "Voyage of the Weddell Fleet."
47. Dated a few weeks after Weddell's fleet had left Macao for the Bogue, the following note of Mundy contains information about this Macao-defector-turned-Courteen-interpreter: "11/21 August 1637: We went ashore to the said town in our barge, and another boat with an interpreter was sent to other places. . . . The aforesaid interpreter was a Chincheo [native of coastal Fujian near Zhangzhou and Quanzhou], runaway from the Portugals at our being at Macao, who spake a little bad language." That is, the Fujianese had a smattering of Portuguese.

The excursion of the *Anne* had also evinced the distinct possibility that there were Chinese interested in establishing short- if not long-term commercial relations with the British. The Courteens could explain to the Chinese that the avaricious Portuguese monopolists were selfishly thwarting all attempts to create mutually beneficial Sino-British trade. For their part the British would offer more generous terms and procure the Chinese higher profits. Since by now the Ming provincial and naval authorities must have felt some reassurance that they were bona fide traders and not mere pirates or marauders in the same mold as the Dutch, Weddell, his fellow captains, and the head merchants supposed that they might be able to engage in some sort of exchange somewhere in the Pearl River estuary if not at Canton—at least some limited buying and selling to be authorized by officials in that city. This was probably the opinion of Captain Carter, Thomas Robinson, John Mountney, and the other factors who had participated in the prospecting trip of the *Anne* that had managed to enter the Bogue and traverse some of the Pearl River towards the provincial capital. At a conference of the fleet's council held on 3 August, a few days after the return of the pinnace, the participants of that reconnaissance trip had reported to the leadership all the incidents and meetings with the Chinese and pointed out the fair prospects of an endeavor of further direct intercourse.[48] They had also proffered a map ("draught") of the river leading to Canton and the terrain they had observed during their exploration. No matter how rough the map they had sketched, or superficial Captain Carter's acquaintance with the weather, winds, tides, and currents, Weddell now had better intelligence to guide him, should he decide to move the fleet beyond its present position off Macao—and to sail the *Dragon* into the Tiger's Mouth.

By the time this consultation was held, the Courteen commander was all the more inclined to venture forth—notwithstanding any protest, obstruction, or armed resistance of the Portuguese. For the food, water, and sanitation conditions of the fleet were nearing desperate. According to the British, the Portuguese had deliberately sold them rotten rice and other tainted or adulterated provisions from Macao. Suspecting the unwholesomeness of the rice, the Courteens had fed some of it to the swine aboard Richard Swanley's *Sun*. Ill-effects of consuming it were noticed in those animals, so few of the men would touch it. As the Lusitanians were preventing any Chinese boats that would come out to sell the anchored British further fresh victuals, the wisdom of sailing up into the Bogue and towards Canton was all the more compelling. Any distinction between audacity and necessity was fading. With sickening and some moribund crew, the status quo of wait-and-see inaction must have begun to feel like suicidal folly. Perhaps such inaction would breed mutiny.

---

48. "Voyage of the Weddell Fleet."

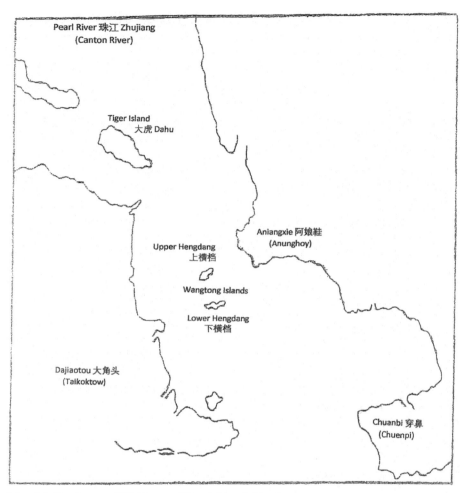

Map 4.1: The Bogue, 虎門 Humen (Tiger's Mouth/Gate)

5

The *Dragon* Enters the Tiger

The Courteen Fleet in the Bogue and Pearl River Estuary, August 1637

On 8 August 1637 the British fleet weighed anchor at Taipa Island below Macao and sailed north towards the Bogue (虎門 Humen).[1] From Taipa ten large Chinese junks followed and hung about them, and many more of these junks were at anchor in the vicinity as the Courteen vessels passed Macao portside on 9 August. Warned just a few days earlier by the Portuguese to beware of some sort of surprise attack, Weddell's fleet was prepared to defend itself. The British ships sailed northeast of Macao a few more leagues where, on 11 August, around the Nine Islands (九洲島 Jiuzhoudao), some Chinese boats approached them. The fleet anchored, the admiral *Dragon*'s barge was sent to communicate with them; the Courteen boat picked up a Chinese officer and his interpreter, a Chinese-Portuguese bilingual. The Ming officer conveyed a message that the British should halt and wait there until they received a message from Canton. He would send word to the authorities that the British wished to make purchases and trade there.[2] Unwilling to subject his men to the anxiety and torture of yet another session of anchored inaction, with water and provisions dwindling, and apprehensive of dangerous weather conditions and extremities (hurricane or typhoon), Captain Weddell and his council resolved not to hover in such a vulnerable position. So on the night of 11 August he sailed the fleet all the way up the estuary into the Bogue, to a spot not far from where the pinnace *Anne* had just recently anchored in her late July excursion led by Captain Carter.

After entering the Bogue, the next few days the British ships had to contend with uncooperative winds and currents as they tried to sail farther up the Pearl River leading to Canton.[3] On 14 August the Courteens were again confronted by

---

1. 29 July / 8 August 1637, Mundy, *Travels*, vol. 3, 183.
2. "The first of this month we came some 2 or 3 leagues farther, when there came unto us certain vessels, unto whom we sent the [*Dragon*'s] barge and brought from them an officer with an interpreter, who desired us to anchor thereabouts and to proceed no farther until order should come from Canton, whither they would send present [immediate] advice of our coming and desire." 1/11 August 1637, Mundy, *Travels*, vol. 3, 184.
3. Mundy noted of this river area just north of the Bogue: "These two days we saw a great number of fisher boats, etc. vessels, so that it may be verified here what is reported of some parts of China, that there are more people on the water than on the land, for what we have yet seen are islands, high, broken, stony, sandy, uneven land, and uninhabited, not 1 acre in 1000 made use of; but these are but the out isles of Canton lying about the river's mouth." 1/11 August 1637, Mundy, *Travels*, vol. 3, 185.

a few dozen ships of the Ming naval fleet. From the Chinese officers they received and complied with a request to anchor where they were, in the vicinity of Chuanbi Island.[4] As the British lay at anchor that night, they were particularly vigilant, or rather, on edge, as vague notions of a Chinese sneak attack could not be dispelled. Two days later, on 16 August, a messenger and a Chinese-Portuguese speaking interpreter from the commander of the Chinese fleet transmitted the message that they proceed no farther up the river towards Canton. They were instructed to turn aside and retreat somewhat south of their current location. If they complied, this "mandarin of the fleet" promised, they would receive provisions. Furthermore, he would try to obtain permission for the Courteens to trade, but it would take several days to return an answer from Canton.[5] Such an interval of time might have been necessary because, according to the British understanding of the situation, the highest-ranking Ming officials in that area were out of town: "Both Chadjan, the supervisor general, and Toutan or Quan Mone, and viceroy, were both absent far off."[6] On this occasion, 16 August, Captain Weddell was also admonished by the messenger that the Chinese had sunk some boats to block the further passage of the fleet up the river.

At this meeting with the messenger on 16 August, the British commander emphasized that they intended no violence or harm and that his merchants simply wanted to exchange their silver money for provisions and Chinese commodities and merchandise: the fleet would depart the moment they completed such transactions. Weddell also informed the Chinese officer's messenger that in order to afford his ships a safer posture—hurricanes and typhoons being possible—the Courteen fleet would go just a little farther and then halt to receive further communications and directions. So in the next two days Weddell proceeded to steer his ships a little more north towards Canton, all the while Chinese junks shadowed them and hollered and made signs for them to stop and anchor.[7] On 18 August, the Courteens arrived at a convenient location, "Fumaon," in the vicinity of Aniangxie, and anchored.[8] It was adjacent to a Ming fort, and a large fleet of men-of-war hung about it.[9]

---

4. "From the first current to this day, the 4th [14th August], we got but little [farther] by reason of strange currents and little winds. There came to us here another fleet of great China junks, the king's men of war, about 40 sail, strange vessels and as strangely fitted." 4/14 August 1637, Mundy, *Travels*, vol. 3, 185.

5. 6/16 August 1637, Mundy, *Travels*, vol. 3, 185.

6. "Voyage of the Weddell Fleet."

7. "Weddell's China Narrative, O.C. 1662."

8. "Anchored in 10 or 11 fathom of water by a town called Fumaon; reasonable good land on both sides, although islands and inlets; town, villages and trees in sundry places." 8/18 August 1637, Mundy, *Travels*, vol. 3. Most likely the Courteens were then somewhere between present-day Aniangxie/Xidatan (西大坦) and Chuanbi/Weiyuandao (威遠島).

9. According to Weddell, he anchored at this location near to the fort "through their much entreaty, upon promise that in 10 days they would procure us free trade with those in Canton, but if we should offer to go above the castle [farther up the river towards Canton] it would give an alarum to the country people which lived upon the islands round about us and would be ill taken by the mandarin of Canton; so we agreed to stay 10 days for an answer from Canton." "Weddell's China Narrative, O.C. 1662." The following passage from Mountney's "Voyage of the Weddell Fleet" seems to describe these events, on or shortly after 18 August: "Being now furnished with some slender interpreters, we soon had speech with divers mandarins in the king's

When the Courteen contingent of Captain Carter, Thomas Robinson, and John Mountney had probed this segment of the Pearl River during the excursion of the pinnace *Anne*, neither cannons nor soldiers could be discerned on the fort. But now they could spot about forty-five iron-cast cannons just recently mounted on its platform. The cannons, each estimated to weigh six or seven hundred pounds, had apparently been transferred from the ships. Assuming that thus fitted the fort would deter the British from venturing farther up the river, the Chinese vessels moved back towards Canton. Flags had also been hoisted on the walls of the fort as if to announce it was poised for combat. The British supposed that the Portuguese had engendered or contributed to this belligerence in the Ming by slandering them as mere pirates: "[On account of] our perfidious friends, the Portugals . . . had in all this time since the return of the pinnace *Anne* so slandered us unto them [the Chinese] became very jealous [mistrustful] of our good meaning, insomuch that in the night time they put 46 pieces of iron cast ordnance into this fort lying close to the brink of the river, each piece being between 6 and 700 weight and well proportioned."[10] While the Chinese naval officers put the fort into such an offensive posture, the British were simply trying to procure desperately needed water and provisions, and waiting for further communication from the Ming side.

The day after arriving there, on 19 August, Captain Weddell sent a delegation to the fort in order to try to make arrangements for the purchase of provisions but received a hostile response to the request.[11] This caused the British to alter their attitude from defensive to offensive: white flags were replaced with red ones on the poops, and on the main topmasts were raised flags bearing the royal arms—the flags which Charles I had authorized them to unfurl in the event of hostilities. On noticing this change in the naval display of the foreigners, the Chinese promptly dispatched a messenger from the fort to plead with the Courteens to practice a little more patience: in six days an answer from Canton would arrive. And the Chinese promised to write again to the authorities in Canton that evening. The messenger from the fort also presented to the British a white flag, with which, he explained, they could obtain provisions from nearby towns and villages along the Pearl River. The following morning, 20 August, they tried to put this flag to use to obtain food and water. The British entered an inlet leading to a village. Despite the exhibit of the white flag, a small imperial sculling junk motioned that they must proceed no farther. Committed to the notion that their newly acquired flag meant something, this signal from the Chinese boat was disregarded. As soon as the Courteens reached

---

junks, to whom we discovered the cause of our coming, viz., to entertain peace and amity with them, to traffic freely, as the Portugals did, and to be forthwith supplied for our monies with provisions for our ships. All which they promised to solicit with Haitau (the lord treasurer), Champin (the admiral of the forces both by sea and land), and the rest of the prime men then resident in Canton."

10. "Voyage of the Weddell Fleet." Captain Weddell noted: "The ordnance they took out of the junks and they being all mounted in the castle, the junks went farther up into the river supposing the castle sufficient to keep us from going further into the river." "Weddell's China Narrative, O.C. 1662."

11. 9/19 August 1637, Mundy, *Travels*, vol. 3, 188.

the village the people flocked about them and sold them such items as hens and eggs. Mundy, one of the factors sent on this errand, chanced upon a market: "Here in the bazaar or market among other provisions there was a snake to be sold, about 4 or 5 feet long, alive, his mouth sewed up for biting, accounted good meat, and dogs flesh also . . . estimated a principal dish."[12] Perhaps achieving the distinction of being the first Englishmen to try tea in China (outside of Macao), at a "pagoda" they briefly visited, the Courteen detachment left that village at about noon and went to another near "Fumaon." There they obtained a bullock and some hens and were promised more vending of victuals the next day.

In their barge they returned the following day, 21 August, while another boat carrying a recently acquired interpreter explored other locations in the vicinity. This interpreter was the Fujianese who had defected from the Portuguese when the British fleet had been anchored just below Macao in July. However, he was far from proficient. For translation the Courteens had also acquired a north African slave, an Ethiopian named Antonio. Originally, he had also absconded from the Portuguese, but was working with Chinese outside Macao when the British encountered him. He seems, however, to have been no more effective as an interpreter. While the Fujianese had only a very limited repertoire of Portuguese, Antonio must have had only very paltry Chinese.[13] Neither of the Courteen boats procured much since the local official, referred to as the "mandarin of Lantao"—whose jurisdiction was thought to cover all the towns and villages in the vicinity and who commanded junks in the area—had issued an order prohibiting all intercourse and trade with the British.[14] While they were disappointed at the meager harvest of their errands run for victuals, the British in one of the boats were treated quite hospitably by some Buddhists from one of the towns. As the Courteens were returning to their boat, these votaries were on their way to temple to attend the ceremonies and feast of the new moon. The foreigners followed them to the "pagoda" where they observed what struck them as a most bizarre ritual. After the ceremony these subjects of Charles I were vouchsafed some chopsticks and given pieces of meat which had been roasted

---

12. "The people there gave us a certain drink called *cha*, which is only water with a kind of herb boiled in it. It must be drunk warm and is accounted wholesome." 10/20 August 1637, Mundy, *Travels*, vol. 3, 191.

13. "The aforesaid interpreter was a Chincheo, runaway from the Portugals at our being at Macao, who spoke a little bad language. There is another named Antonio, a *kafir* Ethiopian Abyssinian, or curled head, that came to and fro about messages as interpreter, little better than the other, runaway also from the Portugals to the Chinois, it being an ordinary matter for slaves on some discontent or other to run away from their masters; and being among the Chinois they are safe, who make use of their service." 11/21 August 1637, Mundy, *Travels*, vol. 3, 192. Later, after more had transpired, Mundy, ever-prone to litotes, observed: "Our interpreter, Antonio the kafir, none of the best of linguists." 28 December 1637 / 7 January 1638, Mundy, *Travels*, vol. 3, 241.

14. "The mandarin of Lantao who is governor of all the towns and villages hereabouts, as also of their junks, sent order all about that nothing should be sold us." 11/21 August 1637, Mundy, *Travels*, vol. 3, 191–92. Temple conjectured that by "Lantao" the Courteen factor was probably referring to the islands of "Wangtung," that is, the small islands south of Tiger Island (大虎 Dahu), what are now called the Hengdang Islands (橫檔島 Hengdangdao), the north-south pair of islands now intersected by the Humen Pearl River Bridge (虎門大橋 Humen Daqiao), built in 1997.

The *Dragon* Enters the Tiger   87

at the temple altar. They were presented with an alcoholic beverage to imbibe, apparently spirits which had been heated in a device resembling a samovar.[15]

The afternoon of the same day, 21 August, Peter Mundy and John Mountney, carrying the white flag and accompanied by their Fujianese interpreter, returned to the fort to complain that the flag had accomplished little in the way of obtaining food and drink: the British had received cold and hostile treatment in most of the places they presented it. The Chinese responded that they would give them one of their own men to accompany them on their next errands for provisions. But the skeptical Mundy and Mountney objected that such an addition would not yield different results; they requested, instead, to communicate with the principal government official in the area. Impossible, replied the Chinese interlocutor; rather, the British must wait another four days for an answer from the authorities in Canton. In disgust and defiance Mountney angrily flung the flag to the ground.[16] As he and Mundy and their Fujianese interpreter walked away, they ignored calls from behind to resume discussion.[17] Instead, they went back to the Courteen ships and related what had transpired. After deliberation by Captain Weddell and the fleet's council, it was decided they should wait out the four days which they understood to be stipulated in the agreement. They concurred that they would now need to be especially alert and prepared for belligerent action from any direction. They imagined that the Chinese could be stalling and using the interval of several days to prepare a large-scale attack.

The next day, 22 August, the barge was sent a little farther up the Pearl River towards Canton in order to test the depths for larger vessels. The larger ships would be less exposed and vulnerable to typhoons or to man-made assaults if they could anchor away from their present location. The fleet also desperately needed access to more potable water. As the small Courteen boat was passing the fort near Aniangxie, it was fired upon three times; one projectile flew over and the other two fell short. The barge immediately returned to the fleet, and Captain Weddell convened a meeting of the captains and head merchants to discuss what action to take in response. The firing of artillery from the Ming fort upon a defenseless barge was regarded as a breach of the peace: "Having (as they thought) sufficiently fortified themselves, they treacherously breaking this agreed truce, discharged divers shot (though without hurt) upon our barge, which passed by them to find out a convenient watering place."[18] The council unanimously decided that in view of all the delays, evasions, and this fresh, craven assault upon the barge, it was time to display their frustration and exhausted patience with a demonstration of force. Their forbearance and self-restraint seem to have gained them nothing. Perhaps, on the contrary, it was grooming them for imminent destruction. In any event, the Courteens felt

---

15. Mundy, *Travels*, vol. 3, 193–94.
16. Mundy, *Travels*, vol. 3, 196.
17. Mundy, *Travels*, vol. 3, 196.
18. "Voyage of the Weddell Fleet."

they no longer had any reason to expect to obtain provisions or any other kind of commerce by pathetic begging and adhering to a patient and passive policy: "The more we suffered the more insolent they grew."[19] Thus it was determined that they would maneuver the ships up to the fort to bombard it in retaliation for the offensive action taken against the barge.

Once again all the combat flags were hoisted and a tide arrived punctually to carry them alongside the fort. As soon as they anchored within a musket shot of the fort, the Chinese fired about a dozen shots. The British observed them to be clumsy at their artillery: many of their balls simply dropped out of the cannons and dribbled over the wall. Only one of the shots did some small damage to one of the ships, albeit it was to Weddell's own *Dragon*.[20] Accompanied by the beating of drums and blasting trumpets and within a pistol shot of the fort, the British commenced firing the cannons of the *Dragon*. The British ordnance struck so accurately, emphatically, and decisively that within half an hour they had frightened about twenty men out of the fort. They sustained firing intermittently another few hours, until they were confident that the fort had been abandoned.[21] Boats transporting about a hundred members of the British fleet were then dispatched for the shore by Weddell. But as they approached, another dozen shots were fired from the fort. Unperturbed by this ineffectual discharge of artillery, they proceeded to land. Those few Chinese who had remained in the fort took flight upon seeing the Courteens landing. Finding the gates of the fort open, the British entered. They took down the Chinese flag and replaced it with the British one of their Stuart monarch Charles I. Then Weddell and the other captains of the fleet came ashore to survey the fort. They found more than forty several-hundred-pound cannons of mixed iron cast. The men who had deserted the fort perched themselves on a hill overlooking it. From this position they hurled large stones; this proved effective in dissuading the British from loitering long or relaxing at the fort. After burning down structures within the fort complex and dismantling some walls, the Courteens took the cannons and some small equipment and weaponry. At night the British contingent returned to their ships a little south of the fort, near Aniangxie.

Reflecting upon the storming of this fort, the factor Peter Mundy considered it a turning point for the British: "We showed our discontent for their refusing our friendly proffers for a peaceable commerce, and seeing all fair means will not prevail, we thought good to make trial of the contrary. In conclusion, the peace is broken and now more than ever it behooves us to stand upon our guard."[22] In his account

---

19. Mountney, Rawlinson A.299.
20. "One shot came and cut a little of the *Dragon*'s main halliards a little above man height, the admiral [Captain Weddell] then walking on the half deck." 12/22 August 1637, Mundy, *Travels*, vol. 3, 197.
21. In both Mundy's and Weddell's accounts, the bombardment of the fort lasted a half hour, whereas in Mountney's "Voyage of the Weddell Fleet" it is noted that two or three hours of cannon shot preceded the taking of the fort.
22. 12/22 August 1637, Mundy, *Travels*, vol. 3, 199. The British notion of the futility of employing "fair means" any further echoed the perspective of the exasperated VOC governor of Taiwan, Hans Putmans, who had written to the Heren XVII in October 1632: "This truly reveals the sort of treacherous and cowardly people

Captain Weddell related that upon completing the disarming and dismantling of the fort an alarm ("alarum") was swiftly sent up to the authorities at Canton.[23] On the afternoon of 23 August the British seized a Chinese junk in the Bogue. Not much was found aboard: only a little rice, some timber, scarcely any weapons, and only a trace of ammunition. Those materials and the Chinese men found aboard the vessel were brought to Weddell. After emptying the junk, the commander appointed members of his crew to combine with some of the Chinese in navigating it, with the design of intercepting other junks that might threaten the British fleet. Some of the Chinese captives were assigned the task of rowing.[24] With food and water now in very short supply and more men beginning to sicken from dehydration and starvation, the skiff (or barge) of Captain Richard Swanley's *Sun* was dispatched to seek such fresh provisions as pigs and fowl.[25] Thomas Robinson directed this mission, displaying a white flag aboard the skiff. Accompanied by only seven musketeers, he visited several villages. About a mile inland the small British detachment found some sort of temple to convert into an impromptu bazaar. Prominently displaying themselves and their silver money on its porch, they employed the small structure as their temporary commercial stall. Chinese in the surrounding area brought such things as hens and hogs to sell to those who must have appeared very odd-looking foreigners.[26] Thus, some inhabitants of the banks and islands of the Pearl River were ignorant of or indifferent to any prohibition of communication and commerce that had been issued by the mandarin governing the area.

But while Robinson was in the middle of supervising the purchase of miscellaneous provisions, he noticed in the distance more than three hundred soldiers approaching with swords, bucklers, and lances. As they drew near the Chinese troops began to bellow menacingly.[27] The British instantly grabbed their firearms and Robinson instructed his men to take care that they not be cut off from a retreat to the shore where they had left the boat. They managed a backward march to their skiff by warding off the Chinese with a concerted maneuver of rotating three-musket volleys. While none of the Courteen contingent was injured, some of the Chinese

---

the Chinese are. . . . The more you deal with them with courtesy, civility, and punctiliousness, the more they make us suffer and the more they push us around in circles and wear us out." Quoted in Cheng, *War, Trade and Piracy*, 85. Putmans, in turn, was echoing a predecessor, Nuijts, who had written in 1627: "For more than twenty years our nation has made friendly requests in the appropriate way to open Chinese trade, but our friendly overtures did not have the desired effect and so we were forced to seek the same through war." Quoted in Clulow, *Company and the Shogun*, 216.

23. "Weddell's China Narrative, O.C. 1662."
24. "We likewise took a junk [13/23 August 1637], and reserving aboard her captain and a little child, his son, put some of our men into her, intending to do the like by all such as we could surprise, until we had fitted each ship with one, who being floated and defended by our men and rowed by such China men as we should take, might more nimbly pursue their junks, and more safely venture over flats and shoals water." Mountney, Rawlinson A.299.
25. "All provisions of refreshing growing scarce in the ships and sick men much necessitated." "Voyage of the Weddell Fleet."
26. "Voyage of the Weddell Fleet."
27. "They began to raise a confused shout after the manner of the Irish hubbub." "Voyage of the Weddell Fleet."

retreated from the musket fire and others were struck down. Meanwhile, hearing the sound of firearms, Captain Weddell had dispatched an auxiliary squad. So when Robinson and his men reached the shore they found succor and reinforcements bringing more arms and ammunition. With this supplement of force, Robinson was able to go back to the temple and recover the provisions they had just purchased. In the process of this retrieval the British neither injured any of the people nor damaged any property.[28]

On the same day as Robinson's provisions detail and its spontaneous skirmish, on 23 August, the British were also able to take a fishing boat, five of whose men jumped out and swam away. After examining the boat and the two men who had remained aboard, the British released them and their small vessel. A large junk carrying salt and timber towards Canton was also seized, and all its crew fled.[29] Weddell used some of the Chinese captured with the first junk to deliver a letter to the chief mandarins in the provincial capital. They traveled up the Pearl River in the cockboat of the junk they had been riding. The letter they were to transport was written in Chinese, but no records indicate how that translation was achieved. It contained a protest at the Chinese breach of the peace in firing upon the British barge at the fort: "Some of the junk's people were in their own cockboat sent with a letter to Canton, written in China characters, showing therein a reason of our thus proceeding with them, and that contrariwise our desire was to have their friendship and free commerce in the country."[30] It also rendered a justification for the ensuing conduct of the British at the Bogue fort, as well as a reminder that they sought nothing but friendship and free trade—most especially, urgently needed provisions—for which they had silver money and merchandise to exchange. It also stated that the Chinese still in their custody would not be released until these others, serving as their messengers, returned.

Just two days after Thomas Robinson's rustic scuffle and the dispatch of the Chinese-rendered communication up to Canton, on 25 August a Portuguese-fluent Chinese, bearing what was interpreted as a flag of truce, arrived at the British fleet inside the Bogue. He explained that he had been sent by the authorities in the provincial capital in order to learn the intentions and demands of the foreigners.[31] Captain Weddell emphasized that while they had all along been committed

---

28. "Voyage of the Weddell Fleet."
29. 13/23 August 1637, Mundy, *Travels*, vol. 3, 201.
30. 13/23 August 1637, Mundy, *Travels*, vol. 3, 201–2. This letter addressed "the chief mandarins at Canton" and "expostulate[ed] their breach of truce, and excusing our assailing the castle [fort], and withal in fair terms requiring the liberty of a free trade." "Voyage of the Weddell Fleet." A cockboat was a small ship's boat, usually a boat towed behind a coasting vessel going up or down river.
31. Mountney's later report provides the detail: "He told us he came from the principal mandarins of Canton." Rawlinson A.299. Mundy's record for 15/25 August notes: "Came a petty mandarin with a flag of truce. He came from the higher powers to know our grievances." In Mountney's other account, "Voyage of the Weddell Fleet," the man bearing the flag is represented as "a mandarin of no great note"; "his masters, who were some of the chief mandarins riding about a point off land not far from us [in the Bogue]." Weddell's account agrees with the others: "He came with warrant from the great mandarins in Canton to know the reason of our coming into their parts, and what we desired." "Weddell's China Narrative, O.C. 1662."

The *Dragon* Enters the Tiger
91

to nothing except mutually beneficial trade, some "petty mandarins" around the Bogue had mistreated them, launching attacks while they were merely seeking trade, most especially water and provisions. The British commander complained that some of his men had been injured and killed in these attacks directed by officials in the Bogue and shores and islands in the Pearl River. That was what had provoked them finally to resort to force.[32] The Portuguese-fluent representative of the Canton mandarins replied that those officials did not know anything about the incidents that Weddell had described to him. Be that as it may, if the British would return the cannons and other equipment and materials taken from the fort, then he would go back to his superiors and do their bidding. That is, he assured Weddell and Mountney that he would personally endeavor to obtain for them not only a commercial permit but also a convenient spot on a shore or island where they could anchor their fleet and set up at least a temporary trading post. Of course, the British would be expected to pay all the same sorts of fees and customs like the Portuguese did at Macao. He also emphasized to them his confidence that these arrangements could be accomplished fairly soon. Captain Weddell graciously replied that he would undertake to compensate the Chinese for any damage his men had done in their recent assaults and raids, and this promise was put into writing and signed. On this same occasion, the British returned the large salt junk they seized just a few days before. After accepting some gifts from the British commander, the representative of the Canton authorities announced that he would return to his superior, who was waiting in a boat not far from where the British fleet was currently anchored.

The following day, 26 August, this bilingual envoy of the higher powers returned to the *Dragon*. He requested that Weddell appoint two representatives to accompany him to Canton in order to present a British petition to open up trade. He informed the Courteen commander that in addressing the authorities on behalf of the British he would emphasize the malice and hostility of their fellow foreigners the Portuguese who, he was well aware, had slandered and thwarted these visitors from the West. He even professed himself very sympathetic to the British. For, as he elaborated, the Portuguese of Macao had badly wronged him on a previous occasion—when he had served as their interpreter and intermediary at a recent Canton trade fair. He further related that he had been employed by those Iberians several years before quitting on account of abuse and mistreatment: "The said mandarin . . . would work the Portugals what mischief he could, by reason, as he said, they had wronged and disgraced him."[33] Captain Weddell and the fleet council decided to comply with all the envoy's requests and take him up on the promising offer to arrange trade for them. Thomas Robinson, John Mountney, Charles Webb, and three young assistants were chosen to go with this representative on the errand to

---

32. "We told him ['petty mandarin'] we were English men and came to seek a trade with them in a fair way of merchandising, but we had been abused by some of the under mandarins and some of our men slain by them, and for that cause we were constrained to do what we had done." "Weddell's China Narrative, O.C. 1662."
33. 16/26 August 1637, Mundy, *Travels*, vol. 3, 208.

Canton. To offer as gifts an embroidered cabinet, an exquisitely wrought basin and ewer of silver, as well as valuable trinkets and handicrafts cast in gold and silver were all put at the disposal of the Courteen envoys to present to their hosts in the provincial capital. As the British trade delegates prepared themselves to be escorted in a Chinese junk up the river to Canton, a sense of optimism began to grow. Captain Weddell and Nathaniel Mountney now felt a great deal more sanguine about their chances of establishing commercial relations with the Ming, independent of any mediation by—nay, in spite of—their perfidious allies the Portuguese. As Peter Mundy concluded at this juncture, after the meeting aboard the *Dragon* with the representative of the chief mandarins: "Now there appeared some hopes of settling a trade in these parts."[34]

---

34. 16/26 August 1637, Mundy, *Travels*, vol. 3, 208.

6

Captives at Canton

The Crisis of the Courteen Fleet at the Bogue, September–October 1637

Thomas Robinson, John Mountney, Charles Webb, and their three assistants rode up the Pearl River and arrived just outside Canton in the evening of 27 August 1637. They anchored a close distance from the residence of the "Champin," the "Admiral General."[1] Now the bilingual "petty mandarin," their escort, drafted for them a petition in Chinese to present at their audience. This document was signed by Robinson and Mountney. At about 3 o'clock in the afternoon of 28 August they were summoned ashore. After passing between long rows of guards, the British trade envoys were made to stand a hundred feet from the Champin and another high-ranking mandarin. Then they were commanded to kneel and bow. The petition ceremoniously hanging from Robinson's neck was taken by the Portuguese-speaking official to hand to his superiors.[2] From the Macao Portuguese translation that was subsequently made of this Chinese petition, drafted on behalf of the British, it is clear that the main point was to protest against the betrayal and malice of those Iberians while pleading for license to carry out commercial transactions like their fellow Europeans. On arrival in China the Courteens had attempted to initiate trade, but the Portuguese proved only "false and treacherous." While clearly insinuating that the Lusitanians had swindled and abused them at Macao, this petition presented to the Champin and the other mandarin at Canton also conveyed the charge that the Portuguese had murdered members of the British fleet: "[They] put poison in the food they gave us, and killed over forty of our men."[3] At their wits' end and in desperation, the petition explained, the British had left Macao for the Bogue to seek kinder treatment and procurement of urgently needed food and water. But here

---

1. "16/26 Aug. 1637: John Mountney and Thomas Robinson passed up the river, and the next evening arrived at the city, anchoring close under the walls in sight of the palace of Champin, the Admiral General." "Voyage of the Weddell Fleet."
2. "Passing through a treble guard placed in 3 courts, and at length coming in sight of the chiefs there assembled, they were willed, according to the country custom, to *sumba* or kneel, and Thomas Robinson, holding the petition at large [unfolded] extended upon his head, delivered it to [the bilingual mandarin] to carry up to Champin." "Voyage of the Weddell Fleet."
3. In the later account of the Portuguese, the number of poisoned claimed by the British is rendered higher: "In Canton, they presented a petition against us, to the Mandarins, in which they spoke of us in most insulting terms, and brought false charges against us, saying . . . that we had put poison into their food killing thereby 60 or 70 of their men and some pigs." Letter from the City of Macao to the King of England, 24 December 1637, *Lisbon Transcripts, Books of the Monsoons*, book 41, fol. 220.

94   *The First British Trade Expedition to China*

they were also treated most discourteously. The local mandarins "refusing to receive us," the British had eagerly accepted the invitation of the "Haitao" and Champin, conveyed and translated by their bilingual intermediary, to send trade representatives to Canton, while the rest of the fleet remained anchored at the Bogue.[4]

Concluding the petition which had been prepared for them by the "petty mandarin," Robinson and Mountney proposed that two of their six-member delegation, along with their escort, the bilingual representative, return to the fleet in the Bogue in order to fetch 20,000 taels (ounces of silver) to pay into the Ming emperor's treasury for license to trade. The other four Courteen delegates would remain in the provincial capital awaiting the commencement of trade. Robinson and Mountney were given to understand that the Champin approved of the arrangement and terms outlined in the British petition. This official also apparently concurred with Robinson and Mountney that the Portuguese of Macao were the true authors of all the trouble and suffering the Courteens had endured: "He presently consented unto [their petition's requests], and promised his utmost assistance, blaming the treachery of the Portugals, whom he taxed as authors, by their slanders, of all the precedent inconveniences."[5] He confirmed that the Lusitanians had been spreading the lie that the British were only pirates and marauders.

Accompanied by their bilingual broker, around midnight on 29 August, the Courteen envoys returned to the fleet in the Bogue to announce the good news that their requests to trade had been granted by the two high-ranking officials, Hai-tao and Champin.[6] They reported that officials in Canton would be appointed to work out the details of trade and supervise commercial transactions. From these two mandarins at Canton who had received the petition, the bilingual intermediary brought a placard composed of large Chinese characters and pasted on a wooden board.[7] In his fluent Portuguese the man summarized its contents for Captain Weddell and the fleet's council: in exchange for paying the Ming emperor's duties (in the same fashion as the Portuguese) the British could trade freely and set up a station in one of three selected places in the Pearl River estuary. The license also specified that the man was authorized to assist the Courteens in managing their commercial affairs during this visit. This representative of the authorities in Canton then requested that Captain Weddell select two or three merchants to go with him up to Canton where they could purchase such commodities as gold, musk, raw and wrought silk, fine handicrafts, porcelain, sugar, green ginger, and China root. It was suggested they go in the next day or two. Before the bilingual representative departed that night, the

---

4. "Copy of the first petition made by the English to the mandarins of Canton this year, 1637," *Lisbon Transcripts*, I.O. Records, Vol. IV, Mundy, *Travels*, vol. 3, 211.

5. "Voyage of the Weddell Fleet."

6. 19/29 August 1637, Mundy, *Travels*, vol. 3, 209.

7. "Our mandarin came again, bringing with him from the hai-tao, chompee, etts., (great men at Canton), a patent or *farman* in China writing, pasted on a great board such as are usually carried before men of office." 21/31 August 1637, Mundy, *Travels*, vol. 3, 212. Where Mundy sometimes uses "chompee" and "hai-tao," the other English records use the alternatives "Champin" and "Hitow." These variant spellings used by the Courteens to refer to Chinese officials are discussed in Chapter 8.

Courteen commander returned to him all the cannons and equipment taken from the fort which the British had stormed. The other captured junk and its occupants were also given back to this official.[8] The next day, 1 September, he came aboard again to inform Weddell that he had been summoned by the recently appointed provincial viceroy, "Tootan," who had just arrived at the capital. He promised the Courteens that when he had obtained an audience with this viceroy he would represent the British as favorably as possible and seek confirmation of the license he had just conveyed to them.[9]

In accordance with the terms of the license as explicated in Portuguese, then English, to Weddell, on 1 September the pinnace *Anne* was dispatched to survey the three designated places for a British anchorage and trade station. For this detail Weddell selected the master of the *Sun*, Thomas Woollman, Peter Mundy, and a Chinese-Portuguese speaking interpreter.[10] The first of the three places designated as a prospective base for the British was rejected for being too close to Macao. The second site, probably an island a little northwest of present-day Hong Kong, was rejected for being too remote and turbulent an anchorage.[11] Instead, they seem to have selected one of the two bays on the eastern shore of the estuary—close to present-day Shenzhen.[12] The water was somewhat too shallow to be optimal, but the location was accepted as a temporary expedient. This spot was also chosen by Woollman for its proximity to several small towns along that shore of the estuary.[13]

When Woollman and Mundy in the *Anne* returned to the fleet in the early hours of 5 September, they learned that Nathaniel Mountney, the head merchant of the fleet, his brother, John Mountney, and Thomas Robinson, along with two attendants, Simon Grey (a sailor from Richard Swanley's *Sun*) and Charles Webb, had two days before, in the morning of 3 September, departed for Canton with the bilingual official.[14] They had carried about a dozen chests of silver dollars (amounting to 22,000 "*real* of eight"), some chests of Japanese silver plate, as well as some cloth and precious, finely crafted objects that could be offered as gifts to the Ming officials. About half of this silver was to be submitted to the chief mandarins at Canton as customs duties; the remainder would be used to purchase commodities and merchandise. It took about two days for the British merchant delegation to reach the outskirts of Canton.[15] Most oddly, on the evening of 5 September their

---

8. 21/31 August 1637, Mundy, *Travels*, vol. 3, 212–13.
9. "Our mandarin came again and said the Tootan who is viceroy of this province of Canton, being new confirmed, was going in circuit to visit his government, and sent for him, so of necessity must go to him, and that he would inform him of us and so procure his confirmation of our patent aforesaid." 22 August / 1 September 1637, Mundy, *Travels*, vol. 3, 213.
10. 22 August / 1 September 1637, Mundy, *Travels*, vol. 3, 215.
11. The island in question might have been Lintin Island, now called Neilingdingdao (內伶仃島).
12. This would place them in the vicinity of that part of the coast now occupied by the Shenzhen Bao'an International Airport.
13. 22 August / 1 September 1637, Mundy, *Travels*, vol. 3, 216.
14. 26 August / 5 September 1637, Mundy, *Travels*, vol. 3, 216; "Voyage of the Weddell Fleet."
15. "Voyage of the Weddell Fleet."

escort had them garbed in Chinese outfits ("China habit") before they disembarked and then ushered them to a house located in a suburb of the city.[16] This, they understood, was the home of a relative of their liaison, and to this residence was brought all the silver and goods appointed for duties, gift, and exchange.[17] The next day, 6 September, Nathaniel Mountney dispatched a note to be carried back to the Courteen fleet; this took only a day to reach Weddell and informed the British commander that all was proceeding well so far.[18] Nathaniel Mountney then submitted 10,000 silver dollars, the customs duties, and proceeded to negotiate prices for Chinese commodities and manufactures.[19] In the next several days, he closed deals to purchase eighty tons of sugar, a large quantity of ginger, musk, raw and wrought silk, gold chains, and miscellaneous provisions for the British fleet.[20] He, his brother John, and Robinson, and their two assistants, Grey and Webb, were confined to the house, so transactions were made at a decided disadvantage: they were permitted to view only samples, not the bulk; nor were they granted any opportunity to observe the weighing of them.[21] But besides those significant drawbacks, operations seemed to be proceeding smoothly. Accordingly, Robinson would be sent back to the fleet in order to fetch more silver dollars to purchase more goods, as well as to bring pachak and incense to sell to Chinese merchants.[22] Pachak, or costus root, was always in demand at Canton and other parts of China for use as a digestive in Chinese medicine. The Courteens must have made sure to acquire some before arriving at Macao at the beginning of July.

In the meantime, on 8 September, Captain Weddell had dispatched Peter Mundy and a companion to communicate with the commander of the Chinese junks anchored in the Bogue. The British requested permission to move the ships a little farther up for better safety. It was feared that a typhoon or hurricane could strike soon, for the weather had turned stormy—the Chinese junks had been placed

---

16. "Seeming cautious that we should be seen, [the bilingual Chinese] caused us to keep ourselves close until our arrival, and about midnight brought us, clothed in China habit, into the suburbs of the town with all our monies and goods." Mountney, Rawlinson, A.299. Although Weddell was not there, his account records that they were escorted into the suburbs in "mandarins' clothes" by the bilingual, who "brought them to a kinsman's house of his, and there lodged them." "Weddell's China Narrative, O.C. 1662."

17. "Voyage of the Weddell Fleet."

18. "A letter came from our principals at Canton, signifying of their safe arrival with health, and how they were introduced into the city in the habit of Chinois, but as yet not a word of trade." 28 August / 7 September 1637, Mundy, *Travels*, vol. 3, 217.

19. Mountney, Rawlinson, A.299.

20. "There were sent 1500 pikul of green ginger at 7 1/2 *reals* the pikul, and the rest (save what for necessary expenses) imprested [advanced on account] for the same commodity, proposing large quantities of sugar, both in regard of its cheapness here and its sale in Europe and India to be most fit for the bulk of our lading, and the rest to be employed in such silk stuffs as are most vendible in India and Europe." Mountney, Rawlinson, A.299. "Having first paid 10 thousand reals of 8, agreed upon for custom and duties, they began to bargain for sugar, ginger, stuffs, etc. insomuch that in 5 days they had procured the quantity of 80 ton sugar, besides ginger and other merchandise and provisions for the ships, and had given out monies according to the use of the country for very great parcels, with much encouragement." "Voyage of the Weddell Fleet."

21. Mountney, Rawlinson, A.299.

22. Mountney, Rawlinson, A.299.

in a sheltering creek in expectation of the arrival of inclement winds and waves. The Chinese commander replied that he had no authority to grant such a request.[23] The next day Weddell disregarded this unsatisfactory response and moved the ships about two miles farther up to Tiger Island (大虎 Dahu) to take cover beside a hill.[24] Then the following day, 10 September, the British rode a favorable current two or three leagues up the Pearl River in hopes of obtaining more desperately needed water and provisions. At a village which the Courteens called "Muncoo" (perhaps a bit beyond the Second Bar at the approach to Canton), they procured nearly nothing.[25]

On 11 September, Captain Weddell received another message from the factors at Canton. Nathaniel Mountney apprized him that news of the fleet's anchoring at Tiger Island had already reached the city. The cape merchant requested that the commander return the fleet to its less intrusive place in the Bogue, a greater distance from Canton—and keep the ships there at least temporarily in order to manifest a less threatening posture.[26] Mountney also informed Weddell that he had already been able to purchase large amounts of white sugar and green ginger, to be brought to the British ships in the Bogue the next day. The captain declined to follow the suggestion by the chief factor in Canton: Weddell did not move the ships back down the river. Instead, he maintained his position as he received another visit from the Portuguese-speaking Chinese who came back with Thomas Robinson from Canton on 15 September to fetch the vendible commodities (including pachak and incense) and silver dollars. The next day there followed two junks carrying the sugar and ginger just purchased by Mountney in Canton.[27] Chinese vessels also arrived to sell victuals including pears, chestnuts, raisins, and lychee.[28] Mountney sent a request with his colleague Robinson that Weddell disburse another six chests of silver dollars. And now their Chinese facilitator assured the British commander that within a month all the Courteen ships could be fully laden. He also arranged for about twenty Chinese carpenters from Canton to come to the British ships to pack all the sugar Nathaniel Mountney had purchased there.[29]

On 16 September three sculling junks from Macao approached the British fleet. They were manned by Portuguese and mestizos and brought a protest signed by

---

23. 29 August / 8 September 1637, Mundy, *Travels*, vol. 3, 218–19.

24. 30 August / 9 September 1637, Mundy, *Travels*, vol. 3, 219.

25. 31 August / 10 September 1637, Mundy, *Travels*, vol. 3, 219.

26. 1/11 September 1637, Mundy, *Travels*, vol. 3, 220–21.

27. "There came down in the said vessel [with Robinson] about 1,000 quintals of sugar at royal [*real* of eight] 3 per quintal and upon 50 quintals of green ginger at about 7 real [of eight] per quintal." Mundy, 8/18 September 1637, Mundy, *Travels*, vol. 3, 222.

28. "The next day came much sugar for lading and provision for the ships, among the rest the Chineses brought to sell pears, chestnuts, dried lychees as sweet as any raisins of the sun." 5/15 September 1637, Mundy, *Travels*, vol. 3, 221.

29. In Weddell's narrative we are told that it was "promised to load us all within a month after his coming down . . . so that our business went very fairly forward, and we had about 20 China carpenters came from Canton to make chests to pack up sugar and sugar candy, which cost 1 1/2*d* per pound and as white as snow." "Weddell's China Narrative, O.C. 1662."

the captain-general Domingos da Camara de Noronha and members of the city council.[30] After the leaders of the municipal government had met to discuss policy to be adopted towards the British, two of its senior members had been delegated to go in the boats to the Courteen fleet.[31] According to the captain-general's later account, the Macao elders "were received with great haughtiness."[32] The document they presented to the British was dated 7 September and was addressed to the "Commander and Factor of the English Fleet," that is, Captain Weddell and Nathaniel Mountney.[33] After reviewing what had transpired between the Portuguese and British at the latter's arrival back in early July, and justifying their subsequent conduct, the captain-general and council complained that the Courteens had made massive and gratuitous mischief by entering the Bogue without consulting them or first receiving permission from Chinese authorities in Canton. In the first place, the Portuguese emphasized, they were not at liberty or authorized to receive and facilitate British trade at Macao because they were within the jurisdiction of the Chinese emperor: "It was not within our power to welcome, treat and serve your worships, either as vassals of so powerful a king [Charles I] deserve, for we are not in a land which belongs to our king."[34] Even if that were not an insuperable barrier, the British well knew that they at Macao had received authorization neither from their monarch, Philip IV, nor their imperial superior, the viceroy of Goa, Pero da Silva. The aggressive actions of the British would cause the Portuguese incalculable harm, not least heavy punitive fines, at the hands of the Chinese; for the latter had, since the fleet's arrival in July, been blaming the Lusitanians for receiving if not inviting these European foreigners into China.[35] By bringing the entire Courteen fleet deep into the Pearl River, Portuguese relations with the Chinese had been rendered uneasy and tense. They themselves, long-time residents of China, had never once dared to sail their ships so far towards Canton—let alone to enter the Bogue with such large, ordnance-packed vessels like the *Dragon*, *Sun*, and *Katherine*. Moreover, holding the Portuguese responsible for this unprecedented and dangerous intrusion, and accusing them of approving or aiding and abetting the British,

---

30. 6/16 September 1637, Mundy, *Travels*, vol. 3, 221.

31. Domingos da Camara de Noronha to the viceroy of Goa, 27 December 1637, *Lisbon Transcripts, Books of the Monsoons*, book 41, fol. 191.

32. Domingos da Camara de Noronha to the viceroy of Goa, 27 December 1637, *Lisbon Transcripts, Books of the Monsoons*, book 41, fol. 191. For a description of the reception of the Macao emissaries almost identical to the captain-general's, see Letter from the City of Macao to the King of England, 24 December 1637, *Lisbon Transcripts, Books of the Monsoons*, book 41, fol. 220.

33. "Given in this city of the name of God in China, commonly known as Macao, on the 7th of September 1637, over our signatures only, Domingos da Camara, Antonio da Silveira Aranha, Estevan Pires, Francisco de Aranjo Darros, Luiz Pais Pacheco, Domingos Dias Espinhel, Matheu Ferreira de Proenca." *Lisbon Transcripts*, I.O. Records, Vol. IV.

34. Macao Protest of 7 September 1637, *Lisbon Transcripts*, I.O. Records, Vol. IV.

35. "Any trade that we might have with you would cost us many vexations and annoyance with the great mandarins, and loss of property; although the ship *London* came with a Portuguese factor and merchants and anchored at a great distance from this city, nevertheless she brought great trouble and loss upon this city." Macao Protest of 7 September 1637, *Lisbon Transcripts*, I.O. Records, Vol. IV.

the Chinese authorities were now commanding Macao to use any means, fair or foul, to expel the British: "The mandarins are much disturbed and anxious, seeing your ships where our vessels have never reached, and they send us many orders that we do command your worships to quit their kingdom, compelling us to make your worships put out to the open sea, and deliver their ports from you."[36] Thus, the Portuguese formally demanded that the British immediately evacuate the Bogue and depart from China. The protest also reminded Captain Weddell that the recent accord made by the Portuguese and the British at Goa could not be construed to intend or entail such direct harm to the Portuguese interests at Macao. But clearly the actions taken by the Courteens were achieving precisely that adverse effect. In other words, the British were blatantly violating the terms of the Goa Convention of 1635. The captain-general and the municipal council wished to register in writing their sense that at least in spirit a breach of the accord had been committed by Weddell and the Courteens; and this formal protest at the British behavior they would convey to Kings Charles I and Philip IV.[37]

On the same day as its receipt, 16 September, Captain Weddell composed a curt and contemptuous reply conveyed in Latin, to be brought back to the captain-general and city council by their envoys.[38] Characterizing the Portuguese protest as exceedingly condescending and offensive, the commander boasted that their present enterprise in the Bogue and at Canton was proceeding very profitably. Noting but brushing aside the sanctimonious remonstration of the captain-general, Weddell hastened to the point: "We shall fight your people with blood and sweat to the end."[39] In a more subtle vein, however, and most pointedly, Weddell expressed his sardonic wonder: if, as the Portuguese so heavily emphasized, these lands and waters were clearly within Chinese sovereignty, then why should the British have begged the permission of the Iberian king or any of his viceroys, whether in India or at Macao: "This land, as you yourself acknowledge, is not yours, but the king of China's. Why then should we wait for license from the king of Castile or his petty viceroys in these parts?"[40] From the British captain's view, if the Portuguese

---

36. Macao Protest of 7 September 1637, *Lisbon Transcripts*, I.O. Records, Vol. IV.
37. Macao Protest of 7 September 1637, *Lisbon Transcripts*, I.O. Records, Vol. IV. The Protest concludes: "And should your worships not comply, we demand by your noble persons that you make report to their Majesties the kings of England and Spain of the losses, damage, and annoyance we have suffered from the mandarins and governors of China through your presence in this port, and from the journey you made to the mouth of the river of Canton. And if it should be necessary to make further requisition and protest to your worships upon this matter, we hold that it is here done, expressed and declared, with all details, clauses and conditions by law required, further protesting in the name of our lord, the king of Spain, that our not receiving your worships in this port for the reasons above declared shall not prejudice his royal position respecting the continuation or rupture of the peace which he so willingly concluded with his Majesty the king of England."
38. Captain Weddell's Answer to Macao 7 September Protest, 16 September 1637, *Lisbon Transcripts*, I.O. Records, Vol. IV. If Thomas Robinson was not present, most likely it was the *Dragon's* chaplain Arthur Hatch who composed the Latin for Weddell.
39. Captain Weddell's Answer to Macao 7 September Protest, 16 September 1637, *Lisbon Transcripts*, I.O. Records, Vol. IV.
40. Captain Weddell's Answer to Macao 7 September Protest, 16 September 1637, *Lisbon Transcripts*, I.O. Records, Vol. IV.

would not help them trade with the Chinese from Macao then there was no decent reason why the British should not make their own separate attempt to undertake it independently: to propose trade to the Chinese authorities in Canton without any assistance of Portuguese mediation. But rather than squander precious time rebutting all the points of the Lusitanians or elaborating upon the reasons for his own conduct, Weddell bragged that he had much better things to do—for commerce with the Chinese in Canton was now advancing at a brisk pace: "We have no leisure at present, because of other occupations, to answer your vulgar letters more at length."[41] As if gloating upon the deep penetration of China via the Bogue and the unprecedented commercial breakthrough, the British commander recorded his location at writing his reply, not accurately as somewhere along a shore or island of the Pearl River, but "from our ships in the *port of Canton*."[42]

On 17 September Captain Weddell produced the six chests of silver dollars requested by Nathaniel Mountney in Canton. This money was placed in the custody of the bilingual Chinese agent to transport up to the provincial capital. Prior to leaving, this representative of the provincial authorities instructed Weddell also to send the rest of the silver and the remainder of the goods that the British would be able sell at Canton.[43] Accordingly, the next day, 18 September, Thomas Robinson, Simon Grey, and one of Nathaniel Mountney's servants used the vessel which had transported the sugar to carry back to Canton fourteen chests of silver dollars, as well as another large cargo of incense and pachak, some cloth and fine goods readily vendible in the Chinese market.[44]

While this Anglo-Chinese commerce now seemed to be gaining momentum if not positively flourishing, on Sunday, 20 September the Courteens almost suffered catastrophe. Their ships anchored at Tiger Island, having just been careened the previous day, at about 2 o'clock in the morning, the crew of the *Anne* noticed some large junks approaching.[45] The mariners of the pinnace hailed them but received no response. Since the crew supposed they might be some more Chinese vessels engaged in carrying goods from Canton to the British fleet, they decided not to fire any shots and instead let them pass. But the junks then sailed swiftly towards Captain John Carter's *Katherine*, whose crew issued a warning shot at them. The shot fired from the *Katherine* served to awaken the other Courteen ships to the

---

41. Captain Weddell's Answer to Macao 7 September Protest, 16 September 1637, *Lisbon Transcripts*, I.O. Records, Vol. IV. The recently initiated commerce supervised by the Mountneys and Robinson in Canton is described as "an undertaking so profitable and so certain."
42. Captain Weddell's Answer to Macao 7 September Protest, 16 September 1637, *Lisbon Transcripts*, I.O. Records, Vol. IV; emphasis added.
43. "Our mandarin returned to Canton, there being 6 chests of real of eight entrusted unto him, which he carried away in his own boat with other goods. But before his departure he persuaded to send up all the treasure [silver] they could and almost all commodities vendible here." 7/17 September 1637, Mundy, *Travels*, vol. 3, 227.
44. "Voyage of the Weddell Fleet." "Mr. Robinson departed also in the great vessel that brought down the sugar. He carried with him much incense and all the pachak in the fleet." 8/18 September 1637, Mundy, *Travels*, vol. 3, 228.
45. 10/20 September 1637, Mundy, *Travels*, vol. 3, 228, 232, 233.

Captives at Canton

possibility of danger. Suddenly two of the Chinese junks burst into flame. Chained together and blazing high, they were now hurtling upon a combustible collision course with the British fleet. Yet another junk burst into flame and lunged towards the fleet in the same manner. The *Dragon*, *Sun*, and *Katherine* instantly cut the cables of their anchors to get out of the way. They shifted in the nick of time to dodge the blazing ships spouting Greek fire, metal projectiles, and flaming arrows. As witnessed first-hand by Peter Mundy: "The fire was vehement. Balls of wild fire, rockets, and fire-arrows flew thick as they passed by us. The fire was very high and violent and the brightness thereof so great in that dark night that the hills reflected light. The confused noise was no less, as well of the mariners on the one side crying and calling to their fellows about the ships, working with their heedless hasty running on the decks, as also of the crackling of the burnt bamboos, whizzing of the rockets."[46] One of the flaming junks crashed on the shores of Tiger Island; another two missed the island and were carried out of sight by a current towards the Pearl River estuary.[47]

At the break of dawn, the British were much relieved to have escaped such a ferocious and monstrous attack by night. But now they had much fresh worry to preoccupy them. Who was behind this fiery fleet launched to annihilate them? Had this been an offensive designed by the Portuguese or Chinese? Or was it a joint-operation? But if the Chinese authorities in Canton were as favorably disposed as the bilingual envoy had represented them to be, why had they just been attacked with such frightful and lethal firepower? It seems the Courteens most suspected that this massive assault had been prompted if not plotted or carried out by the Portuguese. But whatever the role played by the Lusitanians, had Captain Weddell and his council made a mistake to put their trust in the Portuguese-speaking representative who had just been facilitating and supervising their trade? If so, the merchants in Canton could be at serious risk. During the morning Weddell sent parties to scour the island in hopes of finding any who had swum ashore after thrusting the fire-ships. The British had observed many men jumping overboard once the ships had been set ablaze. Immediately following the attack, they captured only one Chinese crew member; the rest were observed swimming ashore. This Chinese combatant had tried to elude them by diving under the water, but they thrust pikes into the river to pluck him out. By the time they got him on board, his limbs, back, and belly were pierced. One lunge of a pike had traversed his torso.[48] As the Courteen surgeons treated him, he coughed up some words, but they had no interpreter on hand to glean any meaning. The best the British could ascertain was that he was from Fujian. Once all his wounds were dressed, he was placed in fetters.[49]

---

46. 10/20 September 1637, Mundy, *Travels*, vol. 3, 228–29.
47. 10/20 September 1637, Mundy, *Travels*, vol. 3, 229.
48. 10/20 September 1637, Mundy, *Travels*, vol. 3, 229–30.
49. The accounts of Mundy and Weddell do not exactly agree on what was learned from the injured Fujianese. According to Mundy in his entry for 10/20 September 1637: "By relation of the surgeons, something he said, but for want of an interpreter could not be understood." According to the captain: "We had taken up a

On Tiger Island they found no Chinese, but they did discover a beached junk.[50] It had been packed to unleash the same explosive flame and projectiles as the others but had evidently been abandoned before being lit. Bags of gunpowder and other combustible matter, as well as grapnel and chests of fire-arrows were found scattered among kindling and dry wood. Attached to these arrows were small pieces of jagged wire to snag masts, sail, or tackling. Other metal projectiles were found aboard, as well as iron chains that hung off the junk in order to latch cables. After salvaging everything useful, the British set the junk on fire. The flames consuming the vessel were mighty enough to scorch the grass of a nearby hill. Meanwhile, one of the boats that had been dispatched by Captain Weddell to seize any leaders or participants of the offensive was surprised by three or four junks on the other side of Tiger Island. These were small junks but fully manned. Members of the Courteen crew thought they saw on board one of these Chinese junks a Portuguese man brandishing a sword and tauntingly waving his hat at them. This sight only deepened their suspicion that if the Portuguese had not designed and orchestrated, then they had at least collaborated with the Chinese in the attack. As Mundy related: "It is presupposed that they join with the Chinois and have instigated them against us not to permit us to trade."[51]

At or on the outskirts of Canton, the Mountney brothers with their attendant, Charles Webb, were awaiting the return of Thomas Robinson, Simon Grey, and an assistant of Nathaniel Mountney. They had been doing so in vain. For with all the silver dollars, merchandise, and commodities, Robinson and his assistants were seized on their passage between the Bogue and the capital. Within four leagues of Canton, they had been intercepted by a junk of the imperial fleet. The three British were hauled aboard the Ming vessel, and all their money and property confiscated and taken into town to be placed at the disposal of the authorities. No communication could be effected between the separated Courteen factors at Canton: the Mountneys and Charles Webb on the one side; Thomas Robinson, Simon Grey, and a young assistant on the other. Nor could any of them send to or receive messages from the Courteen ships still at Tiger Island, so they had no idea how the fleet was faring in the Bogue.[52] But apparently word from some source reached Captain Weddell, informing him that his men had been arrested. Recognizing that his fleet's

---

Chincho [Fujianese] who was swimming to the shore (he having fired the first junk) by our boats, who with half pikes had pierced through his arms and thighs, and was brought aboard half dead. Our surgeons cured his wounds (he being kept in irons), who told us who had set him on work. Moreover, he said there were 3 more [ships] ready and 100 small fisher boats to second them if they missed." "Weddell's China Narrative, O.C. 1662."

50. A fourth junk had been designed for the same assault, but was torched too early so never approached the fleet and crashed against a shore a few miles away. 10/20 September 1637, Mundy, *Travels*, vol. 3, 230.

51. 10/20 September 1637, Mundy, *Travels*, vol. 3, 231.

52. "Nathaniel and John Mountney with one youth [Charles Webb], being in Canton, and Thomas Robinson with a servant of N.M. and a sailor [Simon Grey] of the ship *Sun* detained aboard the king's junk, neither the one nor the other party could procure the conveyance of a letter, nor could come to understand what had passed below with the ships, nor how their own cases stood for many days." 14/24 September 1637, "Voyage of the Weddell Fleet."

Captives at Canton

present position could irritate the Ming officials and apprehensive that another fire-ship attack might be launched, on 21 September the British commander sailed the fleet a little south, down the Bogue, to anchor again below Aniangxie, on the eastern shore of the river, close to where they had stormed the fort a few weeks ago.[53] To maintain their more forward position at Tiger Island, it was supposed, they might cause their detained merchants harsher treatment in the capital. On 22 September British boats took two sculling Chinese men-of-war. They expected to seize Portuguese aboard, but the captured vessels were deserted, all their men having swum ashore. The following day, 23 September, the junks, unspoiled and undamaged, were returned to a Chinese official nearby. Weddell hoped that this conciliatory act might serve to persuade the authorities to act benevolently towards his men in Canton; no message from them had come for eight days.[54]

The British were able to lay their hands on a runaway Portuguese slave called Francisco who had subsequently fled from Chinese masters. According to their new recruit, many both aboard the Chinese fleet and along the shore were reporting that there was a fifteen-member delegation of Portuguese arrived at Canton conspiring to foil and sabotage the British effort to transact commerce with Chinese merchants. Rumor continued to swirl and circulate that all the troubles and harm done to the Courteens had been orchestrated by the Lusitanians at Macao. It was said that the latter were trying to extinguish British trade with the Chinese by offering the latter more money and payment of further customs duties on goods arriving at Macao from India, Melaka, Manila, and Japan.[55] Francisco also told the British that an even more massive fire-ship assault was being prepared: seven huge junks, courtesy of the Portuguese, and a hundred small boats, packed even more explosively than their abortive and miscarried predecessors. All were only awaiting chains and grapnel to be ready for launch by Chinese pilots. Word seems to have spread that the British would also be the target of a fleet brought over from Fujian. According to Francisco, the versatile and fierce "Chincheos" (as the Fujianese mariners and mercenaries are invariably represented in the English accounts) would be supplied with gunpowder and ammunition by the Portuguese. The runaway slave also warned that any food and drink brought to the British from the shore would be poisoned. Yet another rumor indicated that all the Guangdong provincial officials from Macao to Canton were now united in a policy of hostility towards the British. Whether in reaction to this batch of rumors communicated by Francisco or the strong winds of

---

53. 11/21 September 1637, Mundy, *Travels*, vol. 3, 235.

54. "We restored the said junks again unto the mandarins untouched, the better to get our merchants freed from aloft, who now we began to fear were in some trouble, having not heard from them these 8 days." 13/23 September 1637, Mundy, *Travels*, vol. 3, 236.

55. "By Francisco, a Portugal slave, run from them to the Chinois and from them again unto our hands, we understood, according to his own relation (the truth we know not, but as he said was the general report of all sorts of people both aboard their fleet as also on shore), viz., that there were 15 Portugals at Canton negotiating against us and that all our disturbances were wrought by their procurement, who offer large sums and new customs on all goods that should come unto Macao from India, Manila, Japan or any place else unto the Chinois to debar us from trade." 13/23 September 1637, Mundy, *Travels*, vol. 3, 236.

the northeasterly monsoon which had been blowing over the waters in recent days, Captain Weddell moved the fleet a league or two farther down the Bogue away from Canton on 24 September.[56]

Back in the provincial capital, around 24 September, the situation changed drastically for the worse for the Courteen factors. The host of the Mountneys, as well as his son, were arrested and dragged to prison in ropes and chains around their necks.[57] The rest of the host's household, its occupants, food, and fuel, were removed. Placards were posted on the doors to prohibit all entry. A detachment of soldiers was stationed on the street to guard its access. For a few days, the Mountneys and Charles Webb, under house arrest, locked in the dwelling, were left to shift for themselves, to subsist on merely a little biscuit and spirits (*arak*). Growing desperate in such strait confinement, they were compelled to resort to violence in seek of redress. Armed with swords and pistols they then stacked up wood against the doors and prepared to set a fire. As the Mountneys were getting ready to ignite the pile, the guards outside noticed their unusual activity and communicated an order to desist. To the mandarin whom they took to be in charge of them they sent a note to relate this incident. That official responded with a demand for an explanation of their dangerous stunt. The Mountneys complained that having been treated so inhumanely, they had been left no choice but to signify their grievance by setting fire to the town in hopes of escape—or to perish in the attempt. This official consented to unlock the doors of the dwelling, but the guard remained in place as before.[58] Since the soldiers would still not permit any vendors to approach the house, several times John Mountney went out into the street to accost those coming and going from the market. Brandishing a sword with one hand and displaying silver dollars in the other, he induced some passers-by to sell their fish or meat.[59]

Still bereft of any communication from his factors in the provincial capital, on 27 September Captain Weddell convened a meeting of the fleet's council. The majority were of the mind that the fleet should repair to Macao and address the

---

56. 13/23 September 1637, Mundy, *Travels*, vol. 3, 236. Notions of a fleet coming down from Fujian was also recorded in Nathaniel Mountney's report: "hearing of more fireworks a-preparing, and divers rumors of a fleet of Chincheos daily expected." Mountney, Rawlinson, A.299.

57. The phrasing in the account of this incident written by Nathaniel Mountney (Rawlinson, A.299) would permit the notion that it was the bilingual Chinese himself and the host who were arrested and thrown in prison: "Hoyto [elsewhere: "hai-tao" and "Hittow"] or lord chancellor, not contented with the division of the 10,000 reals [silver dollars], claps both him and our host in prison." But the other Courteen report, drafted by him or his brother John, indicates it was the host and his son: "And at this time was the host of their house, together with his son, haled forth to prison with ropes and chains about their necks." "Voyage of the Weddell Fleet."

58. "Voyage of the Weddell Fleet." Mountney does not specify who this official was: whether "hai-tao" or "champin" or someone else.

59. The mandarin's consent to loosen their confinement may have been caused not by, or solely by, the menacing, fire-threatening exhibition by the Mountney brothers: "They [the brothers] made answer that being so treacherously dealt withal, and having no other present redress, they intended to revenge themselves by firing the town, and so with the extreme hazard of their lives, either to force a passage or to die in the attempt; which resolution of theirs being a quality whereof those cowardly people [the Chinese] are not much guilty), *together with the bad success of the fire junks and the revenge which ours in the ships were then prosecuting*, caused him [the official] presently to order the doors to be opened." "Voyage of the Weddell Fleet"; emphasis added.

Portuguese with a protest and demand for reparations—after all, it was those perfidious allies who were fundamentally to blame for all their problems, including the current detention of their men, money, and goods at Canton.[60] On the following day, however, Weddell and the Courteen leadership decided on a contrary set of actions.[61] Instead of confronting the Portuguese at Macao, the British would make an ostentatious and purposive display of force: raiding and plundering the Chinese in the fleet's vicinity. It was calculated that complaints of British marauding and onslaughts in the Bogue would reach the authorities at Canton, who would construe this as a retaliatory protest at the incarceration of the fleet's merchants and confiscation of their property and money. Thus resolved, on the evening of 28 September, Weddell took the offensive again, launching well-armed vessels to inflict damage and obtain provisions from small Chinese boats and towns nearby. By dawn of the next day, the British had torched five small junks, two of which had been loaded with explosive material, apparently readied for deployment as fire-ships. On a shore along the Pearl River, they set fire to the village they had previously visited, "Fumaon," after taking a man and a few dozen hogs and pigs.[62] The next day, 30 September, the Courteens went ashore once more in hopes of hearing from local inhabitants news about their merchants under arrest at the capital. They were told that two local mandarins had gone up to Canton with the hope of bringing the merchants back in a few days in order to placate the rampaging Courteen fleet.[63] Remarkably, despite the provincial authorities' prohibition on intercourse with and hostile stance towards the Courteens, native Chinese in the waters and shores of the Bogue remained willing if not eager to trade with the odd-looking foreigners: "Divers boats and junks would come and sell . . . but they came by stealth."[64]

The British continued the onslaught for another few days. One Courteen detachment proceeded to the previously stormed fort, which they found deserted and unfurnished, as they had left it. Weddell dispatched boats a small distance up the river to Tiger Island, where they succeeded in burning one large junk. From this ship of the imperial fleet, equipped with a dozen ordnance, eight Chinese were captured. The British attempted another large junk in the same manner but were

---

60. 17/27 September 1637, Mundy, *Travels*, vol. 3, 237.
61. 18/28 September 1637, Mundy, *Travels*, vol. 3, 237.
62. 18/28 September 1637, Mundy, *Travels*, vol. 3, 237–38; "No man coming near unto us to tell us what was become of our merchants and money, so that we resolved to get them by force or to lose all our lives, and fitted our long boats with a drake [small ordnance] in each boat's head and our skiffs and barge all well-manned, and at 5 in the morning the 19th [29th] September we set upon 16 sail of the king's man of war and fought with them 1/2 hour, in which time we burned 5 of them (3 of them were fire junks); the rest made their escape. The same day our boats took the town of Fumaon which they pillaged and burnt, and by the [blank] was fired another junk, and returned aboard without any damage on our side." "Weddell's China Narrative, O.C. 1662." "Fumaon" is also used by Mundy. He had recorded the fleet's anchoring near there on 8/18 August. This village was most likely on or in the vicinity of present-day Aniangxie/Xidatan (西大坦), north of Tiger Island (大虎).
63. "We sent ashore to know of the country people whether they could tell us any news of our merchants. They told us that 2 mandarins were gone for them and would be here again within 2 days." 20/30 September 1637, Mundy, *Travels*, vol. 3, 238.
64. "Weddell's China Narrative, O.C. 1662."

prevented from boarding by the hurling of heavy stones, iron bars, and an assortment of other projectiles. On Tiger Island they found deserted dwellings to burn down. Their hope of foraging and pillaging was for the most part disappointed, however. Meanwhile, on the same day, the captains of the British fleet returned to the fort and laid three barrels of gunpowder that exploded most of the remaining wall and damaged the rest of the structure still standing.[65] Presumably this was conceived as yet another protest to be observed by the mandarins in the provincial capital. On 4 October, Captain Weddell received another communication from the authorities there. They instructed the British to stay put, cease their raiding and offensive maneuvers and marauding, and wait another ten days for a resolution of the case concerning their merchants, money, and goods.[66]

This was assumed to be just another attempt by the Ming authorities in Canton to buy time to organize or launch a new defensive or offensive operation. So the next day, 5 October, Weddell resumed the sort of marauding that had been carried out in recent days. When another large junk came near the fleet, Weddell sent the barge and the *Sun*'s skiff in pursuit. This junk not only thwarted the British attempt to board by tossing heavy iron darts but also, with the shot of a harquebus, inflicted a fatal wound on the quartermaster of the *Sun*, Christopher Barker. Perceiving the peril in which the Courteen boats found themselves, and cognizant of their shortage of gunpowder, the *Anne* was dispatched to reinforce those smaller vessels; but the pinnace could not get near enough to make good use of its ordnance. Shortly after this engagement, Antonio, the fugitive Ethiopian slave and Luso-Chinese interpreter, who had been in several places around the Bogue in preceding weeks, returned to Weddell in the *Dragon*. He rendered his opinion to Weddell that when the Canton authorities had issued a communication to the British commander to wait ten more days, it was only a pretext to afford sufficient time for the Fujianese fleet to arrive. Antonio informed the Courteen leaders that rumor had it that these "Chincheo" ships were expected any day now. He further admonished the captains that with a dark moon imminent, another fire-ship attack would probably be launched.[67]

---

65. 21 September / 1 October and 22 September / 2 October 1637, Mundy, *Travels*, vol. 3; "Weddell's China Narrative, O.C. 1662."
66. 24 September / 4 October 1637, Mundy, *Travels*, vol. 3, 240.
67. 25 September / 5 October 1637, Mundy, *Travels*, vol. 3, 240.

7

Negotiation and Liberation

Restoration at Canton and Trade at Macao, October–December 1637

In view of the possibility of more fire-ship attacks and other worrisome contingencies, on 6 October 1637 Captain Weddell led the fleet out of the Bogue and farther down the Pearl River estuary, to anchor at a large island—probably Lintin Island, or what is now called Neilingdingdao (內伶仃島).[1] The Courteen leadership had determined to communicate with Macao again. In their desperation to rescue their factors, if not their confiscated money and goods as well, Portuguese agency was obviously the most viable alternative to their own independent efforts at redress and recovery. Thus, on 7 October, the fleet anchored within four leagues of the Portuguese enclave.[2] Besides putting the British in an expedient place for frequent communication with those Iberians, Captain Weddell would also be in advantageous position to confront or intercept their ships that would soon be returning from Japan.[3] The prospect of the British preying upon the Japan fleet would provide some leverage for the Courteens.[4] Weddell now dispatched the pinnace *Anne* and the admiral *Dragon*'s barge to carry a protest-cum-appeal to the authorities at Macao, specifically the captain-general and the municipal council (Senado da Camara).[5]

After a preamble reviewing the circumstances surrounding its signing and the key clauses ("free entry and trade of your ports") of the Anglo-Portuguese accord made at Goa in 1635—and the treatment received by the British fleet from the Portuguese at Goa the previous year—Captain Weddell described the more recent hostile actions of the Portuguese at Macao. This conduct of the Portuguese was all the more outrageous given the fact that the captain-general himself had received

---

1. 26 September / 6 October 1637, Mundy, *Travels*, vol. 3, 241; "Weddell's China Narrative, O.C. 1662."
2. 27 September / 7 October 1637, Mundy, *Travels*, vol. 3, 241.
3. "The time of the year and winter coming on, we resolved to go for Macao and protest against the governor and council for all such damages as had befallen us, to so berth ourselves that *they could not come from Japan but they must of necessity come through us.*" "Weddell's China Narrative, O.C. 1662"; emphasis added.
4. "Now as the English were disillusioned and imagined that all their misfortunes were due to our machinations, they came and stationed themselves near certain islands five leagues hence, with the intention of lying in wait for the fleet from Japan, which had of necessity to pass that way." Domingos da Camara de Noronha to the viceroy of Goa, 27 December 1637, *Lisbon Transcripts, Books of the Monsoons*, book 41, fol. 191. Likewise, the City of Macao later related: "They intended to take vengeance for the injuries they believed we had done them, by seizing six vessels from Japan." Letter from the City of Macao to the King of England, 24 December 1637, *Lisbon Transcripts, Books of the Monsoons*, book 41, fol. 220.
5. 27 September / 7 October 1637, Mundy, *Travels*, vol. 3, 241; "Voyage of the Weddell Fleet."

such a gracious letter from the British monarch, Charles I. Whatever conduct of the Lusitanians had at first looked cordial or cooperative now appeared mere stalling and obfuscation: "During the whole of our stay, both by letters and by speech in conference with persons of standing in the city, you held out to us the hope of open trade after the departure of the fleet of Japan, which we permitted to depart in peace. And when your worships learnt that it was in safety, you sent a messenger to us to ask what further we required, as we had already received the reply and there was nothing further to wait for."[6] Since the Portuguese had treated them so shabbily and contemptuously at Macao, they had been compelled to go up to the Bogue to obtain provisions and probe the possibilities of trading directly with the Chinese. Contrary to what the Lusitanians instructed them to expect, upon arriving at the mouth of the Pearl River, the Courteens had received courteous treatment from native Chinese—more cordial reception than the perfidious Portuguese had accorded them.

But while the British went it alone with the Chinese authorities and local suppliers and merchants, the Portuguese were busy trying to sabotage their operations and destroy them; the bilingual official, the Courteens claimed, must have been hired by the Portuguese to deceive and ruin the British. According to the Courteen protest, that Portuguese-speaking intermediary had pretended to be a mandarin in order to ensnare, rob, and destroy them: "We therefore departed from thence [Macao] and came to the mouth of the river of Canton, where we were expected and received with much courtesy, and trade was already opened, as your officials were witness when they came to bring us the protest, and saw *your agent*, Paulo Noretti, acting as mandarin, which he was not, but an imposter and *your leader and agent* in all the treachery that occurred."[7] This Chinese, bearing the Portuguese name "Paulo Noretti," had deceived them by the design or soliciting of the Portuguese, the latter bent on completely spoiling the British venture. Likewise, the Courteens accused the Iberians of hatching, organizing, funding, and furnishing the fire-ship attack. In this protest Captain Weddell stated that the British would be able to adduce incontrovertible evidence that the Portuguese had brought the ships to the Bogue and then escorted them up to the point of the attack's execution: "captained and conducted by your ships up to the moment of starting the fire, and then were delivered over to the Chinese, whose vessels were ready and waiting to come up to the wrecks and ruins which would result."[8] The captain-general and Senado da Camara had employed an agent to promise the Chinese a considerable sum of silver dollars to arrest the British merchants ("the king's merchants") at Canton and to confiscate their money and goods. The Portuguese had all along been endeavoring

---

6. Copy of the second letter sent by the British (British Protest against Macao), 27 September / 7 October 1637, *Lisbon Transcripts*, I.O. Records, Vol. IV.

7. British Protest against Macao, 27 September / 7 October 1637, *Lisbon Transcripts*, I.O. Records, Vol. IV; emphasis added.

8. British Protest against Macao, 27 September / 7 October 1637, *Lisbon Transcripts*, I.O. Records, Vol. IV.

Negotiation and Liberation

to dissuade the Chinese from doing any business with the British. They had also been trying to recruit the Fujianese to come over with their ships to extirpate the entire Courteen fleet: "Your worships, by your agent Francisco Carvalho Aranha, promised the Chinese large sums of money and fresh duties to do this and deprive us of all hope of trading in this land, and to encourage the Chincheos [Fujianese] to provide themselves with arms and munitions to come upon and totally destroy us." It was no frivolous, unfounded, or reckless accusation: "This have we discovered by the voluntary confessions of different persons who came to us on various occasions, and other clear evidence, such as Portuguese cloth which fell into our hands [at the time of the fire-ship attack], together with what our men saw and heard your men speak of when they were going about in these parts."[9]

As all the troubles and offenses were engineered or facilitated by the Portuguese, the British demanded that the Macao authorities retrieve their merchants—"detained on your account"—as well as the property and money; and further to pay reparations for all the damages the Courteen fleet had sustained. If the Portuguese performed these acts, the protest stated, the British would immediately leave China. Captain Weddell concluded the protest by emphasizing his royal authority—"Commander of the English Fleet dispatched by his Majesty the King of Great Britain"—and the Portuguese duty to act honorably as subjects of the Iberian king, with whom their king had entertained the accord. Should their reasonable demands be denied—which could be construed as tantamount to defying the wills of their sovereigns—the British would at least have formally registered the gravamen of their grievances that all subsequent ills, consequent upon breach of peace and contempt of royal authority, would be the responsibility and liability of the Portuguese of Macao. This protest was drafted aboard the flagship *Dragon* and signed by Weddell, Captain Richard Swanley of the *Sun*, Captain John Carter of the *Katherine*, Arthur Hatch, the fleet's chief clergyman, and Peter Mundy. In the evening of the same day that this document was delivered, 7 October, a boat came from Macao carrying a message to inform them that an answer by the Portuguese would be transmitted the next day.[10]

On 9 October a boat again came from Macao. It transported two men with whom the British were already well acquainted. A Portuguese Jesuit, Bartholomeo de Roboredo, had ridden as passenger in the Courteen fleet in its passage up from Melaka, as had a Spanish military officer, of the rank sergeant-major, likewise transported aboard the *Sun*. On behalf of the captain-general and Senado da Camara,

---

9. British Protest against Macao, 27 September / 7 October 1637, *Lisbon Transcripts*, I.O. Records, Vol. IV; "Some of the men being taken and detained in our ships, did afterwards at Macao avouch to the faces of divers Portugals coming aboard, that they were the very men that had done this; and had hired the Chineses and certain fugitive kafirs [African slaves] and others, to bring on these fire vessels whilst they in the meantime awaited at hand to murder and destroy our people if they should be forced to take to the water." "Voyage of the Weddell Fleet."

10. "Voyage of the Weddell Fleet."

110 | *The First British Trade Expedition to China*

they categorically denied the merit of all the charges leveled by the British.[11] Roboredo and the Spanish sergeant-major carried a polite note, dated Macao, 8 October, composed by the captain-general, Domingos da Camara de Noronha, introducing them and stating that their burden was to demonstrate the patent falsity and baselessness of the British accusations and to set the record straight on all key points in controversy.[12] Roboredo and the Spaniard were obligated to establish that the Portuguese of Macao had had no contact or communications with the bilingual "Paulo Noretti" and had not in any way collaborated with the Chinese in any of the attacks suffered by the Courteen fleet in the Bogue or Pearl River. Nor, they asserted, had the Portuguese of Macao paid any bribes to the authorities in Canton to arrest and imprison the Courteen merchants and confiscate their money and goods. The Ming officials had taken all such actions independently and without consulting the Lusitanians.[13]

In this conference with the British, Roboredo might well have revealed more biographical details about the Portuguese-fluent man whom Captain Weddell had taken to be a "petty mandarin" when this "Paulo Noretti" introduced himself to the British in the Bogue at the end of August.[14] This Chinese man "had been one of our Christians [at Macao], a renegade who had fled from the city with large sums of money at the last fair."[15] The crooked Chinese defector had served as an interpreter at the Canton fair the previous year (1636), and it was through him that "the mandarins forcibly took from us 80,000 *taels*."[16] He had married, settled, and had a wife in Macao. After cheating the Portuguese, he took refuge in Canton "through fear of us, because of the evil he had done us."[17] From the Lusitanian account, then, the Chinese man in question was a master or serial fraudster who went by the name of "Paulo Noretti" whenever swindling and robbing his European clients. This, at least, is what the Portuguese would have had the British to understand by the exposition of Roboredo.

The same day that he received the short note from the captain-general and visit from the interlocutors from Macao, on 9 October the commander of the British

---

11. 29 September / 9 October 1637, Mundy, *Travels*, vol. 3, 246.
12. Copy of a letter addressed by the Captain-General of Macao to the Commander of the English Fleet, 8 October 1637, *Lisbon Transcripts*, I.O. Records, Vol. IV.
13. As the captain-general himself later stressed: "It was a mistake to suppose that the Chinese needed anyone to incite them to deceit, for they were deceit itself." Domingos da Camara de Noronha to the viceroy of Goa, 27 December 1637, *Lisbon Transcripts, Books of the Monsoons*, book 41, fol. 191.
14. We can only conjecture how much of Noretti's identity the British had learned before the occasion of this briefing by Roboredo.
15. Domingos da Camara de Noronha to viceroy of Goa, 27 December 1637, *Lisbon Transcripts, Books of the Monsoons*, book 41, fol. 191.
16. Letter from the City of Macao to the King of England, 24 December 1637, *Lisbon Transcripts, Books of the Monsoons*, book 41, fol. 220. At this time a silver tael was reckoned about 10 *real* (silver dollar); thus, 80,000 tael would convert to the astronomical 800,000 silver dollars. This approximation of 1 tael = 10 *real* is given in this letter.
17. Letter from the City of Macao to the King of England, 24 December 1637, *Lisbon Transcripts, Books of the Monsoons*, book 41, fol. 220.

Negotiation and Liberation

fleet rendered a reply to the Portuguese.[18] In contrast with the previous communication, Weddell adopted a remarkably conciliatory tone. He conceded that the Jesuit Roboredo and the Spanish sergeant-major had argued cogently for the innocence of the Portuguese. Weddell admitted that he had relied on information from the Chinese. He even confessed that his judgment was adversely affected by the distress of all the vicissitudes, confusion, and turmoil the British had recently endured. He stated that the discourse delivered by the envoys from Macao had placated the Courteens. All of these remarks served as preamble to the commander's articulation of two urgent requests. Firstly, he asked the Portuguese through their contacts and communication channels to negotiate with the Chinese to release his merchants, their silver, and merchandise. Expenditures incurred in such negotiation would be defrayed by the British. Secondly, with the British next to Macao, he requested that the Portuguese offer some of their merchandise and commodities for purchase—in consideration of the large cost that their voyage to China had already exacted. Weddell offered to send two representatives to meet with the captain-general and the Senado da Camara to make arrangements along these lines. Before concluding, the British commander also noted that he would have those representatives exhibit to the Portuguese a letter he received from "the mandarin in Canton" who had promised that he would release his merchants in ten days if Weddell removed the fleet from the Bogue—which he had accordingly done, but had not received his imprisoned colleagues in turn.[19]

As discussion between Macao and the Courteens progressed, the following day, 10 October, a Spanish galleon arrived off Macao.[20] It anchored close to the British fleet, so Captain Weddell dispatched a barge from whose visit he learned that it had come from Manila to obtain metal and munitions on the Iberian monarch Philip IV's account. The galleon carried about five hundred men and came equipped with a couple dozen large brass ordnance. Weddell and the leadership of the fleet debated whether to surround and detain the galleon. However, they conceived several good reasons not to meddle—probably foremost was not to violate the accord nor to jeopardize the already delicate negotiations for release of their merchants. And at next daybreak the galleon weighed anchor and exchanged salutes while passing the British ships. But Weddell's decision not to seize the Spanish vessel upset the

---

18. British Reply to Macao, 29 September / 9 October 1637, *Lisbon Transcripts*, I.O. Records, Vol. IV. This reply was signed aboard the admiral *Dragon* by Weddell, Arthur Hatch (chaplain of the *Dragon*), and Peter Mundy. The dissents of Captain Swanley and Captain Carter can be inferred from the absence of their names.

19. British Reply to Macao, 29 September / 9 October 1637, *Lisbon Transcripts*, I.O. Records, Vol. IV. Neither original nor any copy of the letter from this mandarin has survived. In the Portuguese documents this official is identified as the "mandarin of Lantao," an official in the vicinity of the Bogue: Letter from the City of Macao to the King of England, 24 December 1637, *Lisbon Transcripts, Books of the Monsoons*, book 41, fol. 220. When the Courteen fleet was in the Bogue in August, Mundy seems to have referred to the same official: "The mandarin of Lantao who is governor of all the towns and villages hereabouts, as also of their junks": 11/21 August 1637, Mundy, *Travels*, vol. 3, 191–92. By "Lantao" the Courteen factor and Portuguese were both probably referring to the pair of islands south of Tiger Island (大虎 Dahu) which used to be known as the "Wangtung" and are now denominated the Hengdang Islands (橫檔島 Hengdangdao).

20. 30 September / 10 October 1637, Mundy, *Travels*, vol. 3, 249.

many restless and predatory crew aboard the Courteen ships: "Our not intercepting her bred great murmuring in our whole fleet among the commonalty."[21] Evidently, however, the murmuring did not grow strong enough for Weddell to worry about mutiny.[22]

On 12 October Roboredo returned to the British fleet bearing a letter from the captain-general.[23] After receiving the conciliatory note of request from Weddell, Domingos da Camara de Noronha had convened a meeting of all the municipal authorities of Macao.[24] At his residence, the missive of the Courteens was read aloud to the prelates of the religious orders, councilors and other deputies of the Senado da Camara, aldermen, and other officials and prominent citizens of the city.[25] Every eminent personage and member of the governing body was persuaded that it was sensible and squarely within the enclave's interest to grant the British requests. The small-scale transactions involving goods at Macao would not be prejudicial to Portuguese merchants. Quantities were such that commodities and merchandise like sugar, porcelain, ginger, and silk piece-goods could be spared. This commerce, however, would have to be done discreetly and furtively to avoid Ming objections, further taxes, and duties. Although it promised to be more vexatious, to assist the British commander in recovering his incarcerated merchants and detained property in Canton was also deemed the wise course. After all, should the British believe that the Lusitanians were once again violating the Anglo-Portuguese accord (by refusing to lend a hand in such exigent circumstances), the Courteens would feel justified in conducting retaliatory action. And such decisive and damaging action was readily available—the opportunity was on the horizon: "They might attempt to seize one of the six vessels which have gone to Japan, and now expected back at any moment. This they could effectually accomplish, being at anchor close to the spot where our vessels will necessarily have to pass to put into port, this being the direct route and it being impossible to turn them from that course by any warning from the City, seeing it is at a distance of five miles."[26] Moved by such a major consideration, the captain-general and the rest of the Macao leadership were unanimous in their decision to grant Weddell his two requests.

---

21. 30 September / 10 October 1637, Mundy, *Travels*, vol. 3, 249.
22. As by this point in the English and Portuguese records there are a few hints that Weddell, Swanley, and Carter were not unanimous in some key recent decisions and policy, one can speculate that Swanley or Carter, as against Weddell, favored a seizure of the Spanish ship.
23. 2/12 October 1637, Mundy, *Travels*, vol. 3, 249.
24. Letter from Domingos da Camara de Noronha at Macao to the viceroy of Goa, 27 December 1637, *Lisbon Transcripts, Books of the Monsoons*, book 41, fol. 191.
25. Copy of the decision arrived at [by the City of Macao] respecting the British, 10 October 1637, *Lisbon Transcripts, Books of the Monsoons*, book 41, fol. 213.
26. Copy of the decision arrived at [by the City of Macao] respecting the British, 10 October 1637, *Lisbon Transcripts, Books of the Monsoons*, book 41, fol. 213. The conclusion of the minutes of this meeting reads: "All these just reasons and motives being considered, it was judged expedient (despite the most discourteous letters received from the British and read to the Council) to temporize with them, and secretly because of the Chinese, to give them what they asked, which would cost us little, enhance the reputation of the City and be no discredit to us."

Roboredo presented Macao's positive answer. In addition to the Portuguese appealing to the authorities in Canton for the release of the factors and their property, merchants of Macao would be permitted to engage in a circumscribed trade with the British at a place convenient to the latter.[27] Two days later, 14 October, Captain Weddell prepared a four-member deputation to settle and formalize the terms with the Portuguese. Captain Richard Swanley of the *Sun*; Thomas Woollman, master of the *Sun*; Peter Mundy; and the purser of the *Dragon*, Christopher Parr were chosen to go to Macao to represent the British before the captain-general and the council. The envoys were just on the point of departing when a letter arrived from Roboredo informing Weddell that the British commander must come himself: the captain-general and the Macao officials would not receive any proxy. Thus, instead of pursuing their mission to Macao, Woollman, Mundy, and some attendants were the same day dispatched to survey a possible re-location spot for the fleet, east across the Pearl River estuary from the Portuguese enclave, near Lantau Island (大嶼山 Dayushan), west of present-day Hong Kong.[28]

As the Spanish galleon recently at Macao was now anchored there, Woollman and Mundy took the opportunity to enter into conversation with its captain, a man from Biscayne named Juan Lopez de Andoyna, who shared a meal with and accommodated them for the night. Mundy's Spanish was fully fluent, so it must have been a very pleasant and relaxed chat.[29] Among other fine provisions, the British had their first taste of a delicacy named "chocolate," transported across the Pacific from the Spanish New World. Before leaving the next morning, the Courteens ascertained that the vessel was seven hundred tons, built at Manila, and had already crossed the Pacific twice on a trip to Acapulco and back. To Macao she had brought nine or ten tons of clove, which had come to Manila from the Moluccas; besides silver dollars (used to purchase ordnance and munitions from the Portuguese at Macao), the ship carried dyer's wood (logwood) and some quantity of tobacco.[30] The clove, silver dollars, dyer's wood, and tobacco were all readily vendible at Macao/Canton, where demand for such imports from Chinese merchants was constant during the Ming dynasty.

After this estuary reconnaissance with the Spanish galleon off Lantau, on 15 October, Captain Weddell sent Mundy and several other Courteens to Macao to present a letter stating the reasons why he would not personally come to meet with the captain-general and the municipal council.[31] If the Portuguese would render two hostages (Roboredo and a member of that council), however, then he was prepared to come himself. On this visit, Mundy heard, in private, that mandarins had come

---

27. 4/14 October 1637, Mundy, *Travels*, vol. 3, 249.
28. 4/14 October 1637, Mundy, *Travels*, vol. 3, 251–52. Lantau, now 大嶼山 Dayushan, is the location of Hong Kong Disneyland.
29. As a teenager Mundy spent four years in Spain as a merchant apprentice.
30. 4/14 October 1637, Mundy, *Travels*, vol. 3, 251–52. Mundy was interested to hear from the captain that it took such a ship at least six months to go from Manila to Acapulco but usually only three to return.
31. 5/15 October 1637, Mundy, *Travels*, vol. 3, 253.

from Canton to discuss the British affair. And a rumor was circulating that, were the Courteens to promise never again to return to China, then the factors, silver, and merchandise would be restored. After waiting a while for a reply to Weddell's proposal, Mundy and the British contingent were dismissed with assurance that an answer would swiftly follow them. The same afternoon Macao's captain-general sent one of his pages to deliver a reply to the Courteen fleet—now probably anchored off Lintin Island. On the same day, 15 October, just as the messenger was arriving with the note, Chinese junks passed near the anchored ships. Since the junks were armed, the British were apprehensive; but when they heard the sound of drums and pipes, they construed it as an overture of rapprochement and assumed that the junks might be carrying Canton officials coming to Macao to confer about releasing the factors and property.

While Mundy and his companions were away at Macao, letters from the Courteen captives at Canton had arrived. The Mountneys were remarkably optimistic that they would soon be liberated and their property returned to them—or if not their merchandise, then at least Chinese commodities and goods of comparable value. Their optimism seems to have arisen from learning that the recently appointed viceroy of Canton (Guangdong), if not one of the Chongzhen emperor's secretaries, had come to the provincial capital to deal with the British.[32] In Canton, on 16 October the "admiral general" ("Champin") dispatched a servant to visit the Mountneys still under house arrest.[33] The Champin was curious to try some meat prepared in English style, so the brothers cooked and dressed some hens for him. Along with the platter of roast poultry, they treated the Chinese official to some biscuit and a bottle of sack. Apparently, he was delighted by the modest meal and assured them of his friendship.[34] A couple of days after the Courteen merchants had presented the Champin with a simple repast, on 18 October, Nathaniel Mountney fell ill, and the mandarin sent someone to treat him. That night the "admiral general" permitted Thomas Robinson to visit him, the first time Robinson and the Mountneys had seen each other since their arrests and detention in September.[35]

But however amicably his factors up in Canton were being treated by the Champin, it seems Captain Weddell did not trust that they, along with their goods and money, would be released by the viceroy who was now supposed to be on the spot to resolve matters. Weddell plainly exhibited no confidence that this viceroy would liberate them without the sort of Portuguese intervention for which he had been negotiating in Macao. The British commander continued discussion with the

---

32. 5/15 October 1637, Mundy, *Travels*, vol. 3, 253–54.
33. "Voyage of the Weddell Fleet."
34. This mandarin's relishing of the simple fare of the Mountneys reminds one of a daimyo's appreciation of English cuisine a few decades previous: Richard Cocks, not long after arriving at Hirado in Japan, described how the Matsura requested some English-style cooking, to which "chef" Cocks responded with English pork and beef, prepared with turnips and onions. "Relation of Richard Cocks, 12 October 1613," in *The Voyage of Captain John Saris to Japan, 1613*, ed. Ernest M. Satow (Hakluyt Society: London, 1900), 160.
35. "Voyage of the Weddell Fleet."

Macao captain-general in hopes of achieving an agreement whereby the Portuguese would do his bidding to effect the restoration of merchants and restitution of property. On 18 October the captain-general and the council of Macao sent three messengers to deliver another letter to the British fleet.[36] They pleaded with the commander and the other captains of the fleet (Richard Swanley of the *Sun* and John Carter of the *Katherine*) to come in person to Macao to negotiate. According to Weddell, by reasonable application of cynicism, the captain-general and Senado da Camara were still greatly worried that the British would meddle with or do worse to the Japan fleet expected to arrive any day at Macao.[37] This eventuality could explain their anxious follow-up communication and proposal. Perhaps the Portuguese were pressing hard for the in-person visit to Macao by Weddell, Swanley, and Carter in order to remove them from their ships and, thereby, eliminate the threat of their intercepting the returning Japan vessels.

It may have been for that purpose, then, that the Lusitanians proposed the following deal: if Weddell would come ashore and have the fleet move leeward of Lintin Island, then the British would be permitted to come into the city to buy and sell as they pleased.[38] That leeward anchoring would put them in a less advantageous position to attack the Portuguese ships. Misgivings among the Courteen council were aroused, and the other captains refused. Weddell consented to go, accompanied only by Peter Mundy, the chaplain Arthur Hatch, and the purser of the *Dragon*, Christopher Parr. The Portuguese sent two men to escort them in a sculling junk. As it approached the city, the Courteen delegation was saluted with the firing of five large cannons. On disembarking Weddell was greeted by the municipal council and community leaders who conducted the British to an opulently furnished house. The deputation was then dined sumptuously by the Portuguese. As they ate upon fine silver and sipped Portuguese wine, their ears were caressed with singing accompanied by harp and guitar. After the repast, Weddell and his companions were brought to the captain-general. With him they proceeded to the Senate house where they met a Ming "taccassy" (an official like a recorder or registrar) and some other mandarins dispatched by the "haitao" in Canton to discuss the business of the merchants, property, and money still in custody. It was decided that four Portuguese should be selected to go up the river to that city as delegates to accomplish the release of the Courteen merchants and negotiate all related and outstanding business.[39]

It was at about this time, mid-October, that Captain Weddell must have become convinced that the Chinese bilingual "Paulo Noretti"—the man whom they had greeted as a mandarin in the Bogue in August—had completely deceived

---

36. 8/18 October 1637, Mundy, *Travels*, vol. 3, 254.
37. "Weddell's China Narrative, O.C. 1662."
38. 8/18 October 1637, Mundy, *Travels*, vol. 3, 254.
39. 8 /18 October 1637, Mundy, *Travels*, vol. 3, 256. According to Domingos da Camara de Noronha (Letter of 27 December 1637), at Macao Captain Weddell was put in the presence of "the mandarins" to hear "what they would say in the name of the Aitao." In the Portuguese records the latter rendering is used in contrast with the "haitao" and "hitow" of the Courteens.

the British. For a Jesuit in Macao now rendered a translation of what Noretti had represented to the Courteens as a license from the haitao and Canton mandarins for the British to trade like the Portuguese. The Jesuit informed the British that the document granted nothing of the sort. Rather, the communiqué had expressed the shock and wrath of the Canton authorities at the British proceeding aggressively and without permission entering the Bogue. In that message conveyed by Noretti, the haitao had issued an explicit ultimatum that the British depart immediately or expect a devastating attack that would annihilate their fleet—such that not a "shred of sail" would remain of the Courteen ships. The following text is what Noretti had represented as an *invitation to commerce*, offered by the haitao and champin back on 31 August 1637:

> As it is well to know the instructions given concerning the information communicated to us by the mandarins of Canton, that four ships of barbarians with red hair had come thither from afar, and upon their arrival had anchored within the Mouth of the Tiger [Bogue; 虎門 Humen]; who, upon being questioned as to their business, vomited from their mouth that they had received license from three mandarins to hold intercourse and to trade. And that they now asked those mandarins who had given them this promise, that should there be any other mandarin who with his soldiers should impede them in this matter, they should be held as mortal enemies.

> And the mandarin of the Mouth of the Tiger advised the Cumprim [champin], who is the commander-in-chief, of other matters relating to this question. And the latter upon hearing this, equipped a thousand soldiers and some tens of mortars to drive them out, and intimate to them that entry to buy and sell would not be given them, as is notorious to all.

> And after telling them this many times, and that they must return to their kingdom, and that we would not allow them to come and disturb our lands, this same notice was affixed at the Mouth of the Tiger, where they had asked for means of trading. Because, having to ask this of us, permission should have been asked of the Organchanty, the Aitao and the Cumprim, so that they might consult with the Visitador and Viceroy; and had they given license, then it might have been [confirmed].

> But coming by force and against my will and permission may not be done in this land by those who come hither to trade. And seeing that some profit may be made, they are dazzled and deceive the lower classes. And you do not know the laws of China, for in China there are very strict laws, and he who breaks them knows no pardon; therefore nothing could be stricter.

> And I command as far as I may, and for this purpose I dispatch the mandarin who bears this sentence, who will forthwith give this order to the ships of the red-haired barbarians, and upon receiving this our order they shall instantly weigh anchor and put out to the open sea. For you have shown great daring in attempting to trade by force with us, we having forbidden it; and in so doing you appear to me to be like puppies and goats who have no learning and no reason.

Negotiation and Liberation

One or two of your men, like men without sense, have pressed this business upon me and the commander-in-chief that we should consider what you are doing; therefore I warn you that should you have the great boldness to harm so much as a blade of grass or piece of wood, I promise you that my soldiers shall make an end of you, and not a shred of your sails shall remain, should you do such a thing; and you shall have no time for repentance and your sin shall not be forgiven.[40]

The Courteens must have been stunned and dismayed at how differently, falsely, Noretti had translated this baleful and minatory communiqué of the haitao.

By this point Weddell and his fellow captains should have been disposed to credit the Jesuit's translation, after the fearsome fire-ship attack and all the hostilities in the Bogue. The veracity of this rendering was further commended by a merchant of the Chinese junk they had taken weeks ago, as well as Antonio the Ethiopian, both of whom construed the message in a similar fashion. It now appeared that Noretti was an agent in an elaborate operation that entailed tricking, robbing, and slaughtering the British. Through his guile and subterfuge, the factors, property, and silver had been placed in peril in Canton while in the Bogue the fleet, having let down its guard, was almost destroyed on 20 September by the fire-ship attack. As Peter Mundy put it: "he was the engine whereby it was done."[41] But if an engine needed operating or driving, the Courteens were now relegated to speculation about the identity of the engineer or conductor behind that treacherous bilingual "petty mandarin."[42]

At Macao Captain Weddell was able to negotiate an agreement whereby he would pledge to leave and never return to China, while the haitao and highest-ranking mandarins of Canton would release the merchants, property, and silver:

> I, John Weddell, Commander of the fleet of four English ships at present in the river of Macao by order of my master, the most powerful king of England, declare: that if the Hai-tao of Canton, or his mandarins, deliver to me my six men who are imprisoned by their authority in Canton, and the silver and merchandise they had with them, or any specimens of the products of China in exchange, that I will depart peacefully from Chinese waters, without injuring anyone, and will never return to these shores.

On 19 October this was put into writing and signed by the British commander.[43] Shortly afterwards the Portuguese leaders of Macao, in turn, signed an agreement with the haitao and Canton authorities. This stated that the haitao's *chapa* (official

---

40. "This is a faithful rendering of what is in the Chapa, this day, 27th October 1637 [17 October O.S.], Bento de Matthes." *Lisbon Transcripts*, I.O. Records, Vol. IV. Mundy affirmed that the Portuguese translator was trustworthy and "a Jesuit skillful in the Chinese language." He himself summarized the Jesuit's translation and was much impressed at the haitao's insulting classification of the Courteens as "red-haired barbarians."

41. Mundy later, 25 December 1637 / 4 January 1638, reflected and repeated that Noretti had been "the instrumental cause of all our troubles."

42. Which Ming officials were directing Noretti is a question reserved for Chapter 8.

43. "This I promise and thereto set my hand. Macao, 9th October Old Style. John Weddell." Copy of the undertaking dated 9 [19] October 1637, *Lisbon Transcripts*, I.O. Records, Vol. IV.

118   *The First British Trade Expedition to China*

order) had summoned them to the provincial capital to retrieve the British captives and bring them to Macao. The Portuguese accepted the responsibility to ensure that the British kept their promise of not returning to China. In appreciation of and as obligation for the hospitality of the Ming emperor, Chongzhen, the City of Macao undertook to use deadly force to oppose the British should they return:

> Touching the detention, and to arrange for the liberation of the British who, being ignorant of the laws of China, entered your lands, we were summoned by the Aitao's Chapa to go to Canton and fetch the British, in number five men, and bring them to Macao, from whence they may return to their lands, and not transgress in the future, as in their petitions they promise, which if transgressing, we who are residents in the lands of the king of China and have received from him many favours for well nigh a hundred years, and are natives of his land, undertake to exert all our power as soldiers of the king in his service.[44]

Captain Weddell and the British deputation took their leave of the captain-general and prepared to depart, but a suitable boat was not found to transport them back to the fleet. Instead they stayed the night by the accommodation of Captain Antonio da Silveira Aranha, one of the four governors who composed the Senado da Camara.[45] On 20 October Weddell and his colleagues left Macao and were again saluted by the firing of several cannons as they passed out of the inner harbor. They were greeted with cheers as they returned to the decks of their ships. The following day, 21 October, Weddell, as promised, shifted the fleet to the island, probably Lantau, a little west of present-day Hong Kong—where it would be much less a threat to Portuguese ships returning from Japan. Finding the Spanish galleon from Manila still anchored there, the British and Spaniards exchanged salutes of ordnance.[46]

On 24 October a delegation of five Portuguese from Macao arrived at Canton to secure the release of the Courteen merchants and arrange their return to the fleet.[47] Ostensibly they had come to obtain the liberty of the British merchants, and Captain Weddell had given them a letter to deliver to his colleagues. But the Mountneys claimed that these Portuguese, wishing to seem the sole and magnanimous agents of their liberation, were in reality endeavoring to further defame and undermine the

---

44. Copy of the pledge which Macao made with the mandarins of Canton, regarding the British who were in the said port [undated: ca. October 1637], *Lisbon Transcripts*, I.O. Records, Vol. IV. While this pledge indicates five, it should probably have numbered six still in Canton: Nathaniel and John Mountney, Thomas Robinson, Charles Webb, Simon Grey, and a servant of the Mountneys.

45. 9/19 October 1637, Mundy, *Travels*, vol. 3, 262. The captain-general of Macao had power over the military and in civil cases the prerogative to impose fines. The (1) chief justice (*ouvidor*), (2) the major of the regiment (*sargento-mor*; in October 1637, Antonio da Silveira Aranha), (3) an alderman, and (4) a judge assisted the captain-general. Presumably these four are those to whom Mundy referred as the "Governors of Macao." At least based on the signatories of the protest lodged against the British in the Bogue on 7 September 1637, the most powerful Portuguese at Macao were: Domingos da Camara de Noronha, Antonio da Silveira Aranha, Estevan Pires, Francisco de Aranjo Darros, Luiz Pais Pacheco, Domingos Dias Espinhel, and Matheu Ferreira de Proenca.

46. 11/21 October 1637, Mundy, *Travels*, vol. 3, 264.

47. 14/24 October 1637, "Voyage of the Weddell Fleet."

Negotiation and Liberation

British—characterizing them as scofflaws, thugs, and pirates. While the Mountneys asserted that they had recently arranged for some profitable exchange—and had even begun receiving some of the commodities—these Iberians now impeded and attempted to wreck the proceedings, through slander and bribes. The English brothers claimed that the Lusitanian envoys even tried to have it arranged to haul them to the Ming capital, Beijing, to be tried and punished by the highest authorities of the imperial government. So, according to the Courteen factors, for the first two days the Portuguese agents did nothing but lobby *against* the British, neglecting to give the Mountneys the letter from their captain.[48]

Neither the Mountneys nor Thomas Robinson could have been reliably or confidently informed that a Portuguese contingent had arrived in Canton *for the sake of liberating them*, as previously arranged in the contract made by Weddell down at Macao. On the contrary, they were ready, and conditioned, to perceive the Portuguese as coming only to sabotage their trade by further slandering the British—"rogues, thieves, beggars and what not"—and bribing the mandarins to refuse the Courteens commerce. According to the account penned later by Nathaniel Mountney, on the third day after their arrival at Canton, the Portuguese delegates sent one of their minions to suggest that the merchants draw up a formal request to receive a visit from this Macao deputation. Nathaniel Mountney issued a contemptuous rejection of the proposal. Concurrently, the champin having, on behalf of the British merchants, drafted four petitions addressed severally to the "Chadjan" and other high-level mandarins at Canton, on 25 October submitted the documents to the Mountneys for signature.[49] The petitions requested free trade in the future. Nathaniel Mountney related that the documents were presented to the Ming officials shortly after he and his brother had subscribed. After the Chadjan and the other chief mandarins had received the petitions, they dispatched two inferior mandarins to confirm that the British would consent to pay 20,000 taels annually in customs duties to trade from Macao like the Portuguese. For such a fee they would share the city with the Portuguese and enjoy the same privileges as their fellow

---

48. "[On 24 October there] arrived 5 Portugals at Canton who pretended to Captain Weddell that they had no other business there, but only to solicit the liberty of the merchants, than which they performed nothing less, giving a thousand lying informations against our nation, reporting us to be rogues, thieves, beggars and what not. And whereas the merchants [Mountneys, Robinson] before their coming had promise of a sudden dispatch [and] had received part of what was agreed for upon their monies and goods, these good friends began again by new excessive bribes to hinder their proceedings, and to have them detained and sent up to Peking, the city royal, being 2 months journey in the country, from whence they must never had expected return. Two days they were in Canton and detained the letter they brought from our ships, not so much as once advising the merchants of their arrival." 14/24 October 1637, "Voyage of the Weddell Fleet."

49. "15/25 Oct. 1637: Champin having caused 4 petitions to Chadjan and the other chief mandarins to be drawn in the name of the English, he sent them to the merchants to subscribe, which being done, they were presented on their behalf. Their objects were to obtain a present dispatch and a future trade." "Voyage of the Weddell Fleet." Neither originals nor copies of the petitions have survived.

120   *The First British Trade Expedition to China*

Europeans. The Chadjan requested a prompt answer so that they could immediately submit the proposal to the Chongzhen emperor and his ministers in Beijing.[50] According to Nathaniel Mountney, in the afternoon of 25 October, he and his brother John were summoned to appear at the champin's palace to meet with the Chadjan.[51] While the British merchants came decked out in the finest clothes that could be mustered, they were unable to see this official. Apparently the Chadjan was occupied by other urgent business, so they returned to their dwelling.[52] The following day members of the Portuguese deputation visited them. These envoys brought them several letters from the Courteen fleet and promised to transmit to Macao any letters they wished to send to their commander or colleagues. Two days later, 28 October, Thomas Robinson was conducted from the junk into Canton. On 29 October the Mountneys were summoned to appear with him at a temple on a small island in the Pearl River opposite the city. This was an island frequently used by the Portuguese when they came to do business at Canton.[53] At this temple, in the presence of an audience of what the Courteens claimed were a few "counterfeit" mandarins, the Portuguese delegates formally protested the incivility and ingratitude of the British. Nevertheless, notwithstanding all the abuse, the Lusitanians declared that they had come to liberate the merchants.[54] If the latter and the captains of the Courteen fleet, on behalf of the king of Great Britain, rendered written promise never again to bring ships to China, then the Portuguese delegates would convey them back to Macao.

---

50. "15/25 October 1637: After the audience was broken up, two mandarins of quality were sent from Cham-jan and the rest to know if the English would pay 20,000 *taels* per annum for customs and duties, in consideration whereof they should be possessed of 1/2 Macao and enjoy all freedoms which the Portugals did. And hereof they desired to be resolved, that they might forthwith advertise the king [emperor] and procure his confirmation." "Voyage of the Weddell Fleet." As neither of the other English accounts (Mundy's or Weddell's) nor the Portuguese or Chinese reports corroborate that such an agreement was made between the Courteen merchants and the Cham-jan/Chadjan and other Ming authorities in Canton, there is plenty of latitude for skepticism.

51. "Voyage of the Weddell Fleet."

52. "15/25 October 1637: In the afternoon the merchants were sent for to Champin's palace that Chadjan might (as he desired) see them. They went in the best equipage [display] they could, but he, detained by some other occasions, came not, and so they returned home to their house." "Voyage of the Weddell Fleet."

53. The "little isle" in the "Voyage of the Weddell Fleet" is probably that mentioned in *Purchas His Pilgrimes*, book 1, part 3 (1625), 195: "in the city of Canton in the midst of the river, where was a manner of a monastery of their [Chinese] priests." This island came to be called Napier Island by later British merchants and at the time of the Opium Wars. It is present-day Ersha Island (二沙島 Ershadao). But if Ersha Island is too large to qualify, then it was probably the much smaller and adjacent Haixinsha Island (海心沙 Haixinsha).

54. "18/28 Oct. 1637: [B]efore 3 or 4 counterfeit mandarins, they were by these worshipful gentlemen accused of ingratitude towards them, notwithstanding which, forsooth, in Christian charity (if Jews may have any) would redeem them, and to that end they were come." "Voyage of the Weddell Fleet." The insulting "Jews" epithet is plainly Mountney's way of indicating his notion that these were the parvenu or fake converts of Portugal, the "New Christians" (Cristão-Novo/Marranos). The Courteens in the same fashion smeared the captain-general and other prominent merchants of Macao. C.R. Boxer documented the high proportion of Jews, crypto-Jews, and "new Christians" in Macao: "Many of the wealthiest settlers came from places like Braganza and Beira-Baixa which were notorious strongholds of the *Marranos* (Swine) as the New Christians were popularly if inelegantly termed." *Fidalgos in the Far East*, 144.

Negotiation and Liberation

The Mountneys and Robinson, whether suspicious or paranoid, regarded the proposal as ludicrous. Their response was to reproach the Portuguese for their treachery and spurn their offer of liberation. Nathaniel Mountney pointed out that it was the Portuguese who had caused their incarceration in the first place, by slander, bribe, and otherwise. They would need to be fools to trust the Portuguese to carry them back to their colleagues at Macao; they would sooner trust the Chinese or any other foreigner—anyone besides the perfidious Lusitanians. In the mordant commentary of the Courteen merchant: "These propositions being uttered with their so solid or rather stolid Portugal gravity, and before none but their own counterfeit creatures, wanted not much of begetting an outright laugh with our merchants, who failed not roundly to tell them of their treachery and how little need they stood in of their soliciting their liberty, having enjoyed it before their arrival, and indeed had never been taken from them at all but by their procurement."[55] Nathaniel Mountney's spicy rebuff infuriated the Portuguese. They dispatched letters complaining about his arrogance and impudence to Macao and to Captain Weddell and the fleet now anchored near Lantau.

On 30 October Nathaniel Mountney was summoned by the same mandarins who had sat as audience at the conference between the British and Portuguese held at the temple on the island two days earlier. The chief Courteen factor refused to attend but sent his brother John and Thomas Robinson. They were told by the Chinese interpreter of the Macao delegation that the Canton officials had sentenced them to pay 2,800 ounces of silver (taels), the equivalent of 28,000 silver dollars. This judgment also specified that after this payment they would be put in the custody of the Portuguese, who would return them to Macao to rejoin their compatriots. At Macao they would then be permitted to trade for the rest of the year under the close supervision of the Iberians. After that they must depart, never to return. Yet the Courteen factors, still unable to trust the Lusitanians, suspected this sentence to be a fraud when, within a day of its declaration by that interpreter, the champin, who had retrieved much of their money and goods already, summoned and assured them that if they paid the proper customs duties they would be granted their own place for annual free trade.[56]

In the following early days of November, Thomas Robinson returned to the junk in the Pearl River east of Canton to supervise the measuring of the incense purchased by the Chinese. That night he returned to the city and within a few days oversaw its transport there. It was also at this time that he arranged for his companions in detention on the junk, Simon Grey and another attendant, to come to Canton with him. By the middle of November, the Mountneys received a letter

---

55. 18/28 October 1637, "Voyage of the Weddell Fleet."
56. "This day Champin, who had gathered together most part of the goods and money sent for them and made a real account with them for whatsoever was in his hands . . . promised that, paying the duties accustomed, they should have an annual free trade and a place of residence where they pleased." 20/30 October 1637, "Voyage of the Weddell Fleet."

122   *The First British Trade Expedition to China*

from Weddell and the fleet's council apprising them that it had been decided to sell the worn-out pinnace *Anne* to the captain of the Spanish galleon that had come to Macao from Manila. On the same day as the receipt of this letter, the execution of the contracts was proceeding: in Canton, junks were being laded with sugar, ginger, China root, arak, and provisions to be transported to the British fleet anchored down in the estuary.[57]

The six British captives were freed at last. But according to the account of Nathaniel Mountney, they were liberated *despite*, not because of, any Portuguese intercessory activity in Canton:

> All our people, having free license, departed aboard a junk which they had hired to bring them down to the ships; but they were constrained to stay certain days to accompany the rest, in the meantime enjoying the comfort of the fresh air after their close house, and having free license when they pleased to go ashore on the other side of the river amongst the gardens. Our good friends, the Portugals, perceiving that, in despite of their treacheries, our people had gotten their freedom and goods, sent to excite them with a congratulatory message, and told them there was an order come from Chadjan for their dispatch, with satisfaction for all their monies and goods, which was known long before; but however, *they* [Portuguese] *would have seemed to have been officers in its procuring.*[58]

By the chief Courteen factor's telling, then, the Lusitanians, aware that the British had already regained their liberty and property by the justice and grace of the champin and other mandarins, now hastily communicated a message of congratulation and word that the Chadjan had transmitted to them, the Portuguese, an order for themselves to render to the Courteens, stating that all their money and goods were to be restored. This, as Mountney claimed, had already been achieved by *his own efforts*, with the cooperation and through the favor and benevolence of the champin; so it appeared that the Portuguese were merely trying to obtain unwarranted ex-post-facto credit for effecting their release and recovery of property. Mountney persisted in regarding the Portuguese deputation as the British nemesis, not their savior. On 19 November two low-level mandarins present at the temple meeting the previous month sent a message requesting to confer with the British factors and the Portuguese envoys. The Courteen merchants were busy overseeing the delivery and lading of the sugar, ginger, and China root, so they excused themselves. Then those mandarins and the Macao delegation appeared at the side of the junk where the factors were conducting the business. Would the British not accompany the Portuguese back to Macao? they inquired. No, only if they were dragged, replied the merchants. The Mountneys and Robinson would not put themselves in the custody of the Portuguese and would prefer to arrange their own separate transport.[59]

---

57. "Voyage of the Weddell Fleet."
58. 5–6/15–16 November 1637, "Voyage of the Weddell Fleet," emphasis added.
59. "Two petty mandarins at the pagoda in Canton sent to speak with our merchants and the Portugals; but they being busy in taking in of sugar, ginger, China roots, etc., denied to go to them. Whereupon they, with 4

Negotiation and Liberation

Back at Macao the British had rented a house for several weeks where they could lodge factors to conduct the limited trade the Portuguese authorities had conceded in the recently made agreement that was approved by the Ming officials. Peter Mundy was chosen to supervise a small group to vend such commodities as cloth and incense; purchase sugar, green ginger, and other raw commodities; and make contracts to transport such items for the Portuguese—whether to Melaka or Cochin. From the end of October till the middle of November, Mundy and the Courteens at Macao, and those anchored across the Pearl River estuary off Lantau, could hear only rumors of what was transpiring in the provincial capital: "In this 20 days' space we had variable news of our merchants at Canton, sometimes that they would be here within a day or two, other times that it would be long ere they could come."[60] While Mundy and his colleagues spent their weeks in November at the residence in Macao, they found the food—whether bread, meat, fish, or fruit—remarkably cheap. They were also surprised and impressed by the number of fabulously wealthy inhabitants who belonged to the Portuguese settlement.

At last, on 15 November, the much-anticipated Japan fleet, which had departed from Macao at the end of July, returned.[61] Mundy at Macao heard a rumor that the Portuguese trip to Deshima had not been very profitable this year.[62] He heard that the Dutch had brought a fleet of twelve ships to trade in Japan just before the Portuguese arrived; the market was rendered scarcely profitable for the Iberians as the Dutch had undersold them. Rather likely, however, this account was contrived and fed to the British to prevent envy and obviate something worse than coveting.[63] Mundy also heard that the Iberian Jesuits and other orders of clergy (especially Franciscans from the Philippines) were encountering growing and more lethal hostility in Japan. In this most recent voyage, five clergymen who had come from Manila were put to death: "This Emperor [Tokugawa shogun Iemitsu] beareth mortal hatred to the Jesuits, having of late years put many of them to death by sundry sorts of torments. And now lastly this voyage they killed 5 churchmen that came from Manila; and by relation, if any ship be known to have brought any [clergy], the said ship is to be burned, the goods confiscated, the company imprisoned, the house that harbours them shall be razed, the owner or master forfeits his

---

Portugals came to the junk side and demanded if they would go to Macao with them; but they refused to go forth the junk unless they were forced, the Portugals again telling them that they should go whether they would or no, and so departed." 9/19 November 1637, "Voyage of the Weddell Fleet."

60. By far the largest interval in Mundy's China journal, almost a month, occurs between 11/21 October and 5/15 November. It is thus that he writes of "20 days' space." Mundy, *Travels*, vol. 3, 265.

61. 5/15 November 1637, Mundy, *Travels*, vol. 3, 271.

62. Nathaniel Mountney must have heard roughly the same story: "The Portugals report themselves to have made a bad voyage this year for Japan, the place being so overladen by the Dutch that they have lost 15 percent of their principal; and if it continueth a year or 2 more so, Macao having trade to no other place, cannot long subsist." Mountney, Rawlinson, A.299.

63. This view is offered by Boxer, *Great Ship*, 152–53. Souza concurred with Boxer that the 1637 Japan fleet's voyage was highly lucrative, despite the Dutch market presence. *Survival of Empire*, 62.

124   *The First British Trade Expedition to China*

life and all the neighbors fined."[64] The Portuguese merchants and clergy at Macao were becoming ever more worried that the door to Japan was closing on them—just as it seemed to be opening wider to the Dutch.

While the Mountneys and Robinson were still in Canton supervising transactions, a deal was clinched with the captain of the Spanish galleon to sell the battered pinnace *Anne* for 3,500 *real*.[65] On 20 November a letter from the factors at Canton reached Weddell. They informed the commander that they had procured five or six hundred tons of sugar, green ginger, sugar candy, and China root and had arranged for three large junks to convey all the commodities. With these vessels they expected to come down to Macao very soon. Nathaniel Mountney advised Weddell that he could now release the Chinese captives the British had taken from the junk attacked in the Bogue on 1 October near Tiger Island. Accordingly, the captain now emancipated those eight men as well as another Chinese who had been snared while fleeing ashore. Some money was given to these hostages in compensation, and they took with them a letter to be given to Nathaniel Mountney. Only one hostage was retained by Weddell: the man who was plucked out of the water in the wake of the fire-ship attack. Covered with heavy chains and bolts of iron, he plunged to a death by drowning shortly after the release of his fellow captives. His wounds, having been treated by the fleet's surgeons, had healed; but, seeing his fellow detainees released, perhaps he supposed that some cruel torture lay in store for him.[66]

About a week later, on 28 November, the Mountneys, still at Canton, paid a visit to the champin to present a gift and take formal leave. He requested a receipt for the commodities which had been placed in the junks for transport to Macao. He promised to obtain the rest of the goods owed them and send them to the fleet after their departure from the capital. He also stated that he would issue them his warrant (*farman*), which would expedite their proceeding. The following day the British merchants rendered him the specified receipt for all those goods they had already taken aboard the junks. Since their colleague Thomas Robinson had fallen seriously ill with dysentery, on 2 December, the Mountney brothers visited the champin to hasten the issue of the papers and their departure.[67] The latter requested that in front of two mandarins for witnesses the British merchants formally acknowledge that they had received full satisfaction for their money and goods. They stated that only 1,000 silver dollars (*reals* of eight) remained outstanding. It was promised that this sum would be sent to them at Macao, and so they took their final leave of

---

64. 5/15 November 1637, Mundy, *Travels*, vol. 3, 271–72. The previous year, 1636, by Tokugawa Iemitsu's shogunate edict (allegedly influenced by Dutch lobbying), Portuguese traders were expelled from Nagasaki and were relegated to temporary use of the islet of Deshima. As noted in Chapter 3, on the Courteen fleet's passage from Melaka to Macao, Mundy had learned of recent persecution of Japanese Christians. For the changes of policy in Japan in the 1630s, see Ronald Toby, *State and Diplomacy in Early Modern Japan: Asia in the Development of the Tokugawa Bakufu* (Stanford, CA: Stanford University, 1991), 11–13.

65. Mountney, Rawlinson, A.299.

66. 10/20 November 1637, Mundy, *Travels*, vol. 3, 272–73.

67. Robinson might have been afflicted with the same "flux" that caused one of the five Portuguese envoys to leave a few days before. 16/26 November 1637, "Voyage of the Weddell Fleet."

Negotiation and Liberation

the champin. At this farewell meeting with the "lord admiral," Nathaniel Mountney understood himself to have confirmed his commitment to an undertaking that for free trade and a piece of coastal land for a trading station, the British would pay an annual fee of 20,000 ounces of silver (taels), four iron cannons, and fifty muskets.[68] Just as the Courteen merchants were preparing take leave of this mandarin, a message was brought from the Portuguese envoys. The latter waited outside to confer with the British. The champin would not permit the Portuguese to enter his chamber where he was meeting with the Courteens, so requested a messenger of theirs to inform him of their reason for coming. The Portuguese demanded that the Courteen merchants be placed in their custody. This was flatly refused: as they had already obtained the necessary passes and vessels, the British stood in no need of Portuguese assistance or conveyance. But the Portuguese replied that if the British were not transported under their direct supervision, then the British ships around Macao might make mischief. This was judged a worthy consideration, so the "lord admiral" supervised the drafting of an agreement in which the British and Portuguese promised cordial behavior towards each other as they departed together from Canton. With that, the champin dismissed them all.[69]

Four days later, on 6 December, the six emancipated British set out for Macao to rejoin the Courteen fleet, presumably traveling in Chinese junks appointed by the champin.[70] The same night the four Portuguese envoys followed them closely down the river and the next day caught up with the British and ordered them to halt. The Courteens did not wish their escorting Chinese crew to comply, but by Portuguese threats these Chinese were intimidated into anchoring. The British were thus compelled to travel the rest of the way down the river in tight convoy with the Portuguese. Nearing Macao, the Lusitanians put the merchants, their money, and goods into their own direct custody. The Courteens in the Chinese junks were towed at their sterns into the city, a humiliating arrival amid a large throng of spectators lining the shore. They arrived 8 December.[71] The Mountneys were summoned to disembark; still dangerously ill, Thomas Robinson remained aboard the junk and later that night was conveyed by her skiff to the *Sun* under the command of Richard Swanley. After a few days of recuperation he was able to go into Macao to assist his fellow factors Mundy and the Mountneys in the trading that had already gotten underway in their absence weeks before.

Just a few days before the arrival of the Mountneys and Robinson at Macao, on 5 December, Weddell and the other captains of the fleet were invited by the clergy of the San Paulo to come ashore to watch a musical drama. They declined, but Mundy and other Courteen factors doing business in Macao seem to have enjoyed

---

68. 22 November / 2 December 1637, "Voyage of the Weddell Fleet." Presumably the champin assured Mountney that he would press the Chadjan and higher authorities to approve of this proposed arrangement.
69. 22 November / 2 December 1637, "Voyage of the Weddell Fleet."
70. 26 November / 6 December 1637, "Voyage of the Weddell Fleet."
71. 28 November / 8 December 1637, Mundy, *Travels*, vol. 3.

a memorable show put on at the church. It offered such scenes as a dance by children costumed in Chinese dress and a mock-battle dance between Portuguese and Dutch—presumably meant as a re-enactment of the miraculous and successful defense against the Dutch attack upon Macao in 1622.[72] Subsequently, however, and generally, Mundy, the Mountneys, and Robinson do not seem to have been treated very well in town. According to the report of Nathaniel Mountney written later in December, there were many obnoxious hassles and harassment to hinder their trading. They were forced by the municipal authorities to shift from house to house; at times they were even compelled to return to the fleet to idle before being allowed back ashore. At last and as a great mercy they were afforded the generous hospitality of the captain of the Spanish galleon, temporarily resident in the Lusitanian enclave while his ship remained at anchor across the estuary off Lantau. To the annoyance of the Portuguese municipal officials, the Spaniard lodged them in the same spacious quarters he was renting for himself in Macao.[73]

On 10 December Captain Weddell; Captain Richard Swanley of the *Sun*, the vice-admiral of the fleet; and Nathaniel Mountney, chief merchant, came into Macao to meet with Ming officials. It was arranged for them to sign a statement which had been dictated by the authorities in Canton.[74] The document, composed in Chinese, was brought by a "petty" mandarin represented by the Courteens as a "Taccazzee"—an official far below the haitao and champin. As Mundy testified: "He was brought in an open chair between two men, but much higher from the ground than our sedans; a quitasol [umbrella] carried over his head; music, viz., a kind of hautbois and beating on brass vessels, with several ensigns, went before him."[75] The affidavit entailed the acknowledgment that their offensive actions were done in ignorance of the laws of China, and in it they appealed to the mercy of the Chinese emperor to overlook their trespasses. The statement also enunciated an undertaking never again to conduct themselves contrary to these laws—but, in the event of doing so, they would submit to punishment as determined by Chinese and Portuguese authorities.[76] On the same day that this Chinese document was signed, two more junks arrived laden with goods purchased at Canton to be transferred to the British vessels.

A few more weeks then elapsed as the Courteens continued to trade and procure Chinese commodities and merchandise at Macao.[77] On 30 December the *Katherine*, departed for Aceh, where Weddell and Mountney had established a factory by license of the sultan Iskandar Thani on the way from Malabar to Melaka in the

---

72. 25 November / 5 December 1637, Mundy, *Travels*, vol. 3, 274.
73. 26 November / 6 December 1637, "Voyage of the Weddell Fleet."
74. 30 November / 10 December 1637, Mundy, *Travels*, vol. 3I, 288.
75. 30 November / 10 December 1637, Mundy, *Travels*, vol. 3, 288.
76. 30 November / 10 December 1637, Mundy, *Travels*, vol. 3, 288–89.
77. Another substantial (twenty days') hiatus in Mundy's journal occurs between 30 November / 10 December and 20/30 December 1637.

spring.[78] It was intended that Captain Carter's ship would touch at that northern Sumatra location, arrange for pepper to be ready for the *Dragon* or *Sun*, and then proceed to Bhatkal on India's Malabar coast—where Courteens had been deposited in the spring of 1637 to operate a fledgling factory—and finally to set sail for England before the other two Courteen ships.[79] The factors John Smart and William Baron were selected to go in the *Katherine* with Carter, to be placed at Aceh to manage trade, specifically to arrange for the large consignment of pepper, in preparation for loading onto one or both of the ships to follow. On 5 January, Mundy and Nathaniel Mountney at Macao, trying to conclude transactions, received a note from Weddell instructing them to inform the captain-general, Domingos da Camara de Noronha, that they and all the other Courteens with them would leave town that night.[80] They were also to request that the Portuguese authorities make public proclamation of their departure so that all accounts with the British factors could be settled.

As Mundy was making his way to the captain-general's, he was accosted by one of the latter's minions. This man carried a message addressed to the Courteen merchants; Mundy and the messenger proceeded to walk together to the residence. Just as the English factor was ascending the stairs to his chamber, Domingos da Camara de Noronha descended upon him with a profanity-replete diatribe in Portuguese complaining about the recent behavior of the British merchants. Did they think they were in London? Were they so obtuse and impudent as to be unaware that they were within the jurisdiction of the redoubtable Habsburg monarch of Spain? Denouncing them as rogues, knaves, and traitors ("picaros, borachos, traidores," as Mundy recorded), he commanded them to exit Macao immediately. Any British the captain-general should find still there next morning would be hanged, and any goods which remained in town would be confiscated. Having delivered himself of this fulmination, he walked off without letting Mundy utter a syllable—if the latter had any inclination to do so.[81] Mundy supposed that the Macao executive was so irate because the British had disregarded his rule that no Portuguese or their goods be transported to Melaka or India by the Courteen ships. Back in October Camara de Noronha had issued a proclamation forbidding passage to there or any other place beyond China, except in the case of the clergy and a few other special categories of men. Heavy punishment would follow any violation. Mundy understood that the policy was adopted by the captain-general with a view towards augmenting revenue: that is, in order to be able to assess royal duties on Portuguese who would be forced, without the British option, to employ Macao-licensed vessels. Since would-be Portuguese outfitters of ships for such travel were deterred by fear of Dutch interference and assaults in the South China Sea and Straits of Melaka—where the

---

78. A meeting of the fleet's council had been held 12/22 December 1637, "touching the dispeeding of ship *Catherine* before the rest, with advice and some capital to provide pepper at Achin and the coast of India, against the *Dragon's* and *Sun's* arrival." "Voyage of the Weddell Fleet."
79. 20/30 December 1637, Mundy, *Travels*, vol. 3, 292.
80. 26 December 1637 / 5 January 1638, Mundy, *Travels*, vol. 3, 297–98.
81. 26 December 1637 / 5 January 1638, Mundy, *Travels*, vol. 3, 298.

Hollanders would be maintaining a blockade—the other, the British "red-haired barbarians," appeared to be the best or only option for reaching India: "None [of the Portuguese] durst adventure for fear of the Hollander lying in the straits of Malacca." Apparently, Captain Weddell had just recently broken his promise to abide by the captain-general's order: the Courteen commander had consented to transport not only a considerable number of Portuguese passengers (well over a hundred) but also a large quantity of their silver and goods.[82]

On the night of 5 January, the Macao captain-general sent messengers to the residence of the British merchants to reiterate his grievances and order them to depart instantly. Later a gang of his men armed with swords and guns and bearing torches arrived to expel them. But the merchants insisted that they must have two more days to wrap up business in town, and the captain-general's servants left without doing any violence. However, when the British heard that, in addition to the captain-general, the Senado da Camara was demanding their immediate departure, they reconsidered. The municipal council claimed that several official orders from Canton had recently arrived ("sundry chops new come from Canton"), command-ing the Portuguese authorities to expel the British without further delay. Evidently, this was credible enough to cause most of the Courteens to evacuate that night. The remainder returned to the anchored fleet the next day.[83]

The following day John Mountney and Thomas Robinson entered Macao one last time to lodge a formal protest against the captain-general and Senado's mistreatment of the British throughout their visit of China.[84] This day, 7 January 1638, marked six months since the Courteen fleet had arrived on the doorstep of Macao, when the merchants delivered the letter from Charles I addressed to the captain-general. A few days later, the *Dragon* and *Sun* set sail from where they had first anchored three leagues off Macao. The admiral *Dragon* carried about 140 Portuguese, mestizos, and slaves of the Portuguese, along with their money and goods.[85] Most of them were destined for Melaka, Cochin, and Goa.[86] As the British ships passed the anchored Spanish galleon from Manila, they fired a salute and received a reply in kind. It was warm, and with light winds the Courteen ships sailed south towards Hainan. On 11 January they were ambushed by a storm that robbed both the *Dragon* and *Sun* of their longboats.[87] About ten days later, having passed Annam (south Vietnam) and approaching Melaka, the British encountered three cruising Dutch ships. Among the startling news they received was that Sir William Courteen was dead. Seventeen VOC ships were now choking Goa, and

---

82. 26 December 1637 / 5 January 1638, Mundy, *Travels*, vol. 3, 298–99.

83. 26 December 1637 / 5 January 1638, Mundy, *Travels*, vol. 3, 299–300.

84. 28 December 1637 / 7 January 1638, Mundy, *Travels*, vol. 3, 300.

85. December 1637 / January 1638, Mundy, *Travels*, vol. 3, 317. No doubt the decimation of the Courteen fleet off Malabar in the spring of 1637 had left plenty of room for Portuguese passengers to be taken from Macao.

86. The Macao captain-general's letter to the viceroy of Goa, 27 December 1637, related that a very prominent member of the community, Silveira, arranged for passage with the Courteens, in direct defiance of his order, and that this encouraged many lesser to do the same.

87. December 1637 / January 1638, Mundy, *Travels*, vol. 3, 318–19.

Negotiation and Liberation

another nine were strangling the passage by Melaka. Of most urgent import was the demand presented by the VOC commander, Cornelius Symonsen. His superior, the governor-general at Batavia Anthony van Diemen, required that the British hand over all their Portuguese passengers, as well as the latter's goods and money.[88]

---

88. 12/22 January 1638, Mundy, *Travels*, vol. 3, 321.

8

Lessons Learned

The "Anglology" of the Ming?[1]

At least in the mind of Nathaniel Mountney, the most salient thought as the remnant of the Courteen fleet, the *Dragon* and *Sun*, sailed away from Ming Guangdong was that the British had been outmaneuvered and out-bribed by the wily Portuguese. The conduct of the Chinese may have been nothing beyond what he and Captain Weddell had expected. But before more closely examining the views and attitudes of the departing British (and the now much relieved Lusitanians at Macao), we shift our focus to the perspective and analysis of the Chinese, as revealed in and inferred from the Ming records and reports about the British and Portuguese actions of June–December 1637. Such Chinese primary sources to illuminate the British fleet's sojourn are not numerous and detailed enough to answer all the questions we could raise. The demise of the dynasty just six years later, with the suicide by hanging of its last emperor, Chongzhen, in 1644, helps explain the incomplete annals. In his authoritative survey, Wilkinson summarizes: "In the Ming there were at least 300 provincial and prefectural archives. Most of their contents were destroyed in the fighting at the end of the dynasty. Nothing of them remains today."[2] That the dramatic and tumultuous six months of the Courteens in 1637 is not fully illuminated by Ming records does not occasion a great deal of surprise given such facts as that the Dutch invasion of Macao in 1622 did not leave a trace in surviving registers.[3] Further, in the 1620s and 1630s, as the Ming government in Beijing was forced to concentrate more and more of its attention on northwest domestic and foreign (Manchurian) threats in the northeast, so disregard and neglect of major events and affairs in Guangdong would have been natural if not necessary. Such inattention would help explain any gaps in Ming records pertaining to the activities of maritime

---

1. "Anglology" is my awkward term contrived for the purpose of juxtaposition to "sinology," the subject of the next chapter. Readers of the foregoing chapters will be in no danger of making the faulty assumption that "anglology" has something to do with angels, whose science is called *angelology*.
2. Endymion Wilkinson, *Chinese History: A Manual* (Cambridge, MA: Harvard University Asia Center, 2000), 890; as Wolfgang Franke explained: "Owing to the downfall of the dynasty, no veritable records were compiled for the last [Chongzhen] emperor." *Cambridge Ming*, vol. 8, 746.
3. John Wills, *Cambridge Ming*, vol. 8, 351. However, unlike the Dutch invasion of Macao in 1622, the Chinese engagements off Fujian with Hans Putmans and the VOC at Liaoluo Bay, Jinmen, next to Xiamen, in 1633 are described in some detail in Chinese records, as used by Tonio Andrade in his recent books.

"red barbarians" like the British—who spent six months in China but did so on the Ming's southeast periphery.

As the Chinese scholar of Ming foreign policy Wan Ming has acknowledged, the absence of information in the Chinese sources on the events before the major clashes in September and October 1637 forces us to rely on English and Portuguese ones. Even in the case of September and October we depend upon those European sources for some key meetings and incidents—even those involving high-level Chinese officials. As both of those Western sources, while in conflict on some points, similarly refer to such meetings and incidents, it is implausible that these latter were fabrications—no matter how absent their traces in Ming documents. The most important and complete Chinese record that has survived is badly damaged in the portion that would shed light on the key events of July and August—including the bold and pioneering probe of the pinnace *Anne* up the Pearl River.[4] That record is a compilation of documents from the Ministry of War (兵部).[5] Both Wan and, more recently, Lawrence Wong have used that key document, as well as the published official Ming historical annals, to shed light on the mandarins and their attitudes and conduct vis-à-vis the British and Portuguese.[6] The other highly informative Ming source is the collection of memorials and reports penned by Zhang Jingxin, who was governor of Guangdong and Guangxi (兩廣總督 Liangguang zongdu) in 1637. These writings, composed during and after the Courteen visit of that year, have been edited and presented with erudite commentary by Tang Kaijian and Zhang Kun.[7] Among these and other Chinese historians, the British expedition lasting half a year is known as the "Bogue Incident" (虎門事件 Humen shijian) or more loosely and colorfully, "Incident at the Mouth of the Tiger."[8]

As we approach our review of Chinese primary documents, which expose facts, names, and details unavailable in the English and Portuguese accounts, let us briefly recite some of the key claims and notions articulated by those Europeans. Obviously, the British, at their first entry into China, could never have been certain of which level of Ming and Guangdong government authority they were dealing with. From the Chinese, Portuguese, and Ethiopians (via Macao), they must have haphazardly picked up various titles and rough knowledge of hierarchy which they

---

4. Wan, "First Direct Clash of China and Britain," 58.
5. 兵部題《失名会同两广总督张镜心题》残稿 (明清史料乙编，第八本) (上海：中央研究院历史语言研究所，商务印书馆, 1936).
6. Wong, "The Bogue Incident."
7. Tang and Zhang, "Governor of Guangdong and Guangxi."
8. English "Bogue" comes from the Portuguese Boca do Tigris, which literally translates the Chinese place name 虎門：虎 *hu* (tiger) and 門 *men* (mouth, gate). As dozens of Chinese proverbial sayings (諺語 *yanyu*) and idioms (成語 *chengyu*) employ the tiger as a metaphor, British-in-the-Bogue would yield a rich harvest of tropes in the poetically inclined. The eminent sinologist and authority on the Southern Ming, Lynn Struve, proved unable to resist the charm in one of her titles: *Voices from the Ming-Qing Cataclysm: China in Tigers' Jaws* (New Haven, CT: Yale University Press, 1993).

132 *The First British Trade Expedition to China*

had not learned before arrival in July.[9] As the drama unfolded over the next six months, they had both native and non-native Chinese recruits and conscripts from around the Pearl River estuary to assist them in figuring out who was who, and who reported to whom. They referred to officials generally as "mandarins," and it turns out they did identify, however vaguely, and distinguish some of the most powerful officials in Guangdong, representing them with variant spellings—and ranking them, from highest to lowest:

1. Tootan/Toutan
2. Chadjan/Chamjan
3. Quan Moan/Quan Mone[10]
4. Haitao/Haitau/Hitow/Hittow/Hoyto[11]
5. Campeyn/Champain/Champaine/Champen/Champeyn/Champin/ Cheeompee/Chompee

As the British supposed, it was to the latter, the "champin," that the Portuguese-fluent intermediary "Paulo Noretti" reported: "Champain, his master." Mundy applied to Noretti a title above interpreter (*jurabassa*): "mandarin *tonpuan*."[12]

Besides Noretti, the man they took to be a Portuguese-speaking "petty mandarin," the Courteens interacted and communicated most extensively with the officials they labeled "champin" and "haitao." They had minimal or no direct exposure to the authorities higher than the latter: to those whom they called "Chadjan" and "Tootan." These latter high-ranking officials in Guangdong came onto the scene, to the provincial capital, Canton, only in September or later. The Courteens took

---

9. It would be difficult to figure out which, if any, terms the Courteens had learned, pre-China arrival, from the sinological scholarship contributed by other Europeans (principally Italians, Iberians, and Dutch)—as translated and published in such collections as Hakluyt's and Purchas's in the decades preceding the Weddell expedition. Peter Mundy, for example, had read some of that Hakluyt- and Purchas-purveyed sinology.

10. In Mundy/Courteen orthography: "qu" was kw/gw sound (as in "quandary"); in early seventeenth-century English maps of China, "Quangsi" stood for Guangxi and "Queichiu" for Guizhou. For maps representing Ming place-names in such fashion, see Batchelor, "Selden Map Rediscovered." The sixteenth-century account of China by Martin de Rada used "Quanton" for Canton/Guangdong. See Boxer, *South China*.

11. In the Portuguese documents we find the additional spellings, "aitao" and "aytao." Disappointingly, with the exception of the "aitao," the Portuguese sources usually refer to the Chinese officials vaguely as "mandarins." In one place the City of Macao in its letter to Charles I refers to "a Mandarin from a neighboring village [in the Bogue] of Lantao" and another place "the aforesaid Mandarin of Lantao." The Portuguese also mention "Taquexi, who is governor of seaports among the Chinese, sent us a *chapa* commanding us to summon the Commander [Weddell] on shore in order to negotiate with him and with us for the surrender (which the Aitao desired) of the prisoners who were then in Canton." City of Macao to Charles I, 24 December 1637, *Lisbon Transcripts, Books of the Monsoons*, book 41, fol. 220. As noted below, Mundy seems to refer to this official with the spellings "Tacazzee" and "tacassy." As the City of Macao relates in detail, this official came to Macao to do the bidding of the "haitao" in arranging with the Portuguese and British for the Courteens in Canton to be released: "the Taquexi who had come to settle this business by order of the Aitao."

12. "Mandarin tonpuan, the bearer thereof, otherwise called Paolo Nurette (it is the same who came to parley with us)": 21/31 August 1637, Mundy, *Travels*, vol. 3. For "interpreter" Mundy occasionally used *jurabassas*, a Malay word often applied to bilingual Chinese Christians born in Macao. It came more broadly to cover mestizos and Eurasians who spoke Chinese and Portuguese. C. R. Boxer, *Portuguese Society in the Tropics: The Municipal Councils of Goa, Macao, Bahia and Luanda, 1510–1800* (Madison: University of Wisconsin Press, 1965), 46n5.

the "Chadjan" (also "Chamjan") to be "the supervisor general."[13] "Tootan" (also "Toutan") they took to be "viceroy of this province of Canton": Mundy noted, "Our mandarin [Noretti] came again and said the *Tootan* who is viceroy of this province of Canton, being new confirmed, was going in circuit to visit his government."[14] Subordinate to the "Tootan," the "Quan Moan" (also "Quan Mone") was the official the Courteens understood to be "the subordinate viceroy for trade": "from a message from Hitow, Champen, &c., they were required in friendly manner to proceed no further, but to repair aboard, with promise of all assistance in the procuring of licence from Quan Moan, the subordinate viceroy for trade."[15] Specific reference to other, lower-ranking officials can also be found among the Courteen records. For example, in the Bogue they identified the "mandarin of Lantao," "who is governor of all the towns and villages hereabouts, as also of their junks." The British also referred to the "mandarin of Casa Branca." This was most likely the Ming official who, residing just north of Macao in Xiangshan (香山), directly monitored and supervised the Portuguese enclave and presided over controversies and affairs involving Chinese inhabitants of Macao. We also find recorded in Mundy's journal, while he was in Macao with Weddell to negotiate the release of the factors, a "*Tacazzee*, being a certain degree of mandarin, who now and at other times sat about our business."[16]

The British captains and merchants gained at least a superficial understanding of how these various officials functioned and related to each other within the hierarchy of civil and military branches. Under both the "Tootan" and "Chadjan," the "haitao" Nathaniel Mountney understood to be the "lord treasurer" or "lord chancellor," while Weddell described this official as "the chief justice for the city of Canton."[17] Subordinate to him, they understood, was the "champin": "the admiral of the forces both by sea and land," "Admiral of the Seas," "Admiral General," and "lord admiral"; Weddell styled him both "general of the city of Canton" and "General of the Province by sea"—it was this official whom Paulo Noretti claimed was directly

---

13. This official is most probably what Galeote Pereira had represented in his sixteenth-century account as "*Chaem*, that is a visitor, as it were, whose office is to go in circuit, and to see justice exactly done." Contemporary translation of Richard Willes in Boxer, *South China*, 6.

14. This is likely the official mentioned in the sixteenth century by Galeote Pereira (trans. of Richard Willes): "There is also placed in each ['shire'/province] a *Tutao*, as you would say a governor." In other Portuguese accounts from the sixteenth and seventeenth centuries we find such similar spellings as "Tutão," "Tutam," and "Tutan." Boxer, *South China*, 6 and 89n1.

15. Mountney, "Voyage of the Weddell Fleet." From this line I surmise that they understood "hittow" and "champin" to be subordinate to the "Quan Moan." As noted above, when the British wrote "Quan Moan" it was with the "qu" representing the "gw/kw" sound as in "quandary"—not the pinyin *quan*, which is a sort of "ch" sound as in Massa*ch*usetts.

16. 30 November / 10 December 1637, Mundy, *Travels*, vol. 3.

17. Mountney, Rawlinson, A.299; "Weddell's China Narrative, O.C. 1662." In his sixteenth-century account, Gaspar da Cruz referred to this officer: "To this *Aitao* pertaineth to command the soldiers, and all that is necessary of shipping, victuals, and all other provision against enemies and against pirates. And to this belong also the business of foreigners in cases which belong not to the Revenue." Gaspar da Cruz, *Treatise* (1569), in Boxer, *South China*, 154.

giving him orders. The Courteens also referred to the deputy of the "champin."[18] Mundy recorded the intriguing detail, which seems to have been related by Noretti himself, that the latter "now lives with the Cheeompee ["champin"], a great man in this province."[19]

In his 27 December 1637 letter, the Macao captain-general Camara de Noronha related that: "[the British still anchored at Macao in July] came to an agreement with the Chinese to show them the port of Canton. And being furnished with two pilots, they took soundings of all these islands [in the Bogue and Pearl River], and one of their pinnaces [*Anne*] accompanied the pilots and went quite near to Canton." But none of the Ming records refer to this Anglo-Chinese meeting and agreement. So, according to both the Portuguese and English accounts, weeks before the British encountered the bilingual "mandarin tonpuan" Noretti in the Bogue, in late August, they had received some indication or intimation of Chinese interest in cooperating and trading—from mandarins coming from Macao not long after the arrival of the Courteen fleet in the beginning of July.[20] However, in the accounts left by Mundy, Weddell, and Nathaniel Mountney, we find no note that any "mandarins" at Macao *expressly* advised or invited them to go up to the Bogue. Only obliquely does one of these English accounts refer to encouragement by Macao mandarins, or mandarins from Canton visiting via Macao.

To repeat: the Ming records make no reference to or description of the meetings of the mandarins with the British in July. And again, and even more remarkably, these documents do not even remotely allude to the Thomas Robinson–John Mountney excursion of the pinnace *Anne*. Nor is there any reference—or at least any clear and explicit reference, let alone detailed description—in any of the Ming reports to the Robinson-Mountney-attended ceremony in August where they presented the Noretti-drafted Chinese petition—at what these Courteen factors described as a palatial residence in or on the outskirts of Canton.[21] Indeed, Lawrence Wong has emphasized the lack of Chinese records about Anglo-Chinese interactions in July and August and the paucity of information about Noretti in the *Ming shi* (明史). The *Ming shi* does refer to Noretti by his Chinese name: Li Yerong (李葉榮); and it characterizes him as a 奸民 (*jianmin*) and 奸徒 (*jiantu*), that is, a scoundrel or crafty villain, with the strong connotation of traitor.[22] In the *Ming shi* Li Yerong is called neither interpreter nor official (mandarin).[23] But in the other, much more

---

18. Most probably, by "champin's deputy" the Courteens referred to Li Yanqing (黎延慶), named and identified as 副總兵 (*fuzongbing*; "vice commander") and 南頭副總 (Nantou fuzong) in the 兵部殘稿. As noted below, he was personally involved in supervising the fire-ship attack. Also likely is that Li Yanqing was the officer who, commanding twenty junks on 28 July, halted John Carter and the *Anne* in the Pearl River. He had directly interacted with the British before the "champin" did.

19. 16/26 August 1637, Mundy, *Travels*, vol. 3.

20. For the visits of "mandarins" to the Courteen fleet off Macao in July and August 1637, we assume they brought their own Portuguese-speaking interpreters. Neither the Portuguese nor English records explain how communication was conducted on those occasions.

21. This is a point highlighted by Wong, "The Bogue Incident," 52.

22. Wong, "The Bogue Incident," 50.

23. Wong, "The Bogue Incident," 51.

detailed Ming record, 兵部殘稿 (*bingbu cangao*), that is, in the documents from the Ministry of War (兵部 *bingbu*), he is classified as a 通事 (*tongshi*, interpreter), but not as someone holding any 官職 (*guanzhi*, official position) of any sort; so it was only he himself who told, that is, lied to the British that he was an official.[24]

Along with Wong, Wan Ming has clarified whose responsibility it was to confront the British when Captain Weddell sailed the whole Courteen fleet into the Bogue. The officer was the man the Courteens called the "champin," or "our lord admiral." His Chinese name is what the British were unable to record: Chen Qian (陳謙).[25] The English rendering "champin" obviously approximates *zongbing* (總兵), provincial commander of military-naval forces.[26] The *zongbing* bore direct and principal responsibility for handling the "red-haired barbarian" intruders in the Pearl River.[27] But this *zongbing*, that is, the "champin," Chen Qian's superior, the "haitao" also became involved in disposing of these tenacious European interlopers.[28] Li Yerong/Paulo Noretti was dispatched by this "haitao" and Chen Qian to convey the ultimatum to the British. The English renderings "haitao" and "hittow" were approximations of *haidao* (海道)—which the British glossed variously as "lord treasurer," "lord chancellor," and "the chief justice for the city of Canton." He was the superintendent of customs duties, whose Chinese name was Zheng Jinguang (鄭覲光).[29]

---

24. Wong, "The Bogue Incident," 51.

25. Chen Qian, as *zongbing* (總兵), is identified in the *Ming shi*. See Wong, "The Bogue Incident," 52.

26. Hucker's entry for *zongbing* is *tsŭng-pîng kuăn* 總兵肩 or *tsung-pîng*, and he glosses it "regional commander" and "military head of a territorial jurisdiction generically called a Defense Command." Charles Hucker, *A Dictionary of Official Titles in Imperial China* (Stanford, CA: Stanford University Press, 1985), no. 7146; as elaborated in his later survey: "Those who directed tactical dispositions and operations in a large area were commonly called regional commanders (tsung-ping kuan) [*zongbing guan*]. Officers who controlled smaller areas were called regional vice commanders (fu tsung-ping kuan) [*fu zongbing guan*] or assistant regional commanders (ts'an-chiang) [*canjiang* 參將]." Hucker, "Ming Government," *Cambridge Ming*, vol. 8, 102. More recently, the scholar of southeast coastal affairs in the late Ming / early Qing, Cheng Wei-chung (*War, Trade and Piracy*, Appendix II, 337), has adopted Hucker's translation of *zongbing* as "regional commander." A more famous *zongbing* was the father of Zheng Chenggong (鄭成功 Koxinga): in Fujian a few years after the Courteen fleet's departure from China, Zheng Zhilong (鄭芝龍) was serving as *zongbing*.

27. Wong, "The Bogue Incident," 52–53, 56.

28. The *haidao* (Zheng Jinguang) reported that at the time of the fire-ship attack (September 20), he was still in Duanzhou (端州), a district of Zhaoqing, a significant distance west of Canton: 繳時臣正擬於役端州 (兵部殘稿).

29. John Wills represents the *haidao* (海道) as "vice-commissioner for the maritime defense circuit" and describes this officer's key role in negotiating with the Portuguese at the time of the founding of Macao in the 1550s. Wills, *Cambridge Ming*, vol. 8, 344. While Wills uses vice-commissioner for the "maritime defense circuit," Hucker preferred "Coastal Defense Circuit." *Dictionary of Official Titles*, no. 2126, hăi-fáng tao 海防道. Wills followed Boxer, who related how the Portuguese acquired their first secure base in Guangdong by an agreement with this official. In 1554 the Portuguese captain major Leonel de Sousa successfully negotiated with the *haidao* Wang Bo ("commander of the coastguard fleet"), to reach an oral agreement that let the Portuguese trade in Guangdong on terms identical with those of the Siamese, who were already trading. Boxer, *South China*, xxxiv. For Chinese references to Wang Bo deliberately deceiving his Ming superiors about the true identity of the Iberians and accepting Portuguese bribes to permit them commerce, see 李庆新 [Li, Qingxin], 明代海外贸易制度 [The overseas trade system of the Ming dynasty (北京：社会科学文献出版社 [Beijing: Shehui Kexue Wenxian Chubanshe]), 2007.

As noted above, Noretti / Li Yerong introduced himself to the British as an official, a mandarin. The Portuguese accounts imply that Li's superiors *let* him present himself as a mandarin—not as a mere interpreter or messenger. In other words, the Portuguese suggested that at least the *zongbing* ("champin") Chen Qian, who was directly supervising Li, was well aware that the latter would misrepresent himself on greeting the British in the Bogue in late August. That was pretty obviously their plan. Professor Wong concludes from his own scrutiny of the reports of the Ministry of War that Chen Qian was operating and coordinating very closely with Li Yerong: "陳、李二人是一黨同謀的" (Chen and Li together formed a conspiracy).[30] By Wong's reading, the official above Chen Qian, the *haidao*, Zheng Jinguang, however, is *not* implicated—that is, there is no indication in the Ming records that the latter knew that Li Yerong would lie to the British about his identity or falsify the communiqué that conveyed the ultimatum—for the British fleet to evacuate the Bogue or be annihilated, such that not a "rag of sail" would remain (片帆不留 *pianfan buliu*). Nor, according to my own examination of the 兵部殘稿 (*bingbu cangao*) and Zhang Jingxin's memorials and reports, is there any claim in the Chinese documents that this *haidao* Zheng Jinguang knew that Chen Qian and Li Yerong were carrying out a scheme to trick and rob the British before the fire-ship attack of September 20.[31] Wong maintains that on the Ming side the key question is: Who was the superior interacting with Li Yerong / Paulo Noretti; he answers: Li Yerong was working with Chen Qian, *zongbing*, commander of the navy / military forces of Guangdong. The *zongbing* (the "champin") Chen Qian both conspired with Li Yerong to deceive and rob the British beginning late August and then orchestrated and oversaw the fire-ship attack of September 20. All this can be established or reasonably inferred from the Ming documents.[32] So, it would appear that at least it was Chen's plan to get as much silver and vendible goods from the British (accompanied to Canton by the factors Nathaniel and John Mountney and Thomas Robinson) and then exterminate their colleagues and ships still anchored in the Bogue. But was this plan co-orchestrated, authorized, or known to Zheng Jinguang, the *haidao*, or any mandarins of

---

30. Wong, "The Bogue Incident," 53. Wong uses various Chinese phrases with the import of conspiracy, collusion, machination, and plot to describe the concerted action of Chen Qian and Li Yerong; e.g., "陳謙和李葉榮串謀" where we would translate 串謀 (*chuanmou*) as "to conspire" or "to engage in conspiracy." He also characterizes the criminal scheme of Chen and Li as "個人利益的謀財害命陰謀," that is, "a devious plot to achieve private profit and property by murder." "The Bogue Incident," 55, 56.

31. By Zhang Jingxin's memorials and reports, I am referring to that governor's texts as edited by Tang and Zhang, "Governor of Guangdong and Guangxi."

32. Also evident from the 兵部殘稿 is that the deputy of Chen Qian, Li Yanqing was involved in overseeing the fire-ship attack. Li Yanqing (黎延慶) is identified as 副總兵 (*fuzongbing*; "vice commander") and 南頭副總 (*Nantou fuzong*). In the reports submitted by Chen Qian, among the Ministry of War documents, it is related that Zhang Qi (張奇) and forty other Fujianese soldier-sailors adept at fire-ship attacks (善火閩兵, *shanhuo minbing*) were recruited by Chen Bangji (陳邦基), a lower-level officer (把總) who was taking orders under Li Yanqing to prepare and undertake the operation. Chen Bangji is described as the fire-ship attack commander who rode in one of the vessels and personally directed the assault of September 20: 陳邦基自願認領閩兵沖鋒. The British thought that additional attacks might be conducted by Fujianese ("Chincheos") mercenaries, but were unaware that the abortive one of September 20 had been prosecuted with personnel from that other coastal province.

Lessons Learned: The "Anglology" of the Ming? 137

even higher rank? Departing from Wong and his focus, that is the question that I would pose and shall pursue below.

The British used the word "Chadjan" to refer to the high-ranking official in Canton whom they regarded as the superior of the "haitao" and "champin." They understood him to be "the supervisor general." They were most likely referring to the Guangdong *xun'an* (巡按): imperial inspector / inspector-general, whose name was Ge Zhengqi (葛徵奇).[33] From the reports of the Ministry of War, it appears that officials of the superintendencies of maritime shipping (市舶司 *shibosi*) were ordered by this "Chadjan," Ge Zhengqi, to go to Macao, along with officers from Xiangshan (香山) and Xiangshan Fortress (香山寨), to confer and organize with the Portuguese, and to compel them to come to the provincial capital to dispose of the British merchants and their property. So Ge Zhengqi was in Canton while the Mountneys and Robinson were still in custody, and he was the highest imperial official (next to the "Tootan") handling the affair. Ge issued orders and received reports and updates from Chen Qian and Zheng Jinguang. He was also one of the principal officials who subsequently submitted memorials to the Chongzhen emperor reviewing and commenting upon the events involving the British and Portuguese. After this inspector-general, Ge Zhengqi, arrived on the scene (at least a few weeks after the British had first entered the Bogue), Li Yerong / Paulo Noretti, apparently not yet convicted of malfeasance, became the target of investigation. By the higher authorities—those above *zongbing* Chen Qian and the *haidao* Zheng Jinguang—Li Yerong would later be condemned for colluding with and smuggling British (紅夷 *hongyi*) merchants and their goods and silver into Canton. In the same vein, Chen Qian and Li Yerong would be castigated for taking bribes and using devious means to gain personal profit.[34]

The "Tootan" was the official whom the British took to be "viceroy of this province of Canton." They were under the impression (correct, as it turns out) that he was only quite recently (June 1637) appointed to this top position in provincial governance.[35] While the *xun'an* Ge Zhengqi was already at Canton or nearby, this governor (or "viceroy") was still in Guangxi on circuit.[36] The newly installed viceroy (兩廣總督 *Liangguang zongdu*) was Zhang Jingxin (張鏡心).[37] Along with, but later than, Ge Zhengqi, Zhang came onto the scene to supervise the handling of the British by the

---

33. Throughout the 兵部殘稿, we find orders given to the *haidao* Zheng Jinguang by the Guangdong *xun'an* Ge Zhengqi (廣東巡按葛徵奇). Hucker rendered *xun'an* as "regional inspector" and noted that the most important of the censorial commissions was that of this inspector; one such "regional inspector" was assigned to each province. Hucker, *Dictionary of Official Titles*, no. 2713; and Hucker, *Cambridge Ming*, vol. 8, 93. Cheng has followed Hucker in rendering *xun'an* as "regional inspector." *War, Trade and Piracy*, Appendix II, 337. For Ge Zhengqi's background, see Wan, "First Direct Clash of China and Britain," 56n1.
34. 兵部題《失名会同两广总督张镜心题》残稿（明清史料乙编，第八本）(1936), 752–53.
35. Ge Zhengqi noted the recency of this provincial governor's appointment: 新督臣張鏡心. For the other positions that Zhang Jingxin held concurrently, see Wan, "First Direct Clash of China and Britain," 56n1.
36. According to the report of the *haidao* Zheng Jinguang referring the viceroy's location: 督臣又遠在西粵.
37. Besides "viceroy," *zongdu* is also commonly translated as "governor-general," and Hucker, *Dictionary of Official Titles*, glosses it as "supreme commander" as well.

haidao ("haitao") Zheng Jinguang and *zongbing* ("champin") Chen Qian. After all the subsequent interrogations and investigations, many of those administered by Ge Zhengqi, in January 1638 Zhang Jingxin reported to the emperor the malfeasance of Chen Qian and Li Yerong and recommended their censure and punishment.[38] The Guangdong viceroy chastised Chen Qian and Li Yerong for deceiving and luring the British into Canton for their own private gain.[39] While none of the Ming records indicate what, if any, conviction was made or precisely what punishment Li Yerong and Chen Qian ultimately received for their corrupt and criminal dalliance with the "red-barbarians," the high-level mandarins who supervised the disposal of the British seem to have received approval and even commendation from Beijing. The Guangdong governor ("Tootan") Zhang Jingxin was praised and judged worthy of reward. The inspector-general ("Chadjan") Ge Zhengqi and superintendent ("haitao") Zheng Jinguang were both praised and recommended for bonuses for their exemplary policy and conduct.[40] But as I will suggest below, the Courteens, or at least Nathaniel Mountney, might have been surprised to learn that the latter, Zheng Jinguang, had been recognized for probity and meritorious conduct.

From the Ming records I have reviewed, it appears clear that the plot carried out against the British—to deceive them in the Bogue, take their money and goods, and then destroy them by fire-ships—was a scheme directed if not hatched by the man the Courteens called the "champin," Chen Qian. It was the latter who employed Li Yerong / Paulo Noretti, the Portuguese-fluent "petty mandarin," to communicate a false message—that they had been granted license to trade. But from the Courteen accounts we glimpse the intriguing possibility that official involvement in this scheme went higher than Chen Qian: specifically, that the "haitao" Zheng Jinguang was privy or complicit, if not directly involved. In the account penned by Nathaniel Mountney, while relating details about the fire-ship attack of 20 September, this superintendent (海道副使 *haidao fushi*) Zheng is implicated in the line: "their [Portuguese] most treacherous stratagem [fire-ship attack], which they had privately, *by the connivance of hittow*, contrived against us."[41] In other words,

---

38. The main substance of Zhang Jingxin's memorial 《参鎮臣庇奸之罪疏》 is description of the corruption and misconduct of Chen Qian and Li Yerong. Ge Zhengqi's memorials in 兵部题《失名会同两广总督张镜心题》残稿（明清史料乙编，第八本）contain similar censure of Chen and Li. The *xun'an* Ge in such documents referred to the taking of bribes and misconduct with the British this way: 贿縱接濟.

39. Also implicated and named was Chen Qian's subordinate, Yang Yuan: 香山参将楊元. There can be no doubt that Weddell and the Courteens interacted with Yang Yuan at least a few times in the Bogue, but their references to him are vague—and it is unlikely that they knew his close relationship to the "champin" Chen Qian. Yang Yuan's position (参将) is usually rendered "assistant regional commander." Along with Li Yerong, Zhang Jingxin named a few other individuals who were probably Li's or Chen's associates in the illegal operation conducted in the Pearl River: 揭邦竣 (Jie Bangjun), 葉貴 (Ye Gui), and 林心湖 (Lin Xinhu). 張鏡心《参鎮臣庇奸之罪疏》(Tang and Zhang, "Governor of Guangdong and Guangxi," 123).

40. 兵部题《失名会同两广总督张镜心题》残稿（明清史料乙编，第八本）(1936), 756.

41. Mountney, "Voyage of the Weddell Fleet"; emphasis added. Moreover, in accounting for the detainment of Courteens and their goods and money in Canton, it is asserted that the Portuguese by bribery had "so prevailed with the covetous nature of *Hai-tao* and some others." A similar comment contains the clause: "*Hittow* and some others of the Portugals' bribed friends."

albeit in speculative fashion, the British allege that Zheng Jinguang—not Chen Qian—took bribes from the Portuguese to commission the launch of the fire-ship attack upon the lulled British. To be sure, the various Courteen accounts—those of Peter Mundy, Nathaniel Mountney, and Captain Weddell—are far from unanimous or unequivocal about the authorship and execution of the fire-ship attack. For example, in one place Captain Weddell identified the "mandarin of Casa Branca" as heavily involved: "In the interim the Portugals had wrought with the mandarin of Casa Branca [Xiangshan] to join with the 2 other petty mandarins to procure 7 fire junks to put upon us in the dark of the night whilst we were busy in shifting the *Sun*."[42] In the accounts of Mountney and Mundy, this mandarin is *not* mentioned in relation to the fire-ship attack. Nor, incidentally, can we find specific references to Chinese officials in the Portuguese accounts—only "the Chinese" and "mandarins"—neither titles nor names. Mountney and Weddell both recorded their confident and explicit judgment that the Portuguese bribed the Chinese to launch the attack; Mundy is much more tentative. For Chinese hostile action taken against the British in general—not referring to the fire-ship assault—Mundy considered that it was "through the Portugals' bribery . . . *or* . . . the Chinois observing an ancient custom reported of them in not permitting strangers to traffic in their country."[43] The theory that the Portuguese bribed the Chinese to launch the fire-ship attack can certainly survive thorough examination of all the extant documents—English, Portuguese, and Chinese. But for some or many readers of those documents, that notion will be relegated to mere conspiracy theory.[44]

It would have been one thing for the Ming authorities, at the behest of Portuguese bribes, to order the British to leave immediately; to issue a clear ultimatum and then launch the attack upon any exhibit of defiance. But it was quite another thing to *deceive* the British about the ultimatum—that is, in effect, *not* to issue them a clear warning about the consequences for not departing. The latter operation of guile was attributed to the *haidao* Zheng Jinguang when the British used the term "connivance." Further, language used by the Portuguese is loose enough to suggest or permit the conjecture that authorities higher than the *zongbing* Chen Qian, such as

---

42. "Weddell's China Narrative, O.C. 1662."
43. 8/18 August 1637, Mundy, *Travels*, vol. 3; emphasis added.
44. Further warrant for the British to adhere to the idea that the Portuguese were pulling the strings behind the fire-ship attack could have been provided by their awareness of the kind of tactics the Lusitanians had adopted in dealing with the Spaniards in roughly the same location and in similar sets of circumstances. The Portuguese had in the past launched their own fire-ship attacks in the Pearl River estuary, against even those fellow Iberians and fellow subjects of Habsburg sovereigns. Nor is it likely that the Courteens were ignorant of those previous exercises in sly and fiery violence. The only, but very strong, reason *not* to suspect the Portuguese of commissioning the fire-ship attack on September 20 was that it would have risked too blatantly violating the Anglo-Portuguese accord of 1635. And fair or cordial, at least not openly offensive, treatment of the British by the Portuguese could be expected "for fear of the Hollander." Even while the Courteens were still in the Pearl River Delta, there seem to have been rumors of another Dutch invasion of Macao. In Domingos da Camara de Noronha's letter to the viceroy of Goa, 27 December 1637, the captain-general noted: "The city [Macao] bought from them [Courteens] 3,000 dollars' worth of powder upon the news that a Dutch force intended to attack the place." *Lisbon Transcripts, Books of the Monsoons*, book 41, fol. 191.

Zheng, may have been privy to the subterfuge enacted by Li Yerong: "The Chinese, in order to deceive them, offered them every facility, promising them abundant trade. Meanwhile, they were secretly raising an army against them, so much so that the governor of the neighboring province of Chincheo [Fujian] sent soldiers to Canton for its defence."[45] Of course, the "Chinese" and "they" could be referring to only Chen Qian, his subordinates, Li Yerong, and his associates. But using such a broad term as "the Chinese" in this context could suggest collective and concerted action without distinction or division between lower and higher officials; or without any distinction between Chen Qian and Zheng Jinguang. To be sure, the City of Macao in its letter to Charles I, in December, averred: "[The British in the Bogue were] threatening us with war if we impeded their trade, which they said was already very profitable, whereas they had had little but vain promises from *a Mandarin who wished to rob and eventually did rob them.*" Certainly, the Ming records, as reviewed above, point most clearly to this "mandarin" being Chen Qian. But nothing in all the Portuguese reports or official correspondence rules out the possibility that the Lusitanians were referring to Zheng Jinguang instead. Notably, Nathaniel Mountney persevered in his claim that the "champin" Chen Qian was his loyal trade lobbyist in Canton. The Courteen cape merchant emphasized that Chen remained to the very end "our fast friend."[46] By Mountney's analysis, Chen remained benevolent and loyal while the "haitao" Zheng Jinguang was turned hostile by slander, lobbying, and bribes of the Portuguese.

Whether Chen Qian was a "fast" or actually a veritably false friend of Mountney and the Courteens, might Zheng Jinguang have at least winked at the operation of deceit and theft before the attempted extermination of the British? To be sure, and according to Professor Wong's acute analysis, the Ming reports and memorials from the ministry indicate or imply that Li Yerong and Chen Qian acted *independently* and *contrary* to the will and orders of Chen Qian's superior, that is, Zheng Jinguang. Those records point to Chen Qian as personally managing Li Yerong and supervising the launch of the fire-ship attack; none of them refer to the *haidao* Zheng Jinguang as being involved in Li's subterfuge or in planning or overseeing that attack. But if Zheng had actually been winking at Chen Qian and Li Yerong, then there is not too much reason to expect to find such a damaging and scandalous fact recorded in any documents—let alone in any official ones. In the case of any possible malfeasance or corrupt behavior by Ming officials, surely we cannot always expect to find indications or records—especially when those officials are powerful and well enough connected to control the investigations and writing of audits and reports.[47] Perhaps

---

45. Letter from the City of Macao to the King of England, 24 December 1637, *Lisbon Transcripts, Books of the Monsoons*, book 41, fol. 220.

46. "Voyage of the Weddell Fleet." In Mountney's other account, Rawlinson, A.299, we find lines of the same import: "Our lord admiral . . . had undertaken our protection."

47. Michael Szonyi's point may be somewhat applicable to the review and records of actions taken by officials in Guangdong dealing with the British and Portuguese in 1637: "[Military officers] were also involved, turning a blind eye in exchange for bribes. To appear in the historical record, these men had to have been caught, and

the strongest reason to entertain the notion that the *haidao* Zheng Jinguang knew that Chen Qian and Li Yerong would lie to the British and arrange to transport them and their money to Canton—that Zheng was privy to the whole series of ruses, deceptive and covert actions—is that Chen Qian and Li Yerong could hardly have hoped to undertake this large operation (entailing all the transport of merchants, commodities, and silver back and forth from Canton to the Bogue) *without being detected by such a powerful official*—the "lord chancellor" and "chief justice for the city of Canton," as the Courteens variously styled the *haidao*. Would not the successful prosecution of such an illegal operation—significant trafficking between the Bogue and Canton—require bribery and complicity higher than the *zongbing* Chen Qian? So, again, while the *haidao* Zheng Jinguang did, indeed, issue the ultimatum, it is far from impossible that he *knew* that Li Yerong would falsify it and proceed to engage in maneuvers to obtain silver from the British. In order to comply with the Ming prohibition on foreign trade with non-Portuguese Westerners (still the official policy of the administration of the Chongzhen emperor), Zheng had to issue such a document. But that would not preclude his winking at an attempt to trick and rob the Courteens. I would submit that Zheng Jinguang as well as Chen Qian (most probably not such a "fast friend") may have been monitoring or managing Li Yerong as he undertook the devious subterfuge. But both, especially Zheng Jinguang, would have done so as remotely and surreptitiously as possible, and would be prompt to (and plausibly) deny any inkling of skullduggery. Zheng could have been consulted about and secretly authorized the plot while taking all the requisite steps to ensure that he would be able to deny knowledge and involvement—and, thus, never suffer censure by Zhang Jingxin, Ge Zhengqi, or the Chongzhen emperor.

If we can, in light of both the Chinese and European records, regard the conduct of such a high-ranking officer as the provincial naval-military commander (Chen Qian) as corrupt to an extremely scandalous degree—as being malfeasance of a grave and impeachable character—then we might revisit the old and once venerable notion of "well-governed" Ming China. Juan Gonzáles de Mendoza's monumental and seminal book on China published in 1585 rendered the judgment that the Ming state was "the best-governed kingdom" in the known world.[48] As an eminent authority on early modern sinological literature, Donald Lach, summarized: "No aspect of Chinese society was so uniformly admired by seventeenth-century Europeans as its government and administration. Already in the sixteenth century Mendoza had suggested that China was the best-governed land on earth. Thereafter no one essayed to describe China without devoting an almost disproportionately large share of space

---

to have been caught by superiors who chose to deal with them formally, through bureaucratic mechanisms. Besides those who turn up in the records, there were surely many more who were never caught, and many more who were caught but who managed to stay out of the records." *The Art of Being Governed: Everyday Politics in Late Imperial China* (Princeton, NJ: Princeton University Press, 2017), 94.

48. For the enormous influence of Mendoza, including his readership in Elizabethan England, see Chapter 1.

to government and administration."[49] After devoting half a century to researching Ming society, its political institutions, and administrative functioning, Charles Hucker, peerless Western authority on the subject, concluded with a few pages of reflection on "the quality of Ming governance."[50] He noted that in contemporary novels and plays the government was often depicted as "a morass of arrogance, cupidity, hypocrisy, cowardice, and, at best, high-principled ineffectiveness."[51] He recognized that such literature must be taken with a spoonful of salt, and Hucker's ultimate judgment did not ultimately stray so far from Mendoza's:

> Most Ming emperors were less than admirable rulers and Ming officials included both rascals and worthies in full measure. Many Ming Chinese may well have wished for more enlightened rulers and more uniformly effective officials. Still, for all its faults, when compared to contemporary governments in other major societies, the Ming government apparently put a light burden on ordinary Chinese. It can hardly be supposed that Ming Chinese could have envisioned a more satisfactory institutional system. Hence, considering how it maintained its power and sustained its subjects both morally and materially, the Ming government probably deserves to be reckoned, on balance, the most successful major government in the world in its time.[52]

In the dramatic events involving the British in Guangdong in 1637, we may certainly identify what Hucker might, on the Chinese side, consent to call "rascals": Chen Qian and Li Yerong. If we put aside the general administration of Ming China, to concentrate on southeast coastal China, then our estimate of the efficacy and quality of the government (and navy and military) is considerably reduced in the wake of our review of the first British trade expedition to China.

For surely the expedition that entered the Bogue and Pearl River in the summer and fall of 1637 suggests that at least the coastal regions of late Ming Guangdong were *not* especially well governed or particularly secure—at least that there were perfectly venal, unreliable, and treacherous Chinese officials who would engage in deceitful behavior unauthorized by or in defiance of their superiors; that official policy and rules were blatantly disregarded when a handsome profit could be safely made by its violation. Thus, our analysis of the British encounter with the Ming would bolster an important generalization made long ago by John Wills: "For all its overt anti-commercialism and laws against officials engaging in trade . . . Chinese officials did have extensive private financial interests which very frequently led

---

49. Donald F. Lach and Edwin J. Van Kley, *Asia in the Making of Europe*, Vol. 3: *A Century of Advance, Book Four: East Asia* (Chicago: University of Chicago Press, 1993), 1579.
50. *Cambridge Ming*, vol. 8, 103–5. Among Hucker's magnificent contributions is the yet-to-be-superseded *Dictionary of Official Titles in Imperial China* cited above.
51. *Cambridge Ming*, vol. 8, 103.
52. *Cambridge Ming*, vol. 8, 105.

Lessons Learned: The "Anglology" of the Ming?

them to ignore anti-commercial laws and [Confucian] ideologies."[53] Long before the Caroline British arrived in July 1637, that is, throughout the sixteenth century, one can find persistently venal and recalcitrant Ming officials in the southeast coastal provinces. Whether we consider decades of the sixteenth century or just the year 1637, Ming government does not appear especially effective—if an important criterion of efficacy (if not *quality* of governance) is how much the policy decided at the highest/capital level is heeded and implemented at the provincial and lower levels and coastal areas.[54]

Professor Wong's article on the Anglo-Chinese encounter in the Bogue in the reign of the Chongzhen emperor concentrates on the role of the devious interpreter Li Yerong and the abuse of his position for personal gain.[55] But it was the naval commander, the "champin," Chen Qian, holding a very high position (總兵 *zongbing*), who was guilty of malfeasance—by improvising his own treacherous ploy, employing Li Yerong to trick and rob the British; instead of candidly conveying the ultimatum and categorically refusing their request for commercial exchange. The cunning scheme was calculated to bring a private and untaxed profit to Chen Qian and Li Yerong. If the British expedition commanded by John Weddell exposed not uncommon malfeasance and corruption to be found in provincial, coastal Ming China, what about the related question of that dynasty's provision of order and security? On 16 September 1637, the factor Peter Mundy noted that in the Bogue and all around the Pearl River estuary "there [were] many outlaws and sea-robbers among all those islands and creeks."[56] The British were able to linger and loiter menacingly and intermittently maraud and ravage in the Pearl River Delta for several weeks. One might ascribe this to Ming compassion or mercy if it were not so difficult to harmonize such virtue with the malicious spirit of the fire-ship attack launched in the middle of the night. With that consideration in mind, any such lenity would

---

53. John E. Wills Jr., "Maritime China from Wang Chih to Shih Lang: Themes in Peripheral History," in *From Ming to Ch'ing: Conquest, Region, and Continuity in Seventeenth-Century China*, ed. Jonathan D. Spence and John E. Wills Jr. (New Haven, CT: Yale University Press, 1979), 207.

54. For notable episodes in Zhejiang, Fujian, and Guangdong in the 1520s to 1540s, see Wills, *Cambridge Ming*, vol. 8, 490. Similar cases are covered by Roland Higgins, "Pirates in Gowns and Caps: Gentry Law-Breaking in the Mid-Ming," *Ming Studies* 10 (1980): 30–37. Roderich Ptak notes the phenomenon of corruption and illicit trade occurring in those provinces as early as the first decades of the Ming dynasty: "China and Portugal at Sea: The Early Ming Trading System and the *Estado da India* Compared," in *China and the Asian Seas: Trade, Travel, and Visions of the Other (1400–1750)* (Aldershot: Ashgate Variorum, 1998), 1:23. More recently, Szonyi has summarized: "Coastal people from virtually every social status imaginable, from poor fishermen to salt traders to literati elites . . . were involved in illicit maritime commerce in some way. . . . [S]o were the soldiers and officers of the coastal garrisons. Dozens of entries in the *Veritable Records*, spanning the whole dynasty, demonstrate this." *Art of Being Governed*, 93. Two recent essay collections treat corruption, illicit maritime trade, security policy, and piracy on the coasts in the mid- and late-Ming period: Robert Antony, ed., *Elusive Pirates, Pervasive Smugglers: Violence and Clandestine Trade in the Greater China Seas* (Hong Kong: Hong Kong University Press, 2010); and Y. H. Teddy Sim, ed., *The Maritime Defence of China: Ming General Qi Jiguang and Beyond* (Singapore: Springer, 2017). The most relevant monograph in Chinese that covers many of these issues is 林仁川 [Lin, Renchuan], 明末清初的私人海上贸易 [Private sea trade in late Ming and early Qing] (上海：华东师范大学 [Shanghai: Huadong Shifan Daxue, 1987]), 1987.

55. "通事李葉榮從中營私舞弊": Wong, "The Bogue Incident," 41.

56. 6/16 September 1637, Mundy, *Travels*, vol. 3.

bear a striking resemblance only to appeasement and a strategy of biding one's time. The *haidao* Zheng Jinguang commanded the British to depart immediately or else expect a devastating attack that would annihilate their fleet, such that not a "rag of sail would remain" (片帆不留 *pianfan buliu*). In view of the displays of force and effective forays of the British both before and after the fire-ship attack, that line appears rather hollow—or something along the lines of idle threatening. For besides the fire-ship attack, what was supposed to be devastating? As the British repeatedly noted, fire-ship attacks were the only thing they feared from the Ming side.

It appears that the provincial authorities of Canton maintained a very risky dependence on the Portuguese at Macao to deal with such troublesome and unannounced foreigners as the British. If the Lusitanians could not dispose of such barbarians, did the Canton officers like the *haidao* Zheng Jinguang or the *zongbing* Chen Qian have the means to eliminate and annihilate intrusive and intrepid interlopers like the Courteens led by John Weddell, Richard Swanley, and John Carter? Ultimately, the Portuguese pursuing their self-interest, stonewalling and thwarting (if not sabotaging) the British to maintain monopolistic position, placed the Ming in a decidedly vulnerable posture.[57] As Wan Ming conceded, it was the hostility of the Portuguese in pursuing that narrow commercial interest that caused the British to enter the Bogue.[58] The shocking "red-haired barbarian" (紅夷 *hongyi*) penetration of the Pearl River was a crisis and fiasco for the Ming provincial officials at Canton. It exposed the insecurity and faultiness of one key facet of Ming foreign policy, that is, its Macao-as-gatekeeper or first-line-of-defense arrangement. To permit the Portuguese to monopolize trade with Canton and exercise so much control over the entry to the province of Guangdong was certainly to incur serious security risks—and close some doors of opportunity for commercial and economic growth. After all, there is no question whatsoever that the British had come to trade and not to fight with the Ming (or the Portuguese). The violent actions taken by the British can be regarded as merely retaliation and self-defense inasmuch as it would have made no sense for Weddell to commence engagements in waters and terrain so unfamiliar to the British—and with the perfidious Portuguese lurking in the background and eagerly awaiting, if not trying to facilitate, mishap and debacle.

Instead of dealing personally, directly, and forthrightly with the trespassing British fleet, the Canton "mandarins," in the Macao captain-general's unspecific phrasing, communicated to him a request that the Portuguese "together with some of their officials" should send a protest. But why not act instantly and independently of the Portuguese once the latter had already failed to contain the Courteens—and why not unleash a Ming naval attack in broad daylight as an exercise of defense

---

57. In the City of Macao's letter to Charles I, 24 December 1637, the Portuguese themselves clarified the ultimate stakes: "Trade between the English and the Chinese would be the ruin of this city." *Lisbon Transcripts, Books of the Monsoons*, book 41, fol. 220.

58. "可以說葡人出於自保，不得不採取比較現實的態度，但這也在客觀上促使英人不顧一切闖入虎門." Wan, "First Direct Clash of China and Britain," 69.

Lessons Learned: The "Anglology" of the Ming? 145

against a foreign fleet intruding its sovereign domain? It seems the Ming authorities at Canton decided to practice military and naval frugality. But was such virtue, along with faute de mieux lenity or appeasement, imposed by necessity? To have the Lusitanians at Macao function as a filter and check upon other European foreigners was a cheap but not very reliable defense arrangement: this is what the troublesome visit of the British exposed. The Courteen fleet's intrusion and rampage in the Bogue—marauding, arson, sacking, pillaging—revealed the tenuous if not illusory security of the Ming policy of playing barbarian off against barbarian (以夷制夷 *yiyizhiyi*). At least by the summer of 1637, the Portuguese of Macao had become a doubtful first line of defense, as the Courteens weighed anchor at Macao, entered the Pearl River, and demolished a fortress and ransacked villages on the shores and islands of the Bogue. As the Portuguese themselves acknowledged, they were powerless to expel the British fleet by any application of naval or military force: "The English were *masters of the sea* and . . . this port had no ships to come in force upon them to defend it, still less to take the offensive or to drive them from the coast, nor was there any hope of any assistance coming to it in good time from any quarter."[59]

Rather than fully acknowledging and addressing the grievous and deadly security breach in the Bogue and proposing some significant reform of this Portuguese-preferential commercial, Portuguese-dependent defense policy, the authorities in Canton, Ge Zhengqi and Zhang Jingxin, rendered reports and memorials to Beijing that complacently minimized the harm done by the British and merely concentrated on decrying the culpable avarice and malfeasance of Chen Qian, Li Yerong, and other such knaves (奸徒 *jiantu*).[60] Most of the lines from those accounts by the provincial commissioner Ge and viceroy Zhang make it seem as though the British were pitiable and almost casually disposed of. Yet there are also lines that reveal that these provincial officials perceived this unknown species of foreigner to be very dangerous—and to be pests not so easily swatted or tamed (even with the assistance of the Portuguese). The City of Macao's letter to Charles I also noted the anxiety and fear induced in the mandarins at Canton: "The Chinese took alarm, afraid that in future years they will come here with many more to conquer them."[61] In the last analysis, then, and regardless of what was written in the Ming reports and memorials, it is hard to doubt that Captain Weddell and his Courteen colleagues left a deep impression of naval and military potency—not very different from that of the more notorious Dutch, who by 1637 were secure in their newly built base in southwest Taiwan, Fort Zeelandia. But, to reiterate, in those Ming documents the menace of

---

59. Copy of the decision arrived at by the City of Macao respecting the English, 10 October 1637, *Lisbon Transcripts, Books of the Monsoons*, book 41, fol. 213; emphasis added.

60. Professor Wong has observed how the Ming reports carefully concealed how effective and fatal were Weddell's offensives in the Bogue. "The Bogue Incident," 57. The viceroy Zhang Jingxin refers in his reports to the knaves who aided and abetted the intrusive British loitering in the Bogue: 曠日持久，而更有奸黨爲之窟. Likewise, provincial inspector-general Ge Zhengqi emphasized his apprehension that rogues like Li Yerong were all too numerous: 臣恐姦人之如李葉榮者更不少也.

61. City of Macao to Charles I, 24 December 1637, *Lisbon Transcripts, Books of the Monsoons*, book 41, fol. 220.

this barbarian fleet of only four ships is decidedly understated, to the point of dangerously minimizing the threat it posed—and could pose again.

To be fair, the inadequacy of the Ming naval and military resources in Guangdong probably necessitated the risky reliance on the Portuguese at Macao to deal with unanticipated guests like the British.[62] The frailty and vulnerability of the Chinese military and naval forces has been well-documented and much discussed—if recently somewhat revised.[63] Many high-ranking officers were not appointed for any ability, and many even lacked minimal experience and training.[64] In concluding his assessment of the defense apparatus, Hucker writes: "Considering the hopeless state of the Ming military establishment as reported by contemporary critics and later analysts, it seems almost miraculous that the Ming empire managed somehow to hold out against the Manchus (and the Mongols, who soon became Manchu allies) beyond the Great Wall and simultaneously against massive domestic rebellions until as late as 1644."[65] The final appraisal of Ray Huang was not much different, though certainly more mordantly delivered. Among other things he noted that: "During the Ming period, the prestige of the military sank to the lowest level in Chinese history. With peripheral states too insignificant to be considered rivals, even the deterioration of the armed forces created no imminent danger."[66] Huang's estimate was a little lower than Hucker's: "The dynasty could exist with a minimum of military and economic strength. There was no need to take administrative efficiency seriously. In the sixteenth century, pirates, sometimes numbering less than one hundred in a band, could roam inland for several hundred miles unchecked. The durability of the Ming empire was not based on its merit, but on the lack of an alternative."[67]

---

62. Presumably Cheng Wei-chung would concur, as his broad assessment was that: "the Ming dynasty could not raise enough revenue to pay for the maintenance of a permanent naval fleet to defend the coastal regions in a period of change and foreign intrusion." *War, Trade and Piracy*, 247. Recently, Lu Cheng-Heng has highlighted some key differences between the situations in Fujian and Guangdong—most interestingly, that in the 1630s and during the tenure of Zhang Jingxin, the latter province had much fewer resources, armaments, and personnel for coastal security. Cheng-Heng Lu, "Between Bureaucrats and Bandits: The Rise of Zheng Zhilong and His Organization, the Zheng Ministry (Zheng Bu)," in *Sea Rovers, Silver, and Samurai*, ed. Andrade and Hang (Honolulu: University of Hawai'i Press, 2016), 146–47.

63. For seminal discussions see Ray Huang, *1587, A Year of No Significance: the Ming Dynasty in Decline* (New Haven, CT: Yale University Press, 1981), 157–64, 175–76; and Hucker, "Ming Government," *Cambridge Ming*, vol. 8, 62–70. The consensus of steady naval and military decline beginning as early as the Wanli emperor (1572–1620), as outlined by Huang and Hucker, has been subjected to qualification and revision courtesy of historians like Kenneth Swope and Tonio Andrade. For a judicious evaluation of this revisionist corrective, see Peter Lorge, *War, Politics and Society in Early Modern China, 900–1795* (London: Routledge, 2005), 119. More recently, after his deep scrutiny of Ming military affairs and personnel, Szonyi, *Art of Being Governed*, was *not* provoked to challenge that Huang-Hucker consensus. A fresh set of revisionist (and some non-revisionist) views of Ming naval and military competence can be found in Sim, *Maritime Defence of China*; and Tonio Andrade and Kenneth Swope, eds., *Early Modern East Asia: War, Commerce, and Cultural Exchange* (New York: Routledge, 2017).

64. Wills, *Cambridge Ming*, vol. 8, 490.

65. Hucker, *Cambridge Ming*, vol. 8, 70.

66. Ray Huang, "The Ming Fiscal Administration," *Cambridge Ming*, vol. 8, 169.

67. Huang, *Cambridge Ming*, 165.

The *Dragon* entering the Tiger's Mouth, that is, the four British ships penetrating the Bogue and making mischief and wreaking havoc along the shores of the Pearl River, bears comparison to those sixteenth-century pirates running amok unchecked, as described by Ray Huang. Only a decade before the arrival of Captain Weddell and his small fleet, other sections of the Ming empire's southeast coast were being assaulted and plundered with near impunity. As Tonio Andrade has summarized: "By 1627, he [Zheng Zhilong] was leading four hundred junks and tens of thousands of men. They ravaged the Chinese coast, capturing merchants' ships, raiding cities, even defeating Ming forces."[68] The governor-general of Guangdong and Guangxi, a predecessor of the "Tootan" (*zongdu*) Zhang Jingxin, reported that the coastal fleet in the south was too weak to grapple with Zheng Zhilong. Andrade, preeminent authority on Sino-Dutch military relations and naval clashes in China and Taiwan, felt compelled to pronounce categorically: "Its [the Ming's] navy was useless."[69] Key Sino-Dutch engagements as analyzed by Andrade were not dissimilar in contour or outcome to the combat between the British and Ming in the Bogue in 1637. It is true that in contrast with the operation launched upon the British on 20 September 1637, Zheng Zhilong's fire-ship attack on the Dutch in Liaoluo Bay near Xiamen in 1634 was successful.[70] But in the previous year, 1633, the Dutch had destroyed Zheng's cutting-edge fleet—an armada purportedly comparable to a mighty European one. But no effort was made to replace it: "What is curious is that the Ming never tried to rebuild a fleet like the one destroyed in 1633. Perhaps Zhilong's [fire-ship] victory in 1634, achieved with conventional vessels, convinced him and his successors that one didn't need to emulate the Dutch to defeat them."[71] As the Ming authorities in Canton discovered in the Pearl River in September 1637, fire-ship attacks were quite unreliable against alert and nimble British crews and vessels.

In concluding his discussion of Sino-Dutch naval combat spanning the 1630s to 1660s, Andrade observes: "Dutch ships could stand up to far larger numbers of Chinese warjunks." Of a battle that took place in 1663 at Xiamen and Jinmen on the Fujian coast: "Contemporaries—Chinese, Manchu, and Dutch—all agreed. [VOC] Bort's fifteen ships were capable of standing up to Zheng Jing's entire navy."[72] We can make similar observations and render roughly the same judgment in the case of Weddell and the Courteens in the Bogue in 1637: a mere handful of British vessels were shockingly undaunted while surrounded by dozens of Chinese junks in the Pearl River and its estuary. As the unfailingly modest and diffident-prone Peter

---

68. Andrade, *Lost Colony: The Untold Story of China's First Great Victory over the West* (Princeton, NJ: Princeton University Press, 2011), 28.

69. Andrade, *Lost Colony*, 30. In addition to Andrade's assessment, a very informative survey of the condition of the Ming navy is provided by Peter Lorge in "Water Forces and Naval Operations," in *A Military History of China*, ed. David A. Graff and Robin Higham (Boulder, CO: Westview, 2002), 81–96.

70. That episode is covered by Andrade in both *Lost Colony*, 48–50, and *Gunpowder Age*, 205–6.

71. Andrade, *Gunpowder Age*, 206.

72. Andrade, *Lost Colony*, 312, 315; Zheng Jing was grandson of Zheng Zhilong and son and successor of the more famous Zheng Chenggong ("Koxinga").

Mundy noted, on behalf of all the Courteens, the only Ming operation or device that caused any worry in them was fire-ship attack: "Other hurt from them we feared not, *were they 10 times as many*."[73]

Therefore, the Weddell expedition of the Courteen Association illustrates and confirms the broader truth of European and British naval superiority in the sixteenth and seventeenth centuries. While naval stagnation and weakness obtained in Ming China in those centuries, Westerners were advancing steadily in this domain. As Derek Massarella has summarized the maritime superiority of the early modern era: "Europeans had successfully harnessed advances in naval and military technology to overseas expansion: especially the solid, full-rigged ship and the ability to fire a cannon from the deck of a ship without compromising the stability of the ship or its function as a cargo vessel, a feat which Asian ship-design and construction failed to match."[74] Putting aside this broader European phenomenon, N. A. M. Rodger has provided detailed explanation of British advances and success in these areas. British naval potency emerged out of sophisticated ordnance technology that developed from its domestic iron-founding industry.[75] By the last decades of the sixteenth century, ordnance capable of being deployed in ocean-going vessels was widely available: "Whereas in other countries heavy guns were still vastly expensive princely status symbols, in England by the 1580s they had become an everyday commodity within the pocket of any would-be pirate or explorer. This striking technical advantage, which lasted in certain respects into the nineteenth century, distinctly marked the character of English expansion. It made English ships, however small, unusually ready to fight other ships; it gave the English advantages at sea which they did not have on land."[76]

While the reality of this decisive nautical-naval advantage of the British (and Dutch) in the seventeenth century has not been denied by revisionists in the twenty-first century, Andrade has been in the historiographical vanguard in challenging the conventional notion of broader European military superiority in the early modern era. He has offered a robust challenge to the notion that we must regard the Ming military as flimsy and grossly inferior to its Western counterparts. He contends that from about 1550 to 1700 the military level of East Asians was about equal to that of the Europeans. In this "Age of Parity," he maintains: "Whenever trained military forces from East Asia met those of Europe, the former won decisively. . . . East Asians fielded dynamic and effective forces, defeating European troops not just by superior numbers but also by means of excellent guns, effective logistics, strong leadership, and better (or at least equivalent) drill and cohesion."[77] But at least if we judge from

---

73. 30 July/9 August 1637, Mundy, *Travels*, vol. 3; emphasis added.
74. Massarella, *World Elsewhere*, 36. For European nautical science and naval technology in the sixteenth and seventeenth centuries, see John F. Guilmartin, *Galleons and Galleys* (London: Cassell, 2002); and Andrade, *Gunpowder Age*, 196–210.
75. Rodger, "Guns and Sails," 86.
76. Rodger, "Guns and Sails," 86–87.
77. Andrade, *Gunpowder Age*, 5.

Lessons Learned: The "Anglology" of the Ming?

the limited skirmishes on islands and shores of the Pearl River, like the one involving Thomas Robinson on 23 August 1637 (Chapter 5), the Ming Chinese soldiers did not exhibit any ("dynamic" or "effective") military superiority. The clashes and skirmishes in Guangdong involving Captain Weddell's men and the Chinese did not demonstrate that the latter had any ability on land which was superior or even equal to that of the British.

After noting that in the sixteenth century the Ming adopted cannons from the Portuguese and arquebuses both from them and the Japanese, as well as acquiring cutting-edge European artillery early in the next century, Andrade asserts: "Chinese artillery technology became in some ways superior to European artillery. Guns helped the forces of China defeat Europe's two great seventeenth-century imperial powers: the Dutch and the Russians."[78] However that may be, the British in 1637 did *not* find Chinese guns or artillery at the forts in the Bogue to be very effective—or at least those who operated the ordnance were severely and shockingly incompetent.[79] That episode from August 1637 illustrates and bolsters a point raised by such revisionist scholars of Chinese military history as Peter Lorge and Kenneth Swope: that incompetence of Ming leadership, as well as its faulty strategy, lax discipline, and sloppy operations may have been much greater than any technological disadvantages.[80] In any case, the putative superiority of Chinese artillery that emerges in the seventeenth century, as posited by Andrade, was not displayed to the British in 1637. In January 1638, the Courteen fleet left China rather unimpressed. Flaming ships in the middle of the night, not strong guns or cannons, had been the chief security concern. It was the hostages—Nathaniel and John Mountney and Thomas Robinson, captives in Canton—that turned out to be the most powerful weapon deployed by the Ming against Captain Weddell.

Our scrutiny of the British encounters and engagements with the Ming in 1637 suggests that Andrade's estimate of military capacity is somewhat too high: "parity" appears a little excessive after review of all these clashes in the river, creeks, estuary, islands, and shores between Macao and Canton. At least if we concentrate on (and credit) the accounts rendered by the Courteens (which are not undermined by any of the Portuguese ones), our impression will be *imparity*, in favor of the British. Andrade proceeds to conclude that: "the Age of Parity gave way to a Great

---

78. Andrade, *Gunpowder Age*, 10–11; see also Lorge, *War, Politics and Society*, 125. Both Lorge and Andrade emphasize that the Chinese were very quick to copy and adopt this cutting-edge Western firearms technology. This Ming mode of what we now like to call "technology transfer" is discussed at some length by Albert Chan, *The Glory and Fall of the Ming Dynasty* (Norman: University of Oklahoma Press, 1982), 54–59. For a broad explanation of why Western firearms technology advanced more swiftly and considerably beyond Ming China's, see Kenneth Chase, *Firearms: A Global History to 1700* (Cambridge: Cambridge University Press, 2003).

79. The Ming fort stormed by the Courteens in 1637 proved greatly inferior to the Renaissance fort, whose decided superiority over Chinese structures—and, thus, a key European advantage—is well summarized by Andrade, *Lost Colony*, 316–20. Andrade elsewhere stresses the importance of this type of fort in the success of the Dutch in Taiwan from the 1620s to 1660s.

80. "Like so many dynasties before it, the Ming had great difficulty cultivating military talent institutionally"; "It was not a question of resources but of *leadership*." Lorge, *War, Politics and Society*, 139, 140.

Military Divergence, which became manifest during the Opium War of 1839 to 1842, when British forces consistently outfought the Qing."[81] But the result of our review of the Weddell fleet's performance in the Pearl River estuary would permit us to maintain that some significant "divergence" (imparity) was already clearly on exhibit in 1637—when the Ming seem to have done nothing better than launch an unsuccessful fire-ship attack, while desperately imploring the Portuguese to dispose of this batch of exceptionally tenacious "red-haired barbarians." In the Epilogue, I will pursue this point further, to advance the proposition that between the "Bogue Incident" (虎門事件 Humen shijian) of 1637 and the first engagements of the Opium Wars in 1839, things had not changed so much as is usually assumed—or that "divergence" was more visible than "parity" as Weddell's *Dragon* wreaked havoc in the mouth of the Tiger. That wooden and steamless *Dragon* in the Bogue was a nemesis centuries before the sighting of such a phenomenon as "industrial revolution" or "industrial imperialism"—or the launch of "gunboat diplomacy."[82]

The Ming in Guangdong who interacted with or observed the Courteens in 1637 must have gotten the impression that these pale-skinned foreigners were fierce and formidable whether by water or by land. The Ministry of War reports and memorials characterize the "red-haired barbarians" (紅夷 hongyi) as terribly ferocious: 桀悍 (jiehan). But how else might the Chinese have thought of the novel commercial intruders after the series of encounters during the six months in the Pearl River Delta? Remarkably, the Courteens thought that they had left a good impression—or at least that they succeeded in demonstrating that they were not mere marauders and pirates like, say, the Dutch: "For hereby the honest dealing of our nation, contrary to their [Portuguese] slanderous reports, is apparently manifested and made known, as well to the principal governors of that province [Guangdong] as to the particular merchants and all sorts of people."[83] The last clause conveys the notable claim that the Chinese, from government to "commonality," got the impression that the British were honest—seeking trade not plunder, openly and earnestly pursuing commerce. This is far from implausible: the Chinese in Guangdong surely perceived how forceful and violent the British could be; yet such physical power and audacity was not incompatible with sincerity or probity, "honest dealing." Indubitably, and as solidly certified by the Chinese officials who boarded the Courteen ships, the British had brought cargo to sell and plenty of silver dollars to purchase goods at Macao and Canton. Obviously, they would not have brought so much money if they were merely prowling with a design to probe the Pearl River estuary for plunder opportunities. As suggested above, it would have made little sense for the Ming to think that the British had come with any plan to attack the Portuguese enclave, let alone

---

81. Andrade, *Gunpowder Age*, 5.
82. Although John Wills observed superiority of European seamanship and gunnery vis-à-vis China well before British steamships entered the Pearl River estuary, he was referring to the situation in the late eighteenth century. My effort here and in the Epilogue is to bolster the notion that this advantage obtained even earlier.
83. Mountney, "Voyage of the Weddell Fleet."

invade Canton—in contrast to, say, the Dutch veterans, who had by 1637 made numerous coastal incursions and assaults on Fujian, Guangdong, and Macao itself, from the Pescadores and subsequently their southwest Taiwan base, Zeelandia.

The City of Macao in its letter to Charles I in December 1637 referred to the Ming superstition to the effect that the British "were men with blue eyes, which the Chinese believe bring ill-luck, and that if admitted, they will take their kingdom from them. . . . The Chinese took alarm, fearing that in future years they will come here with many more to conquer them."[84] In the Ming records, including all the Ministry of War reports and memorials, we find no mention of or allusion to this prophecy about the "blue-eyed" barbarians. The mandarins and merchants at Macao and Canton obviously arrived at some level of awareness that these pale-skinned reds (and blondes), however similar in appearance, were not exactly the same as the Dutch, the notorious and more frequently encountered "red-haired barbarians" now settled in Taiwan and contending with the Portuguese in Japan and Spanish in Manila. Those mandarins and merchants must have achieved some understanding that the Portuguese at Macao maintained a different relationship with the British: the latter appeared to be involved in some sort of commercial alliance with the Lusitanians—and presumably with the Spanish, whose Manila galleon had visited Macao while the Courteens were still around; and whose commander had engaged amicably with the British. As the captain-general and City of Macao noted, the authorities in Canton pointed out and complained to them that this batch of intrusive red-hairs had arrived at Macao as the *friends* of the Lusitanians. Inasmuch as the Chinese in Guangdong understood that these red-haired barbarians (紅夷 *hongyi*) were subjects of a different sovereign, not identical to the ruler of the Portuguese, perhaps the Canton authorities as well as Ming naval and military officers did not take more violent, or more massively violent, broad-daylight measures against the Courteens precisely because they did not know how powerful the latter's sovereign might be.[85] Would it have been so unreasonable to worry that the unknown ruler of this different branch or nation of red-hairs could launch something like a retaliatory armada if they, the Chinese, treated the British badly enough? (Consistent with such concern and concomitant prudence, they could always attribute the fire-ship attack to the perfidious Portuguese acting behind the scenes.) Maybe that

---

84. Peter Mundy registered his awareness of the notorious Chinese xenophobia, but not the "blue-eyed peril" in particular: "the old tradition and natural inclination of these people not to suffer strangers to inhabit and traffic in their land." 11/21 August 1637, Mundy, *Travels*, vol. 3, 195–96. It seems variations on the prophecy of bright- or pale-eyed conquerors must have circulated widely. In an EIC letter from Banten, 19/29 January 1618 (O.C. 595), we find the comment: "It was revealed by oracle unto the Emperor that his country should be subdued by a gray-eyed people, and do therefore forbid all Christians his country." The legend and lore of blue-eyed conquerors (or liberators) seem to have been present among aboriginals (non-Han) in Taiwan as early as the seventeenth century. Andrade, *How Taiwan Became Chinese*, 197.

85. Tang and Zhang ("Governor of Guangdong and Guangxi," 131) have noted the important point that in one of his memorials the Guangdong viceroy Zhang Jingxin evinced awareness of the difference between the English and Dutch by citing, in passing, the former's different dynastic relationship with the Portuguese. Thus, they recognize Zhang Jingxin as the first Chinese official to make an accurate reference to England as one of the sovereign states of the West, to be distinguished from Holland / the Netherlands (荷蘭 Helan).

is why they did not dare to retain or execute the Mountneys and Robinson, their captives in Canton—in the way that their predecessors at Canton had dealt with their Portuguese captives in a similar situation that obtained when those Iberians first breached the Bogue in the second decade of the sixteenth century.[86] Might the prince or king of these red-hairs have at his command a large naval fleet, larger than the Dutch, to punish any who mistreated or violated his subjects, who had come in his name and by his official patronage? After all, in the Ming era there seems to have been recurrent apprehension that an Iberian/Habsburg monarch had a large enough navy to attack China—to be assembled at and launched from Manila perhaps.[87] The red-haired Dutch had already proved redoubtable—attacking Macao; occupying the Pescadores, then Taiwan; and launching several assaults upon Fujian. Could these other red-haired barbarians, blue-eyed or gray-eyed, be an even stronger breed, serving an even mightier ruler?

Ming ignorance of the identity of the British, at least before the latter's intrusion into the Bogue in 1637, seems only to have been one dimension of a broader and dangerous Chinese ignorance of European and global affairs.[88] What details if any did the government of the Chongzhen emperor know about the Thirty Years' War raging in Europe—a conflict that directly and indirectly influenced actions of Europeans taken in the Far East and around Asia? Did this last Ming emperor and his ministers in Beijing have clear and accurate notions about the peoples and issues involved in that conflict? By the reign of that emperor (1627–1644), the government seems to have been significantly more ignorant of inter-European affairs than the Japanese—for by that time the latter had been able to consult a variety of barbarians, Dutch and English, as well the much earlier-arrived Iberians and Italians—Protestants as well as Roman Catholics (and rival orders of the latter: Jesuit, Franciscan, Dominican, and Augustinian).

---

86. The story of the first Portuguese embassy to China that reached Canton in September 1517 is outlined by Armando Cortesao in his introduction to *The Suma Oriental of Tome Pires* (London: Hakluyt, 1944); for a recent re-telling, see Michael Keevak, "Failure, Empire, and the First Portuguese Embassy to China, 1517–1522," in *Early Encounters between East Asia and Europe: Telling Failures*, ed. Ralf Hertel and Michael Keevak (London: Routledge, 2017), 142–55.

87. In 1576 the Manila governor Francisco de Sande had sketched plans to invade China. See Birgit Tremml-Werner, *Spain, China, and Japan in Manila, 1571–1644: Local Comparisons and Global Connections* (Amsterdam: Amsterdam University Press, 2015), 182–86. Boxer discusses those and similar Spanish attack schemes and relates that in January 1574 Fernando Riquel wrote to Philip II that China, despite its very large population, could be conquered "with less than sixty good Spanish soldiers." *South China*, lxxviin4.

88. "When the Spanish were in the early stages of their occupation of the Philippines, many Chinese believed that they were indigenous Filipinos and in 1638 a paper written by some leading figures in Foochow [Fuzhou] made no distinction at all between the Portuguese and Dutch." Massarella, *World Elsewhere*, 301. For substantial Ming ignorance of even southeast Asian countries and peoples, see Zhou Yunzhong, "The Retrogression in Overseas Geographical Knowledge during the Mid-Ming Period," trans. Ng Eng Ping, in *Maritime Defence of China*, ed. Y. H. Teddy Sim (Singapore: Springer, 2017): 146: "Such ignorance was not limited to ordinary scholars or even top scholars. Even the officials who were specifically in charge of foreign matters showed little knowledge of the outside world." Keevak has also highlighted the profound Ming ignorance of key differences between Europeans. *Embassies to China*, 10.

The highest Ming authorities at Canton, Zhang Jingxin and Ge Zhengqi, both of whom submitted reports and memorials to Beijing about the British presence in the Pearl River Delta, effectively lumped the British with the Dutch by the term 紅夷 (*hongyi*, red-haired barbarian)—just as the Portuguese at Macao would have preferred them to do. In those Ming documents there is little besides passing and superficial observation of the fact that these red-hairs were different from the ones dealt with on previous occasions in recent decades—the ones who had, most shockingly, invaded Macao in 1622. There is no discourse upon how these particular red-hairs (British) might be so different from the other red-hairs (Dutch) as to justify or require a different denomination. Conspicuously absent from the documents composed by Zhang Jingxin and Ge Zhengqi is a statement and discussion of the key fact in explaining the presence of these red-haired barbarians in the Bogue in 1637: that just two years earlier the head merchant of these foreigners, Nathaniel Mountney, had been among those who signed an accord at Goa with the governor (viceroy) of the foreigners now occupying Macao. Ming ignorance of that crucial point would not have displeased the Lusitanians. For presumably the latter preferred to retain their peculiar pedagogical prerogative and remain the sole tutor of the Ming in such matters as barbarian classification—to preserve a monopolistic position as consultant about all things European, red, blue, gray, and otherwise.

The Chongzhen emperor and his predecessors might have fared better if, like the Tokugawa Japanese shoguns, they had allowed more than one Western people to settle and trade, and had, consequently, learned significantly more about these different peoples—and other peoples, trends, and movements in the Western Hemisphere.[89] The Portuguese of Macao occupied the enviably unique and privileged position of gatekeeper of knowledge, by which they could prevent the Chinese from becoming much more enlightened and sophisticated in dealing with other Westerners—to prevent them, for example, from obtaining the ability to distinguish between (and, thereby, to manipulate) different, rival north European Protestants like the Stuart British and republican Dutch. The visit of the subjects of Charles I in 1637 does not seem to have occasioned any major breakthrough in the Ming government's knowledge of Western affairs, or to have led to the initial development of something along the lines of "anglology"—a field of knowledge that would pertain to the red-haired, blue-eyed island people, whose king maintained a cordial relationship *both* with the king of the Portuguese (*folangji*) at Macao *and* with the States General, governors of the "red-haired barbarians," the Dutch, who were in the middle of a long war against that Habsburg king of the Portuguese (Philip IV/

---

89. Dutch supply of intelligence to Japanese authorities from the 1610s to 1630s is noted by Clulow, *Company and the Shogun*. Annual intelligence reports demanded of the Dutch throughout the Tokugawa period were to be called *Oranda fusetsugaki*. Tremml-Werner has also observed how, compared to Ming governments, the Tokugawa Japanese became much more knowledgeable about Europeans and world affairs in the early seventeenth century. *Spain, China, and Japan in Manila*, 87.

III).[90] As the Courteen mariners and merchants are denominated 紅夷 (*hongyi*) throughout the Ming records, it appears that officials like Zhang Jingxin and Ge Zhengqi did not deem it important to distinguish between the Dutch and British—however much they registered the fact that these red-hairs in the Bogue had apparently come to Macao in July as Portuguese friends—or at least more as friends than as foes. Sufficient it was to note that these were non-Portuguese barbarians.[91] Again, the preservation of ignorance and failure to revise the Ming government's barbarian encyclopedia, if you will, or to create a new file for this different red-haired species, is probably just what the Portuguese desired—in order to maintain a key intelligence advantage over their Chinese overlords.

Whether encouraged and vigorously sustained by efforts of the monopolist Portuguese at Macao, was this Ming ignorance and failure to deepen their understanding of European peoples and culture a very serious liability? Was disregard of such facts and realities of the West so dangerous? Conversely, would it have significantly benefitted the Ming government to perceive and grasp the implications of key differences among the Europeans? If we accept the validity of an analogy taken from our own age, then we might answer that the liability of the ignorance was serious and gains from the knowledge would have been substantial. We might ask, in our twenty-first-century world, does it not benefit Europeans and Americans dealing with the Middle East to understand how groups of Arabs and Muslims (Sunni and Shiite) differ? Would not ignorance of such differences handicap or doom efforts of Europeans and Americans to make sound policies with peoples of the Middle East? The judgment of the late John Wills in his survey of European relations with the Chinese in the sixteenth and seventeenth centuries was that: "the silk-silver trades with Japan and Manila had substantial effects on the Ming economy."[92] If that was so (there is still debate on the question), it behooved the Ming government to know more about the European peoples, including the British, who could seriously and adversely affect such commerce and, thereby, its own economy. Conversely, if the Ming, prior to 1637, and in defiance of the Portuguese, had possessed knowledge about the British (and about European affairs more generally), might the Weddell

---

90. The Ming term *folangji* (佛郎機), frequently applied to the Portuguese, Spanish, and Italians, was derived from an Indian–Southeast Asian word "ferengi," which had been used indiscriminately for any Latin Christian and which had arisen as a way of referring to the "Franks" of the Crusades.

91. John Wills observes the Ming-Qing continuity of this sort of documentary indifference and dereliction in the concluding chapter of his study of Dutch interactions with the Manchu and Chinese from 1662 to 1681. *Pepper, Guns and Parleys: The Dutch East India Company and China, 1662–1681* (Cambridge, MA: Harvard University Press, 1974), 204.

92. Wills, *Cambridge Ming*, vol. 8, 333. For the basis of that judgment, consult William Atwell, "International Bullion Flows and the Chinese Economy circa 1530–1650," *Past and Present* 95, no. 1 (1982): 68–90; and Dennis Flynn and Arturo Giráldez, "Cycles of Silver: Global Economic Unity through the Mid-eighteenth Century," *Journal of World History* 13, no. 2 (2002): 391–427. That the decrease of international silver flows did *not* so adversely impact the Ming military and domestic stability is argued by, among others, Brian Moloughney and Xia Weizhong in "Silver and the Fall of the Ming: A Reassessment," *Papers on Far Eastern History* 40 (September 1989): 51–78. See also the more recent evaluation of Atwell, "Another Look at Silver Imports into China, ca. 1635–1644," *Journal of World History* 16, no. 4 (2005): 467–91.

expedition of the Courteen Association have been greeted and embraced as an opportunity, not suffered as just another "red-barbarian" crisis or "incident" (事件 *shijian*)? Late Ming perception of non-Roman Catholic Europeans like the British was filtered by the Portuguese and (mostly Spanish, Italian, and Portuguese) Jesuits. Receiving and properly engaging with the trade envoys of the British king would have helped to liberate the Ming from the narrow if not distorting Lusitanian, Roman-Catholic tutelage. However "closed-minded" or "anti-foreigner" the Ming were; however unreceptive to Weddell and the British the Chinese were in 1637; was that posture and attitude somewhat or largely a function of Portuguese influence exerted (and bribes paid) from Macao? Were the Lusitanians—and not some innate Han xenophobia or default anti-foreigner Ming tendency—actually the most formidable obstacle to the initiation and development of harmonious Anglo-Chinese relations? In any case, the Weddell expedition of 1637 certainly illustrates how important the Portuguese were in shaping Chinese relations with Westerners, or more broadly, Ming foreign policy.

Figure 8.1: "When the Portugals brought us a protest from Macao unto Fumaon [in the Bogue], where we rode, then sat Noretti [Li Yerong] in state on the *Dragon*'s half deck according to letters L. M. N. O. P. Q. R. V." Mundy, *Travels*, vol. 3, 256–57.

9

Lessons Learned

The Sinology of the Courteens?

At least from consulting the records that exist today, we may infer that the British of the Courteen fleet learned much more about the Chinese in Guangdong than vice versa. Merely from the fact that it was the former who took the trouble to visit the latter, this might follow as a matter of course. These British took detailed notes of their experiences, made drawings of people and things, and sketched maps of land and waterways. If the Chinese at Macao and in the Pearl River Delta did so, such materials remain to be discovered. As noticed in the previous chapter, the extant Chinese documents do not offer anything to compel a major revision of the story assembled from only the Portuguese and English sources—as presented in Chapters 4–7. While Ming knowledge of the British was superficial at best (and scarcely augmented by the Qing), the inability to communicate directly with the Chinese was a substantial impediment to any great advance in fledgling British sinology. The Courteens were thoroughly at the mercy of the Portuguese and Chinese as they tried to navigate and maneuver (physically and strategically) between Macao and Canton and throughout the Pearl River and its islands and creeks. Among other matters, it was impossible for the Caroline British to ascertain such critical things as when the top Ming officials at Canton were merely obeying orders from Beijing and when, exercising some discretion and taking initiative, they were, say, acting by influence of the lobbying and bribes from the Portuguese of Macao. Of course, even with better linguistic resources, and more connections and informants, such a task would have been extremely difficult. After all, the Portuguese at Macao must often have been uncertain whether the authorities at Canton were bluffing when citing orders or decrees from Beijing.

But the British labored under much greater ignorance than did the Lusitanians: Which level of Chinese government were they dealing with at any given time? Who answered to whom? The Portuguese veterans at Macao, old "China hands," had a much firmer grasp of the Ming government hierarchy and provincial and municipal personnel—and, accordingly, were much savvier about who could be trusted and held accountable and who had to be obeyed—at least when it was clear that they could not be bribed. The British were on much more secure footing in interacting with the Portuguese: the Macao captain-general, procurador, and Senado da Camara obviously and authoritatively spoke for the Portuguese at Macao. One conclusion

158   *The First British Trade Expedition to China*

the Courteens must have drawn was that to do business effectively and reliably, they would have to learn a great deal more about the Chinese imperial and provincial government hierarchy and administrative functioning—at the least, which officials had to be bribed and which were not susceptible to such silver persuasions.

While Domingos da Camara de Noronha rendered an account to his imperial superior at Goa, Pero da Silva, as well as a letter to Charles I of Great Britain, to whom the City of Macao also addressed an account justifying its conduct, the British filed a report to the directors of the Courteen Association in London. In the latter, penned shortly after the *Dragon* and *Sun* had left China, the chief merchant Nathaniel Mountney wrote:

> If you intend to prosecute what we have with so much expense to you and hazard to ourselves begun, it will be absolutely necessary to settle and to fortify some island, either by permission or by force, although the first will hardly be effected without the latter. The people of China are naturally ingenious, fearful and cowardly, but very treacherous. Therefore, whosoever treateth with them, it must be with his sword in his hand, always prepared against fireworks, which will be their only offensive weapons. We find the Chineses willing enough of themselves to trade, but that they are hindered by the Portugals. Whosoever therefore shall endeavour a trade in these parts must avoid coming to Macao, but either go to the northward or to the southward, the whole country being full of convenient harbours.[1]

Among the British who had visited Ming Guangdong for six months, it was probably a widespread view that the Chinese were no less deceitful and treacherous than the Portuguese—if not more.[2] Presumably Nathaniel Mountney spoke for many of his fellow Courteens—like captains Richard Swanley and John Carter and fellow factor Thomas Robinson—in this characterization of the Chinese.

Yet it has recently been asserted that in the early modern period: "when Europeans came into contact with the powerful, culturally sophisticated and technologically advanced empires of the Far East, they were struck by a sense of fear, awe, and frustration."[3] Judging by reports rendered by Mountney and Weddell, and the journal of Peter Mundy, frustration, not awe or fear, is the only thing one would ascribe to the commanders Weddell, Swanley, and Carter, or to the factors,

---

1. Mountney, Rawlinson A.299. As will be noticed below, this passage is parallel to the remarks in Mountney's "Notes on the Prospects of Trade in China."
2. Echoing the Courteen chief factor, the Macao captain-general also applied the term "treacherous" to the Chinese when he rendered his account to the viceroy of Goa, 27 December 1637: "For there is no worse or more treacherous people under the sun than these Chinese, who are without truth or law or faith." In the same letter Camara de Noronha stated that "the Chinese are great thieves." In the 1630s the Dutch observed in the same vein: "It is truly a sad state of affairs that the wonderful trade of China can be accessed only through such a deceitful, treacherous, untrustworthy, craven, and lying nation as the Chinese." Hans Putmans (VOC governor in Taiwan, 1629–1636), *De dagregisters van het Kasteel Zeelandia, Taiwan, 1629–1662*, 4 vols., ed. Leonard Blussé, Nathalie Everts, W.E. Milde, and Yung-ho Ts'ao (The Hague: Instituut voor Nederlandse Geschiedenis, 1986–2001), vol. 1, B: 591–92. Putmans also used the epithet "devious nation of sodomites," according to a quotation by Andrade, *Lost Colony*, 45.
3. Lee, *English Renaissance and the Far East*, xv.

the Mountneys, Thomas Robinson, and Mundy. Further, much of that frustration was merely the consequence of the perception that the Chinese uncritically credited Portuguese slander and unscrupulously accepted bribes. The same commentator on the British expedition to China, Adele Lee, also emphasizes "the degree to which East Asia fascinated, inspired, and challenged a relatively weak and peripheral Europe in the early modern period. . . . China . . . triggered feelings of insecurity in the early modern English, forcing them to accept their own marginal status on the global stage."[4] After our review of all the major events that took place during this first British trade venture to China, it is hard to characterize such Europeans as Weddell and the Courteens as weak. The intrusive and tenacious British interlopers were not so much fascinated or inspired—but thoroughly irked by ambivalent and treacherous Chinese, alongside the inhospitable if not perfidious Lusitanians at Macao. In concluding her review of the Weddell expedition, Lee asserts: "In particular, the Chinese succeeded in dramatically undoing perceptions (shaped and governed by the Portuguese-Jesuits) of them as a weak and effeminate race that had already been subdued by a European power." But as the lines written by Nathaniel Mountney (and others by Mundy and Weddell) demonstrate, the prevalent view among the British was one of Chinese guile and cowardice. If the Courteens, upon approaching Macao in July 1637, carried an assumption that the Ming were stronger, braver, and more honest than the Portuguese, that postulate was undone.

In the British accounts one cannot discern awe at the "culturally sophisticated and technologically advanced" China. As fully discussed in the previous chapter, Ming military-naval technology and operational capability left the Courteens thoroughly underwhelmed. Peter Mundy was well aware that the first European missionaries to infiltrate China in the late sixteenth and early seventeenth centuries—particularly Iberian and Italian Jesuits, most notably Matteo Ricci—had impressed if not dazzled the Ming by displays of mathematical prowess, geographical-cartographical precision as well as calendrical exactitude; advanced, systematic knowledge of astronomy and physics; and highly sophisticated technological capability in such domains as fire-arms and artillery. Mundy noted that this had been a major factor in the Portuguese acquisition of their spot in south China: "Macao it seems being permitted long since by insinuation of the Jesuits with the king [emperor] and great men, presenting them with divers rarities out of Europe, as also showing them of our European learning, *until then unknown to them*."[5] So Mundy and the British were well aware, presumably even before arriving at Macao in July 1637, that there was little to no reason to stand in awe of "culturally sophisticated and technologically advanced" China. It was the cultural sophistication

---

4. Lee, *English Renaissance and the Far East*, xv, xxiii. Similarly, it is hard to see how Adam Clulow's generalization for the early modern period can be validated by the British interaction with the Ming in Guangdong in 1637: "The size and power of such polities [Ming China, Mughal India, Tokugawa Japan] filled Europeans with trepidation." *Company and the Shogun*, 7. Trepidation was no cause of the Courteen fleet's entry into the Pearl River and storming of a Bogue fort.

5. 11/21 August 1637, Mundy, *Travels*, vol. 3.

and technological advancement of Europe that had impressed the Ming enough to confer honor and prestige upon the Jesuits in Beijing and to allow the Portuguese to preserve their unique settlement in Guangdong.[6]

Indeed, the Caroline British who came to China in 1637 were so unimpressed and unintimidated that their subsequent accounts and reports contemplated further visits if not invasions. They had found enough receptive Chinese, mandarins, merchants, and otherwise to think it was just a matter of by-passing the obstructive Portuguese and paying/bribing the relevant provincial officials. As Nathaniel Mountney wrote very positively, addressing Charles I: "In conclusion, his Majesty could never have so fit an opportunity to make a conquest, nor yet have more hopes of a gainful trade. The Chinese themselves are very willing to trade with us, though hindered by the Portuguese."[7] This confidence in native Chinese interest in engaging in future commerce with the British is reinforced elsewhere in the report which the cape merchant rendered to the Courteen directors back in London: "We may be able to employ all the shipping we are able to send, for the country aboundeth with merchants and commodities and the Chinese themselves [are] very willing to trade with us, though hindered by the Portugals' indirect proceedings."[8] The entire tone and tenor of the report is remarkably confident: with adequate commitment of force and resolve, a British version of Macao could be established somewhere in or near the Pearl River estuary.

The Portuguese reports and correspondence emphatically substantiate the notion articulated by Mountney that the Chinese might well be receptive to future visits and commercial overtures by the British—notwithstanding the pledge by Captain John Weddell never to return.[9] Reviewing the Anglo-Chinese interactions of the previous months in the report he submitted to the viceroy of Goa, Macao's captain-general Camara de Noronha complained: "It is impossible for us as we are situated to forbid them [the British] anything, for the Chinese are so constituted that, even if they have to go under water, they will carry everything to them to any island where they [the British] may anchor, for their [Chinese] cupidity is their only law."[10] Throughout the British sojourn in the Pearl River Delta, there seem to have been Chinese who were willing to trade—sometimes clearly in direct defiance of Ming authorities. Captain Weddell noted the detail, for instance, that while

---

6. In 1629, only eight years before the arrival of Mundy and the British, Xu Guangqi, as vice-president of the Board of Ceremonies, staged a contest to predict the next solar eclipse. Following the triumph of the precise European method over its Chinese and Muslim rivals, Ming scholars and Jesuits collaborated to reform the imperial calendar based on the Western paradigm.
7. Mountney, "Notes on the Prospects of Trade in China."
8. Mountney, Rawlinson A.299.
9. The proposed scheme of action outlined by Nathaniel Mountney in the report of December 1637 suggests that he and the Courteens did not think that anyone, including the Chinese, had to take seriously their promise never to return to China. Perhaps duress would not even need to be pleaded.
10. Domingos da Camara de Noronha to the viceroy of Goa, 27 December 1637, *Lisbon Transcripts, Books of the Monsoons*, book 41, fol. 191. A recent commentator on the Courteen visit, Ralf Hertel, asserts that "nobody [no Chinese] would trade with the insolent 'red-haired barbarians.'" "Faking It," 33. This claim is incompatible with Portuguese, British, and Chinese primary documents.

Lessons Learned: The Sinology of the Courteens? 161

his merchants were captive in Canton and he and the rest of the fleet were in the Bogue: "Divers boats and junks would come and sell us sugar at easy rates; but they came by stealth."[11] Moreover, clear indication that at least some Ming officials in Canton were receptive to British overtures comes from another Portuguese source, a communication of the Macao municipal leadership: "With the continued coming of the English to this City, since the Chinese have shown themselves propitious because of the entrance granted them by the Mandarins into Canton, we are confident that every time they come they will be allowed to trade, either through bribery or fear."[12] The captain-general of Macao concurred that the Chinese would welcome such interloping traders. For after the Courteens departed in January 1638, in his report to the viceroy at Goa, he noted that the Portuguese might as well make some deal or commercial accommodation with the British in the near future, *for the Chinese would get the profit if they did not.* He stated in the same report that the British would always find willing Ming with whom to trade. At and in the vicinity of Macao the Portuguese did not have the wherewithal to prevent such eager and scofflaw Chinese opportunists and entrepreneurs from mingling with the British, at whichever island or spot the latter happened to anchor. More importantly and very worrying, Camara de Noronha noted that there was division among the Canton authorities and mercantile community on what policy to maintain in the case of these new interlopers. Some among those Chinese had wished the British to trade just as the Portuguese customarily did. Others objected that, even if that were a good idea, the emperor and his ministers would soon learn of it, and then all the mandarins in Guangdong would be punished for acting without authorization.[13] Evidently, those of the latter opinion formed the majority. In the last analysis, we could assume that the Chinese officials at Canton might always invite and welcome the British; but, then later, if the higher imperial authorities investigated or cracked down, these officials at Canton could claim that it was the Portuguese at Macao who had invited and assisted the British. Presumably such a device of deceit and blame-shifting was always in the toolkit, if it was not frequently wielded.

If the Lusitanians at Macao feared that the British might be allowed to plant a factory somewhere in the Pearl River estuary, then the Portuguese claim that the Ming were categorically and unalterably averse to extending trade to other foreigners is rendered dubious. In their communications to the Courteens, the Portuguese

---

11. "Weddell's China Narrative, O.C. 1662." This sort of illicit operation paralleled what the Portuguese regularly referred to by their term *lorchas do risco*, that is, Chinese shipping in the Pearl River estuary that risked confiscation for unauthorized trading with Macao. This was among the clandestine forms of exchange practiced by rogues (奸徒 *jiantu*) that needed preventing and eliminating, as repeatedly emphasized by both Ge Zhengqi and Zhang Jingxin in their reports and memorials about the British incident.

12. Brief reasons showing the great prejudice which would result from allowing the English to come to this City, 30 December 1637, *Lisbon Transcripts, Books of the Monsoons*, book 41, fol. 231. The "fear" mentioned by the Portuguese ("through bribery or fear") implies the wisdom and efficacy of the "sword-in-his-hand" commercial approach to the Chinese as espoused by Mountney in the report quoted above.

13. Domingos da Camara de Noronha to the viceroy of Goa, 27 December 1637, *Lisbon Transcripts, Books of the Monsoons*, book 41, fol. 191.

162   *The First British Trade Expedition to China*

of Macao represented the Chinese as hostile to the British. But in their communications to the viceroy and fellow Portuguese at Goa, they represented the Chinese (or a considerable number of them) as receptive to or at least open to entertaining British overtures. The paradox (if not contradiction) that materializes in the Portuguese commentary is that on the one hand (1) the Chinese *will* trade with the British (and thus spoil Macao's monopoly and prosperity); and on the other hand (2) the Chinese *will not* allow the British to trade (and so it was and would be pointless for the British to ask the Lusitanians to facilitate trade with the Chinese). In the following passage of the City of Macao's letter to Charles I, the second element of the paradox is exhibited:

> We finally assured the English that they might be certain that we would not attempt to prevail upon the Chinese to frustrate their designs of trade, for if they chose to admit them, they would not desist on our account, nor would they permit any trade if they did not choose, however much we might beg them to do so. And we could not give admittance to your people or allow them to trade with the Chinese, as this depends on the Chinese and not on us; nor could we allow them to trade with us, as we depend so entirely on the Chinese, and they will neither admit foreigners to trade with them nor allow us to do so. We know for a certainty from the Chinese that they will not admit foreigners into their kingdom, nor do their laws allow it, and they tell us that they repent of having permitted us to enter.[14]

So the Chinese are represented as hostile to any more foreigners or expansion of trade beyond the status quo. But in other passages the Portuguese bitterly complain that the Chinese are all too ready and receptive to trade with the subjects of Charles, to the ruin of Macao. At least in light of those passages in the Portuguese documents, the Courteens were entitled, if over-optimistically, to believe that they could establish commercial relations with the Chinese—if they could only outmaneuver and out-bribe the Lusitanians at their next visit.

A later line of the same correspondence between the City of Macao and the British king implies that the Ming would eagerly and readily trade with the Spanish, fellow subjects of their Iberian sovereign: "Even the Spaniards who inhabit the country nearby cannot carry on trade in this land, because of the harm it will do to us; and therefore it is not permitted to them."[15] The Portuguese do not aver that the Spaniards from Manila do not trade in China because the *Chinese* will not receive or accommodate them. Rather, the Spaniards do not trade because the *Portuguese* (with the approval of their shared Habsburg monarch) will not permit them. But then the Lusitanians of Macao return to their emphasis upon the conceit that it is the *Chinese* (not themselves) who will never permit the British:

> And your Majesty [Charles I] may rest assured that were you to send ships here every year, you would never obtain from the Chinese a factory and permission to

---

14. City of Macao to Charles I, 24 December 1637, *Lisbon Transcripts, Books of the Monsoons*, book 41, fol. 220.
15. City of Macao to Charles I, 24 December 1637, *Lisbon Transcripts, Books of the Monsoons*, book 41, fol. 220.

trade in their country, for their King [emperor] will not allow it on any account, and his governors of this province cannot permit it without his order, or it would cost them their lives. Although they may verbally promise your Majesty's subjects that they will receive them into their country as they receive us, they only say it for the purpose of deceiving and of getting some silver dollars out of them.[16]

In the same vein, the Portuguese add: "We told them [Courteens] that the Chinese designed by lies and trickery to disgust them with us so that we might not be friends; and that they would tell them (as they did) that all their ills were due to us and that we had prevented their trade."[17] So, according to the Portuguese, the Chinese attempted (successfully) to sow discord between the British and Portuguese by telling the former that the latter had been slandering and conspiring against them. That is, Macao claims that the Chinese put insulting words in the mouths of the Portuguese, framing the Iberians as detractors, antagonists, and saboteurs of the British, in order to sow discord between the two European peoples. From our vantage point of hindsight and benefitting from our access to all the Western and Chinese documents, we may observe that inasmuch as the Ming authorities at Canton did wish the British gone from the Pearl River estuary, the former must have been eager to incite hostility in the Portuguese against the British; more broadly, for strategic reasons the Chinese desired enmity and squabbling between the two groups of barbarians. Accordingly, it would have been reasonable of the mandarins at Canton to make some effort to inflame the anger of the Portuguese, for the sake of inducing greater effort in the residents of Macao to expel the dangerous "red-haired barbarians." But it may be doubted that the Lusitanians needed any prompting in this direction; Nathaniel Mountney, for one, did not think so.

The decision of the Courteen Association and King Charles to solicit trade in China was, in the first place, predicated on the assumption of the mendacity of the Portuguese Ming-monopolists: that these Iberians were concealing or grossly understating Chinese interest in doing business with other Europeans. The East India Company factor Henry Bornford, after his trip aboard the *London* to Macao in 1635, had emphasized: "The averseness of the Chinese to intercourse with foreigners is exaggerated by the Portuguese, who also abuse other nations to the Chinese in order to keep trade to themselves."[18] The bold attempt by Captain Weddell and Nathaniel Mountney can be regarded as ultimately and most significantly an attempt to call the bluff of the Lusitanians—that is, to test the Portuguese claim that the Ming (at least the Chinese in Guangdong) were categorically and unconditionally opposed to commencing commercial relations with another European people. The cape merchant of the Courteen fleet was resolved to test the claim, even at serious risk to himself. As the Portuguese noted of their nemesis: "Nathaniel Mountney declared that he would carry this matter through to the end and proceed

---

16. City of Macao to Charles I, 24 December 1637, *Lisbon Transcripts, Books of the Monsoons*, book 41, fol. 220.
17. City of Macao to Charles I, 24 December 1637, *Lisbon Transcripts, Books of the Monsoons*, book 41, fol. 220.
18. Henry Bornford at Surat to the Company, 19/29 April 1636, Foster, *English Factories, 1634–1636*, 226.

to Canton, even though he died there, if only to discover whether the difficulties we [the Portuguese] had made in admitting them to the cities of China were of our own making, of which he was persuaded."[19]

As observed above and in previous chapters, the Chinese in Guangdong appeared far from unanimous in hostility towards the British—whatever the official *haijin* (海禁) policy still maintained in Beijing. This lack of unity in confronting the Courteens, the non-Lusitanian interlopers, was precisely what inspired hope, even reasonable hope, that some substantial commerce might be had in Canton or nearby, unmediated by the Portuguese. This also helps to explain the confident tone which pervades Mountney's report. Was it so foolish of the Courteens (or the EIC in Surat, contemplating another 1635-*London*-type venture) to think that if they returned in a year or two with much larger sums of silver to "donate" to the "champin," "haitao," "tootan," and "chadjan" that they would be permitted to trade or even set up a temporary factory at one of the places in the Pearl River estuary surveyed by Peter Mundy in the *Anne*? But again, and as the Courteens themselves stressed in all their reports, however many Chinese were eager to trade, and willing to dive under water and defy the emperor to do so, it would be difficult for the British to transact business without being obstructed by the vigorous lobbying and machinations of the crafty Portuguese. Those Iberians would be prompt to inform upon any Guangdong officials disobeying the emperor in trading with a foreign people who had not received official permission. Nor should it have looked especially likely that the Ming government in Beijing would very soon revoke the Portuguese commercial privilege of monopoly and evict them from Macao. After all, it is safe to assume that plenty of profit was still being made by the Chinese at Canton via the Portuguese at Macao.[20]

As Mountney noted in his prospectus of trade in China, however small the island the British occupied in the Pearl River estuary, "the Portugals being so near a neighbor will always be troublesome."[21] While Hong Kong has been synonymous with British-in-China for the past two centuries (and decolonized only two decades ago), at the conclusion of the Courteen venture in 1637 it was the island of Hainan, farther south, that appeared the likeliest spot for a future British settlement in China. Nathaniel Mountney was strikingly sanguine in assessing the prospects of the peripheral island on the outskirts of the Ming Empire:

> In our opinion, therefore, *Aynon* [Hainan] will be the fittest place, lying between Cochinchina [coast of south Vietnam] and China and near to Camboia, very fertile and populous, and being but about 20 leagues long and 17 broad, may without any

---

19. City of Macao to Charles I, 24 December 1637, *Lisbon Transcripts, Books of the Monsoons*, book 41, fol. 220.
20. Among other basic facts, there were very rich Chinese merchants in Canton who regularly shipped their silk and other goods to Japan through the Portuguese. Obviously those merchants still prospering in 1637 would not have been particularly interested in changing the status quo that favored the Lusitanians at the expense of Spanish, Dutch, and British.
21. Mountney, "Notes on the Prospects of Trade in China."

great difficulty be both taken and defended. What pearl likewise China affordeth cometh from thence and are esteemed to be of a very good and clear water; so plentiful it is of grain, as it supplies not only Macao but Canton itself with great quantities of rice. A people careless and secure, void of all discipline and debarred from the use of all sorts of weapons, not being permitted to have so much as a sword in their houses, except some particular men enrolled for soldiers, who may wear one.[22]

As the Dutch were now well-fortified in southwest Taiwan and the Spanish ensconced and thriving in Manila, so the British projected a seizure of Hainan territory, for the island "may without any great difficulty be both taken and defended." Presumably it was not subsequently considered as an option to establish a base there because, upon closer scrutiny, and probably among other good reasons, the waters surrounding it were judged too hazardous and the coasts would not lend themselves to establishing a safe and convenient port. Such might be inferred from Peter Mundy's comment as they had passed it on the way to Macao in early July 1637: "We saw the island of *Aynaon* [Hainan]. Between this and Pulo Caetaon lieth a great inlet or gulf called [blank], and between Pulo Caetaon and Sanchean [St. John Island] by Macao is accompted the gulf of *Aynaon*, sometimes dangerous for great seas, currents, foul weather, etts."[23] Besides possible pirate-infestation contingencies, it might also have been assumed that the Ming would be willing to wage campaigns to prevent any barbarian from occupying or dominating that island, just as Ming naval forces from Fujian had compelled the Dutch to leave the Pescadores for Taiwan in 1623–1624. But, of course, the possibility of launching that sort of large-scale operation for Hainan in the late 1630s might be doubted in light of the fact that the Chongzhen emperor had to concentrate resources and personnel on repelling the invaders in the north of the Ming realm—and suppressing peasant rebels in the northwest. Nor, with Charles I in 1638 facing refractory, covenanting Scottish subjects (and then the Bishops' Wars) in the north of his own realm, could the Stuart king of the "red-haired barbarians" enjoy the luxury of contemplating an exotic enterprise to turn Hainan into a British Formosa.

Few Chinese living today can be aware that Hainan was considered, long before Hong Kong, as a possible location for a British trading post or even colony. By contrast, and like some flotsam and jetsam, there may still be floating around some notion that the Weddell expedition of the Courteen Association did great and lasting harm to Sino-British relations—or at least that it ruined prospects of British trade in China for the remainder of seventeenth century. One suspects that

---

22. Mountney, "Notes on the Prospects of Trade in China." For the context of Hainan in the late Ming period, see Robert J. Antony, "Trade, Piracy, and Resistance in the Gulf of Tonkin in the Seventeenth Century" in *Sea Rovers, Silver, and Samurai*, ed. Tonio Andrade and Xing Hang (Honolulu: University of Hawai'i Press, 2016), 312–34. Roderich Ptak has also shed some interesting light on this enigmatic island in the essay "Hainan and the Trade in Horses, Song to Early Ming" in his volume *Birds and Beasts in Chinese Texts and Trade: Lectures Related to South China and the Overseas World* (Wiesbaden: Harrassowitz, 2011).

23. 22 June/2 July 1637, Mundy, *Travels*, vol. 3, 156.

H.B. Morse's remarks, filtered by many after him, still exert some influence: "From Canton the English were excluded until the last years of the seventeenth century—partly owing to the intrigues of the Portuguese, defending their monopoly; partly, without doubt, because of the memory of Weddell's forcible entry and ignominious expulsion."[24] Austin Coates, once a widely read author on Hong Kong history, concluded that the Courteen fleet "finally departed in all humility, having been eased out jointly by the Chinese and Portuguese; but Weddell's voyage had established the thenceforth unchanging Chinese view that, of all barbarian intruders, the English were the most violent and dangerous."[25] Coates offered no evidence for this claim. Indeed, no scholar has been able (if any have attempted) to document any long-lasting adverse effects caused directly by the Weddell expedition on future trade opportunities suffered by the British in subsequent decades. Some, like Morse and Coates (the latter probably just following Morse), have *assumed*, albeit not absurdly, that in the ensuing decades the Chinese remembered and resented the British fleet's aggression and violence. The Portuguese at Macao scolded and admonished the Stuart British: "The war which they [the Courteens] made upon the Chinese caused the latter to hold the English nation in such odium that your Majesty's [Charles I's] subjects need not attempt to come here in the future."[26] While such a line is very hard to reconcile with all the comments (by the very same Portuguese) to the effect that the British will always find Chinese with whom to trade in the Pearl River estuary, it is no easier to reconcile with the fact that several more trips to Macao by British ships occurred within several years of the Courteen departure in 1638—some of them even facilitated if not proposed and initiated by the viceroy of Goa. After the Weddell expedition, the Portuguese at Goa confronting the ever stronger, blockading, and strangling Dutch (both along the western coast of India and the straits of Melaka), persisted in trying to arrange voyages like the one the EIC *London* had made in 1635.[27] The British do not seem to have worried that they would be unwelcome, punished, or attacked by the Ming (and then Qing) because of any aggressive actions or misbehavior by Captain Weddell or Nathaniel Mountney in the Bogue or Canton. Even more telling than any joint-ventures with the Lusitanians, only six years after the Courteen fleet had departed Guangdong, in August 1644 the EIC *Hinde* was dispatched to Macao in another attempt at opening a new channel of commerce.[28]

---

24. *The Chronicles of the East India Company Trading in China, 1635–1834*, 5 vols. (Oxford: Clarendon, 1926), 1:147. As one can infer from Morse's own review of post-1638 British ventures, there is, on the contrary, *much reason to doubt* that the memory of Weddell's entry made any difference. In none of the post-Weddell seventeenth-century episodes he relates in that volume is there any reference to a citation of the Courteen enterprise in Guangdong in 1637 as a snag.

25. Austin Coates, *Prelude to Hong Kong* (London: Routledge and Kegan Paul, 1978), 58.

26. City of Macao to Charles I, 24 December 1637, *Lisbon Transcripts, Books of the Monsoons*, book 41, fol. 220.

27. Morse, *Chronicles of the EIC in China*, 1:31–32.

28. In the first volume of *Chronicles of the EIC in China*'s third chapter ("Macao and Tongking," 31–40), Morse concisely narrates the *Hinde*'s voyage and subsequent ventures to China in the decades after the Weddell expedition. Rogério Miguel Puga has noted that in 1657 the EIC directors were outlining plans to set up a

The widespread revolts and incursions in the north that shook the Chongzhen administration, preceding the dissolution of the Ming dynasty in 1644, would have dominated government attention which might otherwise have been devoted to discussing more fully the intrusion of the British in 1637. Certainly with all the violence of the Ming–Qing transition in the decades that followed the Courteen visit, such a Chinese (Han or non-Han) grudge against the British for Captain Weddell's conduct in 1637 was unlikely to survive—if it had ever formed. Moreover, as to what Weddell and the Courteens did in 1637 while in the Bogue: what was that to a new and non-Han (even barbarian) regime, the Qing? When a Dutch embassy arrived at Canton in 1655, the Qing did not cite the VOC's decades of violence along China's south coast (and depredation of Chinese junks elsewhere in Asia) as a reason for not discussing trade.[29] A fortiori, if the British had come in the decades after the Weddell expedition, much less likely would the Qing have cited the forceful actions of that commander and the Courteen fleet in 1637. Thus, we may conclude that any absence of British vessels on the China coast after the Weddell expedition is much more to be imputed to domestic circumstances in both the British Isles and in Ming-Qing China and Taiwan than to some Chinese recollection and resentment that the aggressive British had used such lethal force in the Pearl River estuary in 1637.

Although it is hard to find any scholars now arguing, let alone demonstrating, that the Weddell expedition impaired long-term Sino-British commercial or diplomatic relations, some recent summaries of this Courteen venture, echoing the conclusion of Coates, classify it as a humiliating if not disastrous failure. It is true that some scholars have made a novel qualification: that it was a *"telling* failure." While the narrative constructed in previous chapters has revealed mishaps and aspects of failure, we can point out some important ways in which this pioneering enterprise was fruitful, if not as lucrative as had been projected by the Courteen Association in London. None of the following reflections, of course, will alter the fact that the British in 1637 failed to achieve the expedition's most ambitious aim, of establishing something beyond ephemeral and ad-hoc trade relations with the Ming. As the factor Peter Mundy himself summarized: "the success of the voyage not issuing according to our desire."[30] Nathaniel Mountney and Captain Weddell certainly planned and expected to do more trading and less fighting in China.

Just a few months after the Courteen fleet departed China, some of the ships visited the northeast coast of India in Bengal. EIC staff were now cultivating a fledgling factory at Masulipatam. The company's factors were greatly impressed at how handsomely the Courteens seemed to have profited from the China voyage. Captain

---

factory in Canton. *The British in Macau*, 47. Nothing seems to have come of that. But that the EIC would even contemplate such a venture does not suggest that they had any fear that Chinese in Guangdong would remember and cite the ferocious (桀悍 *jiehan*) British of 1637.

29. "The Dutch were very well received, first by local officials in Canton and then by the [Shunzhi] emperor in Beijing." Keevak, *Embassies to China*, 68.

30. 30 November / 10 December 1637, Mundy, *Travels*, vol. 3, 290.

Weddell and Nathaniel Mountney arrived with the *Dragon* and *Katherine*. After noting the robust health of the crew, the EIC factors reported to their colleagues at Surat: "They have been in China, at a place called *Cantam* [Canton], where they have made such a voyage that we conceive never English men were ever richlier laden than they are now with goods; and yet they flow with gold and silver in abundant manner. They will not sell any China merchandise in this place at hand, but disburse for all manner of charges their ready coin. They are very well manned, and complain of no wants."[31] The Portuguese at Macao were also under the impression that the Courteens came off quite well notwithstanding all the trouble and vexation in Canton involving detainment of merchants, goods, and silver. Considering "the boats and merchandise which the Chinese had given them in compensation for the money and goods taken from them," there was "very little remained owing, as the factors themselves admitted."[32] Thus, any loss suffered by the British would appear negligible even though, as the Lusitanians emphasized: "this business was the cause of much annoyance with the Aitao [*haidao*] and Mandarins."[33] While a considerable quantity of silver dollars (*real* of eight) had been taken by Li Yerong and then confiscated by the authorities at Canton, Portuguese, English, and Chinese documents uniformly indicate that all or most of it was recovered.

As for buying and selling at both Canton and Macao, we find substantial documentation to the effect that the Courteens did not come off big losers. At the close of his December 1637 report to the viceroy of Goa, the captain-general Domingos da Camara de Noronha related: "And though I told your Excellency before that they [the British] only brought here [Macao] to the amount of 25,000 dollars, I understand that it was more than 50,000 [that they took away], for the devil himself could not keep pace with the people of this land, as all were concerned in smuggling merchandise to them. And this is not counting what was given them in Canton, which was as much again."[34] At Macao the Courteens even seem to have sold much of the wine and cloth not of any interest to the Chinese at Canton. In light of all these facts, I would submit that it is more accurate to describe the British enterprise in China in 1637 as decidedly disappointing rather than a failure.

Undoubtedly, the Courteens had hoped to transact a much larger volume of commerce—and to do so without resorting to so much force. In Guangdong they were able to purchase 800 tons of sugar and sugar candy,[35] 50 tons of green ginger,

---

31. Thomas Clark, Richard Hudson, Thomas Peniston, and Thomas Winter at Masulipatam to the President and Council at Surat, 17/27 May 1638, Foster, *English Factories, 1637–1641*, 74.

32. City of Macao to Charles I, 24 December 1637, *Lisbon Transcripts, Books of the Monsoons*, book 41, fol. 220.

33. City of Macao to Charles I, 24 December 1637, *Lisbon Transcripts, Books of the Monsoons*, book 41, fol. 220.

34. Domingos da Camara de Noronha to the viceroy of Goa, 27 December 1637, *Lisbon Transcripts, Books of the Monsoons*, book 41, fol. 191.

35. During the seventeenth century the province of Guangdong became one of the world's largest sugar exporting regions, comparable in scale to some of the European plantations in the Caribbean. See Sucheta Mazumdar, *Sugar and Society in China: Peasants, Technology, and the World Market* (Cambridge, MA: Harvard University Asia Center, 1998). The VOC had been purchasing sugar from China early in the century and later devoted considerable effort to promoting cultivation of sugar cane in parts of Taiwan.

Lessons Learned: The Sinology of the Courteens? 169

almost 20 tons of loose gold, 14 gold chains, 24 cases of silks and satin, 6.5 tons of Smilax China ("China roots"), and 53 tubs of porcelain ("China ware").[36] After listing these goods in the report to the Courteen Association directors, Nathaniel Mountney noted: "The 3 former commodities [sugar, sugar candy, green ginger] have been much abused in their carriage and a great part changed. The best we have chested for Europe; the other we have fardled [packed in bundles], and intend to make sale of it at Achin and the [Malabar] coast of India in exchange for pepper or other commodities. We have yet remaining 80,000 *reals* of 8 undisposed of, all which, or what the time will permit us, we intend to invest in stuffs, gold, etc. commodities fit for Europe and India."[37] The original plan appears to have been to procure enough in China to fully lade at least the *Sun*, captained by Richard Swanley: "We likewise promised a large return unto you by your ship *Sun*, intended to be sent you from China, with such commodities as those parts would afford and were most vendible in Europe; but many impediments interposing have since hindered us from complying with that our resolution, so that it will be impossible to dispeed [dispatch] her before our arrival at Achin."[38] Departing Macao in early 1638, the Courteens still had a substantial quantity of unspent silver because access to the Canton market had been so restricted. That was the fundamental and very sore disappointment: lack of opportunity to use much of the money they had brought all the way from England to spend in China.

Apart from the central failure to put Anglo-Chinese commercial and diplomatic relations on a more than temporary footing, the most striking casualty was the plan to send a ship to Japan—aborted as a consequence of the insufficiency of appropriate commodities and goods obtained at Canton and Macao. A voyage to Japan must have been contingent upon lading at least one ship with much silk and porcelain, both still in high demand in the archipelago up north. According to

---

36. "12,086 pikul sugar: each pikul being 130 pounds eng.
   500 pikul sugar candy [sugar and sugar candy combine for almost 800 tons]
   800 pikul green ginger [50 tons]
   30 1/2 pikul loose gold, cost about 4333 *reals* of 8
   24 cases stuffs
   100 pikul China roots
   9,600 pieces of Campeach wood
   53 tubs China ware
   14 gold chains
   88 chests of cloves"
   This is the inventory provided by the Courteen merchants after leaving China, found in Rawlinson A.299. The "Campeach" was most probably procured at Macao and was a logwood from the Spanish port of Campeche, Mexico. Mundy assesses the quality and cites the prices of all the above purchases in his journal entry for 28 December 1637 / 7 January 1638, Mundy, *Travels*, vol. 3.

37. Mountney, Rawlinson, A.299.

38. Mountney, Rawlinson, A.299. The *Sun* was to embark for England from Aceh in March 1638—that is, within three months of departing from China. The commodities procured from Canton and Macao fetched a good price at Aceh, and the money thus obtained was invested in pepper. The EIC *Discovery* reported thus on the *Sun* at Madagascar in July 1638: "Her cargo is 250 tons of sugar, 40 of pepper, 20 of cloves, 5 of green ginger, 2,000 pieces of silk, a chest of musk, and 30 tubs of China ware." Andrew Cogan, aboard the *Discovery* at St. Augustine's [Madagascar], to the Company, 29 July 1638, Foster, *English Factories, 1637–1641.*

Mountney, writing in December 1637, an arrangement had already been made for the Courteens to trade in Japan: "The Portugals report themselves to have made a bad voyage this year [1637] for Japan, the place being so overladen by the Dutch that they have lost 15 percent of their principal. We were expected at Japan and a house ready fitted for our entertainment."[39] Bolstering our belief that Weddell and Mountney had planned to dispatch a ship to Japan—if they could sufficiently and appropriately lade a ship in China—are the lines from the Macao captain-general in his report to the viceroy of Goa. Evidently, the latter was apprized that the Lusitanians at Macao were able to discover this design of the British.[40] The interest of the Courteens in a Japan voyage sprung partly from the impetus to pursue the ever-elusive northeast passage.[41] So, another ambition, by far the most quixotic of all the schemes, had to be abandoned because of meager success in China.

In assessing the value of the Weddell expedition to China, we may conclude with a brief discussion of its more intangible merits—those things which could not be neatly enumerated or quantified by a factor or itemized by an accountant in a balance sheet. Did this six-month venture in Guangdong yield any significant new knowledge or intellectual breakthroughs? Did it produce anything along the lines of a first installment of British *sinology*? To what degree if any did the Courteens contribute to British and European knowledge of China? To preview the answer to these questions in summary fashion: while the captains, mariners, and merchants of Charles I may be recognized for their daring, ingenuity, and resourcefulness, the intellectual, cultural, strategic, and sinological harvest of their expedition was not much larger than their commercial and financial profit. Even that admittedly modest harvest, however, has been insufficiently noted by those who have published commentaries or summaries of this first British trade enterprise in China.

The three Englishmen who had been arrested and imprisoned in Canton—the brothers Nathaniel and John Mountney and Thomas Robinson—all failed to return to the British Isles. The Mountneys vanished in the Indian Ocean with the *Dragon* and *Katherine*; factor and chief linguist Robinson died aboard the *Sun* near Madagascar from an injury inflicted during violent commotions on deck while that vessel was being convulsed by storms off the Cape of Good Hope in the spring of 1638. Most likely, a mast or part of one dealt him a fatal blow to the chest. Besides

---

39. Mountney, Rawlinson, A.299. Mundy, also writing in December, referred to the Japan voyage, or at least the *hope* of "settling trade in Japan." 25 November / 5 December 1637, Mundy, *Travels*, vol. 3, 275. When he edited his journal several years after the China venture, the title of the section ("Relation") covering China still referred to Japan as well: "journal of a voyage of a fleete, consisting of foure shippes and two pinnaces, sett forth by the right worshipfull sir william courteene, knight, the designe for india, china, japan, etts." Mundy, *Travels*, vol. 3, 19. Among the lines in the royal instructions issued to Weddell and Mountney in Dec. 1635 was: "When you shall be arrived at Japan you are in the first place to present our letters to that emperor and to proceed according as you shall receive encouragement there" (Appendix A, 439).
40. Domingos da Camara de Noronha to the viceroy of Goa, 27 December 1637, *Lisbon Transcripts, Books of the Monsoons*, book 41, fol. 191.
41. See Chapter 2, for the northeast passage clause within the Courteen prospectus, as authorized and highlighted by Charles I.

the commander of the fleet, Captain Weddell, the Mountneys and Robinson would have had the most to write about—the most China knowledge to share with their compatriots.[42] Captain John Carter, who sailed the pinnace *Anne* into the Bogue in the July 1637 excursion up the Pearl River, was presumably commanding the *Katherine* when it disappeared without a trace. Along with all the men who drowned when the *Dragon* and *Katherine* sunk in the Indian Ocean, not only journals and notes but expensively and dangerously obtained maps of China's Pearl River and its estuary most likely perished.[43] At a meeting of the fleet's council of mariners and factors held back on 3 August 1637, a few days after the return of the *Anne* from the Bogue, the contingent who undertook the reconnaissance had presented a map of the river leading to Canton and the islands and terrain they observed in that probe. Such a sketch would have been a decent contribution towards the making of, say, the first British nautical chart of Guangdong.

It would be hard to determine with any accuracy how many in Stuart Britain learned the details of what had transpired as Weddell and his fleet maneuvered in Guangdong for half a year. Richard Swanley, vice-admiral of the fleet, second-in-command to Weddell, is notable for being the only one of the captains (of the *Sun*) who survived and, thus, could have written an informative account of his China adventure. Nothing about the expedition from his pen was addressed to his contemporaries or has come down to us. After returning to England, Swanley subsequently sided with Parliament against Charles in the Civil Wars—as did ex-Courteen skipper Robert Moulton (who had embarked in the *Dragon* but returned early in the *Planter*), who distinguished himself commanding squadrons against royalist ships.[44] Apparently neither Courteen mariners nor merchants published anything about their pioneering trip to China. In the following years, undoubtedly there were to be stray published references to aspects or incidents. More notably, a few decades later an anti-Dutch polemical pamphlet enunciated the claim that the Hollanders had overwhelmed the *Dragon* and *Katherine* in the Indian Ocean. The story went that, animated by the vicious spirit of Amboina, some Dutch had

---

42. A faint sense of the loss of Weddell's navigational and geographical intelligence can be gauged by an instance of his rendering advice immediately after departure from China: "*Knowing well the weather conditions of the China seas*, Weddell is convinced that such a vessel would be unfit for the venture": Captain Weddell to Antonio de Moura de Brito, Captain of Cochin [? March 1639?] (O.C. 1663), Foster, *English Factories, 1637–1641*; emphasis added.

43. According to John Appleby, author of the *ODNB* article on William Courteen, the estimated loss of *Dragon* and *Katherine* (presumably ships and cargo but excluding men) was £150,000. "William Courten," *ODNB*. The vast profits that sank with those ships is indicated less precisely by Mundy: "Questionless, had they [Weddell, Captain John Carter, Mountneys] come home, they had made a rich voyage as well for themselves as for their employers."

44. Swanley was to be most valuable to Parliament in dominating the Irish Sea in the 1640s. His exploits in that sphere gained him notoriety: "In June 1644 at the capture of Carmarthen he became the only known captain to carry out the parliamentary ordinance to throw any Irish prisoners into the sea." Michael Baumber, "Richard Swanley," *ODNB*. For that controversial episode and other colorful and allegedly scandalous conduct on the Irish coast, involving one Belinda Steele, see Andrews, *Ships, Money and Politics*, 199–200.

ambushed Weddell—the English captain who had, after all, done a deal with the Lusitanian devils in 1635.[45]

Interest in preserving trade secrets and commercial intelligence was clearly expressed by the EIC at least as early as 1615.[46] Such a consideration might be relevant in accounting for the lack of publication of the preliminary sinology gained by the Courteens in 1637. By far the most informative and opulently detailed account of the China expedition, written by Peter Mundy, seems to have been kept to himself and his family and friends throughout his lifetime.[47] He died around 1667, and his China notes were not published until 1911, though at least several authors in the eighteenth and nineteenth centuries had accessed the journal in manuscript form—which one can still view at the Bodleian, Oxford. But we can easily imagine that many of the EIC personnel learned about what had transpired in China by letters (some of which long disappeared) and word of mouth. The correspondence quoted above from the company's factors at Masulipatam does more than suggest that. In 1638 or 1639, William Fremlen, successor of William Methwold as president at Surat, was probably thoroughly briefed about what had taken place at Macao and in the Pearl River Delta. His letter would have been read or heard by all the EIC directors ("committees"), important employees, and investors in London.[48] As the Courteen Association struggled over the next several years and was absorbed by the EIC in 1649, we may also observe that the knowledge of China gained by the former was inherited and assimilated.[49] No doubt, as well, important content in the account of the China sojourn as rendered to Charles I and his government would also have been spread informally and by word of mouth.

A case can be made to designate Peter Mundy the first British sinologist, even if a heavy asterisk would be attached to indicate that he was neither a professional nor a Mandarin-fluent one.[50] Perhaps "first amateur British sinologist" would be

---

45. *A true and compendious narration or, second part of Amboyna, or sundry notorious or sundry injuries, insolencies, and acts of hostility which the Hollanders have exercised from time to time against the English nation in the East-Indies, &c. and particularly of the totall plundering and sinking of the Dragon & Katharine both ships and men* was published by a "J.D." (John Darell) in 1665 in London. Darell and this pamphlet are briefly discussed by Games, *Inventing the English Massacre*, 156–57.

46. Massarella, *World Elsewhere*, 330–31. For considerations of proprietary rights and secrecy of the EIC, see also the recent discussion in Mishra, *Business of State*, 302–3.

47. Thus, if Marco Polo's *Travels* remained in manuscript for two hundred years, till 1485, then Mundy's journal endured an even longer dormancy. His Hakluyt Society editor Temple doubted that Mundy intended to publish: Mundy, *Travels*, vol. 1, lxii–lxiii. For the fate of the manuscript from Mundy's death, see 1:lxiii. John Aubrey took note of Mundy and his manuscript of many voyages ("Memoirs of all his Journeys, a large folio") but did not make any specific reference to the Courteen factor's account of China.

48. President Fremlen and Council, aboard the *Mary* at the mouth of the Surat River, to the Company, 4/14 January 1639, Foster, *English Factories, 1637–1641*. Correspondence of the EIC from 1638 to 1640 makes clear that the experience of Weddell and Mountney in China had circulated to some degree.

49. For the fate of this EIC rival after the death of William Courteen in 1636, see Appleby, "William Courten," *ODNB*; and Roper, *Advancing Empire*.

50. The highly qualified arbiter C. R. Boxer ranked Mundy's "the best account of the City of the Name of God in China [Macao] during the palmy days of its prosperity." *Fidalgos in the Far East*, 123. For the more conventional candidates on whom to confer the honor, see J.L. Cranmer-Byng, "The First English Sinologists: Sir George Staunton and the Reverend Robert Morrison," in *Symposium on Historical, Archaeological and*

most accurate. Replete with intricate and accurate drawings, the journal he kept during the six-month Chinese venture contains much information that would have been new to his compatriots—and to most Europeans for that matter.[51] Mundy had probably read materials about China long before his trip to Macao in 1637: he had certainly read some original and translated accounts published in collections by Hakluyt and Purchas. Through them he had accessed some of the best travelogues, surveys, and encyclopedias available in England, as well as the most advanced of cartography covering the Far East, like that produced by Hondius.[52] Prior to embarking from the Downs in the spring of 1636, then, Mundy was already familiar with some, at least rudimentary, facts about Ming China. He had acquired solid background knowledge before the opportunity arose to gain his own first-hand sinology.

Mundy described and illustrated "mandarins or China officers" as well as scenes from the Pearl River and its estuary's islands and shores. Along with some sketches of the following, he recorded notes about Guangdong climate and weather, towns, villages, dwellings (like those built of oyster shells), temples, pagodas, ceremonies, holidays, customs (e.g., foot-binding), clothes, occupations, recreations, flora, fauna, foods, drinks, dining habits and manners, export commodities and manufactures, currency, coins, and weights. Obviously a factor well-trusted by both Weddell and Nathaniel Mountney, he was afforded the opportunity to be present at many of the meetings involving Chinese, Portuguese, mestizos, and various interpreters. He was aboard the *Anne* in that pinnace's cruise in the Pearl River towards Canton in July. He was also a leading participant in the ultimately delusive prospecting for a location within the estuary for a British factory—a tour of the estuary that covered islands and shores near present-day Shenzhen and Hong Kong. Approaching the end of the Courteen visit of China, he spent several weeks in Macao as head merchant. Mundy took full advantage of all these first-hand experiences to gain what may be regarded as at least preliminary sinology. It was through this nimble and diligent factor that rudimentary knowledge of the Chinese language was gained by a non-Iberian, non-Italian, non-Jesuit.

Before Mundy came into direct contact with Mandarin and Cantonese, he had used Spanish, French, Italian, Portuguese, Gujarati and other languages in India, as well as Persian (Farsi).[53] His variety of linguistic and cultural experience surely

---

Linguistic Studies on Southern China, South-East Asia and the Hong Kong Region, ed. F.S. Drake (Hong Kong: Hong Kong University Press, 1967), 247–60.

51. Some of Mundy's drawings have been reproduced and discussed in Rogério Miguel Puga, "Images and Representations of Japan and Macao in Peter Mundy's *Travels* (1637)," *Bulletin of Portuguese/Japanese Studies*, 1 (December 2000): 97–109. Andrade in *Lost Colony*, 40, Fig. 8, reproduces and recognizes Mundy's impressive and "rare" sketch of a Chinese war-junk—highlighting Mundy's unique if still very modest sinological contribution in the field of nautical/naval technology. That sketch adorns the cover of this book.

52. Mundy owned more than one map of Hondius, besides that printed with the date 1631: Mundy, *Travels*, vol. 3, 19. There are six double-page maps by Hondius in the Mundy MS, Bodleian: Rawlinson A.315. On these Mundy traced his routes with red dotted lines.

53. Throughout the five volumes of Mundy he edited, relentlessly following the restless traveler across multiple oceans and continents, Temple remarks upon the exceptionally acute ear of this Courteen factor-linguist: "His accuracy in reporting vernacular words is extraordinary and testifies to his remarkably good ear, which

174   *The First British Trade Expedition to China*

prepared him to rise to the challenge of the exotic sounds and complicated script he encountered in Guangdong. Mundy (accurately) reported:

> Most China men can write and cast up accounts which they do by pen, as also by an invention with beads instead of counters, and deciphered when I come to speak of their numbers. Here follow some China characters or letters, as I had them from the merchant, being of those eight that were taken out of a great junk which we fired, as formerly mentioned, with their pronunciation in China and signification in English. Our interpreter, Antonio the *kafir*, none of the best of linguists, and therefore may be conceived not so punctual and perfect, but being for the most part of proper names of things, the error may be the less.[54] The China writing beginning from the right hand toward the left, and their lines from the top downward thus:
>
> | | | |
> |---|---|---|
> | 7 | 4 | 1 |
> | 8 | 5 | 2 |
> | 9 | 6 | 3 |
>
> where they begin with 1 and proceed to 2 and 3 in the first line, then to 4, 5, 6 in the second, etts., beginning their books at the farthest and wrong end as we conceive, or as we use. But these few following words go forward according to our custom. They all write with pencils and black and red ink made into dry paste which they distemper with water when they will use it.

Mundy was not apt, however, to follow Matteo Ricci up the linguistic Everest. As an infallibly practical merchant, he reckoned an alphabetical script to be much more expedient: "Although there are said to be many thousands of these characters and so various, yet a man may much sooner and easier express his mind with our 24 letters, only some are to be pronounced through the nose, for which we have no proper letters. I say my opinion, our 24 letters go before their thousands of characters for brevity and true explaining and our figures in numbering in a far greater degree."[55] Here again, incidentally, in Mundy's judging Chinese orthography/script less commodious than Western alphabetic ones, we find no example of a European of the early modern period seized or overcome by a sense of China's "culturally sophisticated and technologically advanced" civilization vis-à-vis that of the West.

---

    enabled him to discover that there were 'no thirds nor fifths' in Indian 'music as I could hear.'" Mundy, *Travels*, vol. 2, lx, 217.

54. At this point in the manuscript about two hundred Chinese characters are written, with pronunciation, as well as correct English translations, all in Mundy's hand. Temple consulted Cambridge professor H.A. Giles (of Wade-Giles phonetic fame), who judged the Courteen journalist's collection of characters "curious, chiefly because they are identifiable as actual and not bogus words, taken down on the spot by a bona-fide traveller."

55. 28 December 1637 / 7 January 1638, Mundy, *Travels*, vol. 3. It is true that Chinese characters had already been published in Europe: in Mendoza's famous work of 1585. But they persisted as conundrums even among the most erudite of Europe's intelligentsia. While the Bodleian at Oxford, for example, was to accumulate an impressive collection of Chinese books over the seventeenth century, it did not have readers to exploit them. For the Bodleian's wealth of Chinese materials, one should consult David Helliwell's recent (and Herculean) cataloging. In his "Selden Map Rediscovered" and *London*, Robert Batchelor has splendidly described the handling and attempts to decipher those materials in the seventeenth century. As for Mendoza in 1585, he was indebted to Gaspar da Cruz, who, in 1569, had provided an astute anatomy of Chinese language/script. Boxer, *South China*, 161–62.

To Mundy, at least, the language system used by the Ming Chinese seemed inconvenient and inferior to those he had learned in his previous travels and extensive participation in foreign exchange and markets.[56]

As touched on above, Mundy's substantial if casual and en passant contribution to British sinology was not published in his life-time, nor in the remainder of the seventeenth century.[57] Among the reasons for this neglect was that several publications were soon available that provided many more (if not many more important) details. Just a few years after Mundy's death, for instance, in 1669, there appeared Johannes Nieuhof's encyclopedic *Embassy of the Dutch East India Company to the Great Tartar Cham, the Present Emperor of China.*[58] As the Ming had yielded to the Qing, some of Mundy's information was also rendered less relevant or much less critical to dealing with diplomatic, coastal, and commercial circumstances after the 1644 demise of the dynasty founded by Zhu Yuanzhang. As noted in the Prologue, it was not until the twentieth century, courtesy of the Hakluyt Society, that this Courteen factor's outstanding diligence and meticulous toil could be widely recognized. Indeed, the present book stands as testament to and reposes very broadly upon his individual effort—his travels, labors, and prowess and achievement as merchant, linguist, and journalist. At the same time, my volume pays tribute to Mundy's magnificently exacting twentieth-century editor, Richard Carnac Temple. The principal narrator of the story of the first British trade expedition to China is undoubtedly Peter Mundy. But it was Temple who effectively afforded him opportunity to relate the adventure to posterity. If Mundy was the first British sinologist, however amateur, then in Temple we may recognize one of his most obscure twentieth-century successors—an equally non-professional and self-effacing one. Among the purposes of my own effort is to ensure that their unique contributions to sinology suffer less neglect in the twenty-first century.

---

56. This opinion might establish Mundy as precursor of William C. Hannas, *The Writing on the Wall: How Asian Orthography Curbs Creativity* (Philadelphia: University of Pennsylvania Press, 2003).

57. A curiously parallel case of a journal kept by a European traveler-mercenary in Taiwan in the 1620s which was only published hundreds of years later is the Swiss Elie Ripon's *Voyages et aventures du capitaine Ripon aux grandes Indes: Journal inedit d'un mercenaire, 1617–1627*, ed. Yves Giraud (Thonon-les-Bains, Haute-Savoie: Editions de l'Albaron, 1990); see Andrade, *How Taiwan Became Chinese*, 33n1.

58. In London in 1669 appeared this English translation of what was published in Amsterdam in 1665 as *Het gezantschap der Neerlandtsche Oost-Indische Compagnie, aan den grooten Tartarischen Cham, den tegenwoordigen keizer van China.* This book contained not only the narrative of the embassy of 1655 but also myriad miscellaneous items, including almost 150 engravings. I say parenthetically "not many more *important* details" because there were plenty of facts recorded and observations made by Mundy that were original and were not rendered redundant by Nieuhof's sinology—which was, after all, heavily derived from Matteo Ricci, Martino Martini, and Alvaro Semedo. For publication details, translations, and editions of Nieuhof, see Keevak, *Embassies to China*, 69–71. For the same purpose—to explain seventeenth-century indifference to Mundy's manuscript (in any who knew that it contained a detailed China journal)—I could also cite a work like Montanus, *Atlas Chinensis*, which appeared in English translation by John Ogilby in 1671.

Epilogue

The First British Trade Expedition to China: A Precursor of the Opium Wars?

The Pearl River Delta, setting for all the activities of the British in China in 1637, was the same location where the initial battles of the First Opium War (1839–1842) took place two hundred years later. The identical venues of engagements and hostilities by land and sea invite comparison between the (Caroline) British in China in 1637 and the (Victorian) British in China in 1839. Just as the British in 1637 had encountered Chinese interested in conducting trade with them outside the official Macao-Canton channel, so in the decades leading up to that Opium War there were plenty of Chinese involved with the British in profiting illegally and handsomely from traffic in the prohibited drug. As the British Chief Superintendent of Trade in China Charles Elliot and subordinate officers sent to Canton to deal with the opium crisis had to make on-the-spot decisions and spontaneous adjustments without first consulting the government in London, so Captain Weddell and the leaders of the Courteen fleet could consult neither their company supervisors in London nor the government of Charles I and his Privy Council at Whitehall before choosing fateful courses of action. The situation may have been more stressful for Weddell, as presumably he had to exercise more discretion and, thus, bear more responsibility for outcomes. After all, in Victorian Britain, the House of Commons *did* debate the China crisis before Lord Melbourne's Foreign Secretary Viscount Palmerston authorized aggressive action to be taken in the Pearl River estuary. On the other hand, Weddell might well have acted with less apprehension of scrutiny.

As the Ming administrations in the sixteenth and seventeenth centuries struggled to crack down on piracy and illicit trade on the southeast coasts, so the Qing governments of the eighteenth and nineteenth centuries struggled to enforce prohibitions against traffic in opium.[1] Just as trade in that drug was enriching too many Qing officials and merchants, so illegal trade with non-Portuguese foreigners like the "red-barbarian" British could profit too many Ming officials and merchants to

---

1. For the illicit traffic at Lintin Island (內伶仃島 Neilingdingdao), where the opium clippers flocked in the decades before the Anglo-Chinese War broke out and where the Courteen fleet was anchored in 1637, see Peter Perdue, *The First Opium War: The Anglo-Chinese War of 1839–1842* (Cambridge: MIT Press, 2010), 4. For the utter inability of the Qing navy to do anything about this traffic at Lintin, see Peter Ward Fay, *The Opium War, 1840–1842: Barbarians in the Celestial Empire in the Early Part of the Nineteenth Century and the War by Which They Forced Her Gates Ajar* (Chapel Hill: University of North Carolina Press, 1975), 46.

Epilogue 177

render the *haijin* (海禁) policy determined in Beijing easily implemented in remote Guangdong or Fujian. The enforcement of the proscription was only intermittently sustained and inconsistently effective. The British in 1637 were able to find locals in the Pearl River Delta to sell them commodities and provisions. When their silver dollars would not persuade, the Courteens resorted to force. Commerce and combat were mingled in a most uneasy arrangement. In the Bogue in September, as related by Peter Mundy:

> We took a junk with our boats and brought her aboard. She had only in her a few timbers, planks, a *harquebus a croc*, bamboo spears and a little rice, which was all handed in to the admiral with some of their people, who in submissive manner fell on their knees when they came aboard. The said junk was manned with English with some Chinois to scull her, and sent ahead to intercept others that should pass as not mistrusting. Also the *Sun's* skiff was sent ashore to try if they could buy any cattle, provision (*which may seem strange to surprise and take and to seek trade and refreshing from the same people at the same time*); but contrariwise they had some skirmish with the country people, whereupon our boats were sent to succour them; so at last all came well off and returned in safety.[2]

Similarly, and as noted in Chapter 9, Captain Weddell observed that there were Chinese in the area willing to undertake disguise to defy the government and engage in illicit trade. In late September, as the commander himself related: "Divers boats and junks would come and sell us sugar at easy rates; but they came by stealth."[3]

Even after major hostilities of the First Opium War had commenced in 1839, the Victorians found Chinese to supply them with sustenance and provisions. In November 1840, for example, the British fleet commanded by Elliot anchored on the eastern flank of the Bogue. A spontaneous, hovering riverside market sprang up to purvey victuals—even while the Chinese vendors were putting themselves at the peril of punitive action by local mandarins. As Julia Lovell colorfully relates: "When the names of this impromptu comprador community were taken down by a group of police spies, the businessmen besieged and set fire to the police boat. 'These poor wretches were literally roasted alive, their persecutors preventing their escape with long bamboos,' recalled an English lieutenant. 'What a most extraordinary nation this is! . . . They will trade with you at one spot, while you are fighting, killing and destroying them at another!'"[4] More than two centuries after the Courteen fleet had departed China, it was still the case that commerce and combat, trade and scuffles, would oddly combine. The British would carry both handfuls of coins and handfuls of guns. Nor had the linguistic aspect of Sino-British relations changed appreciably between the arrival of the subjects of Charles I in 1637 and the war waged by Victoria's men two hundred years later. The Courteen fleet steered into the Bogue by Weddell carried not one merchant or mariner who could speak a syllable or

---

2. 13/23 August 1637, Mundy, *Travels*, vol. 3; emphasis added.
3. "Weddell's China Narrative, O.C. 1662."
4. Julia Lovell, *The Opium War: Drugs, Dreams and the Making of China* (London: Picador, 2011), 127.

write a stroke of Chinese. Thus, the British had to grope for stones to cross the river—摸著石頭過河 (*mozhe shitou guohe*). To moderns like ourselves, Weddell and Nathaniel Mountney may appear shockingly insouciant as they confronted the colossal language barrier—or linguistic Great Wall. But the British and their fellow Europeans elsewhere in Asia and Africa in the seventeenth century were well-accustomed to doing business, at least initially, without knowing a word of the commercial counterpart's language. On Madagascar, June 1638, on the *Sun's* return voyage to England, Mundy reported a typical case of effective bartering: "For our matter of trading with these people, being only for provisions, there needs not much interpreters, for the utterance of booes, baaes, is as good language for bullocks and sheeps as the best; and so for the rest with the help of signs."[5]

No matter how big a handicap linguistic deficiency was for the British in India in the first half of the seventeenth century, commerce was prosecuted on a considerable scale. From the ignorance of native languages, errors, even serious blunders, were not infrequently committed. It was normal in the first decades of the seventeenth century to embark on ventures and errands armed with little to no linguistic competence whatever. Finding himself in India serving the EIC in March 1633, Mundy complained of his predicament: "Yet with all these hard conditions am I thrust out alone, with little [knowledge of the] language, having nobody that I can trust or cares to take any pains to ease me to look after the Company's goods, to help to compound the unreasonable demands of carters, cammelers, etc., to decide their quarrels, differences, to persuade them to reason."[6] Prior to their arrival in China in 1637 the Courteens had to cope with communication obstacles. On the Malabar coast in the spring of that year, off Cannanore, Captain Weddell anchored while Mundy and a detachment explored an island at its entrance. They failed to get information, as their interpreters "could not be understood by the country people." Even when interpreters could be obtained, they were only unsafely relied upon.

As for the Bogue and the Pearl River Delta, even the old "China hands," the Portuguese at Macao, were vulnerable to and suffered from mistranslations. Having been settled in the Ming realm for several decades, these Iberians had acquired Luso-Chinese bilingual facility, contacts, and resources. But during the British sojourn, as the captain-general of the Lusitanian enclave, Domingos da Camara de Noronha, complained: "The Procurador of this city presented a petition to one of the Chinese mandarins . . . but the interpreter who translated it into the Chinese tongue added what he pleased to it, calling the subjects of your Majesty [Charles I] by an insulting name. This being a way these interpreters sometimes have of working evil to us." So even if the Courteens had been better furnished than merely veteran

---

5. Mundy, *Travels*, vol. 3, 374.
6. Mundy, *Travels*, vol. 2, 281. Instances of William Methwold, EIC president at Surat, bemoaning scarcity of linguistic ability in the company's personnel in India can be found in Foster, *English Factories, 1634–1636*, 208, 272. William Fremlen, successor of Methwold, did possess some facility to avoid "gross tricks [being] practiced upon us." Methwold himself was notably gifted in foreign tongues; and appreciation of his prowess in the Surat post is provided by Furber, *Rival Empires*, 67–68.

Epilogue 179

linguist-factor Thomas Robinson, they may still have been abused and confounded as the Portuguese often seem to have been. Would the British enterprise in China in 1637 have run much more smoothly, more peacefully and profitably, had Weddell's fleet possessed its own competent and scrupulous Sino-Portuguese interpreter?

In light of events and aspects of the First Opium War, one could still doubt that the Caroline British would have fared much better with even a top-notch team of translators and interpreters of, say, Matteo Ricci-caliber. At any rate, a century and a half after Captain Weddell departed China and disappeared in the Indian Ocean, little change could be noticed. When Lord Macartney's embassy arrived in 1793, under more extensive royal aegis and possessed of more imperial confidence, the only one among the dozens of British who could communicate a little in Chinese was Thomas Staunton, twelve-year-old son of Sir George Staunton, Macartney's right-hand man. Staunton had recruited four Roman Catholic priests to serve as interpreters—two from Macao. At the time of the First Opium War, a few decades hence, linguistic impediments were still considerable. Sino-British relations of the 1830s would have to contend with the reality that communication functionality was nearly nil. As Lovell informs us: "A question mark hangs over the competence of Lin Zexu's translators. When Lin showed a version of his letter to Queen Victoria, rendered by his chief interpreter, to a crew of shipwrecked Englishmen, one member of his audience reported that he could 'scarcely command my gravity . . . some parts of it we could make neither head nor tail of.'"[7]

While few in our day have heard of Captain Weddell and his exploits in the Bogue in 1637, plenty of Westerners and Chinese are familiar with controversial incidents and clashes of the Anglo-Chinese wars of the nineteenth century. Even before the first major battles of that conflict took place, there was an incident almost identical to one that occurred during the Weddell expedition. At the beginning of September 1839, the British Captain Elliot asked Chinese naval officers in the straits between what is now Hong Kong and Kowloon to let them purchase provisions. Having been rebuffed, British warships opened fire on war junks anchored off Kowloon. That was just a tiny skirmish before violence escalated and full-scale battles broke out. They did so two months later, early November 1839, at the First Battle of Chuanbi (Chuenpee), exactly where Weddell had taken to the offensive— where the Courteen commander had bombarded and then stormed a fort in the Bogue. Mundy, eye-witness in August 1637, reported how smoothly and safely the British assaulted and neutralized the fort at or near Anunghoy (阿娘鞋 Aniangxie):

> Then from the platform they began to discharge at us also near a dozen shot before we answered one. By their working we perceived what good gunners they were and how well they were fitted, for many of their own shot dropped down out of the mouth of the piece close under the wall. Others were shot at random haphazard quite another way, giving fire to them with wet vents even as the pieces lay on the

---

7. Lovell, *The Opium War*, 75.

round wall, without aiming or traversing them at all. . . . I have set down the taking of this platform somewhat largely because it was so orderly done and . . . this act rather showing the manner than deserving the name of the taking of a fort, it being of no great danger, difficulty or resistance.[8]

When the British ships arrived in 1839, fortifications at that spot in the Bogue had been expanded since the Mundy-narrated offensive of the Courteens in 1637. But while there was now, in the reign of the Daoguang emperor (1820–1850), a network of such forts built of granite and mud, their artillery and arsenal were apparently no less impotent.[9] Just as Weddell with only the *Dragon*, *Sun*, and *Katherine* inflicted severe damage and injury on the Bogue fort (and several Chinese junks), so the British under Captain Elliot in 1839 were swiftly able to annihilate the network of forts at the mouth of the Pearl River: "The British . . . systematically destroy[ed] each of the forts they passed, as Guan Tianpei's structures were exposed as poorly designed, isolated, exposed units, from which his terrified soldiers ran as fast they could."[10] Weddell's conquest of the fort was scarcely less swift than Elliot's. In the case of the latter: "twenty-five minutes after the fleet had begun to shell the highest fort at Chuanbi, the British flag fluttered over its walls, the Qing guns stopped and the forts' defenders scattered in panic."[11]

Similarly, both in the clashes of 1637 and 1839–1842, casualties of the Ming and Qing far outnumbered those of the Carolines and Victorians. The latter were able to inflict death and injury on many with only a few ships and men. The conquest of Chuanbi fort on 7 January 1841, lasting an hour and a half, injured thirty-eight British, while the Qing suffered 280 dead and 462 severely harmed.[12] Next month, 25–27 February 1841, between the Bogue and Canton, it cost the British five injured men to slaughter 600 on the Qing side. In addition to slaying that several hundred, this operation fetched the British 460 cannon. As Captain Weddell had wreaked havoc in the Bogue with just a few ships, so the British in 1841 rampaged and slaughtered with hardly a half-dozen superior vessels—annihilating dozens of war junks and seizing and plundering forts and camps. As Lovell, a scholar with consummate mastery of both the English and Chinese sources, has emphasized: "Repeatedly during the war, Qing armies of thousands would be routed by a few hundred, or even a few dozen well-disciplined British troops with functioning

---

8. 12/22 August 1637, Mundy, *Travels*, vol. 3.
9. "Their cannon were badly cast and immobile, and supplied by poor-quality powder, while their circular walls exposed the forts' defenders to bombardment from above." Lovell, *The Opium War*, 130.
10. Lovell, *The Opium War*, 131.
11. Lovell, *The Opium War*, 131. If it were not homicidal it would be slapstick comedy: "The officers directing operations on Wangtong [橫檔島 Hengdangdao] locked their rank and file inside the forts to prevent them from running away, then fled in small boats as soon as the [British] firing began. As a result, their abandoned subordinates fired their cannon *at their departing superiors*, rather than at the British." Lovell, *The Opium War*, 138; emphasis added.
12. Lovell, *The Opium War*, 133.

Epilogue

181

artillery and battle-plans."[13] As the Caroline Weddell with his few vessels had been outnumbered by dozens of Ming war junks, so the Victorian Captain Elliot with his two British frigates was confronted with sixteen Qing naval junks and thirteen fire-boats—perhaps barely distinguishable from the fire-ships launched against the Courteen fleet back on 20 September 1637. At a later crossroads of the nineteenth-century war, when the British perceived that the Chinese governor Qishan, who had replaced Lin Zexu, would not make further concessions, Chuanbi was again the venue for an emphatic demonstration of British tactical prowess and cutting-edge naval technology. The iron, steam-driven warship *Nemesis*, constructed in Liverpool for the East India Company, terrorized and pulverized at will. While the most massive assault launched by the Ming upon the British in 1637 was a pre-dawn fire-ship attack, two hundred years later the Qing resorted to roughly the same low-tech operations. One scheme given serious consideration by Lin Zexu and Guan Tianpei was: "to hire thousands of locals to form teams of desperadoes that would approach on small boats and hurl flaming jars of oil or stink-pots at the British, or leap onto the warships and massacre the crews in hand-to-hand fighting."[14] A fire-ship attack seemingly not one whit different from the one aimed at the Courteens in September 1637 was also considered by Lin and Guan: "to build fleets of skiffs, heaped with dry grass and gunpowder. In the heat of battle, fearless irregulars would row them out, link them together with iron chains, nail them to the side of British boats, set fire to them, then escape."[15] An attack of this ilk was launched by the Qing with no success in the Pearl River Delta on 21 May 1841, and another was planned at Nanjing in 1842.[16]

While Ming officials at Canton in 1637 addressed the intruding British as "puppies and goats," by 1841 their successors, the Qing, addressed them as "dogs and sheep." On 18 June 1841 the Daoguang emperor wrote: "The nature of these foreigners is like that of dogs and sheep. It isn't worth trying to bargain or reason with them."[17] If the emperor had not been deceived so frequently and grossly by his ministers and subordinates—as thoroughly documented by Lovell—then he might not have thought them so unamenable to reason or bargain. A decisive role was played by ignorance and misunderstanding. Three years after the Opium War had begun that emperor asked: "Where is England?" At the beginning of the conflict, letters of moral appeal addressed to Queen Victoria by Lin Zexu carried the astoundingly erroneous assumption that the sale of opium in England was illegal. Our account of the British in Guangdong in 1637 would also warrant citation of ignorance and misunderstanding—if, even more, their exploitation (subterfuge and skullduggery)—as pivotal. Just as the Ming emperor Chongzhen's government and armies

---

13. Lovell, *The Opium War*, 115. We can conservatively estimate that the Courteens killed a few dozen Chinese, and injured several dozen more, while losing and harming few of their own in the process.
14. Lovell, *The Opium War*, 130.
15. Lovell, *The Opium War*, 130–31.
16. Lovell, *The Opium War*, 152 (Guangdong), 232 (Nanjing).
17. Lovell, *The Opium War*, 165.

were too preoccupied with northern incursions and troubles to be able to give full consideration to an overture of commerce and amity from some envoys of Charles I, or to properly distinguish them from the Dutch "red-hairs," or to re-examine and revise the China trade monopoly of the Portuguese at Macao; so in 1839 the Qing court "was too distracted by fears of social unrest to come up voluntarily with a pragmatic response to Western trade demands[, and] Britain interpreted this political paralysis as inveterate xenophobia."[18]

In concluding her book, Lovell fast-forwards to 2010, just as she was penning the last lines:

> The situation did not look so very different, with the [PRC] government infuriating Western states over its rejection of climate-change legislation that might slow growth, its harsh stance on social control and its aversion to compromise on international trade issues, such as strengthening the yuan relative to the dollar.... From the age of opium-traders to the Internet, China and the West have been infuriating and misunderstanding each other, despite ever-increasing opportunities for contact, study, and mutual sympathy. Ten years into the twenty-first century, the nineteenth is still with us.[19]

Yet in view of the many strikingly similar issues and circumstances that obtained, as I have suggested above, we could "rewind" from 2022 to 1637. Now we could say, "More than twenty years into the twenty-first century, the *seventeenth* is still with us." And by this stroke we may have purchased our corollary, or most irreverent and blasé of all conclusions: *plus ça change, plus c'est la même chose*—or to adapt Shakespeare from the *Sonnets*: "For as the sun is daily new and old / So is *history* still telling what is told." As noted above, in the wake of the devastation wreaked upon the waves and shores, in January 1841, after a battle lasting only an hour, the fort at Chuanbi was captured. A fort in the immediate vicinity had been stormed by Captain Weddell two centuries prior. The flags hoisted upon the two forts were different. But were the attitudes or personalities of the British who flew the flag over the Bogue fort in 1637 and the British who hoisted one over Chuanbi in 1841 appreciably different? One could apply quite a few opprobrious terms to Weddell, Nathaniel Mountney, and the rest of the men aboard the ships of the Courteen fleet in 1637: imprudent, reckless, obstinate, aggressive, and belligerent. But if the British still say, with their Pope of poetry, "fools rush in where angels fear to tread" (and fools rush into China without a syllable of Mandarin?), then they also say, "he who hesitates is lost" and "fortune favors the bold." For such disparaging terms as suggested above, one could substitute the laudatory ones: venturesome, persevering, tenacious, mettlesome, and brave.

That returns us to a point raised at the beginning of this book: It is hard to believe that Britain's commercial, industrial, and imperial expansion in the following two

---

18. Lovell, *The Opium War*, 360.
19. Lovell, *The Opium War*, 360.

Epilogue

centuries would have occurred without the trail-blazing efforts of enterprising and intrepid personalities like Weddell and Mountney—risking, failing, drowning, and being killed all over the globe. Exceedingly perilous expeditions like the one undertaken by the Courteen Association were necessary if only as initial steps towards the knowledge and power of what would come to be called empire. The Portuguese had undertaken comparably risky, even more pioneering and dangerous ventures in the fifteenth and early sixteenth centuries—before they had acquired Macao around 1557. The Lusitanians themselves could recognize the audacity of Weddell as the audacity of their own Afonso de Albuquerque, their legendary maritime conquistador. If the importance or fame of the Elizabethan Sir Francis Drake in some respects might be compared to that of Albuquerque, Weddell, as Drake's Stuart successor, likewise bears some resemblance to that Portuguese Asia empire-builder. While not oblivious to Hume and his post hoc ergo propter hoc objection, it demanded men like Drake and then Weddell, and expeditions like Courteen's, for the British Empire to arise.

When the controversies and clashes of the Opium Wars erupted in the late 1830s, several of the British figures could easily be identified as the imperial descendants of Weddell. Indeed, long before the Industrial Revolution produced ships like the *Nemesis* in the nineteenth century, British juggernauts like Weddell used massive ships, superior cannon, and naval maneuvers to behave in ways not easy to distinguish from those of their Victorian counterparts. Thus, I would submit that there is much more similarity than difference to be noticed as we reflect on the seventeenth- and nineteenth-century collisions between the British and Chinese in the Pearl River Delta. In the last analysis, it appears that the British exhibited the card they would play in the Anglo-Chinese war two hundred years before that violent clash began. If the validity of this point is recognized, then we are entitled to pose the rhetorical question: Was not Captain Weddell's bombardment and storming of the fort in the Bogue in 1637 the first exercise or at least strong foretaste of "gunboat diplomacy"? The Portuguese of Macao in their letter to Charles I in December 1637 described the Ming superstition to the effect that the British "were men with blue eyes, which the Chinese believe bring ill-luck, and that if admitted, they will take their kingdom from them. . . . [T]he Chinese took alarm, fearing that in future years they will come here with many more to conquer them."[20] At least in light of the conclusion of the Opium Wars and establishment of the treaty ports, this superstition does not look so silly. The prophecy seems to have come true. While the Courteens had only a rather vague design upon Hainan in 1637, Hong Kong was British by 1842.

---

20. City of Macao to Charles I, 24 December 1637, *Lisbon Transcripts, Books of the Monsoons*, book 41, fol. 220.

Appendix

Key Chinese Officials in Ming Documents with English Renderings by the Courteens

1. 張鏡心 Zhang Jingxin, 兩廣總督 (*Liangguang zongdu*), Governor/ Viceroy of Guangxi and Guangdong

Courteen approximation and translation: Tootan/Toutan, "viceroy of this province of Canton"

2. 葛徵奇 Ge Zhengqi, 巡按 (*xun'an*), Imperial Inspector / Inspector-General / Regional Inspector

Courteen approximation and translation: Chadjan/Chamjan, "supervisor general"

3. 鄭覲光 Zheng Jinguang, 海道 (*haidao*), Superintendent of Customs Duties / Maritime Defense Circuit

Courteen approximation and translation: Haitao/Hitow, "lord treasurer" / "lord chancellor" / "chief justice for the city of Canton"

4. 陳謙 Chen Qian, 廣東總兵 (*Guangdong zongbing*), Guangdong Commander of Military-Naval Forces

Courteen approximation and translation: Champin/Cheeompee, "admiral of the forces both by sea and land" / "admiral of the seas" / "admiral general" / "lord admiral" / "general of the city of Canton" / "general of the province by sea"

5. 黎延慶 Li Yanqing, 副總兵 (*fuzongbing*), Regional Vice-Commander

Courteen translation: "champin's deputy"

Bibliography

Andrade, Tonio. "The Company's Chinese Privateers: How the Dutch East India Company Tried to Lead a Coalition of Privateers to War against China." *Journal of World History* 15, no. 4 (2004): 415–44.

Andrade, Tonio. *The Gunpowder Age: China, Military Innovation, and the Rise of the West in World History*. Princeton, NJ: Princeton University Press, 2016.

Andrade, Tonio. *How Taiwan Became Chinese: Dutch, Spanish, and Han Colonization in the Seventeenth Century*. New York: Columbia University Press, 2008.

Andrade, Tonio. *Lost Colony: The Untold Story of China's First Great Victory over the West*. Princeton, NJ: Princeton University Press, 2011.

Andrade, Tonio, and Xing Hang, eds. *Sea Rovers, Silver, and Samurai: Maritime East Asia in Global History, 1550–1700*. Honolulu: University of Hawai'i Press, 2016.

Andrade, Tonio, and Kenneth Swope, eds. *Early Modern East Asia: War, Commerce, and Cultural Exchange*. New York: Routledge, 2017.

Andrews, Kenneth R. *Ships, Money and Politics: Seafaring and Naval Enterprise in the Reign of Charles I*. Cambridge: Cambridge University Press, 1991.

Andrews, Kenneth R. *Trade, Plunder and Settlement: Maritime Enterprise and the Genesis of the British Empire, 1480–1630*. Cambridge: Cambridge University Press, 1984.

Antony, Robert, ed. *Elusive Pirates, Pervasive Smugglers: Violence and Clandestine Trade in the Greater China Seas*. Hong Kong: Hong Kong University Press, 2010.

Antony, Robert J. "Trade, Piracy, and Resistance in the Gulf of Tonkin in the Seventeenth Century." In *Sea Rovers, Silver, and Samurai: Maritime East Asia in Global History, 1550–1700*, edited by Tonio Andrade and Xing Hang, 312–34. Honolulu: University of Hawai'i Press, 2016.

Appleton, William W. *A Cycle of Cathay: The Chinese Vogue in England during the Seventeenth and Eighteenth Centuries*. New York: Columbia University Press, 1951.

Atwell, William. "Another Look at Silver Imports into China, ca. 1635–1644." *Journal of World History* 16, no. 4 (2005): 467–91.

Atwell, William. "International Bullion Flows and the Chinese Economy circa 1530–1650." *Past and Present* 95, no. 1 (1982): 68–90.

Batchelor, Robert. *London: The Selden Map and the Making of a Global City, 1549–1689*. Chicago: University of Chicago Press, 2014.

Batchelor, Robert. "The Selden Map Rediscovered: A Chinese Map of East Asian Shipping Routes, c. 1619." *Imago Mundi: The International Journal for the History of Cartography* 65, no. 1 (2013): 37–63.

Bingbu Cangao. 兵部题《失名会同两广总督张镜心题》残稿（明清史料乙编，第八本）。上海：中央研究院历史语言研究所，商务印书馆，1936).

Blake, John W. *West Africa: Quest for God and Gold, 1454–1578; A Survey of the First Century of White Enterprise in West Africa, with Particular Reference to the Achievement of the Portuguese and Their Rivalries with Other European Powers.* London: Curzon, 1977.

Blussé, Leonard. *Strange Company: Chinese Settlers, Mestizo Women, and the Dutch in VOC Batavia.* Dordrecht: Foris, 1986.

Blussé, Leonard, Nathalie Everts, W.E. Milde, and Yung-ho Ts'ao, eds. *De dagregisters van het Kasteel Zeelandia, Taiwan, 1629–1662*, 4 vols. The Hague: Instituut voor Nederlandse Geschiedenis, 1986–2001.

Borschberg, Peter. *The Singapore and Melaka Straits: Violence, Security and Diplomacy in the Seventeenth Century.* Leiden: KITLV Press, 2010.

Bowen, H.V., Elizabeth Mancke, and John G. Read, eds. *Britain's Oceanic Empire: Atlantic and Indian Ocean Worlds, c. 1550–1850.* Cambridge: Cambridge University Press, 2012.

Boxer, C.R. "Anglo-Portuguese Rivalry in the Persian Gulf, 1615–1635." In *Chapters in Anglo-Portuguese Relations*, edited by Edgar Prestage, 46–129. Westport, CT: Greenwood, 1971.

Boxer, C.R. *Fidalgos in the Far East, 1550–1557: Fact and Fancy in the History of Macao.* The Hague: Nijhoff, 1948.

Boxer, C.R. *The Great Ship from Amacon: Annals of Macao and the Old Japan Trade, 1555–1640.* Lisbon: Centro de Estudos Historicos Ultramarinos, 1959.

Boxer, C.R. *Jan Compagnie in Japan, 1600–1817: An Essay on the Cultural, Artistic, and Scientific Influence Exercised by the Hollanders in Japan from the Seventeenth to the Nineteenth Centuries.* The Hague: Martinus Nijhoff, 1936.

Boxer, C.R. *Macau na epoca da restauracao* [Macao three hundred years ago]. Lisbon: Fundacao Oriente, 1993.

Boxer, C.R. *Portuguese Conquest and Commerce in Southern Asia, 1500–1700.* London: Variorum Reprints, 1985.

Boxer, C.R. *Portuguese India in the Mid-seventeenth Century.* Delhi: Oxford University Press, 1980.

Boxer, C.R. *Portuguese Society in the Tropics: The Municipal Councils of Goa, Macao, Bahia and Luanda, 1510–1800.* Madison: University of Wisconsin Press, 1965.

Boxer, C.R. *South China in the Sixteenth Century: Being the Narratives of Galeote Pereira, Fr. Gaspar da Cruz, O.P., and Fr. Martin de Rada, O.E.S.A. (1550–1575).* London: Hakluyt Society, 1953.

Brenner, Robert. *Merchants and Revolution: Commercial Change, Political Conflict and London's Overseas Traders, 1550–1653.* Princeton, NJ: Princeton University Press, 1993.

Brook, Timothy. *Mr. Selden's Map of China: Decoding the Secrets of a Vanished Cartographer.* London: Bloomsbury, 2013.

Brook, Timothy. *Vermeer's Hat: The Seventeenth Century and the Dawn of the Global World.* Bloomsbury: London, 2007.

Canny, Nicholas. "The Origins of Empire: An Introduction." In *Origins of Empire*, edited by Nicholas Canny, 1–33. Oxford: Oxford University Press, 1998.

Chan, Albert. *The Glory and Fall of the Ming Dynasty.* Norman: University of Oklahoma Press, 1982.

Bibliography

Chang, T'ien-Tse. *Sino-Portuguese Relations from 1514 to 1644: A Synthesis of Portuguese and Chinese Sources*. Leiden: E.J. Brill, 1933.

Chase, Kenneth. *Firearms: A Global History to 1700*. Cambridge: Cambridge University Press, 2003.

Chaudhuri, K.N. *The English East India Company: The Study of an Early Joint-Stock Company, 1600–1640*. London: Frank Cass, 1965.

Cheng, Wei-chung. *War, Trade and Piracy in the China Seas, 1622–1683*. Leiden: Brill, 2013.

Clulow, Adam. *Amboina, 1623: Fear and Conspiracy on the Edge of Empire*. New York: Columbia University Press, 2019.

Clulow, Adam. *The Company and the Shogun: The Dutch Encounter with Tokugawa Japan*. New York: Columbia University Press, 2014.

Coates, Austin. *Prelude to Hong Kong*. London: Routledge and Kegan Paul, 1978.

Cocks, Richard. *Diary of Richard Cocks, Cape-Merchant in the English Factory in Japan, 1615–1622*, 2 vols., edited by Edward Maunde Thompson. London: Whiting, 1883.

Cortesao, Armando. Introduction to *The Suma Oriental of Tome Pires*. London: Hakluyt, 1944.

Cranmer-Byng, J.L. "The First English Sinologists: Sir George Staunton and the Reverend Robert Morrison." In *Symposium on Historical, Archaeological and Linguistic Studies on Southern China, South-East Asia and the Hong Kong Region*, edited by F.S. Drake, 247–60. Hong Kong: Hong Kong University Press, 1967.

Disney, Anthony. *A History of Portugal and the Portuguese Empire: From Beginnings to 1807*. Vol. 1. Cambridge: Cambridge University Press, 2009.

Disney, Anthony. *Twilight of the Pepper Empire: Portuguese Trade in Southwest India in the Early Seventeenth Century*. Cambridge, MA: Harvard University Press, 1978.

Drake, F.S., ed. *Symposium on Historical, Archaeological and Linguistic Studies on Southern China, South-East Asia and the Hong Kong Region*. Hong Kong: Hong Kong University Press, 1967.

Farmer, Edward L., Romeyn Taylor, Ann Waltner, and Jiang Yonglin, eds. *Ming History: An Introductory Guide to Research*. Minneapolis: Ming Studies Research Series, 1994.

Fay, Peter Ward. *The Opium War, 1840–1842: Barbarians in the Celestial Empire in the Early Part of the Nineteenth Century and the War by Which They Forced Her Gates Ajar*. Chapel Hill: University of North Carolina Press, 1975.

Flint, Valerie. *The Imaginative Landscape of Christopher Columbus*. Princeton, NJ: Princeton University Press, 1992.

Flynn, Dennis, and Arturo Giráldez. "Cycles of Silver: Global Economic Unity through the Mid-eighteenth Century." *Journal of World History* 13, no. 2 (2002): 391–427.

Foster, William. *England's Quest of Eastern Trade*. London: Adam and Charles Black, 1933.

Foster, William, ed. *The English Factories in India, 1634–1636: A Calendar of Documents in the India Office, British Museum and Public Record Office*. Oxford: Clarendon, 1911.

Foster, William, ed. *The English Factories in India, 1637–1641: A Calendar of Documents in the India Office, British Museum, and Public Record Office*. Oxford: Clarendon, 1912.

Foster, William, ed. *The Voyage of Thomas Best to the East Indies, 1612–1614*. London: Hakluyt Society, 1934.

Furber, Holden. *Rival Empires of Trade in the Orient, 1600–1800*. Minneapolis: University of Minnesota Press, 1976.

Bibliography

Games, Alison. *Inventing the English Massacre: Amboyna in History and Memory*. New York: Oxford University Press, 2020.

Games, Alison. *The Web of Empire: English Cosmopolitans in an Age of Expansion, 1560–1660*. Oxford: Oxford University Press, 2009.

Graff, David A., and Robin Higham, eds. *A Military History of China*. Boulder, CO: Westview, 2002.

Guilmartin, John F. *Galleons and Galleys*. London: Cassell, 2002.

Hair, P.E.H., and Robin Law. "The English in Western Africa to 1700." In *The Origins of Empire*, edited by Nicholas Canny, 241–63. Oxford: Oxford University Press, 1998.

Hang, Xing. *Conflict and Commerce in Maritime East Asia: The Zheng Family and the Shaping of the Modern World, c. 1620–1720*. Cambridge: Cambridge University Press, 2016.

Hannas, William C. *The Writing on the Wall: How Asian Orthography Curbs Creativity*. Philadelphia: University of Pennsylvania Press, 2003.

Hertel, Ralf. "Faking It: The Invention of East Asia in Early Modern England." In *Early Encounters between East Asia and Europe: Telling Failures*, edited by Ralf Hertel and Michael Keevak, 31–49. London: Routledge, 2017.

Hertel, Ralf, and Michael Keevak, eds. *Early Encounters between East Asia and Europe: Telling Failures*. London: Routledge, 2017.

Higgins, Roland. "Pirates in Gowns and Caps: Gentry Law-Breaking in the Mid-Ming." *Ming Studies* 10 (1980): 30–37.

Hsia, Adrian, ed. *The Vision of China in the English Literature of the Seventeenth and Eighteenth Centuries*. Hong Kong: Chinese University of Hong Kong Press, 1998.

Huang, Ray. *1587, a Year of No Significance: The Ming Dynasty in Decline*. New Haven, CT: Yale University Press, 1981.

Hucker, Charles. *A Dictionary of Official Titles in Imperial China*. Stanford, CA: Stanford University Press, 1985.

Jackson, Nicholas D. *Hobbes, Bramhall and the Politics of Liberty and Necessity: A Quarrel of the Civil Wars and Interregnum*. Cambridge: Cambridge University Press, 2007.

Jourdain, John. *The Journal of John Jourdain, 1608–1617*. Edited by William Foster. Cambridge: Hakluyt Society, 1905.

Keay, John. *The Honourable Company: A History of the English East India Company*. London: Harper Collins, 1991.

Keevak, Michael. *Embassies to China: Diplomacy and Cultural Encounters before the Opium Wars*. London: Palgrave Macmillan, 2017.

Keevak, Michael. "Failure, Empire, and the First Portuguese Embassy to China, 1517–1522." In *Early Encounters between East Asia and Europe: Telling Failures*, edited by Ralf Hertel and Michael Keevak, 142–55. London: Routledge, 2017.

Lach, Donald F., and Edwin J. Van Kley. *Asia in the Making of Europe*. Vol. 3: *A Century of Advance; Book Four: East Asia*. Chicago: University of Chicago Press, 1993.

Lee, Adele. *The English Renaissance and the Far East: Cross-Cultural Encounters*. Madison, NJ: Fairleigh Dickinson University Press, 2018.

Lehner, Georg. *China in European Encyclopaedias, 1700–1850*. Leiden: Brill, 2011.

李庆新 [Li, Qingxin]. 明代海外贸易制度 [The overseas trade system of the Ming dynasty]. 北京: 社会科学文献出版社 [Beijing: Shehui Kexue Wenxian Chubanshe], 2007.

林仁川 [Lin, Renchuan. 明末清初的私人海上贸易 [Private sea trade in late Ming and early Qing]. 上海：华东师范大学 [Shanghai: Huadong Shifan Daxue, 1987], 1987.

Bibliography

Lorge, Peter. *War, Politics and Society in Early Modern China, 900–1795*. London: Routledge, 2005.

Lorge, Peter. "Water Forces and Naval Operations." In *A Military History of China*, edited by David A. Graff and Robin Higham, 81–96. Boulder, CO: Westview, 2002.

Loth, Vincent. "Armed Incidents and Unpaid Bills: Anglo-Dutch Rivalry in the Banda Islands in the Seventeenth Century." *Modern Asian Studies* 29, no. 4 (1995): 705–40.

Lovell, Julia. *The Opium War: Drugs, Dreams and the Making of China*. London: Picador, 2011.

Lu, Cheng-Heng. "Between Bureaucrats and Bandits: The Rise of Zheng Zhilong and His Organization, the Zheng Ministry (Zheng Bu)." In *Sea Rovers, Silver, and Samurai: Maritime East Asia in Global History, 1550–1700*, edited by Tonio Andrade and Xing Hang, 132–55. Honolulu: University of Hawai'i Press, 2016.

Markley, Robert. *The Far East and the English Imagination, 1600–1730*. Cambridge: Cambridge University Press, 2006.

Marshall, P.J. "The English in Asia to 1700." In *The Origins of Empire*, edited by Nicholas Canny, 264–85. Oxford: Oxford University Press, 1998.

Massarella, Derek. *A World Elsewhere: Europe's Encounter with Japan in the Sixteenth and Seventeenth Centuries*. New Haven, CT: Yale University Press, 1990.

Mazumdar, Sucheta. *Sugar and Society in China: Peasants, Technology, and the World Market*. Cambridge, MA: Harvard University Asia Center, 1998.

Meilink-Roelofsz, M.A.P. *Asian Trade and European Influence in the Indonesian Archipelago between 1500 and about 1630*. The Hague: Martinus Nijhoff, 1962.

Milton, Giles. *Samurai William: The Adventurer Who Unlocked Japan*. London: Sceptre, 2003.

Mishra, Rupali. *A Business of State: Commerce, Politics, and the Birth of the East India Company*. Cambridge, MA: Harvard University Press, 2018.

Moloughney, Brian, and Xia Weizhong. "Silver and the Fall of the Ming: A Reassessment." *Papers on Far Eastern History* 40 (September 1989): 51–78.

Morse, H.B. *The Chronicles of the East India Company Trading in China, 1635–1834*, 5 vols. Oxford: Clarendon, 1926.

Mote, Frederick W., and Denis Twitchett, eds. *Cambridge History of China, Ming Dynasty*. Part 1, vol. 7. Cambridge: Cambridge University Press, 1988.

Mote, Frederick W., and Denis Twitchett, eds. *Cambridge History of China, Ming Dynasty*. Part 2, vol. 8. Cambridge: Cambridge University Press, 1998.

Mundy, Peter. *The Travels of Peter Mundy, in Europe and Asia, 1608–1667*. Vol. 1: *Travels in Europe, 1608–1628*. Edited by R.C. Temple. Cambridge: Hakluyt Society, 1907.

Mundy, Peter. *The Travels of Peter Mundy, in Europe and Asia, 1608–1667*. Vol. 2: *Travels in Asia, 1628–1634*. Edited by R.C. Temple. London: Hakluyt Society, 1914.

Mundy, Peter. *The Travels of Peter Mundy, in Europe and Asia, 1608–1667*. Vol. 3: *Travels in England, India, China, etc., 1634–1638*. Edited by R.C. Temple. London: Hakluyt Society, 1919.

Newitt, Malyn. *Portugal in European and World History*. London: Reaktion, 2009.

O'Connor, Daniel. *The Chaplains of the East India Company, 1601–1858*. London: Bloomsbury, 2011.

Oxford Dictionary of National Biography. Edited by H.C.G. Matthew and Brian Howard Harrison. Oxford: Oxford University Press, 2004.

Parker, Geoffrey. *Global Crisis: War, Climate Change and Catastrophe in the Seventeenth Century*. New Haven, CT: Yale University Press, 2014.

Pato, R.A. Bulhão, ed. *Documentos remetidos da Índia*. 5 vols. Lisbon: Academia Real das Ciências, 1893.

Pearson, M.N. "The People and Politics of Portuguese India during the Sixteenth and Early Seventeenth Centuries." In *Essays concerning the Socioeconomic History of Brazil and Portuguese India*, edited by Dauril Alden and Warren Dean, 1–25. Gainesville: University Presses of Florida, 1977.

Pearson, M.N. *The Portuguese in India*. Cambridge: Cambridge University Press, 1988.

Perdue, Peter. *The First Opium War: The Anglo-Chinese War of 1839–1842*. Cambridge, MA: MIT Press, 2010.

Pettigrew, William, and Mahesh Gopalan, eds. *The East India Company, 1600–1857: Essays on Anglo-Indian Connection*. London: Routledge, 2017.

Prestage, Edgar, ed. *Chapters in Anglo-Portuguese Relations*. Westport, CT: Greenwood, 1971.

Pritchard, Earl H. *Anglo-Chinese Relations during the Seventeenth and Eighteenth Centuries*. Urbana: University of Illinois Press, 1929.

Ptak, Roderich. *Birds and Beasts in Chinese Texts and Trade: Lectures Related to South China and the Overseas World*. Wiesbaden: Harrassowitz, 2011.

Ptak, Roderich. *China and the Asian Seas: Trade, Travel, and Visions of the Other (1400–1750)*. Aldershot: Ashgate Variorum, 1998.

Ptak, Roderich. "Hainan and the Trade in Horses, Song to Early Ming." In *Birds and Beasts in Chinese Texts and Trade: Lectures Related to South China and the Overseas World*. Wiesbaden: Harrassowitz, 2011.

Puga, Rogério Miguel. *The British in Macau, 1635–1793*. Hong Kong: Hong Kong University Press / Royal Asiatic Society Great Britain and Ireland, 2013.

Puga, Rogério Miguel. "Images and Representations of Japan and Macao in Peter Mundy's *Travels* (1637)." *Bulletin of Portuguese/Japanese Studies* 1 (December 2000): 97–109.

Rabb, Theodore K. *Enterprise and Empire: Merchant and Gentry Investment in the Expansion of England, 1575–1630*. Cambridge, MA: Harvard University Press, 1967.

Ripon, Elie. *Voyages et aventures du capitaine Ripon aux grandes Indes: Journal inedit d'un mercenaire, 1617–1627*. Edited by Yves Giraud. Thonon-les-Bains, Haute-Savoie: Editions de L'Albaron, 1990.

Rodger, N.A.M. "Guns and Sails in the First Phase of English Colonization, 1500–1650." In *The Origins of Empire*, edited by Nicholas Canny, 79–98. Oxford: Oxford University Press, 1998.

Roper, L.H. *Advancing Empire: English Interests and Overseas Expansion, 1613–1688*. Cambridge: Cambridge University Press, 2017.

Sainsbury, Ethel Bruce, and William Foster, eds. *Calendar of the Court Minutes of the East India Company, 1635–1639*. Oxford: Clarendon, 1907.

Satow, Ernest M., ed. *The Voyage of Captain John Saris to Japan, 1613*. London: Hakluyt Society, 1900.

Scott, W.R. *The Constitution and Finance of English, Scottish, and Irish Joint-Stock Companies to 1720*. 3 vols. Cambridge: Cambridge University Press, 1910–1912.

Seiichi, Iwao. "Li Tan, Chief of the Chinese Residents at Hirado, Japan, in the Last Days of the Ming Dynasty." *Memoirs of the Research Department of the Toyo Bunko* 17 (1958): 27–83.

Bibliography

Shaw, L.M.E. *The Anglo-Portuguese Alliance and the English Merchants in Portugal, 1654–1810*. Aldershot: Ashgate, 1998.

Sim, Y.H. Teddy, ed. *The Maritime Defence of China: Ming General Qi Jiguang and Beyond*. Singapore: Springer, 2017.

Smith, Haig Z. "'God Shall Enlarge Japheth, and He Shall Dwell in the Tents of Shem': The Changing Face of Religious Governance and Religious Sufferance in the East India Company, 1610-1670." In *The East India Company, 1600-1857: Essays on Anglo-Indian Connection*, edited by William Pettigrew and Mahesh Gopalan, 93–113. London: Routledge, 2017.

Sousa Pinto, Paulo Jorge de. "Enemy at the Gates: Macao, Manila and the 'Pinhal Episode.'" *Bulletin of Portuguese/Japanese Studies* 16 (2008): 11–43.

Souza, George B. *The Survival of Empire: Portuguese Trade and Society in China and the South China Sea, 1630-1754*. Cambridge: Cambridge University Press, 1986.

Spence, Jonathan D., and John Wills, Jr., eds. *From Ming to Ch'ing: Conquest, Region, and Continuity in Seventeenth-Century China*. New Haven, CT: Yale University Press, 1979.

Stern, Philip J. "Company, State, and Empire: Governance and Regulatory Frameworks in Asia." In *Britain's Oceanic Empire: Atlantic and Indian Ocean Worlds, c. 1550-1850*, edited by H.V. Bowen, Elizabeth Mancke, and John G. Read, 130–50. Cambridge: Cambridge University Press, 2012.

Struve, Lynn. *Voices from the Ming-Qing Cataclysm: China in Tigers' Jaws*. New Haven, CT: Yale University Press, 1993.

Subrahmanyam, Sanjay. *The Portuguese Empire in Asia, 1500-1700: A Political and Economic History*. London: Longman, 1993.

Szonyi, Michael. *The Art of Being Governed: Everyday Politics in Late Imperial China*. Princeton, NJ: Princeton University Press, 2017.

湯開建、張坤 [Tang, Kaijian and Zhang Kun]. "兩廣總督張鏡心《雲隱堂文錄》中保存的崇禎末年澳門資料" [Governor of Guangdong and Guangxi, Zhang Jingxin's reports concerning Macao at the end of Chongzhen's reign]. 澳門研究 [*Boletim de Estudos de Macau / Journal of Macau Studies*] 35, no. 8 (August 2006): 122–32.

Toby, Ronald. *State and Diplomacy in Early Modern Japan: Asia in the Development of the Tokugawa Bakufu*. Stanford, CA: Stanford University Press, 1991.

Tremml-Werner, Birgit. *Spain, China, and Japan in Manila, 1571-1644: Local Comparisons and Global Connections*. Amsterdam: Amsterdam University Press, 2015.

Veevers, David. *The Origins of the British Empire in Asia, 1600-1750*. Cambridge: Cambridge University Press, 2020.

万明 [Wan, Ming], "明代中英的第一次直接碰撞—来自中、英、葡三方的历史记述," [The first direct clash of China and Britain during the Ming dynasty from the historical accounts of the Chinese, English, and Portuguese]. 中国社会科学院历史研究所集刊, 第三辑 [*Chinese Academy of Social Sciences Historical Research Journal*] 3 (2004): 56–69.

Watson, Bruce. "The Establishment of English Commerce in North-Western India in the Early Seventeenth Century." *Indian Economic and Social History Review* 13, no. 3 (1976): 375–91.

Wilkinson, Endymion. *Chinese History: A Manual*. Cambridge, MA: Harvard University Asia Center, 2000.

Wills, John, Jr. *China and Maritime Europe, 1500-1800: Trade, Settlement, Diplomacy, and Missions*. Cambridge: Cambridge University Press, 2011.

Wills, John, Jr. "Maritime China from Wang Chih to Shih Lang: Themes in Peripheral History." In *From Ming to Ch'ing: Conquest, Region, and Continuity in Seventeenth-Century China*, edited by Jonathan D. Spence and John Wills Jr. New Haven, CT: Yale University Press, 1979.

Wills, John, Jr. *Pepper, Guns and Parleys: The Dutch East India Company and China, 1662–1681*. Cambridge, MA: Harvard University Press, 1974.

王宏志 [Wong, Lawrence Wang-chi]. "通事與奸民：明末中英虎門事件中的譯者" [The Bogue Incident translator, 1637]. 編譯論叢, 第五卷, 第一期 (2012年3月) [*Compilation and Translation Review* 5, no. 1 (Mar. 2012)]: 41–66.

Zhou, Yunzhong. "The Retrogression in Overseas Geographical Knowledge during the Mid-Ming Period." Translated by Ng Eng Ping. In *The Maritime Defence of China: Ming General Qi Jiguang and Beyond*, edited by Y. H. Teddy Sim, 145–62. Singapore: Springer, 2017.

Zurndorfer, Harriet. "Oceans of History, Seas of Change: Recent Revisionist Writing in Western Languages about China and East Asian Maritime History during the Period 1500–1630." *International Journal of Asian Studies* 13, no. 1 (2016): 61–94.

Index

Abbot, Maurice, 42, 43, 43n40
Abdy, Anthony, 43
Acapulco, 113, 113n30
Aceh (Achin), 5, 6, 11, 57, 65, 65n64, 65n65,
66, 66n69, 67, 67n72, 126, 127, 127n78,
169, 169n38
Adams, William, 19, 20, 20n26
Afonso V (Avis), 14
Africa, 15, 36n10, 37, 86, 178
Agra, 40n30
Ahmad Shah II, 66n66
Ahmadabad, 55n33, 58n45
Ala-uddin Shah, 66n69
Albuquerque, Afonso de, 4, 22, 66, 183
Aljubarrota, Battle of, 14
Amboina, 24, 24n40, 26, 171
America, 3, 25, 37, 44n45, 113
Amsterdam, 3, 57, 175n58
Andoyna, Juan Lopez de, 113, 122, 126, 151
Andrade, Antonio de, 27n56
Anglo-Dutch Defence Fleet, 23, 23n37, 24,
25, 25n42
Anglo-Portuguese accord: *See* Goa
Convention of 1635
Aniangxie (Anung-hoi), 75, 75n24, 84,
84n8, 87, 88, 103, 105n62, 179
Anjouan, 49, 49n11, 50
Annam (Vietnam), 128
Anne (Courteen), 41n35, 48, 48n4, 50,
50n13, 54, 54n27, 62, 66, 67, 68, 70, 74,
74n21, 75, 75n22, 75n24, 75n25, 76,
77, 77n34, 78, 81, 83, 85, 95, 100, 106,
107, 122, 124, 131, 134, 134n18, 164,
171, 173

Anne (EIC), 23n37
Antonio (Ethiopian), 86, 86n13, 106, 117,
174
Arabia, 61
Arabian Sea, 23
Aranha, Francisco Carvalho, 109
Aranjo Darros, Francisco de, 98n33,
118n45
Aston, Walter, Lord Aston, 34
Atlantic Ocean, 6, 14, 17, 37n12, 48n2
Aubrey, John, 172n47
Augustinians, 152
Avis, House of, 14
Azores, 48n2

Baba Rawat (Babarat), 63, 63n60, 64
Banda Islands, 24
Banten (Bantam), 6, 20, 20n23, 23, 25n42,
30n65, 38, 40, 40n31, 40n32, 52,
52n20, 65, 73n14, 78n38, 151n84
Barbados, 37
Barbary, 36, 48, 48n5
Barker, Christopher, 106
Baron, William, 127
Batavia: *See* Jakarta
Bayley, William, 49n11, 65n63
Bear, 19
Bear's Whelp, 19
Beijing, 11, 13, 20, 31, 119, 119n48, 120,
130, 138, 145, 152, 153, 157, 160, 164,
167n29, 177
Beira-Baixa, 120n54
Bengal, 167
Benjamin, 19

Bhatkal, 57, 58, 58n41, 58n43, 58n44, 60, 61, 61n52, 63, 63n58, 63n59, 65, 66, 67n72, 127

Biscayne, 113

Bishops' Wars, 165

Bocarro, Antonio, 32

Bocarro, Manuel Tavares, 29

Bodleian Library, Oxford, 7, 172, 174n55

Bogue (Humen, Boca do Tigre, Tiger's Gate), 3, 5, 31, 74, 75, 75n22, 76, 77, 78, 78n36, 80n47, 81, 83, 83n3, 89, 90, 91, 93, 94, 96, 97, 98, 99, 99n37, 100, 102, 103, 104, 105, 106, 107, 108, 110, 111, 111n19, 115, 116, 117, 118n45, 124, 131, 131n8, 132n11, 133, 134, 135, 136, 137, 138, 138n39, 140, 141, 142, 144, 145, 145n60, 147, 149, 150, 152, 153, 154, 159n4, 161, 166, 167, 171, 177, 178, 179, 180, 182

"Bogue Incident" (Humen shijian), 131, 150

Bombay (Mumbai), 13

Bonnell, Samuel, 36, 37, 37n11, 37n12

Bornford, Henry, 30, 31, 32, 33, 51n16, 55, 55n33, 163

Bort, Balthasar, 147

Bourbon, House of, 29

Bourne, Richard, 66

Braganza, 120n54

Braganza, House of, 13

Bramhall, John, 13n35

Brazil, 15

British, 2, 6, 17, 18, 19, 22, 24, 25,26, 27, 28, 31, 32, 33, 34, 36, 36n8, 44, 46, 54, 55, 56, 57, 64, 65n64, 66, 67, 68, 70, 71, 72, 73n14, 75n25, 76, 77n32, 78, 78n36, 78n39, 79, 79n40, 80, 81, 85, 87, 88, 88n12, 90, 91, 92, 93, 93n3, 94, 95, 96, 99, 100, 101, 102, 103, 105, 106, 107, 107n4, 109, 110, 110n14, 112, 112n26, 113, 114, 115, 116, 117, 118, 118n44, 118n45, 119, 119n49, 120, 120n50, 121, 122, 123, 124, 125, 126, 127, 127n78, 129, 130, 131, 132n11, 133, 134, 134n18, 135, 136, 136n32, 137, 138, 138n38, 138n39, 138n41, 139, 139n44, 140n47, 141, 142, 143, 144,

144n57, 145, 145n60, 146, 147, 148, 149, 149n79, 150, 150n82, 151, 151n85, 153, 154, 155, 157, 158, 159, 159n4, 160, 160n6, 161, 162, 163, 164, 164n20, 165, 166, 166n24, 167, 167n28, 168, 175, 176, 177, 178, 179, 180, 181, 183

British Empire, 1, 3, 4, 5, 6, 13, 183

British Isles, 167, 170

Calicut, 58, 58n42, 62, 66

California, 44n45

Cambodia, 68

Camoens, Luis de, 4

Campeche, 169n36

Canary Islands, 48

Cannanore, 54n30, 58n44, 62, 63, 63n60, 178

Canton (Guangzhou), 3, 6, 8, 9, 10, 11, 15, 21, 29, 30, 30n66, 31, 31n71, 32, 33, 46, 71, 72, 73, 74, 74n19, 74n20, 75, 76, 76n27, 76n31, 77, 77n32, 78n39, 80, 80n43, 80n44, 81, 83, 83n2, 83n3, 84, 84n9, 85, 87, 89, 90, 90n30, 90n31, 91, 92, 93, 93n1, 93n3, 94n7, 95, 95n9, 96, 96n18, 97, 97n29, 98, 99, 100, 100n41, 100n43, 101, 102, 102n52, 103, 103n55, 104, 105, 106, 108, 110, 111, 112, 113, 114, 116, 117, 118, 118n44, 119, 119n48, 120, 120n50, 120n53, 121, 122, 122n59, 124, 125, 126, 128, 132, 132n10, 132n11, 133, 134, 135n28, 136, 137, 138, 138n41, 140, 141, 144, 145, 147, 149, 150, 151, 152, 152n86, 153, 157, 161, 163, 164, 164n20, 165, 166, 167, 167n28, 167n29, 168, 169, 169n38, 171, 176, 180, 181

Cape of Good Hope, 1, 4, 11, 49, 49n6, 170

Caribbean, 2n3, 6, 27n57, 37, 168n35

Carmarthen, 171n44

Carter, John, 38, 38n16, 38n17, 48, 49n6, 50n13, 66, 73n14, 74, 74n21, 75, 76, 76n31, 77, 77n34, 81, 83, 85, 100, 109, 111n18, 112n22, 115, 127, 134n18, 144, 158, 171

Castile, 99

Catalan Revolt, 13

Index

Catherine of Braganza, 13
Cavendish, Thomas, 16
Ceylon, 54
Chandragiri, 60n46
Charles, 35, 35n3, 38, 41
Charles I (Stuart), 13, 26, 28, 29, 34, 35,
  35n6, 36, 36n7, 36n10, 37, 37n13,
  42, 43, 43n40, 44, 44n44, 44n45, 45,
  45n47, 45n49, 45n50, 48, 49, 50, 51, 53,
  53n21, 53n24, 56, 63, 64, 67n72, 70, 71,
  71n8, 76, 85, 86, 88, 98, 99, 99n37, 108,
  109, 117, 120, 128, 132n11, 140, 145,
  151, 153, 155, 158, 160, 162, 163, 165,
  166, 170, 170n41, 171, 172, 176, 177,
  178, 182, 183
Charles II (Stuart), 13
Chatham, 75n24
Chen, Bangji, 136n32
Chen, Qian, 12, 135, 135n25, 136, 136n30,
  136n32, 137, 138, 138n38, 138n39, 139,
  140, 141, 142, 143, 144, 145
China, 1, 2, 3, 4, 6, 7, 8, 11, 15, 16, 18,
  18n15, 19, 20, 21, 24, 29, 30, 31, 32, 34,
  38, 41, 44, 44n44, 45, 45n49, 46, 52, 55,
  57, 58n41, 63n58, 63n60, 64, 65, 66, 67,
  68, 68n81, 72, 76, 78, 80, 83n3, 86, 98,
  99, 99n37, 100, 109, 114, 116, 117, 118,
  120, 123n60, 126, 127, 128, 131, 132n9,
  132n10, 135n26, 141, 142, 147, 148,
  149, 150n82, 152, 152n86, 152n87, 157,
  158, 158n2, 159, 160, 160n9, 162, 163,
  164, 165, 166n28, 167, 168, 168n35,
  169, 169n36, 169n38, 170, 170n39, 171,
  171n42, 172, 172n47, 172n48, 173, 175,
  176, 177, 178, 179, 182
Chirakall, 62, 63n60
Chocolate, 113
Chongzhen emperor, 13, 30, 30n68, 31, 72,
  76, 94, 98, 99, 114, 118, 120, 120n50,
  126, 130, 130n2, 137, 138, 141, 143,
  152, 153, 161, 163, 165, 167, 181
Christianity, 3
Chuanbi, 75, 75n22, 84, 84n8, 179, 180, 181,
  182
Chuanbi (Chuenpee), Battle of, 179
Church of England, 41n33

Clobbery, William, 48n2
Clove, 20
Cochin, 26, 34, 58n42, 58n44, 62, 66, 71,
  123, 128
Cochinchina (Vietnam), 68, 164
Cocks, Richard, 20, 20n27, 21, 41n36,
  114n34
Coen, Jan Pieterszoon, 23, 25n45
Cogan, Andrew, 169n38
Coke, John, 43, 43n41
Columbus, Christopher, 15
Comoro Islands, 49
Cooley, William Desborough, 7
Cooper, Jakob, 50n14, 54n27, 56, 56n35,
  57
Copland, Patrick, 41, 41n34
Cornwallis, Charles, 36n8
Cornworth, Andrew, 66, 66n70
Coromandel, 40n31
Cottington, Francis, 34, 36n8, 43, 43n41
Counter-Reformation, 2
Courteen Association, 5, 6, 7, 8, 34, 37n14,
  38, 39, 39n20, 39n23, 40, 42, 43, 44,
  44n45, 44n46, 45, 45n50, 46, 48, 50, 51,
  57, 58n44, 62, 63, 64, 65, 66, 148, 155,
  158, 160, 163, 165, 167, 169, 171n43,
  172, 172n49, 176, 183
Courteen, Peter, 37
Courteen, William, 7, 12, 37, 37n12, 37n13,
  37n14, 38, 40, 42, 43n41, 44n46,
  45n47, 45n50, 48n2, 58n44, 63n58,
  128, 171n43, 172n49
Cruz, Gaspar da, 133n17, 174n55

Daoguang emperor, 180, 181
Darell, John, 172n45
Dawes, Abraham, 37n12
Deccan, 58n40
Deshima, 72, 72n13, 74, 78, 123, 124n64
Discovery (Courteen), 48, 48n4, 48n5
Discovery (EIC), 169n38
Digby, John, 36n8
Dolphin, 30n65
Dominicans, 152
Downs, 3, 45, 48, 48n5, 49, 61, 62, 63n58,
  173

Dragon, 1, 13, 48, 48n2, 49, 49n11, 50n13,
    51, 53, 54n27, 54n30, 56, 62, 66, 67, 68,
    70, 72, 74, 77, 78, 81, 83, 88, 88n20, 91,
    98, 99n38, 101, 106, 107, 109, 111n18,
    113, 115, 127, 127n78, 128, 130, 147,
    150, 158, 168, 170, 171, 171n43, 180
Drake, Francis, 16, 183
Duanzhou, 135n28
Dudley, Robert, 19
Dutch, 1, 2, 3, 10, 11, 15, 17, 18, 20, 22, 23,
    24, 25, 26, 27, 27n57, 28, 29, 29n63,
    29n64, 30, 31, 32, 34, 36, 41, 44, 46,
    50n14, 54, 55, 56, 57, 62n56, 63, 63n59,
    63n60, 65, 65n65, 66, 67, 67n74, 68,
    68n80, 68n81, 73n14, 77, 81, 123,
    123n62, 123n63, 124, 124n64, 126,
    127, 127n78, 128, 130, 130n3, 132n9,
    139n44, 145, 147, 148, 149n79, 150,
    151, 151n85, 152, 152n88, 153, 153n89,
    154, 154n91, 158n2, 164n20, 165, 166,
    167, 167n29, 170, 171, 182
Dutch East India Company (VOC), 11, 19,
    21n28, 23, 24, 25, 25n43, 26, 27, 29, 36,
    42n39, 44, 50n14, 54n27, 56, 56n35,
    57, 65, 68, 68n80, 88n12, 128, 129,
    130n3, 147, 149, 158n2, 167, 168n35
Dutch Republic, 3n6
Dysentery, 4, 124, 124n67

East China Sea, 46
East India Company (EIC), 1, 3, 4, 5, 6, 8,
    19, 20, 21n28, 22, 23, 24, 25n43, 26,
    27, 28, 29, 30, 30n66, 32, 33, 34, 35,
    36, 37, 37n13, 37n14, 38, 39, 39n20,
    39n23, 39n25, 39n26, 40, 40n29,
    40n31, 40n32, 41, 41n35, 41n36, 42,
    42n39, 43, 43n40, 44, 44n43, 44n46,
    45, 45n47, 45n50, 46, 48n2, 49, 50, 51,
    52, 54n30, 55, 55n33, 57, 57n39, 58,
    58n44, 60, 63, 63n58, 64, 65, 66n69,
    67n72, 68n78, 71n8, 151n84, 163, 164,
    166n28, 167, 167n28, 168, 172, 172n46,
    172n48, 172n49, 178, 178n6, 181
Eden, Richard, 17n12
Edinburgh, 13n35
Edo, 20

Edward III (Plantagenet), 14
EIC: *See* East India Company
El Caser-el Kebir, Battle of, 15
Elizabeth I (Tudor), 15, 18, 19
Elliot, Charles, 176, 177
Elliot, George, 179, 180, 181
England, 1, 3, 4, 6, 15, 27n56, 28, 29, 34, 41,
    41n36, 42, 48, 48n5, 49, 60n47, 61, 62,
    63n58, 75n24, 117, 127, 141n48, 148,
    151n85, 169, 169n38, 171, 173, 178,
    181
English Channel, 29, 29n64, 35, 48
Escalante, Bernardino de, 17n12
Espinhel, Domingos Dias, 98n33, 118n45
Estado da India, 9, 16, 22, 26, 30, 51, 55, 56,
    64n62, 66
Ethiopia, 86, 106, 131
Europe, 2, 3, 26, 29, 42, 56, 62, 96n20, 148,
    149, 152, 159, 160, 169, 174n55

Falcon, 23n37
Fernando I (Burgundy), 14
Fitch, Ralph, 18
Folangji, 30, 153, 154n90
Fort Agoada, 50, 55
Fortune, John, 61
Foster, William, 8
Fowke, John, 48n2
Frampton, John, 17n12
France, 29, 29n63
Franciscans, 123, 152
Francisco (Portuguese slave), 103, 103n55
Fremlen, William, 54n30, 172, 178n6
French, 2, 3, 29n63, 42n39, 48, 80
Fujian, 17n12, 20, 21, 24n38, 25, 25n46, 26,
    26n48, 26n49, 68, 68n81, 80, 80n47,
    86, 86n13, 101, 103, 104n56, 106, 109,
    130n3, 135n26, 136n32, 140, 143n54,
    146n62, 147, 151, 152, 165, 177
Fuzhou, 152n88

Gama, Vasco da, 4, 58, 66
Ge, Zhengqi, 12, 137, 137n33, 137n35, 138,
    138n38, 141, 145, 145n60, 153, 154,
    161n11
Giles, H.A., 174n54

Glascock, Henry, 39, 40n29
Goa, 2, 9, 10, 11, 12, 15, 19, 22, 23, 26, 27,
    27n56, 28, 28n62, 29, 34, 42, 44n44,
    45n49, 46, 48n1, 49, 49n8, 50, 50n13,
    50n14, 51, 52, 53, 53n22, 54, 54n27,
    55, 55n32, 55n34, 56, 56n35, 57, 58,
    62n56, 64, 65, 66, 70n2, 71, 72, 78, 99,
    107, 128, 153, 158, 162, 166
Goa Convention of 1635, 6n17, 27, 27n52,
    27n56, 28, 28n61, 28n62, 34, 35,
    37n14, 42, 44, 44n44, 45n50, 46, 49,
    51, 53, 54n28, 64n62, 65, 71, 72, 78, 99,
    107, 109, 112, 139n44, 153
Gombroon (Bandar Abbas), 23, 38, 52
Gomes, Gaspar, 30, 57
Great Wall, 146
Grey, Simon, 95, 96, 100, 102, 102n52,
    118n44, 121
Guan, Tianpei, 180, 181
Guangdong, 2, 9, 11, 26n48, 33, 38, 46, 80,
    95n9, 103, 114, 130, 131, 132, 132n10,
    133, 134, 135n29, 136, 137, 137n33,
    138, 140n47, 142, 143n54, 144, 146,
    146n62, 147, 149, 150, 151, 151n85,
    157, 158, 159n4, 160, 161, 163, 164,
    166, 166n24, 167n28, 168, 168n35, 170,
    171, 173, 174, 177, 181
Guangxi, 131, 132n10, 137, 147
Guinea, 15n4
Guizhou, 132n10
Gujarat, 22, 23n37, 63

Habsburg, 2, 13, 15, 26, 29, 29n63, 36, 36n8,
    79, 127, 139n44, 152, 153, 162
Haijin, 30n68, 141, 164, 177
Hainan, 68, 128, 164, 165, 165n22, 183
Haixinsha Island, 120n53
Hakluyt, Richard, 2, 3n5, 17, 17n12, 18,
    18n16, 132n9, 173
Hakluyt Society, 7, 172n47, 175
Hall, Edward, 38, 38n19, 48, 61
Hart, 40n31, 52n20
Hatch, Arthur, 41, 41n35, 41n36, 99n38,
    109, 111n18, 115
Hawley, Henry, 40
Hengdang Islands, 86n14, 111n19, 180n11

Hengqin Island, 70n1, 73
Henrietta Maria, Queen, 53
Henry IV (Lancaster), 14
Henry, Prince, "the Navigator," 14
Hill, John, 61
Hinde, 166, 166n28
Hirado, 18n14, 20, 21, 22, 38, 41, 73n14,
    114n34
Hobbes, Thomas, 2
Hollanders: *See* Dutch
Hondius, Hendrik, 173, 173n52
Hong Kong, 3, 95, 113, 118, 164, 165, 166,
    173, 179, 183
Hong Kong Disneyland, 113n28
Hope, 28n60
Hopkinson, Joseph, 27n56
Hormuz, 15, 22, 23n36, 25, 28, 34, 58
Howard, Thomas, Earl of Arundel, 37
Hudson, Mr., 41n35
Hume, David, 183
Humen Pearl River Bridge, 86n14

Iberians, 2, 3, 11, 15, 18, 24, 26, 123, 132n9,
    152, 159, 173
Iemitsu shogun (Tokugawa), 123, 124n64
Ieyasu shogun (Tokugawa), 20, 20n26, 68
Ikkeri, 57, 58, 58n40, 60, 64
India, 1, 4, 6, 11, 15, 18, 22, 23, 25, 26, 27,
    28, 29, 32, 34, 38, 39, 40, 40n29, 40n31,
    41n35, 42, 44, 45n47, 46, 48n1, 50, 51,
    52, 54, 57, 60, 64, 65, 71, 96n20, 99,
    103, 103n55, 127, 127n78, 128, 159n4,
    166, 167, 169, 173, 178, 178n6
Indian Ocean, 12, 22, 23, 170, 171, 179
Indonesian archipelago, 6, 22, 24, 29, 65,
    67
Irish Sea, 171n44
Iskandar Muda, 65, 65n64, 66, 66n66,
    66n69
Iskandar Thani, 65n65, 66, 66n66, 126
Istanbul, 40n29
Italians, 16, 18, 132n9, 152, 154n90, 155,
    159, 173

Jakarta (Batavia), 23, 24, 24n38, 25n42, 26,
    32, 40, 56, 57, 65, 68n81, 129

James I (Stuart), 18, 19, 20, 20n26, 21, 22, 24, 26, 36, 36n8, 37n13, 42, 65n64

Japan, 2, 3, 6, 15n6, 18, 18n14, 19, 20, 21, 22, 23, 24, 25, 26, 30n68, 31, 31n71, 32, 38, 41, 41n34, 41n36, 44, 45n49, 46, 52, 68, 71, 73n14, 74, 78, 78n39, 79, 79n40, 80n44, 103, 103n55, 107, 107n3, 107n4, 108, 112, 114n34, 115, 118, 123, 123n62, 123n63, 124, 124n64, 149, 151, 152, 153, 153n89, 154, 159n4, 164n20, 169, 170, 170n39

Java, 20, 20n23, 23, 24, 24n38, 39, 52, 65, 66

Jesuit, 3, 17, 18n15, 54n28, 66, 67n76, 68, 68n77, 71, 78, 78n38, 109, 111, 116, 117, 117n40, 123, 152, 155, 159, 160, 160n6, 173

Jie, Bangjun, 138n39

Jilong (Keelung), 79n42

Jinmen, 130n3, 147

John I (Plantagenet-Angevin), 14

John I (Avis), 14

Jonas, 23n37, 28, 28n62, 29, 35, 38, 38n19, 41

Kanara, 58n43, 64

Katherine, 13, 38, 48, 48n2, 49, 49n6, 50, 50n13, 54n27, 62, 66, 67, 68, 70, 73n14, 74, 77, 98, 100, 101, 109, 115, 126, 127, 127n78, 168, 170, 171, 171n43, 180

Kibikida, 21n29

Knipe, Edward, 66

Kowloon, 179

Kynaston, Thomas, 36, 37, 37n11, 37n12

Kyushu, 19, 20

Lambeth Palace, 43n40

Lancaster, House of, 14

Lancaster, James, 65, 66n69

Lantau Island (Dayushan), 113, 113n28, 118, 121, 123, 126

Laud, William, 43, 43n40, 43n41

Levant Company, 48n2

Li, Dan, 20, 20n27, 21, 21n28, 21n29, 41

Li, Yanqing, 134n18, 136n32

Li, Yerong (Paulo Noretti), 12, 108, 110, 110n14, 115, 116, 117, 117n41, 117n42,

132, 132n12, 133, 134, 135, 136, 136n30, 137, 138, 138n38, 138n39, 140, 141, 143, 145, 145n60, 156 (Figure 8.1), 168

Li, Zicheng, 13

Liaoluo Bay, 130n3, 147

Liefde, 19

Lin, Xinhu, 138n39

Lin, Zexu, 179, 181

Linhares, Conde de, Dom Miguel de Noronha, 27, 27n54, 27n56, 28, 28n61, 28n62, 29, 30, 30n66, 32, 42, 45n50, 49, 55, 55n33, 72, 73, 73n14

Linschoten, Jan Huygen van, 17, 18n14, 20n24

Lintin Island (Neilingdingdao), 95n11, 107, 114, 115, 176n1

Lisbon, 3, 9, 10, 14

Liverpool, 181

London, 3, 16, 16n11, 17, 20, 24, 34, 35, 36, 37, 37n12, 40, 42, 50, 52, 57, 127, 158, 160, 167, 172, 175n58, 176

London, 29, 30, 30n65, 30n66, 31, 32, 34, 42, 51n16, 55, 55n33, 57, 68n78, 72, 73, 98n35, 163, 164, 166

Louis XIII (Bourbon), 29n63

Lychee, 71, 97, 97n28

Macao, 1, 2, 3, 5, 6, 9, 10, 11, 12, 13, 15, 17, 18, 19, 20, 21, 25, 26, 26n48, 28, 28n59, 29, 30, 31, 32, 33, 34, 38, 38n17, 42, 51, 51n16, 55, 55n33, 57, 64, 67, 67n76, 68, 68n77, 68n78, 70, 70n2, 71, 72, 73, 73n14, 74n20, 74n21, 75n23, 76, 76n29, 77, 77n32, 78, 78n35, 78n36, 78n38, 78n39, 79, 79n40, 79n42, 80, 80n43, 80n47, 81, 83, 86, 86n13, 91, 93, 94, 95, 96, 97, 98, 98n32, 98n33, 98n35, 99, 100, 103, 103n55, 104, 105, 107, 107n3, 107n4, 109, 109n9, 110, 111, 112, 112n26, 113, 114, 115, 115n39, 116, 117, 117n43, 118, 118n44, 118n45, 119, 120, 120n50, 120n54, 121, 122, 123, 123n59, 123n62, 124, 124n64, 125, 126, 127, 128, 128n85, 130, 130n3, 131, 132n11, 132n12, 133, 134, 134n20,

Index

135n29, 137, 139n44, 140, 144, 145, 146, 149, 150, 151, 152, 153, 154, 155, 157, 158, 158n2, 159, 160, 161, 161n11, 162, 163, 164, 165, 166, 168, 169, 169n36, 169n38, 170, 172, 172n50, 173, 176, 178, 179, 182, 183

Macartney, Lord, George, 179

Madagascar, 36n9, 49, 169n38, 170, 178

Madras, 38n19

Madre de Dios, 17

Madrid, 34, 35, 36n7, 36n8

Madrid, Treaty of (1630), 26, 27n51, 28, 34

Makassar (Macassar), 39, 40, 78n35

Malabar, 1, 4, 22, 25, 26, 34, 45n49, 51, 54, 54n30, 55, 57, 58, 58n40, 58n42, 58n45, 61, 62, 63, 63n58, 63n60, 64, 65, 66, 67n72, 71, 126, 127, 128n85, 169, 178

Malaria, 4, 61, 62

Malay (language), 3, 132n12

Malaysian peninsula (Malaysia), 15, 22, 26, 29, 65, 66, 66n66, 67

Manchu: *See* Qing

Mandeville, John, 16

Manila, 2, 3, 11, 19, 20, 21, 25, 26, 26n48, 68, 70n2, 79, 79n42, 80n43, 103, 103n55, 111, 113, 113n30, 118, 122, 123, 128, 151, 152, 152n87, 154, 162, 165

Mars, 65n63

Martini, Martino, 175n58

Martyres, Francisco dos, 49, 50

Mary, 40n31, 48n1, 49n11, 52n20

Mascarenhas, Filippe, 55, 55n32, 55n34, 56, 62n56, 65

Masulipatam, 167, 172

Matthes, Bento de, 117n40

Melaka (Malacca), 2, 3n5, 11, 15, 19, 26, 27, 29, 34, 46, 56n35, 57, 63n60, 65, 66, 67, 67n74, 67n76, 68, 68n77, 71, 73, 78, 78n38, 103, 109, 123, 124n64, 126, 127, 128, 129, 166

Melbourne, Lord, William Lamb, 176

Mendoza, Juan Gonzalez de, 17, 141, 141n48, 142, 174n55

Methwold, William, 27, 27n56, 28, 28n61, 28n62, 29, 30, 34, 35, 42, 49, 50, 51, 51n16, 52, 54n30, 55, 55n33, 58, 58n45, 68n80, 72, 172, 178n6

Mexico (New Spain), 2, 16n11, 40n32, 169n36

Michelbourne, Edward, 19, 42

Milward, Martin, 48n4, 50n13

Ming, 2, 5, 10, 11, 12, 13, 20, 26, 26n49, 29, 30, 30n66, 30n68, 31, 33, 46, 68, 70n1, 71, 72, 74, 75, 76, 77, 77n32, 78, 78n36, 79, 80, 81, 83, 84, 85, 87, 88, 89, 89n22, 90, 91n32, 92, 93, 93n3, 94, 94n7, 95, 97, 98, 98n35, 99, 99n37, 100, 101, 102, 103, 103n54, 103n55, 104n57, 104n58, 104n59, 105n63, 106, 108, 109, 110, 110n13, 111, 111n19, 112, 112n26, 113, 114, 114n34, 115, 115n39, 116, 117, 117n42, 118n44, 119, 119n49, 120n50, 120n54, 121, 122, 122n59, 123, 124, 125, 125n68, 126, 130, 130n2, 131, 132, 132n10, 132n11, 133, 134, 134n18, 134n20, 135, 135n29, 136, 137, 138, 138n38, 138n41, 139, 140, 141, 142, 143, 143n54, 144, 144n57, 145, 145n60, 146, 146n62, 146n63, 147, 147n69, 148, 149, 149n78, 149n79, 149n80, 150, 151, 151n84, 151n85, 152, 152n88, 153n89, 154, 154n90, 154n92, 155, 157, 158, 158n2, 159, 159n4, 160, 160n6, 160n9, 160n10, 161, 161n12, 162, 163, 164, 164n20, 165, 165n22, 166, 167, 168, 173, 175, 176, 178, 180, 181, 182, 183

Moluccas, 57, 113

Mongols, 146

Monson, William, 35

Montanus, Arnoldus, 175n58

Morocco, 48n5

Moulton, Robert, 53, 56, 62, 171

Mountney, John, 8, 9, 12, 39, 39n24, 39n26, 70, 71, 74, 75, 76, 76n28, 76n31, 77, 77n34, 81, 85, 87, 91, 93, 93n1, 93n2, 94, 95, 96, 100n41, 102, 102n52, 104, 104n57, 104n59, 114, 114n34, 118, 118n44, 119, 119n48, 120, 120n52, 121,

122, 124, 125, 126, 128, 134, 136, 137, 149, 152, 159, 170, 171
Mountney, Nathaniel, 3, 4, 5, 8, 9, 12, 28, 28n60, 28n61, 28n62, 29, 35, 37, 39, 39n26, 40n29, 41, 45, 46, 49, 49n11, 50, 51, 52, 53, 53n21, 54, 57, 58n41, 61, 61n50, 62, 65, 65n65, 66, 67, 67n72, 70, 70n2, 72, 77, 79, 80, 88n21, 90n31, 91, 92, 95, 96, 97, 98, 100, 100n41, 102, 102n52, 104, 104n56, 104n57, 104n58, 104n59, 114, 114n34, 118, 118n44, 119, 119n48, 120, 120n52, 120n54, 121, 122, 123n62, 124, 125, 125n68, 126, 127, 130, 133, 134, 136, 137, 138, 139, 140, 149, 152, 153, 158, 159, 160, 160n9, 161n12, 163, 166, 167, 168, 169, 170, 170n39, 171, 172n48, 173, 178, 182, 183
Mountney, Richard, 39n26
Mughal Empire, 1, 22, 27n54, 40n30, 58, 159n4
Mun, Thomas, 43
Mundy, Peter, 7, 8, 9, 12, 40, 40n29, 40n30, 40n31, 45n47, 48n2, 48n5, 49, 49n8, 55, 60, 61, 62n56, 63n60, 68n77, 70, 71, 74, 74n19, 75n25, 77n34, 78n35, 80n47, 83n3, 86, 86n13, 86n14, 87, 88, 88n21, 90n31, 92, 95, 96, 101, 101n49, 102, 105n62, 109, 111n18, 111n19, 113, 113n29, 113n30, 114, 115, 117, 117n40, 117n41, 118n45, 120n50, 123, 123n60, 124n64, 125, 126, 126n77, 127, 132, 132n9, 132n10, 132n11, 132n12, 133, 134, 139, 143, 148, 151n84, 158, 159, 160n6, 164, 165, 167, 169n36, 170n39, 171n43, 172, 172n47, 172n50, 173, 173n51, 173n52, 173n53, 174, 174n54, 175, 175n56, 175n58, 177, 178, 179, 180

Nagasaki, 2, 3, 20, 68, 72n13, 124n64
Nanjing, 181
Napier Island (Ershadao), 120n53
Nemesis, 181, 183
Netherlands, 29, 29n63, 151n85
"New Christians" (Cristão-Novo), 120n54

Nieuhof, Johannes, 175, 175n58
Nine Islands (Jiuzhoudao), 83
Ningbo, 21
Noretti, Paulo: *See* Li, Yerong
Noronha, Domingos da Camara de, 64, 70, 70n2, 71, 72, 73, 77, 78, 79, 79n40, 98, 98n33, 99, 107, 107n3, 108, 109, 110, 110n13, 111, 112, 113, 114, 115, 115n39, 118n45, 120n54, 127, 128, 128n86, 134, 139n44, 144, 151, 157, 158, 158n2, 160, 161, 168, 170, 178
Noronha, Manuel da Camara de, 70n2
North Sea, 29n64
Nuijts, Pieter, 89n22

Ogilby, John 175n58
Olivares, Count-Duke of, Don Gaspar de Guzmán, 36
Onor, 58n43
Opium Wars, 3, 120n53, 150, 176, 177, 179, 180, 181, 183
Oporto, 14
Ottoman Empire, 40n29

Pacheco, Luiz Pais, 98n33, 118n45
Pacific Ocean, 19, 113
Palmerston, Viscount, Henry John Temple, 176
Palsgrave, 41n36
Parke, Robert, 17
Parr, Christopher, 113, 115
Peacock, Tempest, 20n26
Pearl River, 3, 11, 32, 71, 74, 75n25, 76, 77, 77n32, 81, 83, 85, 87, 89, 90, 91, 93, 97, 98, 100, 105, 110, 120, 121, 131, 134, 134n18, 135, 138n39, 142, 144, 145, 147, 149, 157, 159n4, 171, 173, 180
Pearl River Delta/estuary, 1, 3, 5, 10, 12, 25, 31, 32, 67, 71, 73, 74, 74n21, 76, 77, 79, 80n43, 81, 94, 95, 101, 107, 113, 122, 123, 126, 132, 139n44, 143, 147, 150, 150n82, 153, 157, 160, 161, 161n11, 163, 164, 165, 167, 171, 172, 173, 176, 177, 178, 181, 183
Pennington, John, 63n58
Pereira, António, 27n56

Index

Pereira, Galeote, 17n12, 133n13, 133n14
Pereira, Jose Pinto, 55, 55n33
Persian Gulf, 1, 15, 22, 23, 23n37, 38, 52
Peru, 2
Pescadores Islands (Penghu), 25, 25n46, 151, 152, 165
Philip II/I (Habsburg), 15, 152n87
Philip III/II (Habsburg), 26
Philip IV/III (Habsburg), 2n3, 13, 27, 27n57, 28, 28n62, 29, 31, 34, 36, 44, 46, 53, 53n25, 57, 63, 64, 64n62, 71, 79, 79n40, 98, 99, 99n37, 109, 111, 127, 153, 162
Philippines, 2, 11n30, 16, 19, 21n28, 24, 25, 44, 79, 123, 152n88
Pindar, Paul, 37n13, 45n47
Pires, Catherine, 70n2
Pires, Estevan, 98n33, 118n45
Planter, 38, 48, 48n5, 49n11, 50n13, 54n27, 55, 60, 60n47, 61, 62, 62n56, 63n58, 171
Polo, Marco, 15, 16, 172n47
Pope, Alexander, 182
Porter, Endymion, 35, 35n6, 36, 36n7, 36n8, 36n9, 37, 37n11
Portugal, 13, 14, 26, 27n56, 49, 50n14, 53, 58n43, 120n54
Portuguese/Lusitanians, 2, 3, 4, 5, 9, 10, 14, 16, 19, 20, 21, 22, 23, 25, 26, 27, 28, 29, 33, 34, 35, 36, 38, 42n39, 44, 46, 51, 52, 54, 55, 56, 57, 58, 63, 63n59, 63n60, 64, 65, 65n64, 65n65, 67, 67n74, 68n81, 70, 71n8, 72, 72n13, 76n29, 77n34, 78, 78n35, 78n36, 78n39, 80, 80n43, 80n44, 80n47, 81, 85, 86n13, 91, 92, 93n3, 94, 97, 98, 99, 100, 101, 103, 103n55, 105, 106, 107, 107n4, 108, 109, 109n9, 111, 113, 114, 115, 118, 118n45, 119, 119n48, 120, 120n50, 121, 122, 122n59, 123, 123n62, 124, 124n64, 124n67, 125, 126, 127, 128, 128n85, 129, 130, 131, 132n11, 135n29, 137, 138, 138n41, 139, 139n44, 140n47, 144, 144n57, 146, 149, 150, 151n85, 152, 152n86, 152n88, 153, 154, 154n90, 155, 157, 158, 159, 160, 161, 161n11,

161n12, 162, 163, 164, 164n20, 166, 168, 170, 172, 173, 178, 179, 182, 183
Procurador of Macao, 72, 72n11, 79, 79n41, 157, 178
Proenca, Matheu Ferreira de, 98n33, 118n45
Protestant, 2, 19, 23, 24, 30, 67, 78, 152, 153
Purchas, Samuel, 2, 3n5, 16n11, 18, 18n16, 41n36, 120n53, 132n9, 173
Putmans, Hans, 88n12, 130n3, 158n2

Qing (Manchu), 12, 13, 130, 146, 147, 150, 154n91, 157, 166, 167, 175, 176, 180, 181, 182
Qishan, 181
Quanzhou, 20, 21n28, 25n46, 80n47

Rada, Martin de, 132n10
Ramos, Manuel, 30n66, 31, 32, 33
Rastell, Thomas, 27n56
Rawlinson, Thomas, 7
"Red barbarians" (*hongyi, hongmao*), 11, 26n49, 30, 77, 116, 117n40, 128, 131, 135, 137, 138, 144, 150, 151, 152, 153, 155, 160n10, 163, 165, 176, 182
Red Sea, 22
Reformation, 2
Reijersen, Cornelis, 25
Reimão, Paulo, 27n56, 54, 54n28
Ricci, Matteo, 17, 159, 174, 175n58, 179
Rich, Robert, Earl of Warwick, 37n14
Richardson, Mr., 48n4
Richelieu, Cardinal, 29n63
Ripon, Elie 175n57
Riquel, Fernando, 152n87
Robinson, Benjamin, 28n61
Robinson, Thomas, 3, 4, 5, 9, 12, 39, 40, 49, 53, 56, 60, 61, 62, 70, 71, 74, 75, 76, 76n28, 76n31, 77, 77n34, 81, 85, 89, 90, 91, 93, 93n1, 93n2, 94, 95, 96, 97, 99n38, 100, 100n41, 100n44, 102, 102n52, 114, 118n44, 119, 120, 121, 122, 124, 124n67, 125, 126, 128, 134, 136, 137, 149, 152, 158, 159, 170, 171, 179

Roboredo, Bartholomeo de, 67n76, 68n77, 78, 78n38, 109, 110, 110n14, 111, 112, 113
Roe, Thomas, 22
Roebuck, 36
Roman Catholic, 2, 152, 155, 179
Rome, 3, 17
Romero, Alonso Garcia, 79n42
Royal James, 23, 23n37, 38n19
Russia, 149

Safavid Persia, 22, 25, 27n54, 61
Saint John Island, 165
Samaritan, 36
Sande, Francisco de, 152n87
Santa Maria, 15
Sao Joao de Deus, 53n25
Saris, John, 18n14, 20, 21, 41
Scottish, 42n39, 165
Scottish East India Company, 42, 42n39
Scottish Prayer Book, 13
Scurvy, 4
Sebastian I (Avis), 15
Selden, John, 16n11
Semedo, Alvaro, 175n58
Senado da Camara (of Goa), 53n25
Senado da Camara (of Macao), 12, 71, 78, 79n40, 99, 107, 107n3, 108, 109, 111, 112, 112n26, 113, 115, 118, 128, 157
Seville, 17n12
Shah Abbas, 22, 25
Shakespeare, William, 12, 182
Shenzhen, 95, 95n12, 173
Sherburne, Edward, 43n40
Ship Money, 35, 36
Shunzhi emperor, 167n29
Siamese, 135n29
Silva, Pero da, 32, 33, 49, 51, 53, 54, 55, 55n33, 57, 63, 63n59, 64, 64n62, 65, 67, 68n80, 70n2, 71, 79n40, 98, 128n86, 158, 158n2, 160, 161, 162, 166, 168, 170
Silveira Aranha, Antonio da 98n33, 118, 118n45, 128n86
Singapore, 67, 68n78
Smart, John, 127

Sötern, Philipp Christoph von, 29n63
Sousa, Leonel de, 135n29
South China Sea, 68, 127
Spain, 2, 13, 15, 26, 28, 29, 34, 36, 36n7, 36n8, 40n29, 113n29, 127
Spanish, 2, 3, 11, 16, 19, 20, 21, 23, 25, 27n57, 42n39, 44, 67n76, 78, 78n38, 79, 79n42, 80n43, 109, 110, 111, 113, 118, 122, 124, 126, 128, 139n44, 151, 152n87, 152n88, 154n90, 155, 162, 164n20, 165, 169n36
Spanish Netherlands, 2n3, 29
Spice Islands, 19, 23, 24, 39, 57
Star, 38n19
Staunton, George, 179
Staunton, Thomas, 179
Sumatra, 39, 57, 65, 66, 66n69, 67, 67n72, 127
Sun, 1, 4, 48, 48n2, 49, 49n11, 50n13, 53, 54n27, 60, 61, 62, 67, 67n76, 68, 70, 77, 78n38, 81, 89, 95, 98, 101, 102n52, 106, 109, 113, 115, 125, 126, 127, 127n78, 128, 130, 139, 158, 169, 169n38, 170, 171, 177, 178, 180
Surat, 6, 20n23, 22, 23, 27, 27n54, 27n56, 28, 28n60, 30, 30n65, 31, 32, 34, 35, 38, 40, 40n29, 40n30, 40n31, 41, 42, 45n47, 49, 49n11, 52, 52n20, 54n30, 55, 57, 58, 58n44, 63, 65n63, 164, 168, 172, 178n6
Swallow, 38, 38n16
Swally (off Surat), 30n65
Swan, 40n31
Swanley, Richard, 4, 38, 45n47, 48, 49, 61, 67n76, 77, 81, 89, 95, 109, 111n18, 112n22, 113, 115, 125, 126, 144, 158, 169, 171, 171n44
Swiftsure, 63n58
Symonsen, Cornelius, 129

Taipa Island, 73, 77, 79, 80, 83
Taiwan (Formosa), 3n6, 10, 11n30, 21n28, 25, 25n46, 26, 26n48, 46, 68, 68n81, 79n42, 88n12, 145, 147, 149n79, 151, 151n84, 152, 158n2, 165, 167, 168n35, 175n57

Index 205

Taj Mahal, 40n30
Tea, 86, 86n12
Telles de Meneses, Francisco, 53n22
Temple, Richard Carnac, 7, 8, 9, 10, 172n47, 173n53, 174n54, 175
Thirty Years' War, 13, 26, 29, 29n63, 44, 152
Thompson, Maurice, 37n12
Tiger Island, 75, 86n14, 97, 100, 101, 102, 103, 105, 105n62, 106, 111n19, 124
Timor, 32
Treaty of Defence (1619), 24, 25

Unicorn, 38, 38n17, 73n14, 74n21
United Provinces of Netherlands, 2n3, 29, 44
Utrecht, 54n27

Van Dam, Peter, 61
Van Diemen, Anthony, 129
Vernworthy, Anthony, 40, 40n32, 53, 61
Victoria, Queen, 179, 181
Vijayanagar, 58, 60n46, 61n49
Vira Bhadra, nayak of Ikkeri, 57, 58, 60, 60n46, 60n47, 61, 63n59, 64
VOC: *See* Dutch East India Company

Wang, Bo, 135n29
Wangtong: *See* Hengdang Islands
Wanli emperor, 19, 21, 146n63
Webb, Charles, 91, 93, 95, 96, 102, 102n52, 104, 118n44
Weddell, Elizabeth, 1
Weddell, Frances, 1, 3
Weddell, Jeremy, 1
Weddell, John, 1, 3, 4, 5, 6, 8, 9, 10, 11, 12, 13, 22, 23, 23n37, 25, 27n56, 28, 28n62, 29, 34, 35, 35n3, 37, 38, 38n19, 40n29, 41, 41n34, 45, 45n47, 45n50, 46, 48, 48n1, 48n2, 49, 49n6, 49n11, 50, 51, 52, 53, 53n21, 54, 54n30, 55, 55n32, 55n34, 56, 57, 61, 61n50, 62, 62n56, 63, 63n58, 63n59, 65, 66, 67, 68n80, 70, 71, 74, 75n23, 77, 78, 79, 80, 80n47, 81, 83, 84, 84n9, 85, 87, 88, 88n20, 88n21, 89, 90, 91, 92, 94, 95, 96, 96n16, 97, 97n29,

98, 99, 99n38, 100, 101, 101n49, 102, 103, 104, 105, 106, 107, 108, 109, 110, 111, 111n18, 112, 112n22, 113, 114, 115, 115n39, 117, 117n43, 118, 119n48, 120n50, 121, 122, 124, 125, 126, 127, 128, 130, 132n11, 133, 134, 135, 139, 143, 144, 145, 145n60, 147, 148, 149, 150, 154, 155, 158, 159, 160, 163, 165, 166, 166n24, 167, 168, 170, 170n39, 171, 171n42, 172, 172n48, 173, 176, 177, 178, 179, 181, 182, 183
Weiyuan Island, 75n22, 84n8
West Indies, 27n57
Westminster, 24
Whitehall, 35, 43, 176
Wickham, Richard, 20n26
Willes, Richard, 17n12, 133n13, 133n14
Wills, Matthew, 29, 30, 30n65, 31
Windebank, Francis, 35, 43n41, 45
Windsor, Treaty of, 14
Woollman, Thomas, 95, 113
Wye, George, 61
Wylde, Richard, 40

Xiamen, 20, 130n3, 147
Xiangshan (Casa Branca), 133, 137, 139
Xu, Guangqi, 160n6

Yang, Yuan, 138n39
Ye, Gui, 138n39
Yellow/Dengue fever, 4

Zeeland, 37
Zeelandia, 10, 25, 68, 145, 151
Zhang, Jingxin, 12, 131, 136, 136n31, 137, 137n35, 138, 138n38, 138n39, 141, 145, 145n60, 146n62, 147, 151n85, 153, 154, 161n11
Zhang, Qi, 136n32
Zhang, Xianzhong, 13
Zhangzhou, 80n47
Zhaoqing, 135n28
Zhejiang, 21, 25, 26, 143n54
Zheng, Chenggong, 135n26, 147n72
Zheng, He, 2

Zheng, Jing, 147, 147n72
Zheng, Jinguang, 12, 135, 135n28, 136, 137, 137n33, 137n36, 138, 139, 140, 141, 144
Zheng, Zhilong, 135n26, 147, 147n72
Zhu, Yuanzhang, 175

Milton Keynes UK
Ingram Content Group UK Ltd.
UKHW022108100124
435815UK00006B/144